# Asian Perspectives on Human Evolution

# Asian Perspectives On Human Evolution

*Edited by*

**A.R. Sankhyan**

**SERIALS PUBLICATIONS**

NEW DELHI (INDIA)

First Published – 2009

ISBN: 978-81-8387-318-5



*Published by*

**SERIALS PUBLICATIONS**
4830/24, 1st Floor, Ansari Road
Darya Ganj, New Delhi-110002 (India)
Phone : 23245225. Fax : 91-11-23272135
E-mail: serials@satyam.net.in

# Contents

# Acknowledgements

The editor is grateful to the organizing committee of the International Union of Anthropological & Ethnological Sciences (IUAES ) and the 16th ICAES, held from 27-31 July 2009 at Kunming, China, for giving him opportunity as the Chairperson to organize an international session on *Hominoid and Human Evolution with special Reference to Asia: new Findings & New Interpretations*. This encouraged him to put his scientific efforts and resources in securing good articles to bring out the present book. As author, he is grateful to Dr. V.R. Rao, who has taken keen interest in human evolution and facilitated recent explorations conducted by the author and his team in Central Narmada valley and Susunia area, which find brief representation in the present work. Above all, he thanks all contributors for quick positive response and cooperation in sending articles. The views expressed are of the authors..

# Addresses of the Contributors

*[Arranged as per first appearance of the contributor's name]*

**V.R. Rao,** Anthropological Survey of India, Kolkata-700016, INDIA.
E-mail: <drraovr<drraovr@yahoo.com>

**A. R. Sankhyan,** [Editor & Contributor] Anthropological Survey of India, Kolkata-700016, INDIA.,
E-mail: sankhyan51@rediffmail.com>

**Wang Wei,** Natural History Museum of Guangxi Zhuang Autonomous Region, 530012 Nanning, CHINA.
E-mail: <wangwei<wangwei@public.nn.gx.cn>,

**Rajan Gaur,** Department of Anthropology, Panjab University, Chandigarh-1600014. INDIA.
E-mail: <rajan_gaur7@yahoo.com>,

**Rajeev Patnaik,** CAS (Center of Advanced Study in Geology in Geology), Panjab University, Chandigarh-160014, INDIA.
E-mail: rajeevpatnaik@gmail.com

**L. N. Dewangan,** Anthropological Survey of India, Kolkata-700016, INDIA
E-mail: <laxmi.dewa@rediffmail.com>

**Sheuli Chakraborty,** Anthropological Survey of India, Kolkata-700016, INDIA
E-mail: <sheuli_pinki@yahoo.co.in>

**8. Shashi Prabha,** Anthropological Survey of India, Kolkata-700016, INDIA
E-mail: <shashiprabha01@yahoo.com>

**Suvendu Kundu,** Anthropological Survey of India,
Kolkata-700016, INDIA
E-mail. suvo_ab@yahoo.co.in

**G.L. Badam,** Indira Gandhi National Centre for the Arts, Janpath,
New Delhi, INDIA
E-mail: <glbadam@yahoo.com.

**Anne Dambricourt Malassè,** Department of Prehistory, National Museum of Natural History, UMR 5198 CNRS,
Institut de Paléontologie Humaine, 1, rue René Panhard 75013 Paris, France.
E-mail: Email<iphadm@mnhn.fr

**P. Rajendran,** Department of History, Kerala University, Kariavattom, Kerala- 695 581, INDIA.
E-mail: <drprajendran@yahoo.co.in>

**Peter Koshy**
E-mail: <drpkoshy@yahoo.com>. USA

**Ya-Mei Hou,** Institute of Vertebrate Paleontology and Paleoanthropology, Chinese Academy of Sciences Beijing 100044. CHINA
E-mail: <houyamei@ivpp.ac.cn

**Lingxia Zhao,** Institute of Vertebrate Paleontology and Paleoanthropology, Chinese Academy of Sciences Beijing 100044, CHINA.
E-mail: <zhaolingxia@ivpp.ac.cn

**Poonam Verma,** Birbal Sahni Institute of Palaeobotany
53, University Road, Lucknow- 226 007, INDIA.
E-mail: verma_poonam07@yahoo.co.in

**M. R. Rao,** Birbal Sahni Institute of Palaeobotany
53, University Road, Lucknow- 226 007, INDIA
E-mail: rao_mr_2000@yahoo.com

**Karen Rosenberg,** Department of Anthropology, University of Delaware, Newark, DE 19716, USA.
E-mail: krr@udel.edu

**Lü Zuné,** Department of Archaeology, Beijing University, Beijing, CHINA
E-mail: <yunping@163bj.com>

**Indu Talwar,** Department of Anthropology, Panjab University, Chandigarh-160014, INDIA
E-mail: <talwarindu<talwarindu@yahoo.co.in>

**Anneke H. van Heteren,** Centre for Research in Evolutionary Anthropology, School of Human and Life Sciences Roehampton University, Whitelands College, Holybourne Avenue, London SW15 4 JD, U.K.
E-mail: a.vanheteren@roehampton.ac.uk

**Vidwan Singh Soni,** 444/1, Urban Estate Patiala 147002, INDIA.
E-mail<vidwansoni@rediffmail.com>

**Anujot Singh Soni,** 444/1, Urban Estate Patiala 147002, INDIA.
E-mail: <vidwansoni@rediffmail.com

**S.B. Ota,** National Mission on Monuments and Antiquities, Archaeological Survey of India, 24 Tilak Marg,
New Delhi-110 001, INDIA.
E-mail: simadriota@gmail.com

**Samanti Kulatilake,** Department of Sociology & Anthropology, Mount Royal College, Calgary AB. Canada T3E 6K6, CANADA
E-mail: skulatilake@mtroyal.ca

**S.R. Walimbe,** Department of Anthropology University of Pune, Pune 411 006, INDIA.
E-mail: <.walimbems<walimbems@hotmail.com>

**A. K. Prasad,** Colonel (Retd.); Senior Research Fellow, Indian Council of Historical Research, New Delhi–110001, INDIA.
E-mail: < drakprasad@gmail.com>

**Somnath Chakraverty,** Department of Anthropology, B.E.C. University of Calcutta. 5/1 Suri Lane Kolkata ( Calcutta ). Pin: 700014. INDIA.
E-mail: somraja2008@gmail.com

**Umesh Kumar,** Anthropological Survey of India, Kolkata-700016, INDIA.
E-mail: umeshkumarpb@gmail.com

**B N Sarkar,** Anthropological Survey of India, 27 Jawaharlal Nehru Road, Kolkata -700016, INDIA.
E-mail: drbnsarkar@yahoo.com

**Kanchan Mukhopadhyay**, Anthropological Survey of India, Kolkata-700016, INDIA.
E-mail: <kmukho@yahoo.co.uk>

# Introduction

This book contains 24 chapters or research articles grouped under three sections, respectively on *the Hominoid Antecedents, the Palaeolithic Hominins,* and *the Early Humans.* In the opening (1$^{st}$) article of the Hominoid Section, A.R. Sankhyan focuses on the famous palaeoanthropological debate on "*the Last Common Ancestor*", concluding that the debate is not as yet over, though many hominoid palaeontologists go by the DNA evidence and settle on a few later Miocene African fossils. Nevertheless, yet a few others consider Eurasia as the more likely land of the common ancestors, and Sankhyan extends it further to Eastern and South Asia as well stressing need for more researches.

Along with the early common ancestors, very giant hominid-like creatures also lived in South Asia as early as about eight million years ago in Indian Siwaliks, *Gigantopithecus bilaspurensis.* Another species of such creatures, *Gigantopithecus blacki,* had survived as late as half a million years ago along side early *Homo sapiens* in Southern China. They are even thought of still surviving in the remote corners of the Himalayas as the legendry "Yeti" or the "Himalayan Snow Man". Wang Wei has attempted an exhausted scientific analysis of the teeth of the Chinese species in the 2$^{nd}$ article, quite useful for the experts.

How the hominoid ancestors became extinct in South Asia is a big question, yet palaeontologists give credence to change in ecology as the major factor. Rajan Gaur in the 3$^{rd}$ article tries to find out some reasons in his palaeoecological analysis of the Siwalik mammalian fossils, highlighting the climatic changes leading to the breakdown of the wet woodlands into dry wooded savannahs responsible for the evolution or migration and extinctions of the hominoids, also indicated by Sankhyan in his article/earlier papers elsewhere.

In the 2$^{nd}$ Section on the *Palaeolithic Hominins,* or the 4$^{th}$ article Rajeev Patnaik touches upon the early hominin *(Homo erectus)* dispersals ex-Africa through South Asia during Upper Siwalik Plio-Pleistocene (~2.5 Mya) based on diversification of murid rodents as indicators of the strengthened monsoons, also corroborated with the palynological data of the spread of grasslands and shrinkage of forests. The occurrences of East African mega-mammals in the Upper Siwaliks, such as *Theropithecus oswaldi, Pachycrocuta,* and *Megantereon* point towards long distance inter-continental dispersal and lack of significant geographical barriers.

In the 5$^{th}$ article to follow A.R. Sankhyan discusses the affinities of Narmada valley hominin fossils suggesting presence of two types of early/archaic hominins – a 'large' and a 'short and stocky' (pygmoid), likely supported by the lithic typology as well, besides that it makes a good case for *Homo erectus-Homo sapiens* transition, The richness of the fossil and archaeological evidences indicate that the central Narmada valley was a "paradise of the prehistoric man" in South Asia, again fitting well with the mid-intercontinental place of India having served a East-West corridor for Middle to Late Pleistocene hominin migrations.

In the 6th article AR Sankhyan and associates present the results of their intensive and extensive investigations in the entire Central Narmada Valley. They have discovered rich assemblages of largely *in situ* and complete crania and mandibles of mammalian fauna and numerous massive choppers, handaxes and cleavers for the first time at a "Boulder Bed" below the hominin yielding Unit-1 cemented gravel at Hathnora. Their new data throw important light on early hominin activities and habitat. They have also countered the recent claims of some scholars of the lithic industry in the Dhansi, and the "Earlier Acheulian" industry in the Pilikarar Formations.

In the 7th article G.L. Badam & A.R. Sankhyan deciphered important, hitherto ambiguous, evolutionary trends and affinities in the Narmada fossil mammals. They visualised many lineages, such as: (1) in elephants- *Stegodon insignis ganesa– Elephas namadicus – E. hysudricus;* (2) in hippos- *Hexaprotodon namadicus – H. palaeindicus;* (3) in pigs- *Sus namadicus – S. palaeindicus;* (4) in zebrine horses- *Equus namadicus – E. asinus;* others with Siwalik ancestors are: (5) the bovines- *Bos cutifrons – B. namadicus;* and *Bubalus platyceros – B. palaeindicus;* (6) the rhinos- *Rhinoceros sivalensis – R. unicornis*. In addition, they also indicated the temporal rages of the fauna as: (1) the Lower Pleistocene-Upper Pleistocene: *Elephas hysudricus* and *Stegodon insignis ganesa;* (2) Middle Pleistocene (index fossils): *Elephas namadicus; Hexaprotodon namadicus* and *Sus namadicus;* (3) Middle to Upper Pleistocene: *Elephas namadicus, Sus namadicus, Equus namadicus* and *Bos namadicus;* (4) Upper Pleistocene: *Sus palaeindicus* and *Hexaprotodon palaeindicus;*(5) Upper Pleistocene/Holocene transition: *Elephas namadicus; Hexaprotodon namadicus* and *Sus namadicus; Antelope cervicapra, Cervus unicolor, C. duvauceli, Axis axis, Boselephus tragocamelus, Equus asinus* and *Elephas maximuss.*

In the 8th article Anne D. Malasse uses cranial embryogeny as hominin phylogenetic marker concluding that the human chondrocranium (embryonic development) has not changed since the *Homo habilis-Homo erectus- Homo georgicus*, showing the same embryonic trajectories. Hence, despite the higher cranial vault in some Middle Pleistocene hominins (e.g., Narmada), they are not "archaic" *sapiens* but late *Homo erectus*, distinguished by *torus angularis*, also seen in the Neolithic *Homo sapiens* in Asia- suggesting continuity of a genetic lineage. But, the *torus angularis* is la cking in the oldest African fossil species and the oldest robust *Homo sapiens* (Herto) as well as in the Near East (Kafzeh), besides the European Neandertals. Hence, the cranial base of *Homo sapiens* as well as their axial and appendicular skeletons evolved as a result of architect genes mutations (homeobox genes).

In the 9th article P. Rajendran & Peter Koshy restudied the laterite-entombed "Baby" of Tamil Nadu through X-ray computed tomography (CT), 2D/3D scanning, photo microscopy and SEM, revealing the shadows of the possible existence of a human baby fossil in the womb within the hard matrix. Guessed to be of a 166 Kya "archaic" *Homo sapiens,* the finding is solitary of its kind awaiting realisation of its anthropological potentials.

In the 10th article Ya-Mei Hou and Lingxia Zhao has presented important data and raised very many academia issues on the Oldest Palaeolithic of China, its antiquity, its maker, the spread and intra-continental linkages, etc. in the background of previous studies conducted in china since the discovery of *Homo erectus* (Peking man), especially during the last 20 years. They observed a paradox; some sites in the north or south, dated to around 2 Mya reflect quite different lithic industries, the handaxe being no rarer in numbers and spread there, while the earliest handaxe has been estimated as old as 1.2 Mya in central China. This, probably complicates or implicates that China was possibly a place involving various original cultures, yet the authors remain non-committal on this and in turn present strong new data from Longgupo, Fanchang, Nihewan Basin, Bose Basin, Yunxian and Luonan sites, etc. corresponding to the anthropological stages before, in and after the *Homo erectus.*

In the 11th article Poonam Verma, M. R. Rao and Rajeev Patnaik tried to reconstruct the later Pleistocene climate of Narmada Valley through vegetative evidence from palynological analysis corroborating with the magnetic susceptibility proxies. Their pollen samples from the Baneta Formation (Zone I -VI) with the inferred dates of ~ 12.5 - 25.3 Kya, show that the area was covered with open vegetation of the grasses (Chenopodiaceae/ Amaranthaceae, Asteraceae and *Artemisia),* with sparse trees (*Syzygium, Symplocos, Azadirachta, Diospyros, Emblica, Acacia* and *Holoptelea).* Also, marshy elements, such as sedges (Cyperaceae) and *Polygonum* and the aquatic elements (*Potamogeton* and *Typha*) including algal spores (*Spirogyra* and *Zygnema*), denote existence of water bodies/ ponds / lakes. But overall vegetation assemblage suggests a cool and dry climate regime, and the Magnetic susceptibility BMZ-III corroborates with pollen Zone-III (cooler and direr climate), and the BMZ-II with pollen Zone-II (relatively warmer climate)- corresponding to the Last Glacial Maximum episode

In the 12th article Karen Rosenberg & Lü Zuné seek modern human origins in the Chinese Jinniushan (Liaoning Province) hominin with 1300 cc brain, discovered in 1984 and dated to ~280 Kya. It is of the heaviest female about 78 kg, with short ulna indicating cold adaptation The pelvis is strikingly similar to that of the Arago XLIV (France) and Sima de Los Huesos (Spain), a shared primitive Old World trait. In cranial and dental morphology Jinniushan shares with Dali displaying continuity from archaic to modern *Homo sapiens* in China, suggesting a pattern of latitudinal variation and temporal change as seen in western Old World from which many traditional models of modern human origins have been developed.

In the 13th article A.R. Sankhyan and associates makes new additions to the mammalian fossils and Palaeolithic to Microlithic record of the Susunia area of West Bengal and find similarities and differences from the findings of Narmada valley, suggesting Susunia as the north-eastern migratory route of the fauna and hominins during late Middle to early Late Pleistocene time.

In the 14th article A.R. Sankhyan and Indu Talwar present an overview of Indian Palaeolithic prehistory exposing five major cultural transitions that portray the entire story of human origins and evolution. These are: (1) the earliest was the Oldowan/Early Acheulian transition, limited almost to the African continent and associated with *Homo habilis/Homo erectus* evolution. (2) This was followed by the Early/Late Acheulian transition recorded extensively in Africa, Asia and Europe with the spread of *Homo erectus*. (3) The Late Acheulian/Middle Palaeolithic transition equally extensive in Africa, Europe and Asia, which serves a window to see the emergence and spread of archaic *Homo sapiens* and Neanderthals. (4) Middle Palaeolithic/Upper Palaeolithic transition during late Pleistocene when anatomically modern *Homo sapiens* evolved and dispersed. (5) Upper Palaeolithic/ Mesolithic transition with the emergence of primitive agro-pastoralists. These transitions are evident in Indian or South Asian *three* typo-technological cultural complexes, viz., the sub-Himalayan Soanian, the peninsular Acheulian, and the north-eastern Hoabinhian /Upper Annyathian.

In the 15th article Anneke H. van Heteren and A. R. Sankhyan deal with the mysteries of the ancestry of a recently discovered new human tiny species, the *Homo floresiensis* ("Hobbits") in the Liang Bua Cave of Flores Island of Indonesia. The adult LB1 skeleton of *H. floresiensis* shows features indicative of paedomorphosis (infantalism), and its low body weight is congruent with expectations based on an omnivorous endotherm adapted to an island the size of Flores. The data presented here suggest that *H. floresiensis* differs from adults in several features that suggest heterochrony, and support the hypothesis that the distinctive features of *H. floresiensis* were caused by island dwarfing, whether it be with *Homo erectus s.l* or a Narmada-like archaic pygmy hominin, the only known potential ancestor.

PART III: On the Early Humans

In this section in the 16th article V. S. Soni & A.S. Soni report a flake-rich, OSL-dated to mid-Holocene, industry in excavation of a site on the lowest terrace of a tributary of the River Satluj (H.P., India); nearly; 15% flakes have smooth ground edges; associated weathered wheel-made potsherds, an unique or a probable intrusion of Southeast Asian Hoabinhian-like elements.

In the 17th article S.B. Ota explored *Neolithic* (4,700 BC to 900 BC) *evidence for Transhumance in* the Upper Indus Valley, near Gaik and Kiari in Ladakh, India. The evidences confirm seasonal camps, occupied during summer for pastures for cattle as revealed from the faunal remains suggesting pastoralism, besides hunting and gathering, providing insight to animal domestication, cultural movements and origin of Neolithic transhumance in Trans-Himalayan and sub-Himalayan zone and its relationship with Central Asia.

In the 18th article Samanti Kulatilke studied *early occupations of Coastal Sri Lanka,* though the mid-Holocene shell-Midden prehistoric human remains associated with stone implements and faunal remains, discovered recently in the coastal village "Minee Ethiliya" of southern Sri Lanka. Six human burials including a child burial were analysed for physical features of the individuals. This is of significant interest since the widespread adaptive strategy of modern humans - exploitation of aquatic resources - could be further explored.

In the 19th article S. R. Walimbe overviewed dental changes and evolution in Protohistoric Indians. The findings corroborate with the general evolutionary and pathological changes, seen in the form of dental reduction and simplification, and more infection related pathologies, reported for the other regions and groups with the advent of agricultural life-ways, and improved cooking methods. The available data suggest that pre-agricultural Mesolithic populations have relatively larger and more complex dentition than the later Neolithic and Chalcolithic populations; the total crown area (TCA) and molar crown area (MCA) values are 1258 and 673, respectively, for the hunting-gathering Mesolithic populations while for the later agro-pastoral Neolithic-Chalcolithic groups the values fall in the range of 1218-1203 (TCA) and 668-649 (MCA). There is higher incidence of Y-5 occlusal morphological pattern and more manifestations of rare morphological traits (like C6/C7) on mandibular molars among the Mesolithic than the Neolithic-Chalcolithic groups. Higher incidence of infectious pathologies among the early settled farmers can be interpreted in terms of carbohydrate rich diet with relatively low fibre.

In the 20th article Colonel A.K. Prasad views prehistory to history continuum in Bihar-Jharkhand Rock Art where he discovered 96 rock shelters with numerous rock paintings and engravings. Based on subject matter, styles, superimpositions, colour and encrustation, they are classifiable under 10 phases. The earliest (Phase 1 and 2), probably Upper Palaeolithic, have symbols and geometric designs, the human figures drawn in rigid and static symbolic form. The Phase 2 shows flexibility, the hunters and dancers drawn in stick shape and adorned with animal masks. The Phase 3 (early Mesolithic) show hunters and dancers portrayed carrying large bows of human size; the animals shown in naturalistic outline, generally without decoration. The paintings in Phase 4 (middle Mesolithic) become more dynamic, body decoration in animal figures started; the complex geometric designs / symbols continued; the hunters shown standing behind the animals in triumphant gestures with upraised hands. In the Phase 5 (late Mesolithic) slight stylisation and increase in body decorations are observed, and big maces appeared in addition to the bows. The Phase 6 (Neolithic) shows qualitative degeneration; the depictions of animal and human figures become more geometric and crude. In Phase 7 (Chalcolithic) rare depictions of the cattle are surprising though engraved figures of humped bulls on a granite boulder are noteworthy. In Phase 8 (Mouryan historical era) the horse figures appear along with the Kharosti and Brahmi inscriptions for the first time, followed by horse riders in Scythian dress, which in Phase 9 (Kushan period) are shown associated with Kharoshti, Brahmi and Kharoshti- Brahmi inscriptions; the human and animal bodies drawn in triangular and rectangular forms, respectively. The Phase10 paintings are of the Gupta / post Gupta period which depict figures of animals, birds, etc., beautifully drawn in naturalistic form occasionally associated with ancient inscriptions.

In the 21st article Somnath Chakraverty touches upon the continuum in the rock art of India, and presents slides especially from the prehistoric rock art and tribal art of Sambalpur (Orissa) and Pachmarhi (Madhya Pradesh). He thematically analyses the chrono-cultural context coupled with the customary visual art practised in thirteen different pre-literate and pre-industrial tribal communities, suggesting early development of visual and plastic art during late Pleistocene period. Prehistoric rock art has emerged from the almost terminal phase of forager-hunter-gatherer level and continued in successive cultural stages following evolutionary route towards domestication of plant and animals, subsequently, influenced refined by the introduction of metal and use of scripts. The elements of rock art tradition have survived in folk societies almost unaltered and attest varied human values, sentiments and achievement of technical skill to overcome the challenges evident in the early art heritage of humankind.

In the 22nd article Umesh Kumar studied the ecological *adaptations of the Andaman Pygmy*, the remnant late Pleistocene people, splitted from modern humanity over 100 Kya. Andaman Islands are home to marginalised hunting-gathering tribes. Among the five foraging communities found in Andaman and Nicobar archipelago four are the Negrito pygmy. They provide a situation where the elementary form of economic life exists alongside more complex form of economic life, and what would happen to such societies when come in contact with their immediate neighbours who are at the higher rung of economy in terms of economic progression; how does their economy undergo changes and their adaptive strategy. The author presents a detailed analysis of their adaptive changes in economy and way of life based on the minimal surplus accumulation; absence of agriculture and domestic animals; continuous food-gathering activities by all able-bodied persons throughout the year and a generalized reciprocity.

In the 23rd article B.N. Sarkar analyses the micro-evolutionary changes and adaptations of the Andaman Negritoes- Onge and the *Ang* (Jarawa), and their differentiation similar population groups of Southeast Asia. He observes that the average gene diversity ($G_{ST}$) is high (0.2986) among the "Negrito" populations of Southeast Asia in comparison to many Indian populations. The Andaman Islanders (except the Great Andamanese) are still considered to be the remnant of true 'Negrito' population in Asia. They have dwindled to a size where the chance of extinction is very real. The study on such a population provides unique opportunity to understand the evolutionary history of mankind. The author also discusses the possible ecological, cultural and biological factors and demographic history that may be responsible for declining the population of Andaman Islanders.

In the 24th article Kanchan Mukhopadhyay criticises the theories of organic evolution as applied in the historical understanding of the *progress and development* of human societies stating that the earlier ideas of universal evolution had become part of hegemonic ideology. With these the power elites created and used the notion of *primitiveness* to control the course of change and development of the life-ways of non-privileged people. Often efforts were made to transform contemporary foraging communities into horticulturists or plantation workers, nomadic communities were expected to become sedentary. Thus the idea of progress primarily persisted as a political programme outside the domain of anthropology. Once it is suggested that different phases of human history can be perceived in different contemporary human societies, it is also accepted that we know the future of those who belong to some archaic point of history. Governments in different parts of the world came up with programmes of assimilation or of integration for those who were stuck in some history-hole; all such programmes had a sense of direction. Such programmes were invariably smeared with ethnocentrism; the primitives were the past of the developed and the developed were the future of the primitives. Empirical studies have shown how foraging people made to work as plantation workers remained foragers in their thoughts and actions. Even if anthropologists think that they do not subscribe to the idea of unidirectional progress academically, they cannot remain aloof of the fallout of the ensuing programmes. Through active participation of anthropologists and other activists a policy was developed for the Jarawa of the Andaman Islands primarily based on principle of non-interference by the state.

# PART I

# ON THE HOMINOID ANTECEDENTS

CHAPTER–1

# Which was the Last Common Ancestor?

*A. R. Sankhyan*

## INTRODUCTION

Great progress in molecular phylogenetics during the last over two decades has radically influenced our understanding of the fossil-based hominoid phylogeny. The impact has been so much that many notable palaeoanthropologists have taken molecular evidence as sacrosanct believing that it presented a real branching pattern of the extant great apes and humans (see Ciochon and Corruccini, 1983; Pilbeam, 1986; Kelley and Pilbeam, 1986). Traditionally hominoid/hominid fossil evidences were interpreted as suggested early origins of the hominid lineage (Simons and Pilbeam, 1965, 1972). But, the molecular "clock" advocated a very late branching of the human and chimpanzee *(Pan)* lineages from a unique 'Last Common Ancestor' (LCA) after a relatively early split of the Gorilla *(Gorilla)* and preceded by the Orangutan (*Pongo pygmaeus*) lineages. However, subsequently, it has been understood that the molecular dates vary from one system to another, e.g., the albumins yield 0–4 million years dates for Chimpanzee-human divergence- which become meaningless in view of the pre-existence of australopithecines /paranthropines/ praeanthropines-all hominids or akin to the hominids. Then, the DNA-DNA hybridisation dates of 7-8 mya were relied upon in consideration of some fossils from Lothagam in Sumburu Hills thought of representing the LCA (Andrews, 1982, Pilbeam, 1982, Pilbeam, 1986, Kelley and Pilbeam, 1986). However, there is no agreement among palaeoanthropologists on these fossils. Paradoxically, numerous fossil collecting from all over the Old world reveals a peculiar distribution pattern of the Late Miocene hominoids and Plio-Pleistocene hominids. While African continent shows a meager yield of late Miocene hominoids between 13 to 7 mya- a period crucial for the existence of the 'LCA', both Asia and Europe have demonstrated rich occurrences and greater diversity of the hominoids during this time span. Thus, began a hot debate and a crazy search for the purported *"hominid-Pan"* LCA even beyond Africa (Sankhyan, 2009).

**General Hypothesis**

To necessitate a compromise between fossil and molecular evidences the "human-African Ape" or strictly speaking "human-Chimpanzee" LCA has been conceived as "dentally *Sivapithecus-like* and cranio-facially *Chimpanzee-hominid-like"* (Lipson & Pilbeam, 1982; Pilbeam, 1986; and others). Among *Sivapithecus* dental traits, the most important and commonly talked about is the thickness of the molar enamel as noted in Plio-Pleistocene hominids to modern humans, and thought to be a part of the dental-gnathic complex- the mandibular and maxillary robusticity, shallow mandibular corpora, molarisation of premolars, megadonty, etc. The basic assumption is that the *thick* enamel is a primitive retention (sympleisiomorphy) in the hominids, whereas the thin enamel in the African apes is a derived (secondarily reduced) condition (Martin, 1985) due to a ecological shift to a soft / foliage/ frugivorous diet. Consequently, the 'African Ape-hominid' cranio-facial similarities are interpreted as synapomorphies- inherited from their LCA. Following this common rule, a brief overview of the African, Eurasian, South Asian and East Asian Miocene hominoids would enable us to identify the LCA.

In the search for the LCA, it is pertinent to take note of the recent hominoid reviews, e.g. Harrison's review (2002) on African, Kelley's (2002) review on Asian and Begun's (2002, 2004) review on Eurasia hominoids. These reviews have thrown open the following hominoid taxa to be thought of in this context: *Dryopithecus, Griphopithecus, Ouranopithecus* in Europe and Turkey, *Ankarapithecus* in Anatolia, *Equatorius, Nacholapithecus, Afropithecus, Turkanopithecus, Otavapithecus, Samburupithecus, Sahelanthropus* in Africa, and *Lufengpithecus, Sivapithecus* (including *Ramapithecus*) and *Gigantopithecus* in south and east Asia.

## AFRICAN HOMINOID SCENARIO

The current African hominoid scenario is constituted by the following taxa:

*Proconsul (P. heseloni, P. majus, and P. nyanzae)*

*Afropithecus*

*Turkanopithecus*

*Otavapithecus*

*Equatorius*

*Nacholapithecus*

*Kenyapithecus*

The some of the above are recalled for understanding the origins of African Plio-Pleistocene hominids, though the latter appeared after a great gap or sporadic occurrences of the hominoids. The following hominids currently classified under various genera and species constitute a great diversity in African Plio-Pleistocene:

*Australopithecus: (i) A. africanus, (ii) A. aethiopicus*

*Kenyanthropus: (i) K. rudelfensis (ii) K. platyops*

*Paranthropus: (i) P. walkeri (ii) P. bosei (iii) P. robustus*

*Praeanthropus: (i) P. anamensis (=A. anamensis), (ii) P. afarensis* [=*A. afarensis* (Lucy)], *(iii) P. garhi = (A. garhi), (iv) P. bahrelghazali (=A. bahrelghazali)*

*Ardipithecus: A. ramidus*

*Orrorin: O. tugenensis*

*Sahelanthropus: S. tchadensis*

**Which One Represents the LCA?**

Following Begun (2004), who in his more recent attempt has re-classified the various Miocene hominoids, the author would like to simplify his view as "primitive" and "advanced" hominoids. The "primitive" group includes most of these, e.g., *Proconsul, Afropithecus, Griphopithecus, Equatorius, Nacholapithecus, Afropithecus, Turkanopithecus,* and *Otavapithecus*. Morphologically and temporally these could be excluded from the candidature of the LCA. The well-known *Kenyapithecus* falls on the threshold of the "advanced" hominoids. Begun, believes that the confirmation of a taxonomic and phyletic distinction between *Kenyapithecus* and *Griphopithecus*, and the proposed link between *Kenyapithecus* and earlier hominoids from Pas¸alar, strengthen the Eurasian-origins hypothesis by providing yet another example of related hominoids that appear in Eurasia before they appear in Africa. Thus, African *Kenyapithecus* may not qualify for the LCA.

The Sumburu Hill jaw, now recognised as *Samburupithecus*, superficially resembles gorilla in premolars and in heavily enamelled molars with peg-like puffy appearance, and retains many primitive dental and maxillary traits (Begun, 2001). Also, the talked about isolated teeth from Ngorora are more like the *Proconsul* and *Equatorius* (Begun, 2004). Hence, these most probable fossils are unlikely African candidates for the LCA.

A 7- mya *Sahelanthropus tachadensis* from Chad (Brunet *et al.*, 2002) has also attracted attention for the candidature of the LCA. But, it is debated as a unique chimpanzee or a female gorilla or even a hominid. Pilbeam and Young (2004:14) have specifically contended that "based on derived features such as small and apically worn canines, and postcanine teeth and basicranium resembling later hominins, the specimen clearly represents a hominin...but it was a tropical rainforest knuckle-walker". Accordingly, *S. tchadensis* suggests early origins of the hominin lineage, such that the Chimpanzee-hominin LCA could have been much older and unknown. Thus, both on morphological and temporal considerations Africa has so far not yielded the purported 'Chimpanzee-hominid' LCA.

## EUROPEAN /EURASIAN SCENARIO

The above would allow us to hunt for the LCA outside Africa among the known European and Eurasian hominoids, which are as follows:

*Dryopithecus (=Rudapithecus)*

*Oreopithecus*

*Ankarapithecus (=Sivapithecus meteai)*

*Graecopithecus (=Ouranopithecus)*

*Griphopithecus*

*Heliopithecus*

Among these the *Heliopithecus* is distinctly closer to the Hylobates and *Oreopithecus* more a monkey or a paraphyletic hominoid; the Middle Miocene *Griphopithecus* from southeastern Europe is relatively primitive and may also be excluded from the LCA discussion. Bernor (1983), Begun *et al.* (2003) and others observed frequent faunal exchanges between Africa and Eurasia during early to late Miocene. Therefore, Begun (2004) has staked claim on Eurasian Middle to late Miocene *Drypoithecus* and *Ouranopithecus,* being relatively "advance" and suited for the late common ancestry of the chimpanzee-hominid lineages. But, other Eurasian taxa are equally potential, viz., *Graecopithecus (=Ouranopithecus)*, the Hungarian *Dryopithecus (=Rudapithecus)*, as well as the Asian *Sivapithecus* and *Lufengpithecus.*

Moya-Sola & Kohler (1996) claimed the 9.5-mya *Dryopithecus laietanus* from Spain as the LCA of the three great apes. But, it conflicts with other earlier claims based on the Hungarian *Dryopithecus* or the Greek hominoid, *Graecopithecus*, putting it at 12-13 million years ago. Further, the *Dryopithecus (D. laietanus*) is also claimed to be a primitive member of the great ape–human clade in the lack of a sub-arcuate fossa, robust zygomatics, the number and position of the zygomatico-maxillary foramina, and the temporal ridges bring *D. laietanus* to the Orangutan along with other hominoid taxa *Sivapithecus, Lufengpithecus,* and *Graecopithecus* as suggested by Schwartz (1990).

Begun (1992 staked claim of the LCA on the thin-enamelled Hungarian *Dryopithecus (= Rudapithecus)*, but more recently Begun (2004) has argued that *Dryopithecus* radiated *in situ* into at least four species distributed from Spain in the west to Hungary, and possibly Georgia, in the east (or may be in East Asia as well?). At the same time *Sivapithecus* radiated in Asia between 10 to 7 mya. Begun (2004) has repeatedly argued for the *Dryopithecus* as probable candidates for Chimp-human clade. But, *Dryopithecus,* though dental-facially quite suitable for the ancestry of the African apes (Sankhyan, 1988, 1991, 1998 and 2003), violates the essential requirement of the LCA by having thin-enamel on the molars (as in chimpanzee) but lacks the thick enamel of hominids. More probably, *Dryopithecus* does not prove to be a unique last common ancestor of the African ape–human clade. More likely, it was a potential generalized late Miocene hominoid both dentally and postcranially from which both African as well as Asian great apes and Plio-Pleistocene hominids can be derived more parsimoniously.

As regards *Ouranopithecus,* previously synonymised with *Sivapithecus* on dental evidence (Kay and Simons, 1983) or lumped in *Graecopithecus* on cranio-facial as well as the traditional dental evidence (Lipson and Pilbeam, 1982; Ward and Pilbeam, 1983; Ward and Kimbel, 1983, etc.), has also been claimed (Begun, 2004) to be a unique late Miocene hominid ancestor. These characters include prominent glabellas, frontal sinus and brow ridges, broader inter-orbital distance, elongated nasoalveolar clivus ("African pattern"), molars squared, low-cusped and thick-enamelled, premolars molarized, canines reduced in size and the jaws robust and shallow ("sivapithecine dental pattern"). Though it is claimed to be male face, its reduced canine size is attributed to a female individual, questioning therefore its hominid status. Further, the similarities in the upper cranio-facial region of *Graecopithecus* are of primitive catarrhine in nature and that of the lower face (elongated premaxilla) including the brow ridge development are interpreted to be associated with the downward turning of the face with respect to the neuro-cranium (klinorhynchy), therefore, of low phyletic valence. Andrews (1992) classified *Graecopithecus* in Homininae indet. However, an extremely klinorhynch face of the Greek specimen is more closely allied to the gorilla, but it cannot be regarded as an ancestor of gorilla without assumption of anatomical (dental) reversions. The phyletic status of *Graecopithecus,* therefore, remains outside the purview of the 'African ape-hominid' LCA.

The large Turkey hominoid *Ankarapithecus,* earlier known as *Sivapithecus (S. meteai)* (Andrews and Tekkaya, 1980), may also need a re-consideration as LCA, but dismissed by Begun (2004) as it also shows *Sivapithecus* and orangutan-like features.

## SOUTH ASIAN/EAST ASIAN SCENARIO

In fact, India or South Asia had emerged first in the study of palaeoanthropology of the earliest man-like apes- "*Ramapithecus*" that ranged in time from 13 to 5 mya. Numerous hominoid taxa were created which are now of historical interest and reduced to the following taxa only:

*Sivapithecus (S. parvada, S. indicus, S. punjabicus= Ramapithecus, S. simonsi)*

"Sivasimia" (=Sivapithecus)

*Krishnapithecus* (= *Pliopithecus)*

*Gigantopithecus* (*"Indopithecus"*)

Lufengpithecus

The *"Sivasimia"* is founded on a single third molar tooth (even an immature one), which may not differ from *Sivapithecus,* hence may not merit separate generic status but a mere synonym of *Sivapithecus.* The *Krishnapithecus* (= *Pliopithecus)* is a small gibbon-like hominoid and needs no consideration in the LCA debate. *Gigantopithecus* (*"Indopithecus"*) is a very large hominoid or an "aberrant" hominid, which has fired popular (unscientific) speculations of being the legendary "Yeti"–"Himalayan Snow Man" or "Bigfoot", and stands beyond the present debate.

*Ramapithecus* has survived as late as about 5.5 mya (Sankhyan, 1985) but has since been lumped with *Sivapithecus* as its species, *S. punjabicus.* Thus, the present debate narrows down to a discussion on *Sivapithecus* as its species as well as the Chinese *Lufengpithecus.* The author (Sankhyan, 1990, 1998, 2004, 2007) in his various reviews has shown that the Siwaliks inhabited the more advance type hominoids, critical for the understanding of the last hominid-ape split, i.e., they are anatomically quite suitable for the common Ape-hominid ancestry. However, a partial skull of *Sivapithecus* (*S. indicus*) from Potwar Siwaliks (Pilbeam *et al.,* 1982) slaughtered the half-century "star" *Ramapithecus* as it was united with *Sivapithecus* and relegated to the Orangutan lineage. Of course, it was sunk into *Sivapithecus* on the basis of a shared dental dietary 'adaptive pattern' and allometry (Greenfield, 1979, 1980) and partly also for sexual dimorphism (Greenfield, 1979; Kelley & Pilbeam, 1986; Sankhyan, 1988b, 1990, 1998, 2003), besides being synchronic (Sankhyan, 1991).

**The Ramapithecus Debate**

However, the removal of *Sivapithecus* and *"Ramapithecus"* had perplexing repercussions on the anatomical identity of the "chimpanzee-human" LCA, and they eluded the experts differently as follows:

(i) Greenfield (1979, 1980) and Wolpoff (1982) retained these as 'generalized hominoid' ancestors to all the three great apes and humans.

(ii) But, many palaeoanthropologists joined Pilbeam *et al.* (1982) and Andrews (1982), e.g., Lipson and Pilbeam (1982), Ward and Pilbeam (1983), Ward and Kimble (1983), Kelley (1988, 2002, 2005), Kelley & Pilbeam (1986), followed by Begun (1992, 1994, 2001, 2002, 2004) and others viewed *Sivapithecus* and *"Ramapithecus"* exclusively on the Orangutan lineage, such that the first appearance of *Sivapithecus* is taken as the evidence of splitting of the Orangutan lineage from the African ape-hominid common stem. However, Pilbeam *et al.* (1997) followed by Larson (1998), later suspected the *Sivapithecus-Pongo* unique relatedness on postcranial fossil evidence, also acknowledged by Begun (2004) and Benefit and McCrossin (1995).

(iii) Still there were not less numbers of experts who continued to view and "*Ramapithecus*" as hominid even if merged, e.g., Kay & Simons (1983), Kay (1983), Oxnard (1987), De Bonis *et al.* (1990), and many Indian scholars, notably, Prasad (1983), Vasishat (1985), Chopra (1987), Mohapatra (1990), Gaur and Vasishat (2007).

(iv) To a minority, e.g., Schwartz (1984) and Sankhyan (1988, 1990, 1998, 2003, 2007) the merger of *Ramapithecus* with *Sivapithecus* eluded as potential stock for the unique common ancestry of the Orangutan and the hominids since the broad genus *Sivapithecus* possessed both 'pongid and 'hominid' morphologies. Of course, it was sensational diametrically opposite view to the popular molecular viewpoint because the 'Chimpanzee-hominid' LCA could be expected in Africa only. Of late, however, there are notable champions who have dared to challenge the African myth (e.g. Begun, 1992, 1994, 2001, 2002, 2004; Dennel & Roebroeks, 2005).

Leaving aside the South Asian hominoids *(Sivapithecus-Ramapithecus)* for the moment, it may be worthwhile to view the Chinese *Lufengpithecus* (Wu, 1987). It was earlier known as *Ramapithecus* and *Sivapithecus*, subsequently lumped together in *Sivapithecus* on dental criteria but later treated as a single highly sexually dimorphic species different at generic level in facial and palatal morphology.

The detailed phylogenetic analysis of *Lufengpithecus* done by Schwartz (1990) puts it next to *Sivapithecus* in the Orangutan clade, followed by the *Graecopithecus* and *Dryopithecus* (=*Rudapithecus)* in the same broad clade by the synapomorphies of a superiorly expanded maxillary sinus, and lack of a supraorbital sulcus (except in *Graecopithecus).* No characteristics 'African' subnasal pattern is shown by *Lufengpithecus* but it shows rather 'Asian pattern', and likely a primitive catarrhine and placed this genus outside the mainstream of the Hominidae. Later, *Lufengpithecus* is viewed to have greater species diversity, having at least three species- *viz., L. lufengensis* (from Shihuiba) and *L. keiyuanensis* (from Xinaolongtan and Yuanmou), and *L. hudienensis* (from Yuanmou) [see Harrison *et al,* 2002; Schwartz *et al,* 2003, Qi, *et al.*, 2006]. Zhao and He, 2005) observed that the crown formation rates of the Yunnan *L. lufengensis* are close to the African Apes-*Australopithecus afarensis* and *H. sapiens-* indicating as if *L. lufengensis* represented the LCA. Overall, based on dental features Harrison (*et al,*

2002) regarded *Lefengpithecus* as either a 'primitive hominid' falling on the African ape-hominid clade, or as a 'pongid' falling on the orangutan clade- preferred by him. In both ways however, *Lefengpithecus,* like *Sivapithecus,* unites the hominids as well as pongids. The apparent paradox about the pongid affinities in *Sivapithecus* and *Lufengpithecus* also speak for the same. For instance, *Sivapithecus* is mid-facially closer to the orangutan, whereas *Lufengpithecus* is so dentally. Nevertheless, *Sivapithecus* lacks a number of postcranial traits of the orangutan (benefit and McCrossin, 1995; Pilbeam, 1997, Larson, 1998, Begun, 2004), such that a specific relationship is not established. In sum, it may be understood that both *Sivapithecus* and *Lufengpithecus* are primitive members of the hominid-orangutan common clade.

## Character Polarity: Primitive *vs* Derived

The debate primarily centres round whether the dental or the facial traits are more dependable for phyletic affinities, i.e., whether the thick-enamelled dental pattern is convergent in orangutan and hominids or shared phylogenetically. Or the facial traits shared between chimpanzee and hominids are shared phylogenetically or convergent. Without resolving this, it is not possible to pinpoint any particular hominoid as the most likely LCA.

Earlier, Martin (1985) had proposed a developmental model to explain hominoid molar enamel thickness or thinness based on "slow" and "fast" enamel formation rates by a hypothesis of "secondary reduction" in the African ape lineage. However, there is no consistent large secondary reduction of the enamel formation in the African apes (Beynon *et al.*, 1991). Likely, it was not the 'thick' enamel but the 'thin' enamel, which was primitive for the hominids and the African apes or for that matter all great apes. So, a "*Sivapithecus*-like" 'African ape-hominid' LCA as well as "late divergence" is not supported. This would imply that their cranio-facial similarities could either be primitive or parallel developments, and therefore, meaningless for the stake of a common ancestry. Moreover, invoking parallel evolution of hominoid enamel thickness makes little sense since this trait occurs restrictedly among hominids as well among some taxa falling in the orangutan clade. A rather more straight and parsimonious explanation of thick enamel among hominids and the orangutans would be that both inherited this trait from a thick-enamelled common ancestor, and on the same logic the African apes inherited their thin enamel from a thin-enamelled (like *Dryopithecus*) ancestor. The enamel thickness is apparently relatively a conservative trait and the dental-gnathic apparatuses with 'thin' or 'thick' (including intermediate thickness) enamel reflect diagonally opposite dietary adaptations of two types of hominoids, and different dietary regimes, home ranges or dispersal patterns, etc., in different ecological systems.

The thick-enamelled masticatory apparatus of the *Sivapithecus* had been an advantageous selection for utilising a wider range of dietary resources, including the hard stuffs (Kay, 1981) available mainly in terrestrial and semi arboreal woodland niches. This is probably why the thick-enamelled hominoids were widespread during the late Miocene, likely representing the ancestors of the orangutans as well as of the hominids. On the contrary, the thin-enamelled ("dryopithecines", the term here used for *Dryopithecus* and other Middle to late Miocene thin-enamelled hominoids) dental-gnathic apparatus, seen in the African apes, is of relative less selective advantage, and therefore could have been the adaptation to the soft fruit or foliage diet in the tropical forests. This interpretation explains why such hominoids ("dryopithecines") were of limited occurrences during Late Miocene and extremely rare by the end of Miocene (evidence evidences yet un- recovered) when woodland/savannah habitats and drier and colder conditions set in. And, this could probably have been one of the reasons why the immediate ancestors of the African apes are still unknown.

It becomes more obvious that the dental and gnathic characters are better sorters of the Miocene hominoid lineages than are the cranio-facial characters. The latter constitute a mixture of primitive and parallel/ convergent similarities (Andrews, 1992; Brown and Ward, 1988; Schwartz, 1990; Shea, 1988). A nümber of these characters could be related to airorhynchy in the orangutan and the siamang, and to a larger degree in the gibbons, and in the African pygmy chimpanzee to a moderate/ low degree as seen in *Sivapithecus* and *Afropithecus*. Or the same could be related to klinorhynchy, present in extreme from in African apes and *Graecopithecus*, and to a moderate degree in *Australopithecus*, as convergences to terrestrialism. The extent of these adaptations depends on the biomechanics/balancing of the facial loading on the appendicular base in different arboreal or terrestrial postural and locomotory modes. Hence, the characters associated with airorhynchy or klinorhynchy have little phyletic valence in dentally different hominoid taxa, though these are useful in sorting out species on a given lineage.

### Advantage of Sivapithecus as LCA

Since the "Chimp-hominid" LCA still not supported by the fossil evidence, *Sivapithecus* and "*Ramapithecus*" still remain open for debate. *Sivapithecus* was a highly diversified hominoid in the middle to late Miocene and encompassed the Old World. The Siwaliks alone harvested at least four species, ranging from a tiny *S. simonsi* to a giant *S. parvada* with the intermediate *S. punjabicus/S. sivalensis (=Ramapithecus)* and *S. indicus* (mid-facially akin to the orangutan) as seen from the partial skull from Potwar Siwaliks (Pilbeam *et al.*, 1982), where we notice a *mosaic* of both 'hominid' (in the lower face) and 'pongid' (in the mid-face) characters.

To be more specific, the characters of the lower face, i.e., the maxilla and mandible including the dentition, are quite hominid-like as observed in "*Ramapithecus*", viz. megadont cheek teeth, the molars squared, low-cusped and thick-enamelled, the lower third premolars molarized with metaconid development, transverse orientation of the maxillary canines, relatively reduced canines, and shallow and robust mandibular ramii and symphyses with strong external buttresses. Collectively, these features are referred to as "sivapithecine or Asian dental pattern". The mid-face on the other hand, resembles that of the Orangutan in having: 'a narrow inter-orbital distance, tall orbits, prominent brow ridges and glabellar eminences, robust and flaring zygomatics, smooth nasal entrance, the arched and overlapping almost equally thickened hard palate and alveolar process resulting in a narrow incisive canal (see Lipson and Pilbeam, 1982; McCollum *et al.*, 1993). Should then we regard *Sivapithecus* (including *Ramapithecus*)- a 'hominid' or a 'pongid' or both, i.e., the common ancestor of hominids and pongids? If both, then the LCA was "dentally *Sivapithecus* and hominid-like but cranio-facially Orangutan-like".

From the standpoint of the postcranial evidence (Pilbeam *et al.*, 1990) also *Sivapithecus* present a unique postural and locomotor repertoire: 'a slow climbing ape with grasping hands, weight bearing feet (which the Orangutan lacks), freely mobile hip, and lack of special traits for either knuckle–walking (African apes) as well as the quardrumanual acrobatics of the Orangutan and the terrestrial bipedalism of the hominids'. It sounds what could be anticipated for the LCA of both the hominids and the Orangutan, since this type of the repertoire is a pre-adaptation for both arboreal as well as terrestrial ways of living. This could lead to two different lineages under different ecological conditions. For example, a prolonged dependence on trees for survival in the rain-forest tropics (e.g., that of Borneo and Sumatra) could lead such a hominoid to acquire an Orangutan-like quardrumanual acrobatic life style .On the other hand, the same hominoid if continued to exploit the terrestrial niches in the woodland-savannas (of Africa), its vertical climbing faculties would enable it to evolve an erect bipedal gait. It has been demonstrated by many studies (Fleagle *et al.*, 1981; Rose, 1984, 1986) that vertical climbing is pre-adaptive for hominid erect posture. For instance, a biomechanical study of vertical climbing and bipedal walking in gibbons (Yamazaki and Ishida, 1984) concluded that early hominid erect posture might have evolved in an arboreal context. This conclusion corroborates with that arrived at by Prost (1980) that *Australopithecus* was 'pre-eminently arboreal and facultatively bipedal'. Speculation of knuckle walking in the LCA (Begun, 1992) is, therefore arguably not supported nor the evidence for the same in the putative hominid–African ape LCA, though Pilbeam and Young (2004) do maintain this view.

## THE FOSSILS *VS* MOLECULES: CONFLICT OR COMPROMISE?

Ruta and Coates (2003:224) maintain that the "fossils and molecules should be treated as complementary approaches rather than as conflicting and irreconcilable methods". Donoghue and Smith (2003:3) conclude that it is of no use to correlate the molecular and palaeontological clock estimates as all are hostage to a geological timescale that is under continual revision, and unless, all sources of error are taken into account, errors will propagate, potentially beyond the age of the events been estimated. There are obvious fundamental differences in the scale of evolution that occurs at morphological and at molecular; the two are different and ought to follow different rates or even opposite courses, such that their affinities may not convey the same polarity or meaning. Hence, except for the broad anthropoid radiations, viz., Cercopithecoidea, Ceboidea and Hominoidea, the molecular differences within the Hominoidea are less sharp and may not reveal a true/correct picture of hominoid cladogenesis. If humans and chimpanzees have shared a unique late common ancestry, why are the DNA sequencing of the micro mini-satellite of the chromosome reveals that humans and orangutans had shared a common genetic path, whereas the African apes followed a different evolutionary path (Deinard *et al.*, 1998)? This either means that humans and chimpanzees have retained many primitive characters, for which the orangutan has diverged or both orangutan-human as well as chimpanzee-human DNA similarities are a result of parallel evolution. This leads us to nowhere.

One escape is that we may argue that dentally hominid lineage is more *primitive* than the extant great ape lineages; the latter likely became distinct at the end of the Miocene, as if "up from the hominid." As becomes obvious from the preceding discussion, the lumping of *Sivapithecus* and *Ramapithecus* simply reveals a common ancestry of hominids and "pongids" (the term now used only for the orangutans). It is of course, a diametrically opposite view unpalatable to a "chimpocentric" majority seeking origins only in Africa, though the author believes that it is now sufficiently apparent that it was an inter-continental event. As pointed out earlier, if the dental-gnathic similarities in *Sivapithecus-Pongo-Australopithecus* could evolve in parallel, the mid-facial/premaxillary similarities in *Pan-Australopithecus* could also be convergent/parallel developments. Hence, contrary to the general presumption, the first appearance of *Sivapithecus* in the Siwaliks at 12.3 million years ago does not attest the splitting of the extant orangutan lineage, but continuity of a common hominid-Great ape lineage; the three modern Great apes differentiated quite late in the end of Miocene. More fossil evidences and adequate understanding of the causes of extinction/inter-continental migrations of the Late Miocene hominoids (barring *Gigantopithecus*) due to tectonic and climatic (Patnaik and Cameron, 2007) and ecological changes (Gaur, 2007) would greatly clarify the scenario of hominoid/

hominid evolution. The LCA would continue to be debated as a big challenge to all palaeoanthropologists.

## REFERENCES CITED

Andrews, P. (1985), Family Group Systematics and Evolution Among Catarrhine Primates. In *Ancestors: The Hard Evidence.* E, Delson (ed.) New York: Alan R. Liss, pp. 14-22.

Andrews, P. (1986), The Molecular Evidence for Catarrhine Evolution. In *Major Topics in Primate and Human Evolution.* B. Wood, L. Martin and P. Andrews (eds.) Cambridge: Cambridge University Press, pp. 107-129.

Andrews, P. (1987), Aspects of Hominoid Phylogeny. In *Molecules and Morphology in Evolution: Conflict or Compromise?* C Patterson (des). Cambridge: Cambridge University Press, pp. 23-53.

Andrews, P. (1990), Lining Up the Ancestors. *Nature* 345: 664-665.

Andrews, P. and J.E. Cronin (1982), The Relationships of *Sivapithecus* and *Ramapithecus* and the Evolution of Orang-Utan. *Nature* 297: 541-546.

Andrews, P. and L. Martin. (1987), Cladistic Relationships of Extant and Fossil Hominoids. *Journal of Human Evolution* 16: 101-118.

Andrews, P. and L. Tekkaya (1980), A Revision of Turkish Miocene Hominoid *Sivapithecus Metaei.* Paleontology 23: 85–95.

Begun, D.R. (1992), Miocene Fossil Hominids and the Chimpanzee-Human Clade. *Science* 257:1929-1933.

Begun, D.R. (1994), Relations Among the Great Apes and Humans: New Interpretations based on the Fossil Great Ape Dryopithecus. *Yearbook of Physical Anthropology* 37:11-63.

Begun, D.R. (2001), African and Eurasian Miocene Hominoids and the Origins of the Hominidae. In de Bonis L., Koufos, G. and Andrews, P. (eds), *Hominoid Evolution and Environmental Changes in the Neogene of Europe, Volume* 2. Cambridge University Press, pp. 231-253.

Begun, D.R. (2002), Eurasian Hominoids. In Hartwig, W. (ed.), *The Primate Fossil Record.* Cambridge University Press, pp. 339-368.

Begun, D.R. (2004), Sivapithecus is East and Dryopithecus is West, and Never the Twain Shall Meet. *The Anthropological Society of Nippon* (published online as Anthropological Science on 30 September 2004), pp. 1-12.

Begun, D.R., E. Gulec, and D. Geraads (2003), Dispersal Patterns of Eurasian Hominoids: Implications from Turkey. In Reumer, J.W.F. and Wessels, W. (eds.), *Distribution and Migration of Tertiary Mammals in Eurasia: A volume in honour of Hans de Bruijn. DEINSEA* 10: 23-39.

Benefit, B.R. and M.L. McCrossin (1995), Miocene Hominoids and Hominid Origins. *Annual Review of Anthropology* 24: 237-256.

Benveniste, R.E. and D G. J. Todaro (1976), Evolution of Type C Viral Genes: Evidence for an Asian Origin of Man. *Nature* 261: 101-108.

Bernor, R.L. (1983), Geochronology and Zoogeographic Relationships of Miocene Hominoidea. *In New Interpretations of Ape and Human Ancestry, R.L.* R.L. Ciochon and R.S. Corruccini (eds.). New York: Plenum Press, pp. 21-64.

Boaz, N. T. (1983), Morphological Trends and Phylogenetic Relationships from Middle Miocene Hominoids to late Pliocene Hominids. In *New Interpretations of Ape and Human Ancestry*. R. L. Ciochon, and R. S. Corruccini (eds.). New York: Plenum Press, pp. 705-720.

Chopra, S.R.K. (1987), Fossil Apes and Men in India- Status and Prospects. *Panchanan Mitra Memorial Lecture. Calcutta: Asiatic Society of Bengal*, pp 1-16.

Chopra, S.R.K., S. Kaul and R.K. Pathak (1982), Morphometric Affinities in Innominate Bones of Old World Primates including Man. *J. Human Evolution 11: 105-108.*

Ciochon, R. L. and R. S. Corruccini (1983), *New Interpretations of Ape and Human Ancestry*, New York: Plenum Press.

Constans, J., C. Gouaillard, C. Bouissou and J.M. Dugoujon (1987), Polymorphism of the Vitamin D Binding Protein (DBP) Among Primates: An Evolutionary Analysis. *Am. J. Phys. Anthrop.* 73: 365-377.

De Bonis, L. (1983), Phyletic Relationships of Miocene Hominoids and Higher Primate Classification. *In New Interpretations of Ape and Human Ancestry*. R. L. Ciochon and R. S. Corruccini (eds.). New York: Plenum Press, pp. 625-649.

De Bonis, L. G. Bouvrain, P. Geraads and G. Koufos (1990), New Hominoid Skull Material from the late Miocene of Macedonia in Northern Greece. *Nature 345: 712-714.*

Delson, E. (1985), Catarrhine Evolution. In *Ancestors, The Hard Evidence*. E. Delson (ed.). New York: Alan R. Liss, pp 9-13. – 1985. The earliest *Sivapithecus*. *Nature* 318: 107-108.

Dennel, R. and W. Roebroeks (2005), An Asian Perspective on Early Human Dispersal from Africa. *Nature* (Review) 438: 1099-1104.

Donoghue, P.C.J. and M.P. Smith (2003), Introduction-Molecular Clocks and the Fossil Record. In *"Telling the Evolutionary Time"*: Edited by P.C.J. Donoghue and M.P. Smith. London: CRC Press, Taylor & Francis.

Gantt, D. G. (1983), The Enamel of Neogene Hominoids: Structural and Phyletic Implications. In *New Interpretations of Ape and Human Ancestry*. R. L. Ciochon and R.S. Corruccini (eds.). New York: Plenum Press, pp. 249-298.

Gingerich, P.D. (1985), Non-linear Molecular Clocks and Ape-Human Divergence Times. In *Hominoid Evolution: Past, Present and Future*. P.V. Tobias (ed.). New York: Alan R. Liss, pp. 411-416.

Goodman, M. (1976), Towards a Genealogical Classification of the Primates. In *Molecular Anthropology*. M. Goodman and R.E. Tashian (eds.). New York: Plenum Press, pp. 321-264.

Goodman, M. (1982), Bimolecular Evidence on Human Origins from the Standpoint of Darwinian Theory. *Human Biology* 54: 247-264.

Goodman, M. (1989), Update to "Evolution of the Immunologic Species Specificity of Human Serum Proteins". *Human Biology* 61: 925-934.

Goodman, M. and R.E. Tashian (1976), *Molecular Anthropology*. New York: Plenum Press.

Goodman, M., M.L. Baba and L.L. Darga (1983), The Bearing of Molecular Data on the Cladogenesis and Times of Divergence of Hominoid Lineages. In *New Interpretations of Ape and Human Ancestry*. R. L. Ciochon and R.S. Corruccini (eds.). New York: Plenum Press, p. 67-86.

Greengield, L.O. (1979), On the Adaptive Pattern of " Ramapithecus". *American Journal of Physical Anthropology* 50: 527-548.

Greengield, L.O. (1980), A Late Divergence Hypothesis. *American Journal of Physical Anthropology*. 52: 351-365.

Greengield, L.O. (1983), Towards Resolution of Discrepancies Between Phenetic and Palaeontological Data Bearing on the Question of Human Origins. In *New Interpretations of Ape and Human Ancestry*. R. L. Ciochon and R.S. Corruccini (eds.). New York: Plenum Press. pp. 695-703.

Harrison, T. (2002), Late Oligocene to Middle Miocene Catarrhines from Afro-Arabia. In Hartwig, W. (ed.), *The Primate Fossil Record*. Cambridge University Press, pp. 311-338.

Harrison, T. Xueping, Ji and D. Su. (2002), On the Systematic Status of the Late Neogene Hominoids from Yunnan Province, China. *Journal of Human Evolution 43* (2) 207-227.

Hartman, S. E. (1988), A Cladistic Analysis of Hominoid Molars. *Journal of Human Evolution* 17: 489-502.

Kappelman, J. J. Kelley, D.R. Pilbeam, K.A Sheikh, S. Ward, M. Anwar, J.C. Barry, B. Brown, P. Hake, N.M. Johnson, S.M. Raza, and S.M.I. Shah (1991), The Earliest Occurrence of *Sivapithecus* from the Middle Miocene Chinji Formation of Pakistan. *Journal of Human Evolution* 21: 61–73.

Kay, R.F. (1981), The Nut-Crackers: A New Theory of the Adaptations of the Ramapithecinae. *American Journal of Physical Anthropology* 55: 143-151.

Kay, R. F. and E. L. Simons (1983), A Reassessment of the Relationship Between Later Miocene and Subsequent Hominoids. In *New Interpretations of Ape and Human Ancestry*. R. L. Ciochon and R. S. Corruccini (eds.). New York: Plenum Press. pp. 577-624.

Kelley, J. (1988), A New Large Species of *Sivapithecus* from the Siwaliks of Pakistan. *Journal of Human Evolution* 17:305-324.

Kelley, J. (2002), The Hominoid Radiation in Asia. In Hartwig, W. (ed.), The Primate Fossil Record. Cambridge University Press, pp. 369-384.

Kelley, J. (2005), Misconceptions Arising from the Misassignment of Non-hominoid Teeth to the Miocene Hominoid *Sivapithecus*. *Society of Vertebrate Paleontology* PE Article No.8.1.16A.

Kelley, J.and D. Pilbeam (1986), The Dryopithecines: Taxonomy, Comparative Anatomy and Phylogeny of Miocene large Hominoids. In *Comparative Primate Biology. Vol. I: Systematics. Evolution and Anatomy*. D. Swindler and J. Erwin (eds.). : New York. Alan R. Liss. pp. 61-411.

Koop, B.R., M. Goodman, P. Zu, K. Chan and J.L. Slinghton (1986), Primate K-globin DNA Segments and Man's Place Among the Great Apes. *Nature* 319: 234-238.

Larson, S.G. (1998), Parallel Evolution in the Hominoid Trunk and Forelimb. Evolutionary Anthropology 6 (3): 87-99.

Leakey, R.E. and M.G. Leakey (1986), A New Miocene Hominoid from Kenya. *Nature* 324: 146-148.

Lipson, S. and D. Pilbeam (1982), *Ramapithecus* and Hominoid Evolution. *J. Human Evolution* 11: 343-348.

Li, W. H. and M. Tanimura (1987), The Molecular Clock Runs More Slowly in Man than in Apes and Monkeys. *Nature* 326: 93-96.

Mai, L. L. (1983), A Model of the Chromosome Evolution and Its Bearing on Cladogenesis in the Hominoidea. In *New Interpretations of Ape and Human Ancestry*. R. L. Ciochon and R. S. Corruccini (eds.). New York: Plenum Press, pp. 87- 114.

Martin, L. (1985), Significance of Enamel Thickness in Hominoid Evolution. *Nature* 314: 260-263.

Martin, L. (1986), Relationships Among Extant and Extinct Great Apes and Humans. In *Major Tropics in Primate and Human Evolution*. B. Wood, L. Martin and P. Andrews (eds.). Cambridge: Cambridge University Pres, pp. 161-187.

Martin, L. (1986), A Book Review of: *New Interpretations of Ape and Human Ancestry*. R. L. Ciochon and R. S. Corrucinnin (eds.). *J. Human Evolution*. 15: 219-221.

Martin, R.D. (1990), *Primate Origins and Evolution: A Phylogenetic Reconstruction*. London: Chapman and Hill.

Oxnard, C.E. (1975), The Place of the Australopithecines in Human Evolution: Grounds for Doubt? *Nature* 258: 389-395.

Oxnard, C.E. (1977), Morphometric Affinities of the Human Shoulder. *American Journal of Physical Anthropology* 46: 367-374.

Oxnard, C.E. (1984), *The Order of the Man*. London: New Heaven.

Oxnard, C.E. (1987), *Fossil, Teeth and Sex: Perspectives on Human Evolution*. Washington: Hong Kong University Press.

Pickford, M. (1983), Sequence and Environments of the Lower and Middle Miocene Hominoids of Western Kenya. In *New Interpretations of Ape and Human Ancestry*. R. L. Ciochon and R. S. Corruccini (eds.). New York: Plenum Press. pp. 411-439.

Pickford, M. (1985), A New Look at Kenyapithecus Based on Recent Discoveries in Western Kenya. *J. Human Evolution* 14: 113-143.

Pilbeam, D. (1985), Patterns of Hominoid Evolution. In *Ancestors: The Hard Evidence*. E. Delson (ed.). New York: Alan R. Liss, pp. 51-59.

Pilbeam, D. (1986), Distinguished Lecture: Hominoid Evolution and Hominoid Origins. *Am. Anthropologist* 88: 295-312.

Pilbeam, D. (1997), Research on Miocene Hominoids and Hominid Origins: The Last Three Decades. In Begun, D.R., Ward, C.V. and Rose, M.D. (eds), Function,

Phylogeny and Fossils: Miocene Hominoid Evolution and Adaptation. Plenum Press, New York, pp. 13-28.

Pilbeam, D. and L. L. Jacobs (1978), Changing Views on Human Origins. *Plateau* 51: 18-30.

Pilbeam, D., M.D. Rose, C. Badgley and B. Lipschutz (1980), Miocene Hominoids from Pakistan. *Postilla* 188: 1- 95.

Pilbeam, D., M. D. Rose, J. C. Barry and S.M.I. Shah (1990), New *Sivapithecus* Humari from Pakistan and the Relationship of *Sivapithecus* and *Pongo*. *Nature* 348: 237-239.

Prasad, K.N. (1983), Historical Notes on the Geology, Dating and Systematics of the Miocene Hominoids of India. In *New Interpretations of Ape and Human Ancestry*. R. L. Ciochon, and R. S. Corruccini (eds.). New York: Plenum Press, pp. 559-574.

Prost, J. (1980), The Origin of Bipedalism. *American Journal of Physical Anthropology* 52: 175-190.

Raza, S.M., J.C. Barry, D. Pilbeam, M.D. Rose, S.M.I. Shah and S. Ward (1983), New Hominoid Primates from the Middle Miocene Chinji Formation, Potwar Plateau, Pakistan. *Nature* 305: 52-54.

Rodriguez-Trelles, F., R. Tarrio and F.J. Ayala (2003), Molecular Clocks: Whence and Whither? In *Telling the Evolutionary Time*. P.C.J. Donoghue and M.P. Smith (eds), London: CRC Press, Taylor & Francis.

Rodman, P. S. and H.M. McHenry (1980), Bioenergetics and the Origin of Hominoid Bipedalism. *American Journal of Physical Anthropology* 52: 103-106.

Romero-Hererea, A.E., H. Lehman, K.A. Joysey and A.E. Friday (1976), Evolution of Myoglobin Amino Acid Sequences in Primates and Other Vertebrates. In *Molecular Anthropology*, M. Goodman and R.E.Tashian (eds.),, pp. 289-300.. New York: Plenum Press.

Rose, M.D. (1983), Miocene Hominoid Postcranial Morphology Monkey-like, Ape-like, or Both? In *New Interpretations of Ape and Human Ancestry*. R. L. Ciochon and R.S. Corruccini (eds.). New York: Plenum Press, pp. 405-417.

Rose, M.D. (1984), Hominoid Postcranial Specimens from the Middle Miocene Chinji Formation, Pakistan. *J. Human Evolution* 13: 503- 516.

Rose, M.D. (1986), Further Hominoid Postcranial Specimens from the Late Miocene Nagri Formation of Pakistan. *J. Human Evolution* 15. 333-367.

Ruta, M. and M.I. Coates (2003), Bones, Molecules, and Crown-Tetrapod Origins. In *"Telling the Evolutionary Time"*, P.C.J. Donoghue and M.P. Smith (Eds), pp224-262. London: CRC Press, Taylor & Francis.

Sankhyan, A.R. (1985), Late Occurrence of *Sivapithecus* in Indian Siwaliks. *J. Human Evolution* 14: 573-578.

Sankhyan, A.R. (1988), On Human Ancestry: A New Perspective. In *Current Anthropological and Archaeological Perspectives*. K.L. Bhowmik (ed.), *Vol.-I, Man*. New Delhi: Inter-India Publication, pp. 57-88.

Sankhyan, A R. (1990), A Re-thinking on the 'Human Great Ape' Cladogenesis and the Last Common Ancestor. *Journal Anthropological Survey of India* 39: 169-190.

Sankhyan, A.R. (1991), An Anthropological Look on *Ramapithecus and Sivapithecus* Siwaliks Hominoids. *J. Himalayan Geology* 2 (2): 169-177.

Sankhyan, A.R. (1998), A Re-appraisal of the Phylogenetic Status of the Neogene Hominoids in Human Ancestry: In V. Bhalla Festchrift Volume *Physical Anthropology & Human Genetics: Contemporary Perspectives*, (Ed. I. J. S. Jaiswal), pp 128-146. Ludhiana: Asia Vision.

Sankhyan, A.R. (2003), Indian *Sivapithecus* and *Homo*: A Re-thinking Before a Linking. *In: "Understanding People of India: An Anthropological Insight*, A.K. Kalla & D.K. Bhattacharya (Eds), pp. 207-216. Delhi: Department of Anthropology, University of Delhi.

Sankhyan, A.R. (2007), What is Wrong with *Ramapithecus?* In *Human Origins, Genome & People of India: Genomic, Palaeontological & Archaeological Perspectives*, A.R. Sankhyan & V.R. Rao (eds), pp. 120-137. New Delhi: Allied Publishers.

Sankhyan, A.R. (2009), On the Status of Indian Hominoid and Hominid Fossils. In *Status of Prehistoric Studies in the Twenty-first Century in India*, R. Ray & V. Jayaswal (eds), pp. 13-23. Proceedings of the UISPPXV CONGRESS, held in September_2006 in Lisbon, Portugal. BAR International Series 1924, Archaeopress, England.

Sarich, V. M. and J. E. Cronin (1976), Molecular Systematics of the Primates. In *Molecular Anthropology*. New York: Plenum Press, pp. 141-170.

Schwartz, G..T., Liu Wu and L. Zhang (2003), Preliminary Investigation of Dental Microstructure in the Yunnan Hominoid (*Lufengpithecus hudienensis*), Yunnan Province, China. *Journal of Human Evolution* 44 (2): 189-202.

Schwartz, J. H. (1984), The Evolutionary Relationships of Human and Orangutans. *Nature* 308: 501-505.

Schwartz, J. H. (1984), Hominoid Evolution: A Review and Reassessment. *Current Anthropology* 25: 655-672.

Schwartz, J. H. (1987), *The Red Ape*. Boston: Houghton Mifflin Co.

Schwartz, J.H. (1990), *Lufengpithecus* and Its Potential Relationship to an Orangutan Clad. *Journal of Human Evolution* 19: 591-605.

Schultz, A.H. (1986), The Recent Primates. In *Perspectives on Human Evolution*. S.L. Washburn and P. C. Jay (eds.) New York: Holt Renehart and Winston, pp. 122-195.

Sibley, C. G. and J.E. Ahlquist (1984), The Phylogeny of the Hominoid Primates as indicated by DNA-DNA Hybridization. *Journal of Molecular Evolution*: 371-389.

Simons, E.L. and D.R. Pilbeam (1965), Preliminary Revision of Dryopithecines (Pongidae, Anthropoidea). *Folia Primatologica* 3: 81-152.

Simons, E.L. and D.R. Pilbeam (1972), Hominoid Palaeoprimatology. In *The Functional and Evolutionary Biology of Primates*. R.H. Tuttle (ed.). Aldine: Atherton, pp. 36-70.

Stanyon, R. and B. Chiarelli (1982), Phylogeny of the Hominoidea: The Chromosomal Evidence. *J. Human Evolution* 11: 493-504.

Swarts, J.D. (1988), Deciduous Dentition: Implication for Hominoid Phylogeny. In *Orangutan Biology*. J.H. Schwartz (ed.) Oxford: Oxford University Press, pp. 263-282.

Tuttle, R. and G. W. Cortright (1988), Positional Behavior, Adaptive Complexes, and Evolution. In *Orangutan Biology*. J. H. Schwartz (ed.). New York: Oxford University Press, pp. 311-330.

Vasishat, R.N. (1985), *Antecedents of Early Man in Northwestern India: Palaeontological and Paleaoecological Evidences*. New Delhi: Inter-India Publications, 230 pp.

Vrba, E.S. (1979), A New Study of the Scapula of *Australopithecus*. *American Journal Physical Anthropology*. 51: 117-130.

Ward, S. C. and D. Pilbeam (1983), Maxillo-facial Morphology of Miocene Hominoids from Africa and Indo-Pakistan. In *New Interpretations of Ape and Human Ancestry*. R. L. Ciochon and R.S. Corruccini (eds.) New York: Plenum, pp. 211-238.

Ward, S. C. and W. H. Kimbel (1983), Subnasal Alveolar Morphology and the Systematic Position of *Sivapithecus*. *American Journal of Physical Anthropology* 61: 157-171.

Wolpoff, M. H. (1982), Ramapithecus and Hominid Origins. *Current Anthropology* 23: 501-522.

Wu, R. (1987), A Revision of the Classification of the Lufeng Great Apes. *Acta Anthrop. Sinica* 6: 265-271.

Yamazaki, N. and H. Ishida (1984), A Biomechanical Study of the Vertical Climbing and Bipedal Walking in Gibbons. *J. Human Evolution* 13: 563-571.

Zihlaman, A. L. and J.M. Lowenstein (1983), *Ramapithecus* and *Pan Paniscus*: Significance for Human Origins. In *New Interpretations of Ape and Human Ancestry*. R. L. Ciochon and R. S. Corruccini (eds.) New York: Plenum, pp. 677-698.

Zuckerkandl, E. (1976), Programmes of Gene Action and Progressive Evolution. In *Molecular Anthropology*. M. Goodman and E.E. Tashian (eds.). New York: Plenum, pp. 387-447.

Zuckerkangle, E. and L. Pauling (2003), Molecular Disease, Evolution and Genic Heterogeneity in M. Kasha and B. Pullman (eds.) Horizons in Biochemistry, New York: Academic Press, pp189-225 [Cited from Rodriguez–Trelles, F., Tarrio, R and Ayala, F.J. 2003].

CHAPTER–2

# The Chinese Giant Ape Gigantopithecus

*Wang Wei*

## INTRODUCTION

*Gigantopithecus blacki* –the 'Giant Ape' was first named by von Koenigwald in 1935 in term of a huge lower third molar collected from the pharmacy at Hongkong (von Koenigswald, 1935). Subsequently discoveries *in situ* come from nine Karst caves from 1956 to 2006, including Daxin, Liucheng, Wuming, Bama, Jianshi, Longgupo, Mohui and Bijie locality in south China, and Tham Khuyen locality in north Vietnam (Pei *et al.*,1956; Woo, 1962; Zhang *et al.*,1973 and 1975; Xu *et al.*,1974; Huang *et al.*,1995; Zhang *et al.*,2004; Wang *et al.*,2005 and 2007; Zhao *et al.*, 2006; Ciochon *et al.*,1996).

The first locality producing *G. blacki* is the Daxin (or Heidong, means dark cave) in southwest Guangxi, where three *Gigantopithecus* teeth were collected from reddish clay by Jia and his team in spring 1956 (Pei *et al.*, 1956). The following locus is the Liucheng (or *Gigantopithecus* cave), which was primely found by local farmer in 1956 and excavated by Pei and his team during 1956 to 1963. As a result, three mandibles and 1057 isolated teeth of *G. blacki*, and numerous other mammalian specimens, had been recovered after four times of excavations. The Wuming cave, located at mountainside of Bulali of suburb of Nanning City, was first found by a hydrogeological survey team in 1965 and test excavated by Institute of Vertebrate Paleontology and Paleoanthropology (IVPP) in the same year. Twelve *G. blacki* teeth with small number of mammal fossils had been collected from the yellow hard sandy-clay. These materials were reported by Zhang in 1973. Similarly, the Bama locality was also discovered by the hydrogeological survey team in northwest Guangxi in 1973, and reported by Zhang et al. in 1975. One $M_3$ was identified from 16 species of mammal fossil teeth. The Jianshi locality (Longgu cave, means dragon bone cave), situated at west Hubei Province in central China, was initial found and excavated by a field team of IVPP in summer of 1970, and recent excavated by a joint team of IVPP and the Hubei Museum for two times during 1999 to 2000. Twenty-seven *G. blacki* teeth with rich mammal fossils were collected from the cave. Three teeth from earlier collection had ever been thought to be *Australopithecus* (Gao, 1975), while three later found teeth are allocated to *Meganthropus paleojavanicus* (Zhang *et al.*, 2004). In fact, the phylogenetic position of some early Asian hominid is ambiguous and disputed, thus these teeth seem to possibly more like *Homo erectus*. Fourteen *G. blacki* teeth from the Longgupo were discovered by Huang during 1984 to 1988 (Huang *et al.*, 1991), along with them, a fragmental mandible and another isolated incisor were allocated to *Homo*. But now they are broadly considered to be ape with genetic relationship with the Miocene *Lufengpithecus* (Schwartz *et al.*1996; Wu, 2000). The Mohui cave was recovered by during 2002 to 2004, yielding 16 teeth of *G. blacki* and 25 species of mammal fauna (Wang *et al.*, 2005, 2007). The recent report of *G. blacki* is one $P^4$ which was previous collected by the IVPP paleontologists from a drug storehouse in Bijie, west Guizhou Province of southwest China in 1964, however, its provenience is unclear. Fortunately, when the first author of the paper visited Bijie in November 2006, he picked out five *G. blacki* teeth among numerous of mammal fossils, including two incisors, one canine, one upper and another lower molar. These fossils were collected by a local fossil hunter from a quarry, named Baeryan, about 12 km west the Bijie City. The Tham Khuyen in North Vietnam, documented by Ciochon et al. in 1996, is well-known for its co-occurrence of *Homo erectus* and *G. blacki*. One lower left canine was morphologically and metrically similar to the Liucheng counterparts (Ciochon *et al.*, 1996).

All the above *G. blacki* materials consist of three fragmental mandibles and 1057 isolated teeth in Liucheng, and 75 isolated teeth from other eight localities. Based on several dated localities (Huang *et al.*,1995; Ciochon *et al.*,1996; Rink *et al.*,2008) and the biostratigraphical analysis (Huang, 1979; Han, 1985), the *G. blacki* is estimated to exist during early to middle Pleistocene, roughly from 2 to 0.5 Ma.

Sequence of mammalian fossils, including hominoid teeth, at karst caves of the Bubing basin had been systematically studied. Our previous research indicate that at least six layers of caves in this basin vary in elevations, and of the four caves were well documented to be faunal variations related to climate change, biogeographic events and evolutionary change over the past two million years (Wang *et al.*, 2007).

Here, we report a recently new found and careful excavated Chuifeng cave at the Bubing basin. This new found cave is about 227 m above the sea level, 12 m above the Mohui cave, which also produces *G. blacki* teeth and late Pliocene to early Pleistocene mammal fauna. Our excavation was undertaken for five weeks from June to July in 2006. As a result, ninety-three *Gigantopithecus blacki* teeth, associated with 914 pieces of mammal teeth were recovered.

## METHOD

Excavation is focused on northwest part of the Chuifeng cave (Fig. 1). The poorly cemented deposits are mainly formed by light-brown sandy clay with a few limestone breccia. On basis of the distribution of the sediment, four areas have been designed to excavate, as Area-A, B, C and D. There are about 5.5 $m^2$ of the sediment were excavated down to limestone bedrock in 10 cm intervals. Visible fossils were mapped, recorded, and collected, and about 100 kg of sediment each layer were sieved by 0.5 mm mesh screens to gather microfossils at a stream down the hill. In the dark inner cave, a gas-generator of 2000 watts was used for lighting. Electric Distance Measure was used to make the measurements.

Pliocene to middle Pleistocene, and Pliocene *G. bilaspurensis* mandible with most of the teeth attached from north India (Simons *et al.*, 1970). Other *G. blacki* tooth samples, collected from drug stores, are not used for comparison here for their unclear provenience, which potentially mask their important temporal and spatial variations (Table 1).

**Table 1**
**List of the *G. Blacki* teeth *in Situ* whose Mesiodistal and Buccolingual Measurements are Used for Comparison with the Chuifeng Sample**

| *Locality* | *Material* | *Resources* |
|---|---|---|
| Daxin | Three teeth ($P_3$, $M^{1-2}$, $M_3$) | Pei WC *et al.*,1956 |
| Liucheng | Three mandibles and 1006 teeth ($11I^1$, $7I_1$, $6I^2$, $6I_2$, $24C^1$, $27C_1$, $65P^3$, $89P_3$, $104P^4$, $100P_4$, $174M^{1-2}$, $140M_{1-2}$, $141M^3$, $103M_3$, $2DM^2$, $7DM_2$) | Woo RK, 1962 |
| Wumin | Twelve teeth ($4P^3$, $2P^4$, $1P_3$, $2M^{1-2}$, $1M_{1-2}$, $2M_3$) | Zhang YY *et al.*,1973 |
| Bama | One $M_3$ | Zhang YY *et al.*,1975 |
| Jianshi | Twenty-seven teeth ($1I^1$, $1C^1$, $1P^3$, $1P^4$, $3M^1$, $2M^2$, $2M^3$, $4C_1$, $2P_3$, $5P_4$, $2M_1$, $2M_2$, $2M_3$) | Xu *et al.*,1974; Zhang *et al.*,2004 |
| Longgupo | Fourteen teeth ($1C_1$, $1P^3$, $2P^4$, $3P_3$, $3P_4$, $4M_{1-2}$) | Huang *et al.*,1995 |
| Mohui | Sixteen teeth ($1I_1$, $2C^1$, $1C_1$, $3P^3$, $1P_3$, $5M_{1-2}$, $1M^{1-2}$, $1M^3$, $1M_3$) | Wang *et al.*,2005 and 2007 |
| Bijie | One $P^4$ | Zhao *et al.*,2006 |
| Tham Khuyen | One $C_1$ | Ciochon *et al.*,1996 |
| India | One mandible | |

## HOMINOID SAMPLE SETTING AND DESCRIPTION

Totally 118 isolated teeth have been identified to hominoid among the Chuifeng sample. One small-sized tooth resembles that of the extant *Hylobates* morphologically, thus it can be assigned to this genus. Twenty-four relatively large-sized teeth possess of higher crown with simple occlusal pattern, differing to the known lower crown and complicate occlusal wrinkles of *Pongo*, or the especially large-sized *G. blacki*. So, these teeth are provisionally assigned to Hominoidea gen. et. sp. Indet. There are 91 extremely larger-sized teeth can be allocated to *Gigantopithecus* morphologically, however, two relatively smaller incisors could be assigned to this genus too. Among all of the unearthed 1007 pieces of mammal teeth, *Gigantopithecus* plays a dominant role, making up a relatively high proportion of 9% of the total fauna in this collection. Eleven teeth of *Gigantopithecus* have been diagnosed as the decayed-tooth, with a percentage of about 12%. Among this *Gigantopithecus* sample, 78 teeth are well-preserved with crown, but their roots are mostly missing for porcupine activities. General descriptions are as follows:

### Upper Lateral Incisor

The left $I^2$ of Z008532 is well-preserved, except the root tip was tiny bitten by porcupines. The single root is MD compressed, curving distally, with a length-breadth index of 55.46. The mesial side is relatively flat, whereas, the distal side shows shallow longitudinal groove. The crown is excessively worn to expose a large subrounded dentine plane, surrounded by thin linear enamel. In lingual view, the remained basal crown is convex and inclined towards buccal. Viewed buccally, the labial face is vertically convex and inclined lingually. A small mesial interproximal wear facet presents, however, the distal counterpart is residual.

### Upper Canines

The crown of two left $C^1$ of Z008535 and Z008536 are at good condition, but the root of Z008535 is missing. The Z008536 preserves a small cervical portion of the distal-lingual part of the root. The Z008535 is especially robust, nearly two times larger than the Z008536 in size. Their crowns are relatively low, slightly worn and conical in shape, with height of 23.81 mm and 14.55 mm corresponding to MD of 20.80 mm and 14.79 mm. The buccal surfaces of the crown are strongly convex. The lingual surfaces are slightly bulging. The distal edges are comparatively sharp and the mesial sides are blunt. The bases of the crown are surrounded by broad cingulums, but more prominent lingually.

### Upper Third Premolars

The upper third premolars contain six teeth, including four left $P^3$ of Z008585-8 and two right $P^3$ of Z008589-90. The crowns of these teeth are well-preserved, the roots are mostly missing.

In occlusal view, two teeth of Z008588 and Z008590 are just slightly worn, the Z008589 is heavy worn, and other three are moderately worn to expose a relatively large dentine point on apex of paracone and small one on summit of protocone. All these $P^3$ are morphologically similar, the occusal outlines are rounded-trapezoid, and the buccal half is broader than the lingual one. The area of the paracone is markedly greater than that of the protocone. The median longitudinal groove is flexuous, separating the labial and lingual cusp at median basin, however, terminating at the mesial and distal marginal ridges. The lingual slope of the paracone is much more declining than the buccal slope of the protocone. The mesial and distal marginal ridges are well developed. The anterior fovea is deeper than the posterior fovea, which is clearly represented at the slightly worn specimen of Z008588.

In lingual view, the summit of the protocone is mesially placed, while the summit of the paracone occupies a distal position. Enamel folds are presented on lingual and buccal faces. In mesial or distal view, the strong development of the buccal basal prominence is remarkable, producing a characteristic lingual inclination of the labial face.

**Upper Fourth Premolars**

The upper fourth premolars are formed with seven teeth, including three left $P^4$ of Z008592, 3, 5, and four right $P^4$ of Z008591, 4, 6, 7. The crowns of these teeth are well-preserved; the roots are mostly or entirely missing.

In occlusal view, two teeth of Z008591, 3, 5, 6 are slightly worn, the Z008597 is heavy worn to exposing two large planes at paracone and protocone positions, the Z008592, 4 are moderately worn to expose two dentine points on apex of paracone and protocone. All the $P^4$ are also morphologically similar. The occusal outline is rounded rectangle. The area of the paracone is greater than the area of the protocone. The anterior fovea is similar to the posterior fovea, which is clearly represented at the slightly worn specimen of Z008595.

**Upper First/Second Molars**

The upper first/second molars include eleven teeth, consisting of five left $M^{1-2}$ of Z008598 & 8602 and six right $M^{1-2}$ of Z008603-8. The crowns are in good condition, but the roots are mostly missing, except the Z008600 which is only the apex portion absent.

Viewed occlusally, four teeth of Z008598, 8605, 7 & 8 are unworn or slightly worn, six teeth of Z008599, 8600, 2, 3, 5& 6 are moderately worn to expose one or two dentine craters, one tooth of Z008601 is seriously worn, which lingual half is erased to large sunken area.

The occusal outline of the crown is some rhomboidal in shape, generally BL-elongated. Four cusps of protocone, hypocone, paracone and metacone are well developed. The mesial cusps of protocone and paracone are gently higher than the distal cusps of hypocone and metacone. The buccal cusps of paracone and metacone rise erectly, while the lingual cusps of protocone and hypocone are inclined buccalward. Two lingual cusps, as well as two buccal cusps, are clearly separated by vertical furrowÿwhich extends to cervical crown on the buccal and lingual surface respectively, being connected by median longitudinal groove at central crown basin. The protocone and paracone are lager than the hypocone and metacoen, in general, the hypocone is the smallest cusp. The paracone occupies a BM position and the hypocone, LD place. So, the four cusps are delimited by Y-shaped fissure.

In the unworn or slightly worn teeth, the mesial and distal marginal ridges is prominent, the fovea posterior is deeper than fovea anterior. On the slope of the paracone, a large middle wrinkle expends from the apex of the cusp to the median longitudinal groove, linked with the MB marginal ridges, forming a "flower-bud pattern". On the slope of the metacone, a main ridge extends from the apex of the cone toward the Y-shaped fissures, giving out samller secondary wrinkles. On either side of the main ridge is the distinct crenated rim or marginal ridge, producing a "clover-leaf pattern". On the slope of the protocone, the main ridge is divided into two or three branches as it extends toward the longitudinal groove. On either side of these are marginal ridges. The wrinkle of the hypocone is similar to the protocone, however smaller in size. These characteristics are similar to the described Liucheng specimens (Woo, 1965).

There is slight basal prominence of crown around all sides, but it more conspicuous on the lingual side. The lingual slope is much more declining than the buccal counterpart.

Viewed from Z008600, the root consists of three separated branches, two buccal and one lingual. The L branch is BL-compressed, extending lingually. The MB and DB branches diverge from each other from the cervical enamel junction. They are BL broad, MD compressed, generally vertical extending, and inclining lingualward near the apex portions.

**Upper Third Molars**

The upper third molars are composed of two teeth, one left $M^3$ of Z008611 and another right $M^3$ of Z008609. The crowns of the two teeth are well-preserved. The Z008611 is slightly worn, while the Z008609 is moderately worn, no dentine exposing. The root of the former is entirely missing, but partially preserved in the latter.

In occlusal view, their outlines are rounded trapeziform, remarkably smaller than the $M^{1-2}$ in size. Four cusps are developed; two mesial cusps are extremely larger than the distal counterparts. The paracone is vertical prominence, markedly protruding buccally. The protocone is the largest cusp, followed by paracone, metacone, and hypocone is the smallest one. The metacone and the hypocone are greatly reduced, forming an utterly dissymmetrical shape mesio-distally. Thus only a small portion of the distal moiety remains.

The slopes of the cusps are covered with ridges generally similar to those of the $M^{1-2}$. In mesial and distal view of Z008611, the highest cusp is paracone, while hypocone the lowest. The mesial face is large and moderately convex, marked with the interproximal wear facet. The distal face is small and strongly convex. Viewed lingually, the lingual slope is distinctly declining buccally.

The root of Z008609 divided into three branches, two buccal and one lingual. The lingual branch is BL compressed, the mesio-buccal branch is MD compressed, but the distal-buccal one is missing.

### Lower Deciduous First Molar

The lower deciduous first molar is only one tooth of Z008540. The size of this tooth is distinctly smaller than its corresponding permanent tooth. The crown of the $DM_1$ is subrectangular in occlusal outline, with a length-breadth index of 105.5. Its occlusal surface is moderately worn. The metaconid is the largest cusp, the protoconid is similar to the hypoconid in size, but lager than the entoconid which has a cavity at its distal face. The buccal face sways markedly towards the lingual side. The metaconid and entoconid is more elevated than the two buccal cusps, the hypoconulid is absent. The roots are totally missing.

### Lower Deciduous Second Molar

The second lower deciduous molar of Z008539 is rectangular in occlusal view, with a length-breadth index of 139.5. The occlusal surface is tiny worn, with five cusps. The metaconid is the largest and elevated cusp, while the hypocónulid is the smallest cusp, while the entoconulid is developed. The Lingual side is straight; nevertheless, the buccal side is lingually oblique for the protuberant base. Numerous of cristaes originate from five main caups and extend to various orientations, forming a typical *Gigantopithecus* occlusal pattern. The mesial fovea is transversely and moderately narrow; the distal fovea is much small and triangular. The roots are broken off at the base, much weaker than the permanent tooth.

### Lower Lateral Incisor

The lower lateral incisor is represented by two teeth of a right $I_2$ of the Z008533 and a left $I_2$ of Z008534. Their crowns are well preserved, but most of roots are missing. They are heavy worn to expose the dentine. In lingual view, the basal crowns are convex and inclined towards buccal. Viewed buccally, the labial face is vertically convex and inclined lingually.

### Lower Canine

Z008537 is the only one right lower canine. The crown is well-preserved, but the root is missing. This tooth is slightly worn. In mesial and distal view, the crown is wedge-like with a sharp cutting edge. The buccal surface is strongly convex. The base of the crown is surrounded on all sides by a cingulum. Viewed lingually, the lingual-tubercle extends to apex.

## Lower Third Premolars

The lower third premolars are composed of ten teeth, including eight Left $P_3$ of Z008545-52 and two Right $P_3$ of Z008543-4. The crowns of these teeth are well-preserved, but roots of the Z008545 & 51 are partially missing, the Z008543, 7, 8, 9 & 52 are mostly roots missing, and the Z008544, 6 & 50 are entirely missing. Slightly occlusal wear are taken on six specimens of Z008544, 5, 7, 9, 50 & 51, moderately wear are presented at Z008548 & 52, and heavy wear are appeared on Z008543 & 6, exposing continuous dentine plane between protoconid and metaconid.

The outline of the crown is irregular pyramid and asymmetrical, the main axis runs obliquely from mesio-buccalward to disto-lingualward. The protoconid is well-developed and markedly larger than the metoconid. The protoconid and metaconid are conical, the former is higher and situated forward than the latter, the posterior half of the crown is much bigger than the anterior half, the two cusps are separated by the median longitudinal groove, the fovea anterior and posterior are deep, but the anterior is a small pit, the posterior is a large groove, transversely developed. The crown is surrounded by a basal swelling of cingulum. In lingual view, the basal crown is slightly convex and inclined towards buccal. Viewed buccally, the libial face is also slightly convex, but distinctly inclined lingually, with enamel elongation downwards.

The roots are mostly preserved at Z008545, 51. In these specimens, the roots are divided into an anterior and a posterior branch. The former is compressed buccolingually, distributing two shallow longitudinal grooves at both mesial and distal sides. The latter is flattened buccolingually, but its BL dimension is much more broader than the former, with a more wider longitudinal groove developed mesially. In the broken apex of roots of the Z008545, one small rounded canal presents at the anterior branch, correspondingly, two small canals appears at buccal and lingual side of the posterior.

## Lower Fourth Premolars

The lower fourth premolars are comprised of eleven teeth, including seven left $P_4$ of Z008553-9 and four right $P_4$ of Z008560-3. The crowns of these teeth are well-preserved, but roots of six teeth of Z008554, 55, 58-61 are mostly missing, five teeth of Z008553, 56, 57, 62 & 63 are partially missing at apexes portion. Slightly occlusal wear are taken on three specimens of Z008554, 58 & 62, moderately wear are presented at two of the Z008553 & 63, and strongly wear are appeared on other six of the Z008555, 56, 57, 59, 60 & 61, exposing large dentine plane at protoconid.

The outline of crown is nearly rounded quadrate, with its BL dimension slightly larger than the MD, except the Z008553. The protoconid and metaconid are cone-shaped, located on the mesial 2/3 of the crown and the remaining distal 1/3 of the crown is the talonid. The trigonid portion is higher than the talonid. The protoconid is gently larger and lower than the metoconid, these two cusps are separated by a median longitudinal groove, which is MD prolonged, cutting the mesial and distal marginal ridge. The fovea anterior and posterior are transversely developed, however, the former is smaller than the latter. As a whole, the $P_4$ shows great degree of molarization.

Both lingual and buccal views, the surfaces of the crown are divided by vertical furrows into a larger mesial and a smaller distal portion. The furrow on the buccal surface is longer and deeper than the lingual surface.

The roots of the Z008563 are mostly-preserved. It is divided into branch anterior and posterior. Both branches are flat and wide with the BL diameter much larger than the MD diameter.

**Lower First/Second Molars**

The lower first/second molars are formed by seventeen teeth, including nine left $M_{1-2}$ of Z008564-72 and eight right $M_{1-2}$ of Z008573-80. The crowns of these teeth are all well-preserved. The root of the Z008567, 70, 72, 75 & 79 are missing, the Z008565, 68, 69, 71, 73, 74 & 80 are partially preserved, while the Z008564, 66, 76, 77 & 78 are mostly preserved. The occlusal wear presented at four teeth of Z008564, 66, 74 & 80 are slight without dentine exposing, appeared at ten teeth of Z008565, 67, 68, 69, 72, 73, 75, 76, 77 & 79 are moderate, whereas, at three teeth of Z008570, 71 & 78 are strong, with relatively large scale of dentine exposing.

The occlusal outline of these teeth is clearly MD-elongated, rounded oblong. The five cusps, arranged in a Y-pattern, are from the largest to smallest: metaconid, protoconid, entoconid, hypoconid, and hypoconulid. These cusps are rouned and blunt, with a few narrow furrows distributed. The buccal, lingual, and median longitudinal grooves and the three foveae are visible, while the buccal and lingual grooves vertically extend to the whole crown, separating the buccal protoconid and hypoconid, lingual metaconid and entoconid respectively. The buccal surface of the protoconid and hypoconid are quite prominent for the weak cingulum existent. The slightly worn sample show that the metaconid is the highest cusp, followed by protoconid, hypoconid and entoconid, the hypoconulid is the lowest.

The root Z008576 is relatively the well-preserved sample among all of the $M_{1-2}$, which was only a little bitten by porcupine at the apex. They divide clearly into two branches, a mesial and a distal. The two branches are MD compressed, declining distalward. Measurements of the mesial branch are as follows: MD diameter of 6.02 mm, BL diameter of 13.11 and height of 26.57 mm. The distal branch is measured to 7.43 mm in MD diameter, 13.30 mm in BL diameter and 26.15 mm in height.

**Lower Third Molars**

The lower third molars include three left $M_3$ of Z008610, 8581 & 8584 and two right $M_3$ of Z008582 & 83. The crowns of these teeth are in good condition. The root of the four teeth of Z008581, 8583, 8584 & 8610 are partially preserved, but the root of Z008582 is missing. The occlusal wear of Z008582 is quite tiny, the Z008581, 83 & 84 are slight to moderate, but the Z008610 is extremely strong, exposing to a large dentine concavity.

The occlusal outline of these teeth is also MD-elongated. The trigonid is broader than the talonid for the posterior BL compressed. Five cusps are separated by a Y-pattern furrow. The metacoind is the largest one, follows the protoconid, hypoconid, entoconid, and the hypoconulid is the smallest. There is a very small accessory internal tubercle between the metaconid and entoconid of the samples of Z008584 and Z008582, a small tubercle exists also between the entoconid and the hypoconulid of specimens of Z008581, 82 & 84. Three foveae are visible. Observation from the tiny worn tooth of Z008582 shows that the metaconid is the highest cusp, followed by protoconid, hypoconid, hypoconulid, and the entoconid is the lowest.

In mesial view, the mesial face is vertical flatten, BL-elongated. The interproximal wear facet is well marked. Viewed distally, the distal face is remarkable convex, BL-compressed. The lingual and buccal surfaces are convex, while the buccal one is much more distinct. The root of Z008610 divides into two branches. The mesial one is vertical flat, MD compressed, with two independent radicular canals at the open root apex. The distal branch is mostly missing for the porcupine activity.

## MEASUREMENTS AND COMPARISON

Measurements are focused on the seventy-eight *G. blacki* teeth with well-preserved crown. Their mesiodistal and baccolingual dimensions have been taken, with an exception of the Z008594 for its basal portion broken and BL dimension absent. The values of the crown height have been taken from fourteen unworn teeth; in addition, twenty slightly worn counterparts have also measured for referring. All of the available values are listed in Table 2, metric comparisons of the maxillary and mandibular teeth of *G. blacki* in Table 3, 4.

**Table 2**
**Measurements of *G. Blacki* teeth from Chuifeng Cave (mm)**

| *Number* | *Dentition* | *MD* | *BL* | *Height* | *Number* | *Dentition* | *MD* | *BL* | *Height* |
|---|---|---|---|---|---|---|---|---|---|
| Z008532 | $LI^2$ | 7.68 | 12.02 | - | Z008550 | $LP_3$ | 16.92 | 21.43 | 15.45 |
| Z008533 | $RI_2$ | 7.50 | 9.83 | - | Z008551 | $LP_3$ | 14.39 | 17.57 | 12.30* |
| Z008534 | $RI_2$ | 7.47 | 9.68 | - | Z008552 | $LP_3$ | 16.51 | 19.54 | - |
| Z008535 | $LC^1$ | 20.80 | 17.99 | 23.85* | Z008553 | $LP_4$ | 17.41 | 15.26 | 141.7* |
| Z008536 | $LC^1$ | 14.79 | 14.52 | 14.55* | Z008554 | $LP_4$ | 13.77 | 14.68 | 14.26*×*×× |
| Z008537 | $RC_1$ | 11.97 | 17.35 | 23.01 | Z008555 | $LP_4$ | 15.17 | 17.35 | - |
| Z008585 | $LP^3$ | 13.13 | 16.54 | - | Z008556 | $LP_4$ | 13.76 | 16.60 | - |
| Z008586 | $LP^3$ | 13.84 | 18.49 | - | Z008557 | $LP_4$ | 15.01 | 18.95 | - |
| Z008587 | $LP^3$ | 13.55 | 18.77 | - | Z008558 | $LP_4$ | 15.75 | 16.77 | 15.71 |

*Contd.*

| *Number* | *Dentition* | *MD* | *BL* | *Height* | *Number* | *Dentition* | *MD* | *BL* | *Height* |
|---|---|---|---|---|---|---|---|---|---|
| Z008588 | $LP^3$ | 15.46 | 20.60 | 17.33 | Z008559 | $LP_4$ | 14.30 | 16.39 | - |
| Z008589 | $RP^3$ | 15.27 | 21.36 | - | Z008560 | $RP_4$ | 13.41 | 15.57 | - |
| Z008590 | $RP^3$ | 15.70 | 21.64 | 15.48* | Z008561 | $RP_4$ | 16.44 | 19.85 | - |
| Z008591 | $RP^4$ | 13.05 | 19.75 | 13.22 | Z008562 | $RP_4$ | 14.67 | 17.14 | 15.41* |
| Z008592 | $LP^4$ | 12.59 | 19.86 | - | Z008563 | $RP_4$ | 17.36 | 18.20 | 151.6* |
| Z008593 | $LP^4$ | 11.63 | 19.34 | - | Z008564 | $LM_{1-2}$ | 18.92 | 15.43 | 12.97 |
| Z008594 | $RP^4$ | 13.11 | - | - | Z008565 | $LM_{1-2}$ | 19.44 | 17.32 | - |
| Z008595 | $LP^4$ | 14.27 | 21.50 | 16.25 | Z008566 | $LM_{1-2}$ | 18.73 | 15.81 | 11.17* |
| Z008596 | $RP^4$ | 13.70 | 21.93 | 16.11* | Z008567 | $LM_{1-2}$ | 20.54 | 18.37 | - |
| Z008597 | $RP^4$ | 13.07 | 22.63 | - | Z008568 | $LM_{1-2}$ | 19.39 | 18.01 | - |
| Z008598 | $LM^{1-2}$ | 17.95 | 19.65 | 12.60 | Z008569 | $LM_{1-2}$ | 18.25 | 17.03 | - |
| Z008599 | $LM^{1-2}$ | 17.12 | 20.20 | - | Z008570 | $LM_{1-2}$ | 19.24 | 15.87 | - |
| Z008600 | $LM^{1-2}$ | 15.95 | 20.86 | - | Z008571 | $LM_{1-2}$ | 17.83 | 14.69 | - |
| Z008601 | $LM^{1-2}$ | 17.66 | 22.59 | - | Z008572 | $LM_{1-2}$ | 18.59 | 16.30 | - |
| Z008602 | $LM^{1-2}$ | 16.35 | 20.78 | | Z008573 | $RM_{1-2}$ | 22.52 | 19.09 | - |
| Z008603 | $RM^{1-2}$ | 20.38 | 22.95 | 14.35* | Z008574 | $RM_{1-2}$ | 20.91 | 17.83 | 123.8* |
| Z008604 | $RM^{1-2}$ | 15.90 | 18.67 | - | Z008575 | $RM_{1-2}$ | 18.47 | 16.87 | - |
| Z008605 | $RM^{1-2}$ | 16.88 | 18.75 | 14.96 | Z008576 | $RM_{1-2}$ | 17.25 | 14.04 | - |
| Z008606 | $RM^{1-2}$ | 16.81 | 20.30 | - | Z008577 | $RM_{1-2}$ | 18.81 | 16.66 | - |
| Z008607 | $RM^{1-2}$ | 17.98 | 17.00 | - | Z008578 | $RM_{1-2}$ | 17.38 | 15.79 | - |
| Z008608 | $RM^{1-2}$ | 21.08 | 23.97 | 19.35 | Z008579 | $RM_{1-2}$ | 19.02 | 16.20 | - |
| Z008609 | $RM^3$ | 14.82 | 17.58 | 12.91* | Z008580 | $RM_{1-2}$ | 22.84 | 20.00 | 14.45* |
| Z008611 | $LM^3$ | 17.29 | 17.53 | 12.93 | Z008581 | $LM_3$ | 21.65 | 19.24 | 12.18* |
| Z008543 | $RP_3$ | 14.78 | 18.32 | - | Z008582 | $RM_3$ | 24.41 | 21.11 | 15.65 |
| Z008544 | $RP_3$ | 13.87 | 17.13 | 13.42* | Z008583 | $RM_3$ | 20.30 | 17.25 | 11.32* |
| Z008545 | $LP_3$ | 14.90 | 17.43 | 13.60 | Z008584 | $LM_3$ | 20.99 | 17.21 | 11.12* |
| Z008546 | $LP_3$ | 18.45 | 20.33 | - | Z008610 | $LM_3$ | 18.19 | 16.48 | - |
| Z008547 | $LP_3$ | 13.81 | 15.03 | 13.48* | Z008538 | $LDM^2$ | 12.45 | 14.24 | - |
| Z008548 | $LP_3$ | 15.73 | 16.71 | - | Z008539 | $LDM_2$ | 17.16 | 12.30 | 9.10 |
| Z008549 | $LP_3$ | 17.89 | 20.40 | 16.18* | Z008540 | $LDM_1$ | 14.43 | 13.68 | - |

* Values of crown height of slightly worn teeth

## INFERENCES

In general, the Chuifeng *G. blacki* teeth resemble all the found samples of this species morphologically. The similarities includes that the posterior teeth are markedly larger than the reduced anterior, the incisors are small and peg-like, the canines are reduced and low-crowned, the unworn posterior teeth are polycuspidation, the premolars are broad, flat and molarized, the molars are low-crowned and flat with very thick enamel caps.

Metrically, the crown areas of the Chuifeng incisor of *G. blacki* are smaller than that of the Liucheng and the Mohui sample. The crown sizes of two $C^1$ are close to the Mohui and Jianshi sample, but smaller than mean of the Liucheng. Crown area of $C_1$ is distinctly larger than *G. bilaspurensis*, but smaller than that of the Longgupo, Mohui, Tham Khuyen, and the mean of the Liucheng. Its B/L value exceeds the lower limit of any *G. blacki*, appearing much MD compressed, while the *G. bilaspurensis* is much more. The crowns of $P^3$ are close to the Liucheng, Longgupo, Mohui and Jianshi samples, but remarkably smaller than that of the Wuming.

**Table 3**
**Metric Comparisons of the Maxillary Teeth of *G. blacki* (mm)**

| | *Liucheng* | | *Longgupo* | | *Mohui* | | *Jianshi* | | *Wuming* | | *Chuifeng* | |
|---|---|---|---|---|---|---|---|---|---|---|---|---|
| | Mean (Range) | N | Mean (Range) | N | Mean (Range) | N | Mean (Range) | N | Mean (Range) | N | Mean (Range) | N |
| $I^2$ | | | | | | | | | | | | |
| MD | 8.58 (7.9-9.0) | 6 | | | | | | | | | 7.68 | 1 |
| BL | 11.52(10.2-12.8) | 6 | | | | | | | | | 12.02 | 1 |
| Area | 99.13(80.58-111.36) | 6 | | | | | | | | | 92.31 | 1 |
| L/B | 74.92(67.97-81.08) | 6 | | | | | | | | | 63.89 | 1 |
| $C^1$ | | | | | | | | | | | | |
| MD | 19.05(14.1-23.9) | 17 | | | 15.00(14.4-15.6) | 2 | 15.3 | 1 | | | 17.80(14.79-20.80) | 2 |
| BL | 16.87(13.0-20.8) | 15 | | | 14.00(13.5-14.5) | 2 | 14.5 | 1 | | | 16.23(14.52-17.99) | 2 |
| Area | 325.49(183.30-497.17) | 14 | | | 210.3(194.4-226.2) | 2 | 221.9 | 1 | | | 244.47(214.75-274.19) | 2 |
| L/B | 112.98(101.88-131.14)9090 | 14 | | | 107.15(106.7-107.6) | 2 | 105.5 | 1 | | | 108.74(101.86-115.62) | 2 |
| $P^3$ | | | | | | | | | | | | |
| MD | 14.65(12.5-17.4) | 39 | 15.6 | 1 | 14.4(13.6-14.8) | 3 | 15.5 | 1 | 16.4(15.8-17.1) | 4 | 14.49(13.13-15.70) | 6 |
| BL | 18.98(16.3-22.6) | 39 | 19.7 | 1 | 19.2(18.2-20.6) | 3 | 21.2 | 1 | 23.2(22.1-24.0) | 4 | 19.57(16.54-21.64) | 6 |
| Area | 279.47(213.75-393.24) | 39 | 307.32 | 1 | 276.87(247.5-304.9) | 3 | 328.6 | 1 | 380.51(369.07-410.4) | 4 | 285.3(217.17-339.75) | 6 |
| L/B | 77.13(67.68-85.00) | 39 | 79.19 | 1 | 75.1(71.9-78.7) | 3 | 73.1 | 1 | 70.75(67.52-75.57) | 4 | 74.25(71.49-79.38) | 6 |
| $P^4$ | | | | | | | | | | | | |
| MD | 14.29(11.0-15.6) | 63 | 14.15(13.6-14.7) | 2 | | | 15.4 | 1 | 17.5 | 1 | 13.06(11.63-14.27) | 7 |
| BL | 19.43(17.0-24.0) | 63 | 20.15(20.1-20.2) | 2 | | | 24.7 | 1 | 25.0 | 1 | 20.84(19.34-22.63) | 6 |
| area | 259.47(187.00-345.60) | 63 | 285.15(273.36-296.94) | 2 | | | 380.4 | 1 | 437.5 | 1 | 271.64(224.92-306.81) | 6 |
| L/B | 68.45(60.00-79.06) | 63 | 70.22(67.66-72.77) | 2 | | | 62.3 | 1 | 70.00 | 1 | 62.70(57.76-66.37) | 6 |
| $M^{1-2}$ | | | | | | | | | | | | |
| MD | 17.81(14.4-21.9) | 105 | | | 16.5 | 1 | 18.5(16.8-20.8) | 3 | 21.45(20.8-22.1) | 2 | 17.64(15.90-21.08) | 11 |
| BL | 19.72(16.5-24.0) | 105 | | | 19.5 | 1 | 20.19(18.2-22.5) | 3 | 24.7(24.2-25.2) | 2 | 20.52(17.00-23.97) | 11 |
| area | 353.07(247.50-489.95) | 105 | | | 321.8 | 1 | 374.78(322.1-449.28) | 3 | 530.14(503.6-556.92) | 2 | 363.93(296.85-505.29) | 11 |
| L/B | 90.43(78.69-108.47) | 105 | | | 84.6 | 1 | 91.78(82.4-97.3) | 3 | 86.83(85.95-87.70) | 2 | 86.38(76.46-105.76) | 11 |
| $M^3$ | | | | | | | | | | | | |
| MD | 17.12(13.2-20.4) | 88 | | | 18.4 | 1 | 19.1 | 1 | | | 16.06(14.82-17.29) | 2 |
| BL | 19.1(15.2-24.0) | 87 | | | 21.8 | 1 | 21.95(21.2-22.7) | 2 | | | 17.56(17.53-17.58) | 2 |
| area | 329.97(229.46-475.20) | 87 | | | 401.1 | 1 | 433.6 | 1 | | | 254.82(206.54-303.09) | 2 |
| L/B | 89.83(67.69-105.92) | 87 | | | 84.4 | 1 | 84.190 | 1 | | | 91.47(84.30-98.47) | 2 |

($P^4$ of Bijie: MD=12.8, BL=19.6, Area=250.9; $M^{1-2}$ of Daxin: MD=17.7, BL=19.2, Area=229.84)

**Table 4**
**Metric Comparisons of the Mandibular Teeth of *Gigantopithecus* (mm)**

| | Liucheng | | Longgupo | | Mohui | | Jianshi | | Wuming | | Chuifeng | | India |
|---|---|---|---|---|---|---|---|---|---|---|---|---|---|
| | Mean (Range) | N | Mean (Range) | N | Mean (Range) | N | Mean (Range) | N | Mean (Range) | N | Mean (Range) | N | Mean |
| $I_2$ | | | | | | | | | | | | | |
| MD | 7.86(7.2-8.3) | 10 | | | 7.6 | 1 | | | | | 7.49(7.47-7.50) | 2 | |
| BL | 10.30(9.6-11.3) | 10 | | | 10.6 | 1 | | | | | 9.76(9.68-9.83) | 2 | |
| area | 81.06(70.56-93.79) | 10 | | | 80.6 | 1 | | | | | 73.02(72.31-73.73) | 2 | |
| L/B | 76.42(71.43-84.38) | 10 | | | 71.7 | 1 | | | | | 76.74(76.30-77.17) | 2 | |
| $C_1$ | | | | | | | | | | | | | |
| MD | 12.97(10.4-15.0) | 15 | 12.6 | 1 | 13.3 | 1 | 10.93(9.8-12.1) | 4 | | | 11.97 | 1 | 9.3 |
| BL | 17.14(14.5-21.0) | 14 | 17.2 | 1 | 18.4 | 1 | 15.15(12.8-17.5) | 4 | | | 17.35 | 1 | 16.0 |
| area | 221.90(152.88-306.60) | 12 | 216.72 | 1 | 244.7 | 1 | 167.63(125.4-211.8) | 4 | | | 207.68 | 1 | 148.8 |
| L/B | 72.98(69.23-82.22)9090 | 12 | 73.26 | 1 | 72.3 | 1 | 72.45(69.1-76.6) | 4 | | | 68.99 | 1 | 58.13 |
| $P_3$ | | | | | | | | | | | | | |
| MD | 15.83(12.9-18.8) | 67 | 17.57(16.6-18.8) | 3 | 15.2 | 1 | 172.67(16.2-18.3) | 3 | 16.5 | 1 | 15.73(13.81-18.45) | 10 | 11.8 |
| BL | 15.97(12.9-21.0) | 67 | 13.33(12.4-14.3) | 3 | 14.0 | 1 | 18.26(16.2-19.5) | 3 | 17.0 | 1 | 18.39(14.22-21.43) | 10 | 14.6 |
| area | 254.21(174.20-378.00) | 67 | 234.92(205.84-268.84) | 3 | 212.8 | 1 | 315.2(282.0-347.7) | 3 | 280.5 | 1 | 286.36(207.56-375.09) | 10 | 172.28 |
| L/B | 99.36(85.71-111.64) | 67 | 131.81(130.08-133.87) | 3 | 108.57 | 1 | 95.17(83.1-106.1) | 3 | 97.06 | 1 | 85.70(78.96-94.14) | 10 | 80.82 |
| $P_4$ | | | | | | | | | | | | | |
| MD | 14.73(12.1-17.3) | 120 | 16.10(14.3-17.5) | 3 | | | 16.98(16.0-18.6) | 4 | | | 15.19(13.41-17.41) | 11 | 13.1 |
| BL | 15.79(13.1-18.7) | 119 | 15.67(14.4-17.1) | 3 | | | 18.7(17.6-20.2) | 5 | | | 16.98(14.68-19.85) | 11 | 14.5 |
| area | 233.99(170.30-317.90) | 119 | 253.64(205.92-299.25) | 3 | | | 322.7(280.0-366.4) | 4 | | | 258.63(202.14-326.33) | 11 | 189.95 |
| L/B | 93.40(81.25-103.23) | 119 | 102.70(99.31-106.45) | 3 | | | 89.58(82.2-94.4) | 4 | | | 89.86(79.21-114.09) | 11 | 90.35 |
| $M_{1-2}$ | | | | | | | | | | | | | |
| MD | 19.13(16.0-23.6) | 41 | 19.48(17.9-20.6) | 4 | 19.12(16.9-20.8) | 4 | 21.18(18.5-23.7) | 4 | 21.00 | 1 | 19.30(17.25-22.84) | 17 | 18.05 |
| BL | 16.55(13.1-20.5) | 41 | 17.50(16.2-18.8) | 4 | 164.75(14.8-17.6) | 4 | 17.98(15.1-20.2) | 5 | 20.00 | 1 | 16.78(14.04-20.00) | 17 | 15.1 |
| area | 319.14(209.60-475.6) | 41 | 341.96(317.72-289.98) | 4 | 316.38(250.1-352.0) | 4 | 374.09(279.4-478.74) | 4 | 420.00 | 1 | 325.98(242.19-456.80) | 17 | 272.56 |
| L/B | 115.61(105.64-127.74) | 41 | 111.28(109.58-113.81) | 4 | 116.05(112.6-123.8) | 4 | 121.18(117.33-124.2) | 4 | 105.00 | 1 | 115.81(107.16-122.86) | 17 | 119..55 |
| $M_3$ | | | | | | | | | | | | | |
| MD | 19.19(16.0-23.0) | 51 | | | 19.2 | 1 | 22.47(19.0-25.0) | 3 | 23.00(20.00-26.00) | 2 | 21.11(18.19-24.41) | 5 | 19.6 |
| BL | 16.07(13.7-19.0) | 51 | | | 16.4 | 1 | 19.0(16.0-21.2)()90 | 3 | 20.55(18.1-23.0) | 2 | 18.26(16.48-21.11) | 5 | 16.2 |
| area | 310.43(228.79-430.10) | 51 | | | 314.9 | 1 | 431.7(304.0-496.1) | 3 | 480(362-598) | 2 | 379.61(299.77-515.30) | 5 | 317.52 |
| L/B | 119.55(105.26-128.57) | 51 | | | 117.1 | 1 | 118.48(110.4-126.3) | 3 | 111.77(110.5-113.04) | 2 | 115.64(110.38-121.96) | 5 | 120.99 |

($C_1$ of Tham Khuyen: MD=13.0, BL=18, Area=234; P3 of Daxin: MD=19.3, BL=17.6, Area=339.68; M3 of Daxin: MD=22.0, BL= 18.3, Area=402.6; M3 of Ba

The $P^4$ crowns are match to the Liiucheng, Bijie, and Longgupo specimens, however, smaller than that of the Jiangshi, and much less than Wuming counterpart. Same as the Liucheng *G. blacki*, the crowns of $P_3$ from the Chuifeng are in great range of variation in size. Its mean of the crown area is larger than all that of the *Gigantopithecus*, except to the Jianshi. The crown areas of $P_4$ are close to the Liucheng and Longgupo, but smaller than that of the Jiangshi, and larger than *G. bilaspurensis*. The sizes of $M^{1-2}$ are much close to the Liucheng, Hohui and Jianshi samples. The MD and BL diameters well fall within the range of Liucheng, but close to the lower limit of Wuming specimens. The Chuifeng $M_{1-2}$ are quite suitable to Liucheng and Mohui in means and ranges, but less than Jianshi and Wuming sample. The crown of Chuifeng $M^3$ are relatively smaller than that of Liucheng, Mohui and Jianshi sample, its mean area falls within the range of Liucheng, but quite close to the lower limit. The $M_3$ are clearly smaller than that of Jianshi, Wuming, Bama and Daxin, but larger than the Liucheng and Mohui sample.

The contrast of the upper teeth of *G. blacki* from the Chuifeng, Liucheng, Mohui, Jianshi and Wuming are presented by means for crown area at Figure 2. The comparisons of the lower teeth of *G. blacki* from the Chuifeng, Liucheng, Longgupo, Mohui, Jianshi and Wuming and *G. bilaspurensis* of Inida are shown by same way in Figure 3.

As a result, the $I^2$ of Chuifeng and Liucheng are almost same in size, the $C^1$ of the Chuifeng is smaller than that of Liucheng, but slightly larger than means of Jianshi and Mohui specimens. The $P^3$ and $P^4$ are in quite similar situation, the Chuifeng samples are very close to the Liucheng, however, markedly smaller than Jianshi, and much less than Wuming counterparts. The comparisons of $M^{1-2}$ show that the Chuifeng and Liucheng, Mohui and Jianshi have relatively closer crown sizes than the largest Wuming one. The $M^3$ present clear trend of variation in size, Jianshi sample is the largest, followed by Mohui, Liucheng and Chuifeng. Anyway, the teeth anterior of *G. blacki* from all the localities do not vary in size, whereas, the posterior show distinct increasing trend from the Chuifeng, Liucheng, Mohui to Jianshi, and Wuming. This trend is potentially corresponding to the temporal variations.

As to the lower teeth, the $I_2$ of Chuifeng, Liucheng and Mohui are very close in their crown sizes. The $C_1$ of Longgupo is also close to the mentioned three samples, but the Jianshi specimens are quite smaller, more less the *G. bilaspurensis*. The posterior lower teeth of the Chuifeng, Liucheng, Longgupo, Mohui do not vary too much in sizes. However, these samples are remarkably smaller than Jianshi, Wuming, Bama and Daxin, but larger than the *G. bilaspurensis*. So, the comparisons of the lower teeth posterior of *Gigantopithecus* display similar increasing trend of size variation to the upper one.

## REFERENCES CITED

Ciochon RL, Long VT, Larick R, González L, Grün R, de Vos J, Yonge C, Taylor L, Yoshida H, Reagan M. (1996), Dated Co-occurrence of *Homo Erectus* and *Gigantopithecus* from Tham Khuyen Cave, Vietnam. Proc Natl Acad Sci USA 93: 3016-3020.

Gao J. (1975), *Australopithecine* Teeth associated with *Gigantopithecus*. Vert. PalAs 13: 81-88.

Han DF, Xu CH. (1985), Pleistocene Mammalian faunas of China. In: Wu RK, Olsen JW editor. Paleoanthropology and Paleolithic Archaeology in the People's Republic of China. New York: Academic Press. p 267-286.

Huang WP. (1979), On the Age of the Cave-faunas of South China. Vert PalAs 17: 327-343.

Huang WP, Ciochon RL, Gu YM, Larick R, Fang QR, Schwarcz H, Yonge C, de Vos J, Rink W. (1995), Early *Homo* and Associated Artifacts from Asia. Nature 378: 275-278.

Huang WP, Fang QR. (1991), *Wushan Hominid Site*. Beijing: Ocean Press. p 1-230.

Pei WC. (1956), New Materials of Gigantopithecus Teeth from South China. Acta Palaeont Sin 4: 477-490.

Rink WJ, Wang W, Bekken D, Jones HL. Geochronology of *Ailuropoda-Stegodon* Fauna and *Gigantopithecus blacki* in Guangxi Province, Southern China. Quat Res in review.

Schwartz JH, Tattersall I. (1996), Whose Teeth. Nature 381: 202.

Simons EL, Ettel PC. (1970), *Gigantopithecus*. Sci Am 222: 76-85.

von Koenigswald, GHR. (1935), Eine Fossile säugetierfauna mit Simia aus Südchina. Proc Kon Akad Weten Ser C 38: 872-879.

Wang W, Potts R, Hou YM, Chen YF, Wu HY, Yuan BY, Huang WW. (2005), Early Pleistocene Hominid Teeth recovered in Mohui Cave in Bubing Basin, Guangxi, South China. Chin Sci Bull 50: 2777-2782.

Wang W, Potts R, Yuan, BY, Huang WW, Chen H, Edwards L, Ditchfield P. (2007), Sequence of Mammalian Fossils, including Hominoid Teeth, from the Bubing Basin Caves, South China. J Hum Evol 52: 370-379.

Wang W, Tian F, Mo JY. (2007), Recovery of *Gigantopithecus blacki* Fossils from the Mohui Cave in the Bubing Basin, Guangxi, South China. Acta Anthropol Sin 26: 329-343.

Woo JK. (1962), The Mandibles and Dentitions of *Gigantopithecus*. Paleont Sin N S D, No.**11**: 1-94.

Wu XZ. (2000), Longgupo Hominoid Mandible belongs to Ape. Acta Anthropol Sin 19: 1-10.

Xu CH, Han KX, Wang LH. (1974), *Gigantopithecus* Fossils and Associated Fauna from West Hupei. Vert PalAs 12: 294-309.

Zhang YY, Wang LH, Dong XR, Chen WJ. (1975), *Gigantopithecus* Tooth from Bama, Kwangsi. Vert PalAs 13: 148-153.

Zhang YY, Wu ML, Liu JR. (1973), *Gigantopithecus* Teeth Discovered in Wuming, Kwangsi. Chin Sci Bull 18: 130-133.

Zhang YY, Zhang ZB, Liu W. (2004), Paleaoanthropology. In: Zheng SH, editor. Jianshi Hominid Site. Beijing: Science Press. P 26-36.

Zhao LX, Tong HW, Xu CH, Yuan ZX, Cai HY. (2004), New Discovery of *Gigantopithecus balcki* Tooth Fossil from Bijie, Guizhou and Its Significance. Quat Sci 26: 548-554.

CHAPTER–3

# Siwalik Palaeoecology and Hominoid Extinctions

*Rajan Gaur*

## INTRODUCTION

Investigations of the palaeoecological and palaeoenvironmental conditions then prevailing can be very helpful in understanding the selection processes that determined the course of hominoid and hominid evolution. In the context of hominoid evolution, the Siwalik sediments of the Indian subcontinent hold a special status because these deposits have yielded a diversity of primate fossils that document significant stages of hominoid evolution. This paper presents, in brief, a reconstruction of the palaeoecological scenario of the Mio-Pliocene Siwalik sediments of India with special reference to the prospects for the fossil hominoids.

The Siwalik deposits of the Indian Subcontinent comprise an exceptionally long and well-documented record of terrestrial mammalian evolution from early Miocene to Pleistocene. Spanning a distance of roughly 2,400 kilometers between river Indus in the west and the river Brahmputra in the east, these continental molassic deposits are over 7000 meters thick and predominantly fluvial in origin (Johnson and Vondra, 1972; Johnson, 1977). These deposits originated as detritus shed by the rising Himaḷaya, a product of collusion and subsidence of the Indian plate with the Asian Plate some 40-45 million years ago (Powell and Conagham, 1973). The deformation of the Siwaliks is an attribute of further movement of the Indian plate. Lithologically, the Siwalik sediments generally comprise clay, silt and sandy-silt units in various shades of orange, brown and grey alternating with greyish or brownish sandstones. The results of palaeomagnetic investigations of the Pakistan Siwaliks by Opdyke *et al.* (1979) and Johnson *et al.* (1985) reveal that these rocks range in age from 18.3 Million years to 0.6 million years–a span of more than 17 ½ million years. Over the years these rocks have yielded a variety of Strepsirhine Primate genera (*Sivaladapis, Indraloris, Nycticeboides*), Cercopithecoid genera (*Macaca, Procynocephalus, Theropithecus, Presbytis*) and Hominoid genera (*Krishnapithecus, "Sivasimia", Sivapithecus and Gigantopithecus*). Among these, the middle to late Miocene hominoids are of special interest to palaeoanthropologists.

In India, several primate fossil sites are distributed in the Siwaliks of Jammu and Kashmir, Himachal Pradesh, Panjab Haryana and Uttaranchal. The main fossil primate bearing localities in the Indian Siwaliks include Ramnagar Basin (J & K), Haritalyangar Basin (H.P.), Ranital Basin (H.P.), Dera Gopipur area (H.P.), Mirzapur (Panjab), Bunga (Haryana), and Kalagarh Basin of Uttaranchal State. The present paper reconstructs the palaeosynecology of the fossil mammalian assemblages from the Mio-Pliocene fossil hominoid sites of the Indian Siwaliks. The palaeoecological reconstruction described here is based primarily on the analysis of the fossil mammalian fauna. For this purpose the fossil mammalian taxa collected by the author himself as well as those reported by other workers have been employed for faunal analysis.

Though the mammalian fauna from the Indian Siwaliks is well documented, their palaeoecology is yet to be completely understood. Some of the early efforts to reconstruct the Siwalik environment and ecology were made by Tattersall (1969a,b), Prasad (1971,1975), Johnson (1977), Suneja and Gaur (1977), Suneja and Singh (1980), Suneja and Kaul (1980), Gaur *et al.* (1978). Majority of the earlier studies on the ecological reconstruction of the Siwaliks heavily relied upon a few indicator mammalian species, some of which could have been introduced into the assemblage just by chance, without analyzing the mammalian fauna as a whole that may sometimes indicate a different ecology than that suggested by the indicator species. Further, the emphasis was more on broad generalizations for the Siwaliks as a whole and the spatial variations in regional habitats were not attempted. Moreover, most of these studies did not elaborate many lesser habitats, which might have been present. It is only in the last couple of decades that some well-investigated reports on Siwalik environment and ecology have been published by Badgley and Behrensmeyer (1980), Gaur (1981, 1987, 2003), Behrensmeyer and Tauxe (1982), Gaur and Chopra (1983, 1984), Gaur and Vasishat (1989), Scott *et al.* (1999), etc. Some of these reports were focused on Pakistan Siwaliks and a couple of them employed geological and sedimentological data for environmental reconstruction (Badgley and Behrensmeyer, 1980; Behrensmeyer and Tauxe, 1982). Therefore, only a limited amount of information is available about the habitat and palaeoecology of the Indian Siwaliks based on the analysis of mammalian fauna. Despite these studies there still exist gaps in our understanding of the palaeoecology of the fossil hominoid primates from the Indian Siwaliks. These gaps can only be bridged through proper analyses of the fossil fauna and flora from the Siwalik deposits. The present report is an attempt in this direction.

It is now well known that the ecosystem shapes the organisms that live in it. Therefore any serious effort to understand the evolution of a fossil form or a fossil lineage must take into account the ecosystem and the environment and ecology in which this process occurred. Much as the modern day ecology concerns the relationship of the living organisms with their environment, palaeoecology deals with the relationship between the past organisms and their life medium. Palaeoecology may be simply defined as "the study of past biota on a basis of ecological concepts and methods in so far as they can be applied" (Cain, 1944).

## METHODOLOGY

The present study is based on the habitat spectra analysis of the fossil mammals from the primate-yielding localities of the Indian Siwaliks. The fossil mammalian taxa collected by the author as well as those already known from the Siwalik localities under consideration have been used in this study. Habitat spectra analysis is a sensitive method of reconstructing the palaeohabitats and palaeoecology. It was developed and used for the first time by Van Couvering in 1980. The method takes into consideration the morphology and the closeness of a fossil form to its nearest extant relative to deduce past habitats. The method is based on two basic assumptions, viz. (1) morphology of forms reflect habitats and (2) the closer a fossil taxon is to a living taxon the greater is the similarity between their habitats. For the present work, the habitat spectra analysis of the fossil mammals was carried out following the procedures suggested by Van Couvering (1980). The fossil species were assigned a range of possible habitats and given a weighting from zero to six in accordance with the level of the lowest living classificatory category. The weighted total for each habitat type was then depicted as histograms, which clearly indicated the dominant habitats along with the lesser ones.

## THE FAUNAL ASSEMBLAGES

The mammalian faunal assemblage from the Siwaliks of India is very rich and a diversity of mammalian taxa, ranging from rodents to hominoids, is represented. In addition to mammals other vertebrate groups such as reptiles, fish and amphibians are also present. Among the non-mammalian vertebrate groups, the reptiles, such as crocodylidae and chelonidae, are more common. The major hominoid-yielding localities of Indian Siwaliks include Ramnagar Basin (J & K), Haritalyangar Basin (H.P.), Kalagarh Basin (Uttaranchal) and Ranital Basin (H.P.). Among these localities, the Ramnagar and the Haritalyangar Basins have been the most prolific.

**Table 1**
**Fossil Mammals from Major Lower and Middle Siwalik Primate Localities of India**

| | *Lower Siwaliks* | | | *Middle Siwaliks* | | |
|---|---|---|---|---|---|---|
| | *Kalagarh* | | *Ramnagar* | *Ranital* | *Haritalyangar* | |
| *Fossil Taxa* | *Kamlial Form.* | *Chinji Form.* | *Chinji Form.* | *Nagri Form.* | *Nagri Form.* | *Dhokpathan Form.* |
| INSECTIVORA | | | | | | |
| Sivalikosorex parsadi | – | – | – | – | – | x |
| PRIMATES | | | | | | |
| Palaeotupaia sivalicus | – | – | – | – | x | – |
| Indraloris himalayansis | – | – | – | – | x | – |
| Sivaladapis palaeindicus | – | – | x | – | – | – |
| Sivaladapis nagrii | – | – | – | – | x | – |
| Indoadapis shivaii | – | – | – | x | x | – |
| Krishnapithecus krishnaii | – | – | – | – | x | – |
| Gigantopithecus giganteus | – | – | – | – | x | x |
| Sivasimia chinjiensis | – | – | x | – | – | – |
| Sivapithecus sivalensis | – | – | x | x | x | – |
| Sivapithecus Indicus | – | x | x | – | x | x |
| Ramapithecus punjabicus | | x | x | – | x | – |
| RODENTIA | | | | | | |
| Rhizomyoides sivalensis | – | x | – | x | – | – |
| Rhizomyoides nagrii | – | – | – | – | x | – |
| Rhizomyoides pilgrimii | – | – | – | – | x | – |
| Rhizomyoides punjabicus | – | – | x | – | – | – |
| Dakamys nagrii | – | – | – | – | x | – |
| Kanisamys indicus | – | – | – | – | x | – |
| Kanisamys nagrii | – | – | – | – | x | – |
| Parapodemus hariensis | – | – | – | – | x | – |
| Progonomys choprii | – | – | – | – | x | – |
| Siwalikomus nagrii | – | – | – | – | x | – |
| Sayimys sivalensis | – | – | x | – | – | – |
| Sayimys perplexus | – | – | – | – | x | – |
| Mastomys colberti | – | – | – | – | x | – |
| Muridae indet. | – | – | x | – | – | – |
| CARNIVORA | | | | | | |
| Dissopsalis sp. | – | – | x | – | – | – |
| Sivanasua himalayensis | – | – | – | – | x | – |
| Sivanasua nagrii | – | – | – | – | x | – |
| Amphicyon sindiensis | x | – | – | – | – | – |
| Amphicyon sp. | – | – | x | – | – | – |
| Viverra chinjiensis | – | x | | | – | – |
| Viverra nagrii | – | – | – | – | x | – |
| Vishnuictis hariensis | – | – | – | – | x | – |
| Lutrinae indet. | – | – | x | – | – | – |
| Lycyaena macrostoma | – | – | – | – | x | – |
| Crocuta mordax | – | – | – | – | x | – |
| Crocuta gigantea | – | – | – | – | x | x |
| Ictitherium nagrii | – | – | x | – | – | – |
| Vishnufelis sp. | – | – | x | – | – | – |

*Contd.*

| | *Lower Siwaliks* | | | *Middle Siwaliks* | | |
|---|---|---|---|---|---|---|
| | *Kalagarh* | | *Ramnagar* | *Ranital* | *Haritalyangar* | |
| *Fossil Taxa* | *Kamlial Form.* | *Chinji Form.* | *Chinji Form.* | *Nagri Form.* | *Nagri Form.* | *Dhokpathan Form.* |
| Maganterion praecox | – | – | – | – | x | – |
| Vinayakia intermedia | – | – | – | – | x | – |
| PROBOSCIDEA | | | | | | |
| Deinotherium pentapotamiae | – | – | x | – | x | – |
| Deinotherium sindiense | x | – | – | – | x | – |
| Deinotherium indicum | – | – | – | x | x | x |
| Deinotherium sp. | – | x | – | x | – | – |
| Gomphotheridae indet. | – | x | x | – | – | – |
| Trilophodon pandeonis | x | – | – | – | – | – |
| Trilophodon indicum | – | – | – | – | – | x |
| Tetralophodon falconeri | – | – | – | – | – | x |
| Synconolophus cf. dhokpathanensis | – | – | – | – | – | x |
| Stegolophodon bombifron | – | – | – | – | – | x |
| PERISSODACTYLA | | | | | | |
| *Equidae* | | | | | | |
| Hipparion antelopinum | – | x | – | x | x | x |
| Commohipparion theobaldi | – | – | – | – | x | x |
| Equs sivalensis | – | – | – | – | – | – |
| Equus sivalensis minor | – | – | – | – | – | – |
| RHINOCEROTIDAE | | | | | | |
| Brachyopotherium perimense | – | – | x | – | x | – |
| Gaindatherium brownii | – | – | – | – | x | – |
| Caementodon sp. | – | – | x | – | – | – |
| Chilotherium intermedium | – | – | x | – | – | – |
| Aceratherium perimense | – | – | x | – | – | – |
| ARTIODACTYLA | | | | | | |
| *Suidae* | | | | | | |
| Listriodon pentapotamiae | x | – | x | – | – | – |
| Tetraconodon mirabilis | – | – | – | – | x | – |
| Conohyus sindiense | x | x | x | – | – | – |
| Conohyus parsadi | – | – | – | – | x | – |
| Conohyus chinjiensis | – | – | x | – | – | – |
| Conohyus sp. | – | x | – | – | – | – |
| Propotamocherus salinus | – | – | – | – | x | x |
| Propotamochoerus sp. | – | x | x | x | – | – |
| Dicoryphochoerus robustus | – | x | – | – | x | – |
| Dicoryphochoerus titanoides | – | – | – | – | x | – |
| Dicoryphochoerus vagus | – | – | – | – | x | – |
| Sus advena | – | – | – | – | x | – |
| Sus sp. | – | x | – | – | – | – |
| Lophochoerus nagrii | – | – | – | – | x | – |
| ANTHRACOTHERIIDAE | | | | | | |
| Anthracotherium punjabiense | – | x | x | x | x | – |
| Anthraconema dangarii | – | – | – | – | x | – |
| Anthracodon hariensis | – | – | – | – | x | – |
| Hyoboops minor | x | x | – | – | – | – |

*Contd.*

| | *Lower Siwaliks* | | | *Middle Siwaliks* | | |
|---|---|---|---|---|---|---|
| | *Kalagarh* | | *Ramnagar* | *Ranital* | *Haritalyangar* | |
| *Fossil Taxa* | *Kamlial Form.* | *Chinji Form.* | *Chinji Form.* | *Nagri Form.* | *Nagri Form.* | *Dhokpathan Form.* |
| TRAGULIDAE | | | | | | |
| Dorcabune anthracotherioides | - | - | x | - | - | - |
| Dorcabune sp. | - | - | x | x | - | - |
| Dorcabune negrii | - | x | x | x | x | x |
| Dorcatherium majus | - | x | x | x | - | - |
| DIRAFFIDAE | | | | | | |
| Giraffokeryx punjabiensis | - | x | x | - | x | x |
| Hydaspitherium megacephalum | - | - | - | - | x | - |
| Vishnutherium iravaticum | - | - | - | - | x | - |
| BOVIDAE | | | | | | |
| Gazella lydekkeri | - | - | - | - | x | x |
| Gazella sp. | - | - | x | - | - | - |
| Protrgocerus glutens | - | - | x | - | - | - |
| Miotragoceros sp. | - | - | x | x | - | - |
| Dorcadoxa porrecticomis | - | x | - | - | - | - |
| Tragocerus punjabiensis | - | - | - | - | x | x |
| Selenoportax vaxillarius | - | - | - | - | x | x |
| Pachyportax nagrii | - | - | - | - | x | x |
| Pacyportax latidens | - | - | - | - | x | - |
| Sivacobus palaeindicus | - | - | - | - | - | - |

Form = Formaton —

Table-1 shows the diversity of the mammalian taxa known from different formations of the major fossil hominoid-bearing localities of the Lower and Middle Siwaliks in India. This list is based on the fossil mammalian taxa reported by numerous workers since 1845 (see references). It is evident from the table that Lower and Middle Siwaliks in the Haritalyangar Basin and Lower Siwaliks of Ramnagar Basin depict the maximum diversity of fossil mammalian fauna. As far as the fossil primates are concerned, a majority has been recovered from the Chinji Formation of Lower Siwaliks and the Nagri Formation of Middle Siwaliks. Some fossil primate material has also been reported from the Dhokpathan Formation of Middle Siwaliks and from Pinjor Formation of Upper Siwaliks. A single cercopithecoid specimen is also known from the Boulder Conglomerate Formation of Upper Siwaliks. From the distribution of primate fauna in the various Siwalik formations of India, it appears that Chinji and Nagri times probably provided an environment, which was apparently favourable for the diversification of prosimians and hominoid primates.

## HABITAT SPECTRA AND PALAEOECOLOGY

In the present report palaeoecological deductions have been made on the basis of the habitat spectra analysis of the fossil mammalian fauna known from the various formations of the Siwaliks of northwest India. The habitat spectra analysis of the mammalian fauna is a very useful method to infer the range of palaeohabitats (Van Couvering, 1980; Gaur and Chopra, 1984; Gaur, 1987). The past habitats are deduced by taking into consideration the morphology and the closeness of the fossil taxa to their nearest living relatives. Following the methods of Van Couvering (1980), fossil mammals from the major primate bearing localities of the Indian Siwaliks have been analysed for the habitat spectra to infer past ecology.

The primate fauna was more diverse during the Chinji Formation of Lower Siwaliks and the Nagri Formation of Middle Siwaliks. Similarly, the hominoids were also more abundant during this time period. The palaeoecological reconstruction of the Miocene hominoid-bearing localities of the Indian Lower (Chinji) and Middle Siwaliks (Nagri) indicates a more or less similar habitat with slight regional and temporal variations. The habitat spectra analyses of the mammalian fauna reveals that at most localities with abundant hominoid or other primate fauna, the dominant habitat consisted of woodlands and forests. The Chinji fauna is suggestive of thick woodlands with dense bush cover and warm and humid climate with a more or less closed cover habitat. The forest cover component was

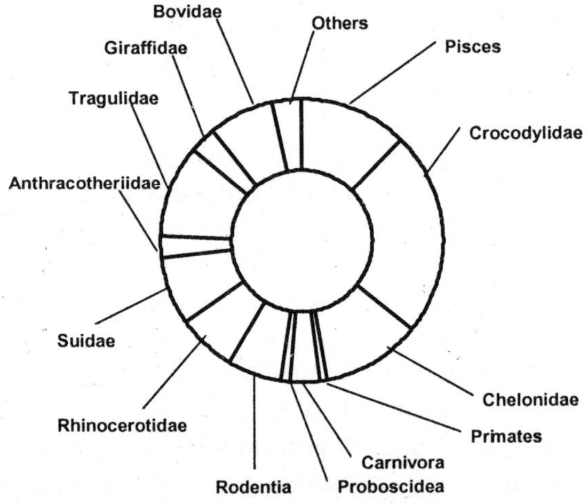


Figure 1: Relative Frequencies of Various Fossil Group from the Chinji Formation of Lower Siwaliks at Ramnagar, J & K (Redrawn after Gaur and Chopra, 1983).

greater for Ramnagar area than that for Kalagarh area. The palaeoecology of Chinji deposits at Ramnagar is similar to that of Chinji localities of Pakistan, which also appear to suggest more uniformly forested conditions with a continuous canopy (Scott *et al.*, 1999). As compared to Fort Ternan locality of African hominoid *Kenyapithecus*, which is considered similar in age to the Chinji deposits (Scott et al., *op cit.*), the Chinji and Nagri hominoids lived in a more closed environments. The closed canopies may not have been available to *Kenyapithecus* dated to about 14 Million years, thus implying the occurrence of geographic variations in palaeoecology of African and Eurasian Miocene hominoids.

The Nagri mammalian fauna at Haritalyangar shows a change from a general forested Chinji ecology to ecology with open woodlands and subordinate bush land. The Ranital Nagri ecology was roughly similar to that of Haritalyangar with a slightly larger proportion of forests. The habitat spectra of Nagri mammals favour a dominant and somewhat open woodland habitat.

The Nagri palaeoecology at Haritalyangar was more or less similar to that of *Sivapithecus parvada* reported by Scott *et al.* (*op cit.*) from the Nagri deposits of Pakistan. The other important components of the Nagri landscape were the forests, wooded-grasslands and bush land, in a decreasing order. It is evident that the Nagri hominoids had a greater range of habitats available to them as compared to hominoids from Chinji Formation. By the Nagri times, the thick forests and woodlands of Chinji times had broken down and become more open, probably due to the increased seasonality of the climate caused by the continuous uplifting of the Himalayas, which gave rise to a seasonal monsoon type of climate. Thus from Chinji to Nagri times there was a trend of increasing habitat

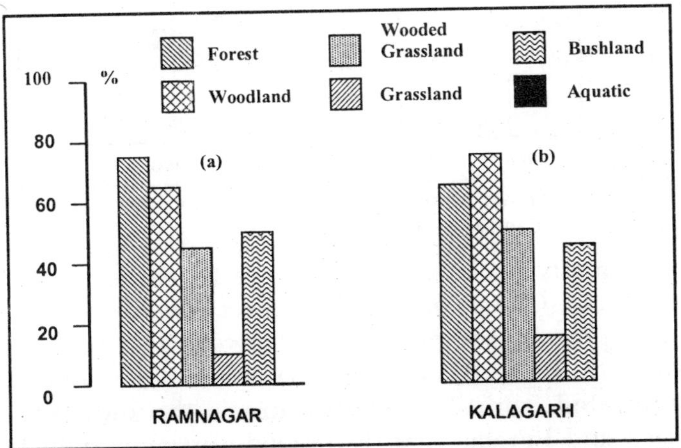


Figure 2: Habitat Spectra of Fossil Mammals from the Chinji Formation of Lower Siwaliks at Ramnagar (a) and Kalagarh (b)

fragmentation and diversity. Though the forests may have declined but open plains did not develop.

The woodlands of Nagri times were broken down during Dhokpathan times and the fauna at Haritalyangar is suggestive of a more open country habitat, similar to savannah (or wooded savannah), probably due to increased seasonality of climates and aridity. The occurrence of grazing mammals further suggests that some grassland type areas were also present and that grasses had probably entered into the Dhokpathan vegetation.

The closed habitats of Chinji and Nagri hominoids had dwindled during Dhokpathan times and this habitat change probably affected the course of evolution of hominoids, which are mainly represented in the Dhokpathans of India by a large-bodied and probably terrestrial *Gigantopithecus*. The habitat during Tatrots opened up further but the climate was still warm and humid with a mosaic habitat dominated by wooded grassland with bush land and grassland (Gaur and Chopra, 1984). The once diverse primate fauna of Chinji and Nagri times drastically declined during Dhokpathan and subsequent phases and only terrestrial cercopithecoids have been found in the Siwalik deposits younger than Tatrots.

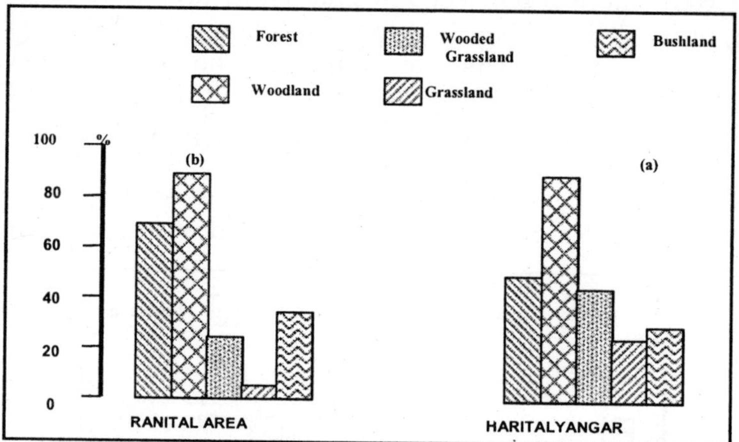


Figure 3: Habitat Spectra of Fossil Mammals from the Nagri Formation of Middle Siwaliks of Ranital Area (b) and Haritalyangar Basin (a)

Given the currently available fossil evidence, the earliest record of fossil hominoids is from the Chinji Formation of Lower Siwaliks, which has been magnetostratigraphically assigned an age between 14.3 and 10.8 Million years (Johnson *et al.*, 1985). It is believed that hominoids, along with other mammals, migrated from Africa into Eurasia through land bridges between Africa and Eurasia that developed approximately 16.5 to 17 million years ago, as a result of global cooling during Miocene. A favourable warm and humid climate with abundant forest cover allowed a diversification of hominoids and other primates during the Chinjis, which is attested by the recovery of prosimian (*Sivaladapis*) and hominoid (*Sivapithecus*) taxa from these deposits. By the end of Chinjis and the beginning of Nagris, the forest cover had begun to be fragment, probably due to a change in climate from tropical-subtropical to more seasonal. That monsoonal system had begun to take its effect at the beginning of Nagris at 10.7 Million years is indicated by the analysis of oxygen isotope data obtained from the fossil unionids and bovid teeth from the Middle Siwaliks of Nepal (Dettman *et al.*, 2001). This implies that the Tibetan

Plateau at that time had been sufficiently high and broad to drive the monsoon and cause strong wet-dry seasonality. A change in climate to a more seasonal one in the Nagris probably caused fragmentation of the forests and a trend of increased habitat diversity as compared to more uniformly forested conditions of the Chinjis. The increased habitat diversity of the Nagris probably acted as a spur for the further diversification of prosimian (*Sivaladapis, Indraloris, Nycticeboides*) and hominoid fauna (*Krishnapithecus, Sivapithecus, Gigantopithecus*). Scott *et al.* (*op cit.*) are of the opinion that hominoid taxonomic diversity may be tied to environmental diversity.

At the end of Nagri times, roughly 8.5 Million years ago, a marked change in climate and flora is indicated by the data on carbon isotopes from palaeosol samples and tooth enamel studies from Pakistan Siwaliks. The palaeosol carbon isotope data from Pakistan provides a strong evidence for a vegetation shift from C3 plants to C4 grasslands between 8 and 6 Million years (Cerling *et al.*, 1997; Quade *et al.*, 1989; Quade and Cerling, 1995). This shift from C3 to C4 plants was probably a global phenomenon (Cerling *et al.*, 1997). At this time (7.5 Million years ago), a drier landscape is clearly indicated by the changing nature of the palaeosol in the Pakistan and Nepal Siwaliks (Quade *et al.*, 1995; Quade and Cerling, 1995). These late Miocene climatic changes also influenced the hominoid evolution in the Siwaliks.

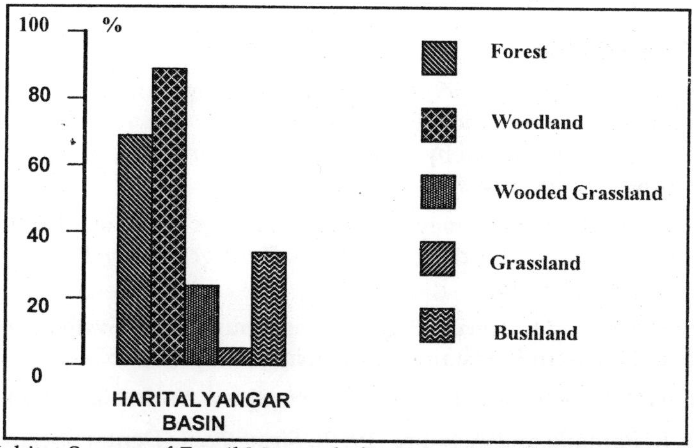


Figure 4: Habitat Spectra of Fossil Mammals from the Dhokpathan Formation of Middle Siwaliks of Haritalyangar Basin

The Dhokpathan Formation shows a sharp decline in the hominoid fauna. Barring *Gigantopithecus* and a single specimen of *Sivapithecus* from Haritalyangar area by Sankhyan (1985), no other primates are reported from the post-Nagri deposits of the Indian Siwaliks. The breakdown of the woodlands and the appearance of wooded savannah in the Dhokpathans and increasing aridity and seasonality of the climate along with the disappearance of the preferred habitat of the hominoids might have caused the decline of hominoid and other primate fauna during late upper Miocene.

The subsequent Pliocene witnessed a further increase in seasonality of climate and increases in aridity with the gradual replacement of savannahs and bush land of Tatrots with dominant grasslands during Pinjors (Gaur and Chopra, 1984), conditions which were unfavourable for the forest adapted hominoids. It is thus not surprising that that the post-Dhokpathan Siwalik deposits are totally devoid of hominoid fossils. The only primate fossils that we get in Pliocene Siwalik deposits are the open country and more terrestrial cercopithecoids such as macaques and baboons. The situation in Siwaliks is similar to that obtaining in other parts of Eurasia, where in late Upper Miocene, i.e. after 7 Million years, no or very rare hominoids (i.e. clades of humans and great apes) remained north of the Tropic of Cancer (Kordos and Begun, 2002). One of the responses of hominoids to climatic changes was probably extinction, as has been suggested by Andrews and Bernor (1999). The other response could have been evolution and dispersal into Africa from Eurasia by some hominoids and also into tropics of Southeast Asia by a relative of the orangutan clade, by the end of Miocene (Kordos and Begun, *op cit.*). Thus, it is probable that, by the close of Miocene, the once flourishing Siwalik hominoid primate fauna either became extinct or, at least some forms, migrated to other regions, such as the tropical Southeast Asia.

## REFERENCES CITED

Andrews, P. and R. L. Bernor (1999), "Vicariance Biogeography and Palaeoecology of Eurasian Miocene Hominoid Primates". In *The Evolution of Neogene Terrestrial Ecosystems in Europe*. Edited by J. Agusti, L. Rook and D P. Andrews. pp. 454-487 Cambridge: Cambridge University Press.

Badgley, C. and A.K. Behrensmeyer (1980), Palaeoecology of Middle Siwalik Sediments and Faunas, Northern Pakistan. *Palaeogeography, Palaeoclimatology, Palaeoecology* 30: 133-155.

Behrensmeyer, A.K. and L. Tauxe (1982), Isochronous Fluvial Systems in Miocene Deposits of Northern Pakistan. *Sedimentology* 29(3): 331-352.

Cain, S. A. (1944), *Foundations of Plant Geography*. New York: Harper and Bros.

Cameron, D. R. Patnaik, and A. Sahni (1999), *Sivapithecus* Dental Specimens from Dhara Locality, Kalagarh District, Uttar Pradesh, Siwaliks, Northern India. *Journal of Human Evolution* 37:861-868.

Cerling, T.E., Y. Wang and J. Quade (1993), Expansion of C4 Ecosystems as an Indicator of Global Ecological Change in the Late Miocene. *Nature* 361: 344-345.

Chopra, S.R.K. (1978), New Fossil Evidence on the Evolution of Hominoidea in the Sivaliks and Its Bearing on the Problem of the Evolution of Early Man in India. *Journal of Human Evolution* 7: 3-9.

Chopra, S.R.K. 1983. "Significance of Recent Hominoid Discoveries from the Siwalik Hills of India". In *New Interpretations of Ape and Human Ancestry*. Edited by R. L. Ciochon and R. S. Corruccini. pp. 539-557.New York: Plenum.

Chopra, S.R.K. and S. Kaul (1979), A New Species of *Pliopithecus* from the Indian Sivaliks. *Journal of Human Evolution*. 8 : 475-477.

Chopra, S.R.K. and R.N. Vasishat (1979), Sivalik Fossil Tree Shrews from Haritalyangar, India. *Nature*. 281: 214-215.

Chopra, S.R.K. and R.N. Vasishat (1980), A New Mio-Pliocene *Indraloris* Primate) Material with Comments on the Taxonomic Status of *Sivanasua* (Carnivora) from the Sivaliks of the Indian Sub-continent. *Journal of Human Evolution*. 9:2.

Chopra, S.R.K. and R.N. Vasishat (1984), Fossil Adapids from Kangra District of Himachal Pradesh, India. *10th Congress International Primatological Society Nairobi, Kenya*, Abstract Papers.

Colbert, E.H. (1935), Siwalik Mammals in the American Museum of Natural History. *Transactions of American Museum of Natural History*. 74:255-436.

Dettman, D.L., M. Kohn, J. Quade, F.J. Ryerson, and T.P. Ojha (2001), Seasonal Stable Isotope Evidence for a Strong Asian Monsoon through the Past 10.7 M. Y. *Geology*. 29(1): 31-34.

Dutta, A.K., P.K. Basu, and M.V.A. Sastry (1976), On the New Finds of Hominoids and Additional Finds of Pongidae from the Siwaliks of Ramnagar Area, Udhampur District, J & K State. *Indian Journal of Earth Sci*ence. 3 (2): 334-335.

Falconer, H. and P.T. Cautley (1845-1849), *Fauna Antiqua Sivalensis: Being the Fossil Zoology of the Siwalik Hills in the North of India*. London: Smith, Elder and Co.

Gaur, R. (1981), *Palaeontology and Palaeoecology of Plio-Pleistocene Upper Sivalik Sediments in the Northeast of Chandigarh*. Ph.D. diss., Panjab University, Chandigarh.

Gaur, R. (1987), Environment and Ecology of Early Man in Northwest India: Geological and Palaeontological Evidences. Delhi: B. R. Publishing Corporation.

Gaur, R. (1992), On *Dorcatherium Nagrii* (Tragulidae, Mammalia) with Review of Siwalik Tragulids. *Rivista Italiana di Paleotologia Stratigraphia*, 98 (3): 353-370.

Gaur, R. (2003), "Mammalian Faunal Analysis and the Palaeoecology of Fossil Primates from the Siwaliks of Northwest India". In *Understanding People of India: Anthropological Insight*. Edited by A.K.Kalla and D.K.Bhattacharya, pp. 186-206. Delhi : Department of Anthropology, University of Delhi.

Gaur, R. and S.R.K. Chopra (1983), Palaeoecology of the Middle Miocene Sivalik Sediments of a part of Jammu & Kashmir State (India). *Palaeogeography, Palaeoclimatology, Palaeoecology*. 43:313-327.

Gaur, R. (1984), Taphonomy, Fauna, Ecology and Environment of Upper Sivaliks (Plio-Pleistocene) near Chandigarh, India. *Nature*. 308:353-355.

Gaur, R. and R.N. Vasishat (1989), "Hominoid Palaeoecology of the Indian Siwaliks". In: *Perspectives in Human Evolution*. Edited by A. Sahni and R. Gaur. pp. 195-222.Delhi: Renaissance Publishing House.

Gaur, R., A. K. Sablok, S.R.K. Chopra and I.J.S. Suneja (1978), A palaeoenvironmental Study of the Siwalik Formations in Parts of Bilaspur District (Himachal Pradesh). *Man and Environ*ment. 2: 69-71.

Gaur, R. R.N. Vasishat and A.R. Sankhyan (1980), The First Record of *Dorcatherium* (Tragulidae) from the Pinjor Formation, East of Chandigarh. *Bull. Ind. Geol. Assoc., Vol. 13 (1):* 67-90.

Gaur, R. R.N. Vasishat, I. J. Suneja and S.R.K. Chopra (1983a), Palaeoenvironment and Palaeoecology of the Hominoid-bearing Sivalik Sediments of the Nurpur-Ranital Terrain, Kangra District (H.P.), India. *Publication Centre of Advanced Study in Geology, Punjab University, Chandigarh.*13:113-118.

Gaur, R., R.N. Vasishat, I. J. Suneja and S.R.K. Chopra (1983b), Fossil Mammals (Tragulids, Giraffids and Bovids) from the Neogene Sivalik Deposits Exposed in the Nurpur-Ranital Terrain, Western Himachal Pradesh, India. *Publication Centre of Advanced Study in Geology, Punjab University, Chandigarh.* 13:180-187.

Gaur, R., R.N. Vasishat and S.R.K. Chopra (1985), First Record of *Dorcatherium nagrii* (Tragulidae, Mammalia) from Lower Sivaliks of Ramnagar Area (J&K), India. *Journal Palaeontological Society of India. 30: 59-62.*

Gupta. S.S., V.C. Verma and A.P. Tewari (1982), New Fossil Hominoid Material from the Siwaliks of Kangra District, Himachal Pradesh. *Journal Palaeontological Society of India.* 27: 111-115.

Gupta, V.J. (1969), Fossil Primate from the Lower Siwaliks of Kangra. *Research Bulletin Panjab University, Chandigarh.* 20: 577-578.

Johnson, G.D. (1977), Palaeopedology of Ramapithecus-bearing Sediments, North India. *Geologische Rundschau.* 66 (1): 192-216.

Johnson, G.D. and C.F. Vondra (1972), Siwalik Sediments in a Portion of the Panjabre-entrants: The Sequence at Haritalyangar, District Bilaspur, H.P., *Himalayan Geology.* 2: 118-144.

Johnson, G.D., N.D. Opdyke, S.K. Tandon and A.C. Nanda (1983), The Magnetic Polarity Stratigraphy of the Siwalik Group at Haritalyangar (India) and a New Last Appearance Datum for *Ramapithecus* and *Sivapithecus* in Asia. *Palaeogeography, Palaeoclimatology, Palaeoecology.* 44:223-249.

Johnosn, M. M., J. Stix, L. Tauxe, P.F. Cerveny and R.A.K. Tahirkheli (1985), Palaeomagnetic Chronology, Fluvial Process, and Tectonic Implications of the Siwalik Deposits near Chinji Village, Pakistan. *Journal of Geology* 93 (1): 22-40.

Kappelman, J. (1991), The Palaeoenvironment of *Kenyapithecus* at Fort Ternan. *Journal of Human Evolution.* 20:95-129.

Kordos, K. and D. R. Begun (2002), Rudabanya: A Late Miocene Subtropical Swamp Deposit with Evidence of the Origin of the African Ape and Humans. *Evolutionary Anthropology.* 11:45-57.

Lydekker, R. (1880), Siwalik and Narbada Proboscidea. *Palaeontologica Indica.* Series 10, 1:181-300.

Lydekker, R. (1881), Siwalik Rhinocerotidae. *Palaeontologica Indica.* Series 10, 2:1-62.

Lydekker, R. (1882), Siwalik and Narbada Equidae. *Palaeontologica Indica.* Series 10, 2:67-98.

Lydekker, R. (1884a), Siwalik and Narbada Bunodont Suina. *Palaeontologica Indica.* Series 10, 3(2): 35-104.

Lydekker, R. (1884b), Siwalik and Narbada Carnivora. *Palaeontologica Indica,* Series 10, 2(6): 100-134.

Lydekker, R. (1898), Wild Oxen, Sheep and Goat of All Land Living and Extinct. London: 318 pp.

Opdyke, N., E. Lindsey, G.D. Johnson, N. Johnson, R.A.K. Tahirkheli (1979), Magnetic Polarity Stratigraphy and Vertebrate Palaeontology of the Upper Siwalik Subgroup of the Northern Pakistan. *Palaeogeography, Palaeoclimatology, Palaeoecology,* 27:1-34.

Opdyke, N., E. Lindsay, G.D. Johnson, N. Johnson, R.A.K. Tahirkheli (1982), Magnetic Polarity Stratigraphy and Vertebrate Palaeontology of the Upper Siwalik Subgroup of Northern Pakistan. *Palaeogeography, Palaeoclimatology, Palaeoecology* 37: 1-35.

Pandey, J. and V.V. Sastry (1968), On a New Species of *Sivapithecus* from the Siwalik Rocks of India. *Journal Geological Society of India.* 9(2) : 206-211.

Pilgrim, G.E. (1911), The Fossil Giraffidae of India. *Palaeontologica Indica, N.S.* 4(1):1-29.

Pilgrim, G.E. (1911-1926), The Fossil Suidae of India. *Palaeontologica Indica, N.S.* 8(4): 1- 65.

Pilgrim, G.E. (1911-1932), The Fossil Carnivora of India. *Palaeontologica Indica, N.S.* 18:1-232.

Pilgrim, G.E. (1911-1939), The Fossil Bovidae of India. *Palaeontologica Indica, N.S.* 26:1-356.

Powell, C.M.A. and P.J. Conagham (1973), Plate Tectonics and the Himalayas. *Earth Planet Science Letter.* 20: 1-12.

Prasad, K.N. (1970), The Vertebrate Fauna from the Siwalik Beds of Haritalyangar, Himachal Pradesh. *Palaeontologica Indica.* 39: 1-79.

Prasad, K.N. (1971), Ecology of the Fossil Hominoidea from the Siwaliks of India. *Nature* 232: 413-414.

Prasad, K.N. (1975), "Observations on the Palaeoecology of South Asian Tertiary Primates". In *World Anthropology Palaeoanthropology, Morphology and Palaeoecology.* Edited by R. H. Tuttle, pp.21-30. Paris: Mouton.

Prasad, K.N. (1977), Review of Miocene Anthropoidea from India and Adjacent Countries. *Journal Palaeontological Society of India.* 20: 382-390.

Prasad, K.N. (2001), *An Introduction to the Mammalian Fauna of the Siwalik System: Biodiversity of the Siwalik Fauna.* Chennai: Prasad Publications.

Quade, J.T. Cerling and J.R. Bowman (1989), Development of Asian Monsoon Revealed by Marked Ecological Shift During the Latest Miocene in Northern Pakistan. *Nature.* 342: 163-166.

Quade, J. and T. Cerling (1995), Expansion of C4 Grasses in the Late Miocene of Northern Pakistan: Evidence from Stable Isotopes in Paleosols. *Palaeogeography, Palaeoclimatology, Palaeoecology. 115: 91-116.*

Quade, J., M.L. Carter, T.P. Ojha, J. Adam and T.M. Harrison (1995), Late Miocene Environmental Changes in Nepal and the Northern Indian Subcontinent: Stable Isotopic Evidence from Palaeosols. *Geological Society of America Bulletin*. 107: 1381-1397.

Sahni, A., V. Kumar and V.C. Srivastava (1974), *Dryopithecus* (Subgenus: *Sivapithecus*) and Associated Vertebrates from the Lower Siwaliks of Uttar Pradesh. *Bulletin Indian Geological Association*, 7(1): 54.

Sahni, A. and S.K. Khare (1977), A Middle Siwalik Fish Fauna from Ladhyani (Haritalyangar) Himachal Pradesh. *Biological Memoirs*. 2(1&2): 187-220.

Sahni, A. and B.N. Tiwari (1979), Lower Siwalik Vertebrates from Kalagarh District, Pauri Garhwal, H.P. *Himalayan Geology*, 9: 339-347.

Sahni, A. and V.J. Gupta (1980), *Deinotherium Indicum* from the Middle Siwaliks of the Kangra Foot-hills, Himachal Pradesh. *Recent Researches in Geology*, 8: 351-355.

Sahni, A., B.N. Tiwari and K. Kumar (1980), An Additional Lower Siwalik Vertebrate Fauna from the Kalagarh Area, District Pauri Garhwal, Uttar Pradesh. *Proceedings 3rd Indian Geological Congress, Poona*. pp 81-90.

Sahni, A., B.N. Tiwari and K. Kumar (1983), A Report on the Occurrence *Ramapithecus Punjabicus* (Hominoidea) from Uttar Pradesh Siwaliks. *Himalayan Geology* 11: 193-197.

Sahni, A. and R. Gaur (Eds) (1989), *Perspectives in Human Evolution*. Delhi: Renaissance.

Sahni, M.R. and L.P. Mathur (1964), Stratigraphy of Siwalik Group. *Proceedings 22nd Session International Geological Congress*, India. pp. 1-24.

Sankhyan, A.R. (1981), The First Record of *Dorcatherium Nagrii* (Tragulidae) from the Dhokpathan Formation (Middle Siwaliks) of Hartalyangar Area, Himachal Pradesh. *Himalayan Geology 12*:91-97.

Sankhyan, A.R. (1985), Late Occurrence of *Sivapithecus* in the Indian Siwaliks. *Journal of Human Evolution*, 14: 573-578.

Schwarzbach, M. (1963), *Climates of the Past: An Introduction to Palaeoclimatology*. London: D. Van Nostrand Company, Ltd.

Scott, R.S., J. Kappelman and J. Kelly (1999), The Paleoenvironment of *Sivapithecus Parvada. Journal of Human Evolution. 36: 245-276.*

Suneja, I.J. and R. Gaur (1977), On the Continental Deposits in Relation to Palaeoenvironments. *Everyday Science*, 22: 33-38.

Suneja, I.J. and G. Singh (1980), A Palaeoenvironmental Study of Part of Tawi Valley Sediments, Jammu and Kashmir. *Man and Environment*. 4:85-87.

Suneja, I.J. and S. Kaul (1980), Ecology of Miocene Hominoids at Ramanagar (North India). *Man and Environment*. 4: 88-89.

Tattersall, I. (1969a), Ecology of North Indian *Ramapithecus*. *Nature*. 221: 451-452.

Tattersall, I. (1969b), More on the Ecology of *Ramapithecus*. *Nature*. 224:821-822.

Tewari, B.N. (1983), Lower Siwalik Faunas of the Indian Subcontinent with Special Reference to the Kalagarh Fauna. *Publication Center of Advanced Study in Geology, Panjab University, Chandigarh.*13: 207-215.

Thomas, H. and S.N. Verma (1979), Decuverte d'un Primate Adapiforme (Sivaladapinae subfam. nov.) dans le Miocene moyen des Siwaliks de le region de Ramnagar (Jammu et Cachemire, Inde). *C.R. Acadamy de Sciences, Paris.* 289: 883-836.

Thomas, H., J.J. Jaeger, and M.V.A. Sastry (1980), Geologie et paleontology des Siwaliks Inferieus (Miocene Moyen) a Ramnagar (Jammu et Cachamire, Inde). *8e Reunion Annuelle des Sciences de la Terra, Marsseille,* P. 346.

Van Couvering, J.A.H. (1980), "Community Evolution in East Africa During the Late Cenozoic". In *Fossils in the Making* Edited by A.K. Behrensmeyer and A.P. Hill. pp. 272-305. Chicago: University of Chicago Press.

Vasishat, R.N. (1985), *Antecedents of Early Man in Northwestern India: Palaeontological and Palaeoecological Evidences.* New Delhi: Inter-India.

Vasishat, R.N., R. Gaur and S.R.K. Chopra (1978), Community Structure of Middle Sivalik Vertebrates from Haritalyangar (H.P.), India. *Palaeogeography, Palaeoclimatology, Palaeoecology.* 23:131-140.

Vasishat, R.N., I.J. Suneja, R. Gaur and S.R.K. Chopra (1983), Neogene Mammals (Equids, Rhinocerotids, Suids and Anthracotherids) from the Siwalik Beds of Kangra District, Himachal Pradesh, India. *Publication Center of Advanced Study in Geology,Panjab University, Chandigarh.*13: 207-215.

PART II

# THE PALAEOLITHIC HOMININS

CHAPTER–4

# Siwalik Palaeoecology and Early Hominin Dispersals

*Rajeev Patnaik*

## INTRODUCTION

Plio-Pleistocene freshwater sediments in India are mostly confined to the well known Siwalik Group of the sub-himalayan region, which in turn is divided into Tatort, Pinjor and Boulder Conglomerate Formations of the Upper Siwaliks. Though, these Formations are found from Pakistan in the west (Figure 1) to Myanmar in the east they are better exposed in the Indian part mainly in the vicinity of Chandigarh (Figure 2). A great wealth of vertebrate fossil remains has been unearthed from these fairly well dated sections (Ranga Rao *et al.*, 1988, 1995; Nanda, 2002; Kumaravel *et al.*, 2005, Patnaik and Nanda, in press). Because the boundaries between Tatrot and Pinjor and Pinjor and Boulder Conglomerate Formations have been found to be time transgressive, various workers now rely on Upper Siwalik biostratigraphic interval zones. Since first and last appearances of large mammals are fairly well known, their occurrences have been tied to well dated (by magnetostratigraphy and tephrachronology) sections both in Pakistan and India to build these interval zones (Keller *et al.*, 1978; Opdyke *et al.*,1979; Barry *et al.*, 1982; Hussain *et al.*,1992; Ranga Rao *et al.*,1988, 1995; Nanda, 2002).

## PLIO-PLEISTOCENE SIWALIK MAMMALS

To begin with, Plio-Pleistocene Siwaliks were divided into the following large mammal interval zones by Barry et al. (1982): 1) The extinct hippo, *Hexaprotodon sivalensis* Interval-Zone ranged from 5.3 to 2.9 Ma and that of *Elephas planifrons* ranged from 2.9 to 1.5 Ma. Further studies (Hussain *et al.*,1992) changed the range of the *Elephas planifrons* Interval-Zone from 2.9 - 1.5 to 3.4 - 2.7 Ma and led to formation of a third interval zone, the

*Elephas hysudricus* Range-Zone (2.7 - ? Ma). *Elephas hysudricus* Range-Zone is now considered to range from 2.7-.6 Ma (Nanda, 1997). Nanda (2002) renamed *Elephas hysudricus* Interval - Zone as *Equus sivalensis* Interval-Zone ranging in age from 2.6 Ma to 0.6 Ma. The long ranging *Equus sivalensis* Interval- Zone in the Indian part comprises *Elephas hysudricus, Stegodon insignis, Equus sivalensis, Rhinoceros palaeindicus, R. sivalensis, Coelodonta platyrhinus,* species of *Cervus* including *Rucervus, Sus* spp., *Sivatherium giganteum, Hemibos* spp. and *Bos acutifrons* (Nanda, 2002). More data from well dated sections in the Upper Siwaliks exposed near Pabbi Hills, Pakistan has prompted Dennell *et al.*,(2006) to further revise *E. hysudricus* faunal zone. Now we have *E. hysudricus-Sivatherium* part ranging from 2.7 to 1.7 Ma, which is defined by the local extinction of *Sivatherium gignatum,* hippopotamids, anthracotheres and a large canid. The younger part *E. hysudricus- Crocuta-Ursus-Panthera* represents the time period between 1.7 to 0.9 Ma. Integration of magnetostratigraphy and large mammal occurrences reveal that *Equus, Elephas, Bos* and *Cervus* make their first appearance at the Gauss - Matuyama (Chron C2An\C2r) magnetic boundary at 2.48 Ma (2.58 Ma, Cande and Kent, 1995, Opdyke *et al.*,1979).

In the Chandigarh region, there are now four fairly well dated sections that contain Plio-Pleistocene mammals. These are Patiali Rao, Ghaggar, Nadah and Haripur Khol sections (Figure 3). West of Chandigarh lies the Jammu region, where, the Upper Siwalik succession have been divided into three Formations – the Parmandal Sandstone, the Nagrota and Boulder Conglomerate Formations. The biostratigraphy of the Nagrota Formation is well constrained because two bentonitic tuff beds, which have been dated to 2.8 $\pm$ 0.56 Ma and 2.31 $\pm$ 0.54 Ma occur in this section (Ranga Rao *et al.*,1988). Combining Jammu and Chandigarh regions the important Plio-Pleistocene taxa include *Canis pinjorensis, Elephas hysudricus, Equus sivalensis, Rhinoceros palaeindicus, R. sivalensis, Coelodonta platyrhinus* (= *Punjabitherium platyrhinus*), *Cervus punjabiensis,* and *Leptobos falconeri.* If we go further west and take into account the richly fossiliferous locality of Pabbi Hills, Pakistan, early Pleistocene mammals include *Hemibos triquetricornis, Damalops palaeindicus,* Cf. *Cervus,* Cf. *Dama, Sivatherium giganteum,* Suid (*Sus,* Opdyke, 1979), *Equus* cf. *sivalensis, Rhinoceros sivalensis, Elephas hysudricus, Stegodon,* Hippopotamid, Cf. Cercopithecidae, *Crocuta crocuta, Pachycrocuta brevirostris,* Hyaenidae, *Felis,* Cf. *Panthera uncia* and *Megantereon cultridens,* Cf. *Canis cautleyi,* Herpestid and Usrid (Dennell, 2004). On the whole we find similar assemblages within the Upper Siwalik deposits of India and Pakistan. But there are few regional differences, such as absence of Indian Siwalik taxa *Theropithecus* and *Camelus* in Pakistan Siwaliks. As per Dennell et al. (2006) taxa that are present in Pakistan and absent in India are *Megantereon, Pachycrocuta, Ursus* and anthracotheres. This assumption may not be true because *Megantereon, Pachycrocuta, Ursus* and anthracotheres have been recorded from the Indian part by previous workers (Patnaik and Nanda, in press).

Among the small mammals murids and gerbillids are the dominant Plio-Pleistocene families. In fact murids replaced cricetids in the Late Miocene. A large gerbillid, *Abudhabia* occurs at ~4 Ma and ~2.5 Ma and later gives rise probably to *Tatera* occurring at 2 Ma (Patnaik, 1997). Beginning of Pliocene saw only 3 murid species, around 4 Ma they start diversifying into 8 species. But the most prominent speciation occurs at approximately 2.5 Ma, where at least 13 murid species emerge. Then a slight decline (numbering to 10) in the number of murid species occurs at ~2-1.8 Ma (Figure 3).

**Plio-Pleistocene Ecological Set Up**

If we follow the principal of actualism, the above mentioned Plio-Pleistocene large mammals are indicative of presence of grasslands and a well-watered landscape (Gaur, 1987). But, this broad scenario probably does not reflect the true picture. The Pliocene is marked by presence of hippo, *Hexaprotodon*, the *Rhinoceros* and anthracotheres which must have required permanent water bodies throughout the year. Presence of this type of condition is further supported by occurrence of a variety of turtles, crocodiles and Channid (snake heads) fishes in the Pliocene Tatrot and Basal Pinjor Formations (Patnaik in preparation). Climate probably started changing in the early Pleistocene, indicated by the extinction of large browsers such as *Sivatherium*, hippopotamids and anthracotheres. With plenty of grasers around, the early Pleistocene fauna points towards presence of dry-season grasslands (Dennell, 2003; Dennell *et al.*,2006).

Small mammals with their small home ranges and sensitiveness to climatic fluctuations are considered better ecological indicators. Murid rodents today are particularly adapted to monsoonal conditions (see Patnaik, 2003 for a review). When we look at the distribution and abundance of modern grade murids in the Pliocene, they perfectly overlap that of the present day murids (Figure 4). This indicates that monsoonal conditions very similar to that of today ware there in the Siwaliks of Pliocene time. In fact if we plot the distribution of *Homo erectus* onto this map, most of the sites will fall in the monsoonal region. Most of the Pleistocene murid taxa such as *Golunda, Bandicota, Nesokia, Dilatomys, Millardia* and *Hadromys* were predominantly grazers, again pointing towards presence of arid conditions.

Palaeovegetation is considered the best indicator of palaeoecological and palaeoclimatic conditions. A diverse palynoassemblage has been recovered from the from the Nadah section (Rao and Patnaik, 2001) dating to ~2-1.8 Ma. This assemblage comprises algal fungal, pteridophytic spores, gymnospermous and angiospermous pollen fossils. It is interesting to note that this assemblage belongs to 13 modern families. 4 of these families are cosmopolitan, 3 are tropical to subtropical, 3 are tropical to temperate, and 3 are temperate. Both pteridophytic and fungal spores are indicative of moist, warm and humid conditions. Climatologically, the overall vegetation pattern indicates, a tropical-subtropical humid climate Presence of nearby upland montane areas is supported by the occurrence of the temperate flora belonging to Magnoliaceae (*Magnolia*) and Pinaceae (*Pinus*), predominantly at the top of the section. During the dry part of the year occurrence of forest fires is indicated by presence carbonised wood and grass.

On a regional scale, Pleistocene in the Indian Siwaliks is marked by tectonic activity, which led to an increase in gradient. It has been suggested that due to this increase in slope instability trees were probably not well supported (Hoorn *et al.*, 2000). It is well known now that on a global scale the inception of northern hemisphere glaciation in the Late Pliocene (Shackleton *et al.*,1984) may have facilitated intensification in the monsoon climate system (Gupta and Melice, 2003; Gupta and Thomas, 2004). On the other hand, early Pleistocene saw a marked decrease in faunal composition (Patnaik and Nanda, in press).

### Homo Erectus Co-travelers

It have been suggested that in the Plio-Pleistocene time grasslands probably covered a large area right from west Africa to China and the conditions were quite conducive for *Homo erectus* and associated mammalian fauna to disperse (Dennell, 2003). An assertion Patnaik (2000, 2001 and 2003) also made based on occurrence of murids in Ethiopia, Kenya, Tanzania and Indo-Pakistan (also see Figure 4). Patnaik (2000) had suggested that during the Late Pliocene time there were no physical barrier between Indian sub-continent and east Africa to prevent faunal migrations. There are several mammalian taxa that may have used the same corridor to travel out of Africa as was done by *Homo erectus*. For instance, East African forms such as *Oryx*, *Hippopotamus* and *Crocuta crocuta* also occur in Pinjor deposits (Tchernov, 1992). A North Africa hominid site, Ain Hanech, (Algeria) which is of early Pleistocene age has *Equus*, gazelle and *Hippopotamus* in its fauna (Dennell, 2003). So is the faunal composition of famous hominid localities Ubeidiya, Israel and Dmanisi, Georgia (Anton and Swisher, 2004). Elements of Pinjor fauna have also been recorded from Lower Pleistocene site of Xiaochangliang, China (Zhu *et al.*, 2001). European early Pleistocene carnivores such as *Megantereon* and *Pachycrocuta* are also found in Pinjor (Turner, 1992; Rook *et al.*, 2004). Another co-traveler of *Homo erectus* is the cercopithecid *Theropithecus*, which has been found to occur in Plio-Pleistocene sediments of South, East and North Africa, Israel, Spain, Italy and India (Delson, 1993; Delson *et al.*, 1993; Gibert *et al.*, 1995; Belmaker, 2002; Rook *et al.*, 2004; Patnaik and Nanda, in press).

## CONCLUSIONS

This review of Plio-Pleistocene mammalian assemblages in India and Pakistan and their correlation with those found at hominin yielding sites of Africa and Eurasia allows new insight into the past migration corridors. The various fossil data suggest that the palaeoecological conditions in Siwaliks at the time of Late Pliocene and early Pleistocene were indeed conducive enough to allow early hominins to make a foothold. Though controversial Palaeolithic evidence of presence of early hominins in the Siwaliks does exist (Dennell, 2004; 2003), indirect indications of hominin presence can be drawn from the presence of so-called co-traveler mammals such as *Megantereon, Theropithecus* and *Hippopotamus*, but it is high time we should find the "hard evidence" of presence of *Homo erectus* in the Siwaliks.

## REFERENCES CITED

Anton Susan C. and Swisher Carl, C. (2004), Early Dispersals of *Homo* from Africa Annu. Rev. Anthropol. 33: 271–96

Barry, J.C., Lindsay, E.H., Jacobs, L.L. (1982), A Biostratigraphic Zonation of the Middle and Upper Siwaliks of the Potwar Plateau of Northern Pakistan. Palaeogeography, Palaeoclimatology, Palaeoecology 37, 95-130.

Belmaker, M. (2002), First Evidence of the Presence of *Theropithecus* sp. in the Southern Levant. Israel J. Zool. 48 (2), 165.

Cande, S.C. and Kent, D.V. (1995), Revised Calibration of the Geomagnetic Polarity Timescale for the Late Cretaceous and Cenozoic. Journal of Geophysical Research 100 (B4), 6093- 6095.

Dam, Van J.A. (1997), The Small Mammls from the Upper Miocene of the Teruel-Alfambra Region (Spain): Palaeobiology and Palaeoclimatic Reconstructions. Geologica Ultraiectina, 156, 13-204.

Delson, E. (1993), Theropithecus Fossils from Africa and India and the Taxonomy of the Genus. In: Jablonski, N.G. (Ed.), Theropithecus: The Rise and Fall of a Primate Genus. Cambridge University Press, Cambridge, pp. 157e189.

Delson, E., Eck, G.G., Leakey, M.G., Jablonski, N.G. (1993), A Partial Catalogue of Fossil Remains of Theropithecus. In: Jablonski, N.G. (Ed.), Theropithecus: The Rise and Fall of a Primate Genus. Cambridge University Press, Cambridge, pp. 499-525.

Dennell, R.W. (2003), Dispersal and Colonisation, Long and Short Chronologies: How Continuous is the Early Pleistocene Record for Hominids Outside East Africa? Journal of Human Evolution 45: 421–440

Dennell, R.W. (2004), Early Hominin Landscape in the Northern Pakistan. Investigations in the Pabbi Hills. BAR International Series 1265:1-454.

Dennell, R.W. Coard, R. Turner, A. (2006), The Biostratigraphy and Magnetic Polarity Zonation of the Pabbi Hills, Northern Pakistan: An Upper Siwalik (Pinjor Stage) Upper Pliocene-Lower Pleistocene fluvial sequence. *Palaeoecology, Palaeoclimatology and Palaeogeography*. 234:168-185.

Gaur, R. (1987), Environment and Ecology of Early Man in Northwest India. B. R. Publishing Corporation, Delhi.

Gibert, J., Ribot, F. Gibert, L., Leakey, M., Arribas, A.,Martinez-Navarro, B., (1995), Presence of the Cercopithecid Genus *Theropithecus* in Cueva Victoria (Murcia, Spain). J.Hum. Evol. 28, 487-493.

Gupta A.K. and Melice J.-L. (2003), Orbital Forcing of the Plio–Pleistocene Indian Monsoons: Benthic Foraminiferal Proxies from ODP Site 758. Current Science, 85:179–184.

Gupta, A.K. and Thomas, E. (2004), Initiation of Northern Hemisphere Glaciation and Strengthening of the Northeast Indian Monsoon: Ocean Drilling Program Site 758, Eastern Equatorial Indian Ocean Geology; January 2003; v. 31; no. 1; p. 47–50.

Henderson-Sellers, A. and Robinson, P.J. (1994), Contemporary Climatology. Longman, Harlow.

Hoorn C., Ojha T., and Quade J. (2000), Palynological Evidence for Vegetation Development and Climatic Change in the Sub-Himalayan Zone (Neogene, Central Nepal). Palaeogeography, Palaeoclimatology, Palaeoecology, 163: 133–161.

Hussain, S.T., Van Den Bergh, G.D., Steensma, K.J., De Visser, J.A., De Vos, J., Arif, M., Van Dam, J., Sondaar, P.Y., Malik, S.B., (1992), Biostratigraphy of the Plio-Pleistocene Continental Sediments (Upper Siwaliks) of the Mangla-Samwal Anticline, Azad Kashmir, Pakistan. Proceedings Koninklijke Nederlandse Akademie van Wetenschappenn, Amsterdam 95, 65-80.

Keller, H. M., Tahirkheli, R. A. K., Mirza, M. A., Opdyke, N. D. (1978), Magnetic Polarity Stratigraphy of the Upper Siwalik Deposits, Pabbi Hills, Pakistan. Earth and Planetary Science Letters 36, 187 -201.

Kumaravel, V. Sangode, S.J. Kumar, R. and Siddaiah, N.S. (2005), Magnetic Polarity Stratigraphy of Plio-Pleistocene Pinjor Formation (type locality), Siwalik Group, NW Himalaya, India. *Current Science, 88*(9):1453-1461.

Misonne, X. (1969), African and Indo-Australian Muridae, Evolutionary Trends. *Annals Mus. Afr. Cent. Zool. Ser. 8*. 172, 1-219.

Nanda, A.C. (1997), Some Biostratigraphic Observations based on the Upper Siwalik Faunas of the Siwalik Group of India and Nepal. In: Wijayananda, N.P., Cooray, P.G. and Mosley, P. (Eds.), Geology in South Asia - II. Geological Survey & Mines Bureau, Dehiwala, Sri Lanka, pp. 171-189.

Nanda, A.C. (2002), Upper Siwalik Mammalian Faunas of India and Associated Events. Journal of Asian Earth Science 21:47-58.

Opdyke, N.D., Lindsay, E., Johnson , G.D., Johnson, N., Tahirkheli, R.A.K., Mirza, M.A. (1979), Magnetic Polarity Stratigraphy and Vertebrate Paleontology of the Upper Siwalik Subgroup of Northern Pakistan. Palaeogeography, Palaeoclimatology, Palaeoecology 27, 1-34.

Patnaik, R. (2000), Siwalik Murid Rodents: Origin and Dispersal. Himal. Geol. 21, 145-151.

Patnaik, R. (2001), Late Pliocene Micromammals from Tatrot Formation (Upper Siwalik) exposed near village Saketi, Himachal Pradesh, India. Palaeontographica 261, 55-81.

Patnaik, R. (2003), Reconstruction of Upper Siwalik Palaeocology and Palaeoclimatology using Microfossil Palaeocommunities. *Palaeoecology,Palaeoclimatology and Palaeogeography* (special volume).197(1-2): 133-150.

Patnaik, R. and Nanda, A.C. (in press) Early Pleistocene Mammalian Faunas of India and Evidence of Connections with Other Parts of the World. Ed. John Fleagle. Springer N.Y.

Ranga Rao, A., Agarwal, R.P., Sharma, U.N., Bhalla, M.S., Nanda, A.C. (1988), Magnetic Polarity Stratigraphy and Vertebrate Palaeontology of the Upper Siwalik Subgroup of Jammu Hills, India. Journal Geological Society of India 31 (4), 361-385.

Ranga Rao, A., Nanda, A.C., Sharma, U.N., Bhalla, M.S. (1995), Magnetic Polarity Stratigraphy of the Pinjor Formation (Upper Siwalik) near Pinjore, Haryana. Current Science 68 (12), 1231-1236.

Rao, M.R and Patnaik, R. (2001), Palynology of Pliocene Sediments of Pinjor Formation, Haryana, India. *Palaeobotanist.* 50:267-286.

Rook, L., Martý´nez-Navarro, B., and Howell, F.C. (2004), Occurrence of *Theropithecus* sp. in the Late Villafranchian of Southern Italy and Implication for Early Pleistocene "Out of Africa" dispersals. *Journal of Human Evolution,* 47:267-277.

Shackleton, N.J., Backman, H., Zimmerman, D.V., Kent, M.A., Hall, D.G., Roberts, D., Schitker, J., Baldauf, A., Despaires, R., Homrighausen, P., Huddlestun, J., Keene, A.J., Kaltenback, K.A., Krumsiek, A.C., Morton, J.W., Murray, Westberg-Smith, J.,1984. Oxygen Isotope Calibration of the Onset of Ice-rafting and History of Glaciation in the North Atlantic Region.. *Nature 307,* 620–623.

Tchernov, E. (1992), Eurasian-African biotic exchanges through the Levantine Corridor during the Neogene and Quaternary, in: von Koenigswald, W., Werdelin, L. (Eds.), Mammalian Migration and Dispersal Events in the European Quaternary, ngsinstitut Senckenberg, Frankfurt a.M. 153, pp. 103–123.

Turner, A., (1992), Large Carnivores and Earliest European Hominids: Changing Determinants of Resource Availability during the Lower and Middle Pleistocene. *Journal of Human Evolution 22,* 109–126.

Zhu, R.X., Ho.man, K.A., Potts, R., Deng, C.L., Pan, Y.X., Guo, B., Shi, C.D., Guo, Z.T., Hou, Y.M., Huang, W.W., (2001), Earliest Presence of Humans in Northeast Asia. *Nature, 413,* 413–417.

CHAPTER–5

# Affinities of Narmada Hominin Fossils

*A.R. Sankhyan*

## INTRODUCTION

Compared to the hominoids, hominins have evolved very fast into a number of species over time during the last about 2 million years, such as: *H. sapiens, H. floresiensis, H. neanderthalensis, H. heidelbergensis, H. antecessor, H. erectus, H. pekinensis, H. georgicus, H. ergaster* and *H. habilis*, while counting from present to the earliest. The commonly followed evolutionary scheme is: *Homo habilis- Homo ergaster- Homo erectus- Homo sapiens*, though it is still debated who were the immediate ancestors of the first *H. sapiens. Homo habilis*, who lived between 2.5 to 1.8 millions years ago in Africa, though small-brained were intelligent scavengers and toolmakers, and probably ancestors of *H. sapiens*. They were followed (or even co-existed in different econiches with, as per the latest small finding) by *Homo erectus* (= *ergaster*) about 1.55 million years ago and were confined to Africa. They had relatively larger brains and were more skilled toolmakers and hunters. Their descendants spread into Eurasia / east Europe, e.g., the Dmanisi *Homo georgicus* (Gabunia, *et al.*, 2002) and later the Homo erectus, who preceded *H. sapiens*. Subsequently, Neanderthal man, *Homo neanderthalensis* appeared around 700-500 kya in Europe and western Asia. They were the dominant hominid species in Europe for much of the last Ice Age, and met extinction in the hands of *Homo heidelbergensis*- also known as "archaic *Homo sapiens*". They were heavily muscled and made sophisticated tools and were fierce hunters. Scholars following the Single Origin (Out of Africa) hypothesis regarded them a widely spread species in Africa, Europe and Asia as well during 200-30 kya, which may have also been ancestral to Neanderthals in Europe and to *H. sapiens* in Africa. Another species, *H. antecessor* is similar to the same type in Europe. Multiregionalists view this group as evidence of a transition toward modern *H. sapiens*.

### Indian Scenario

Of course, the Quaternary hominid fossil record of South Asia is very poor with the Central Narmada Valley having yielded the unequivocal fossil evidence. There is another report from coastal Tamil Nadu of the fossilized "Baby in the womb" entombed in a laterite block (Rajendran *et al.,*, 2003), though it remains beyond morphological comparisons as yet. The claim of a *Homo erectus* incisor from the Upper Siwaliks in association with pebble tools has not yet been scrutinized by others. Similarly, the Plio-Pleistocene antiquity of the Potwar stone tools has not been substantiated or adequately datede elsewhere in South Asia. So, at present, what ever little we know is only from the Central Narmada Valley.

Figure 1: The Hominin Site Hathnora in Central Narmada Valley

Narmada valley appears to be the paradise of the prehistoric man South Asia since most of the Middle Pleistocene Siwalik fauna took refuge in the valley at a time when colder/glacial conditions prevailed in most of the northern hemisphere and made survival difficult there. The climate of the region had been warm and equable and also favoured the fossilization of the human bones–a rare event in South Asia. Additionally, due to its strategic mid-continental place between South-East Asia and West Asia, it might have served as one of the east-west passages to the prehistoric populations across Asia and Africa. It is now fairly clear that the valley was a meeting place for diverse human ethnic and cultural elements since the Palaeolithic times as has been documented by different Stone Age industries and the prehistoric rock-paintings preserved in numerous rock shelters of the Satpura and Vindhyan hills, confining the valley. Hundreds of painted rock shelters at Bhimbetka have now been recognized as a world heritage site.

### THE NARMADA HOMININ FOSSILS

Cutting the long story short, the available fossil evidence suggests two types of archaic hominins:

1. A large-sized "archaic" *Homo sapiens,* represented by calvaria (partial Skullcap).

2. A "pygmy-sized"-short and stocky "archaic" H. *sapiens* represented by three postcranial bones, viz., a complete right and a partial left clavicle (Collarbone) and the left 9th rib.

### The Skullcap (Calvaria)

The Narmada cranium has since attracted the attention of several experts in the debate of origins of *Homo sapiens* / modern humans, who are divided on broad theoretical lines. While a few still continue to regard it as the so-called "evolved" *Homo erectus* (Lumley and Sonakia, 1985b; Sonakia, 1999, 2005), some view the calvaria as of the "archaic" *Homo sapiens* (e.g., Kennedy *et al.*, 1991, Kennedy, 1992, 1999, 2000, 2005). Later, Cameron *et al.* (2004) have taken out Narmada calvaria from the *H. erectus* domain without assigning or referring to a particular species, which again, is a stand not much different from that of Kennedy and others, i.e., the so-called "archaic" *H. sapiens*. They however, categorically suggested Narmada hominin's European ancestry with the Neanderthals or pre-Neanderthals, in particular with the Steinheim man, and concluded that Narmada hominin was a European migrant to South Asia earlier to 250 ka. In any either case the usages of "evolved" or "archaic" are redundant with the current cladistic phylogenetics, which recall the debate between the 'Multi-regional' vs. 'Single Origins' hypotheses dealt with the author elsewhere (Sankhyan, 1999). It may also not be acceptable to many if the Narmada calvaria are assigned to *H. heidelbergensis* (Rightmire, 1988), which is believed to have ruled Europe and Africa, and probably East Asia as well. The author's own observation on the partial cranium (see below) suggests it as quite unique and not affined specifically to any European and African middle to late Pleistocene hominins.

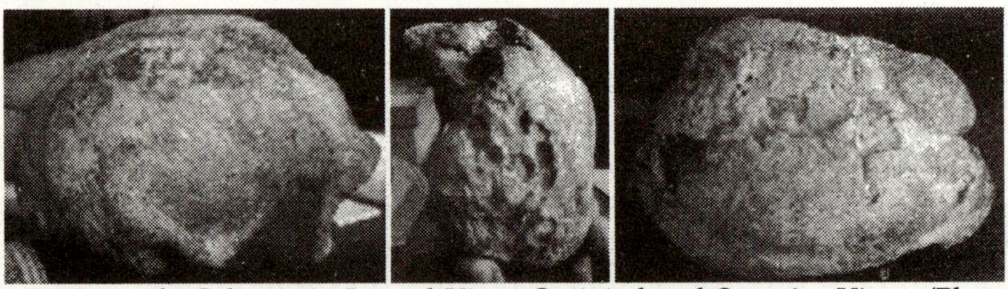

Figure 2: Narmada Calvaria in Lateral View, Occipital and Superior Views (Photograph taken by the Author in GSI, Kolkata (courtesy Bhaskar Chakraborty and S. Sen) on the Original Specimen in presence of Dr. Lingxia Zhao, IVPP, China) in January 2009

Several scholars reviewed/ studied or commented on the phylogenetic status of the skullcap as stated earlier. The author (Sankhyan, 2005, 2007) has recently studied it by examining both, the good replica as well as the original specimen and made observations on 26 metrical traits besides 20 non-mensural traits. The non-mensural traits are reproduced here below (Table 1) from the Table 10 of Sankhyan (2007). A gist of the study is as follows:

**Table 1**

| | | | 1 | 2 | 3 | 4 | 5 | 6 | 7 | 8 | 9 | 10 | 11 | 12 | 13 | 14 | 15 |
|---|---|---|---|---|---|---|---|---|---|---|---|---|---|---|---|---|---|
| | | | *Nar* | *Hh* | *H.er* | *H.g* | *eH.e* | *lH.e* | *H.p* | *H.a* | *AT$^{SH}$* | *Ce* | *St* | *H.he* | *H.n* | *eH.s* | *mH.s* |
| | *Degree of Development* | | | | | | | | | | | | | | | | |
| *Trait* | *Coding Scheme of Cameron et al (2004)* | *Present Coding Scheme* | | | | | | | | | | | | | | | |
| SOT | 0= Strongly developed and arched1= moderately developed and arched2=strong bar-like torus3 =Weak to absent | 0=Absent/week 1=Moderate 2= Strong-arched /strong-bar | 1 | 2 | 1 | 1 | 2 | 3 | 2 | 1 | 2 | 2 | 2 | 2 | 2 | 0 | 0 |
| MTT | 0=Intermediate (0.15-0.29) 1=Thick (>0.29)2=Reduced (<0.15) | 1= Reduced 2= Intermediate 3=Thick | 2 | 2 | 2 | 2 | 3 | 3 | 2 | ? | 3 | 3 | 3 | 3 | 2 | 2 | 1 |
| OS | 0=Round 1=Rectangular 2= Rhomboid | Same | 0 | 0 | 0 | 0 | 0 | ? | ? | ? | 1 | ? | 2 | 2 | 0 | 1 | 1 |
| POC | 2= Abso lutely reduced (>0.80) 1=Reduced=1(0.74-08) 0=Moderate (<0.74) | 0=Abso lutely Reduced 1=Reduced 2=Moderate | 0 | 2 | 1 | 1 | 1 | 0 | 2 | 0 | 0 | 0 | 0 | 0 | 0 | 0 | 0 |
| FS | 0=Well developed throughout 1= Moderately developed throughout 2=Weekly developed throughout 3=Absent or present laterally | 0=Absent/ Lateral 1=Weak 2=Moderately developed throughout 3=Well developed throughout | 0 | 3 | 2 | 2 | 1 | 1 | 2 | 2 | 2 | 2 | 0 | 2 | 0 | 0 | 0 |

*Contd.*

| | | | 1 | 2 | 3 | 4 | 5 | 6 | 7 | 8 | 9 | 10 | 11 | 12 | 13 | 14 | 15 |
|---|---|---|---|---|---|---|---|---|---|---|---|---|---|---|---|---|---|
| | | | *Nar* | *Hh* | *H.er* | *H.g* | *eH.e* | *lH.e* | *H.p* | *H.a* | *AT^SH^* | *Ce* | *St* | *H.he* | *H.n* | *eH.s* | *mH.s* |
| | *Degree of Development* | | | | | | | | | | | | | | | | |
| *Trait* | *Coding Scheme of Cameron et al (2004)* | *Present Coding Scheme* | | | | | | | | | | | | | | | |
| FB | 0=Absent<br>1=Present | Same | 0 | 0 | 0 | 0 | 0 | 0 | 0 | ? | 0 | 0 | 1 | 0 | 0 | 0 | 1 |
| FO | 0=Intermediate<br>1=Low<br>2=High | 1=Low (l) 2=Moderate (m) 3=High (h) | 2 | 2 | 2 | 2 | L1 | L1 | 2 | ? | 2 | 2 | ? | 2 | 2 | H3 | h3 |
| MB | 0=Close to cranial base<br>1=Cranial base/ biparietal similar<br>2=At biparietal | 1=Basal (b)<br>2=Basal/Parietal (b/p)<br>3=Parietal (p) | 0 | 0 | 0 | 0 | 0 | 0 | 0 | ? | 1 | 0 | 1 | 0 | 2 | 0 | 2 |
| AT | 0=Absent<br>1=Present | Same | 1 | 0 | 0 | 1 | 1 | 1 | 1 | ? | 1 | 1 | 0 | 0 | 0 | 0 | 0 |
| SMC | 0=Distinct and separate features<br>1=Unite anteriorly | 1/u=United anteriorly2/ s=separate/ distinct | 2 | 2 | 2 | 2 | 2 | 2 | 1 | ? | 2 | 2 | 2 | 2 | 2 | 2 | 2 |
| OSS | 1=Absent<br>0=Present | 0=Absent<br>1=Present | 1 | 1 | 0 | 0 | 1 | 1 | 1 | ? | 0 | 1 | 1 | 0 | 1 | 0 | 0 |
| O/NP | 0=Weakly flexed<br>1=Strongly flexed | Same | 0 | 0 | 1 | 1 | 1 | 1 | 1 | ? | 0 | 1 | 0 | 1 | 0 | 0 | 0 |
| I/O | 0=Below opisthocranion [meaning separate]<br>1=At opisthocranion [meaning Coincident] | 0=Coincident ( c)<br>1/s= Separate (s) | 1 | 1 | 0 | 0 | 0 | 0 | 0 | ? | 1 | 0 | 1 | 0 | 1 | 1 | 1 |

*Contd..*

| | | | 1 | 2 | 3 | 4 | 5 | 6 | 7 | 8 | 9 | 10 | 11 | 12 | 13 | 14 | 15 |
|---|---|---|---|---|---|---|---|---|---|---|---|---|---|---|---|---|---|
| | | | *Nar* | *Hh* | *H.er* | *H.g* | *eH.e* | *lH.e* | *H.p* | *H.a* | *AT*[SH] | *Ce* | *St* | *H.he* | *H.n* | *eH.s* | *mH.s* |
| | *Degree of Development* | | | | | | | | | | | | | | | | |
| *Trait* | *Coding Scheme of Cameron et al (2004)* | *Present Coding Scheme* | | | | | | | | | | | | | | | |
| OP | 1= Occipital plain shortened<br>0=Occipital plain lengthened | 0=Shortened (S)1=Long (L) | 1 | 1 | 1 | 0 | 0 | 1 | 0 | ? | 1 | 0 | ? | 1 | 1 | 1 | 1 |
| CHL | 0=Long-Low (LL)<br>1=Short-High (SH) | Same | 1 | 0 | 0 | 0 | 0 | 0 | 0 | ? | 1 | 1 | ? | 0 | 1 | 1 | 1 |
| MP | 0=Reduced<br>1=Small<br>2=Large | 0=Small<br>1=Large | 1 | 1 | 0 | 0 | 1 | 1 | 1 | 1 | 1 | 2 | 2 | 2 | 2 | 2 | 2 |
| CC | 0-Small;<br>1=Intermediate;<br>2=Increased;<br>3=Large;<br>4=Absolutely large | Same | 3 | 0 | 1 | 0 | 1 | 2 | 2 | ? | 3 | 2 | 2 | 3 | 4 | 3 | 4 |
| No. (%) of traits shared with Narmada | | | - | 847.06 | 741.17 | 741.17 | 741.17 | 850 | 850 | 375 | 1164.71 | 847.06 | 640 | 635.29 | 1270.59 | 1270.59 | 635.29 |
| **N** (No. of traits compared in different hominins) | | | 17 | 17 | 17 | 17 | 17 | 16 | 16 | 4 | 17 | 17 | 15 | 17 | 17 | 17 | 17 |

SOT=Supraorbital Torus, MTT=Mid-Toral Thickness, OS=Orbit Shape, POC=Post Orbital Constriction, FS= Frontal sulcus, FB=Frontal bossing, FO=Frontal Orientation, SK=Sagittal keeling, MB=Maximum breadth, AT= Angular Torus, SMC= Supra-mastoid/ Mastoid Crest, OSS=Occipital Supratoral Sulcus, O/NP=Occipital/nuchal planes, I/O= Inion/ opisthion location, OP= Occipital plane, CHL= Cranial height/length, MP= Mastoid process, CC=Cranial Capacity. NR=Narmada, H.h=*H. habilis*, *H.er*=*H. ergaster*, *H.g*=*H.georgicus*=WA *H.ergaster*, *EH.e*=Early *H.erectus*, *LH.e*=*Late H.erectus*, *H.p*=*H.pekinensis*, *a*=*H.antecessor*, AT[SH] =Atapuerca Sima de los Huesos, Ce=Ceprano, St=Steinheim, *H.he*=*H.heidlebergensis*, *H.n*= *H. neanderthalensis*, *EH.s*=Early *H. sapiens*, *MH.s*=Modern *H.sapiens*.

The inferences from *Table 1* may be summarized as follows:

1. *Supraorbital torus* is moderately developed as in WA *H. ergaster, H. antecessor,* and modern *H. sapiens.*
2. *Mid-toral thickness* is intermediate as in *H. habilis,* African *H. ergaster,* WA *H.ergaster, H.pekinensis, H. neanderthalensis,* and Early *H. sapiens*
3. *Orbit Sshape* appears round in Narmada and shared with *H. habilis,* African *H. ergaster,* WA *H.ergaster,* Early *H. erectus, and H. neanderthalensis*
4. *Post Orbital Constriction* is absolutely reduced in Narmada; a condition shared with Late *H.erectus,* and many European hominins, eg, *H. antecessor,* Atapuerca, Ceprano, Steinheim, and *H. heidelbergensis.*
5. *Frontal sulcus* is lacking in Narmada as in Steinheim, *H. neanderthalensis,* Early and modern *H. sapiens.*
6. *Frontal bossing* is absent in Narmada and in most of the early hominins, except its presence in Steinheim and modern *H.sapiens.*
7. *Sagittal keeling* is not present in Narmada, but instead a mid-sagittal furrow is present as a unique feature.
8. *Frontal orientation* is moderate in Narmada as in many hominins, eg, *H. habilis,* African *H. ergaster,* WA *H.ergaster,* Atapuerca, Ceprano, *H. heidelbergensis, H.pekinensis,* and *H. neanderthalensis.*
9. *Maximum cranial breadth* in Narmada is near the base and closer to the mastoid. This trait occurs in many Pleistocene hominins, eg., *H. habilis,* African *H. ergaster,* WA

*H.. ergaster,* Early and Late *H. erectus, H. heidelbergensis, H.pekinensis,* and Early *H. sapiens.*

10. *Angular torus* is developed in Narmada and shared with WA *H.ergaster,* Early and Late *H. erectus,* Atapuerca, Ceprano, and *H.pekinensis.*
11. *Supra-mastoid and the mastoid crests* are distinctly separate in Narmada as in almost all Pleistocene and modern hominins, except the *H pekinensis* in which they unite anteriorly.
12. *Occipital supratoral Sulcus* is present in Narmada, *H. habilis,* Early and Late *H. erectus,* Ceprano, Steinheim, *H.pekinensis, H. neanderthalensis* and modern *H. sapiens.*
13. *Occipital/nuchal plane* is weakly flexed in Narmada, Atapuerca, Steinheim, *H. neanderthalensis,* and Early and modern *H. sapiens*
14. *Inion/opisthion location* is separate in Narmada as in *H. habilis,* Atapuerca, Steinheim, *H. neanderthalensis,* and Early and modern *H. sapiens.*

15. *Occipital plane* is long in Narmada, *H. habilis*, African *H. ergaster*, Late *H.erectus*, Atapuerca, *H. neanderthalensis*, and Early and modern *H. sapiens.*
16. *Cranial length* is short and high in Narmada, Atapuerca, Ceprano, *H. neanderthalensis*, and Early and modern *H. sapiens.*
17. *Mastoid process* is small (and stubby) in Narmada, similar to *H. habilis*, African *H. ergaster*, Early and Late *H. erectus*, and *H.pekinensis*. Only European hominin sharing this trait is *H. antecessor*. This contrasts with observation of Cameron *et al.* (2004) who regard Narmada mastoid as "large".

It has been observed that the Narmada calvaria shows greater similarities with the European classical Neanderthals as well as with the so-called "archaic" *Homo sapiens*, like Petralona, Arago 21-47, Dali, Ngandong and Kabwe. Out of the 26 mensural traits, the maximum overall affinities of the Narmada calvaria is noted with Petralona in 11 traits, followed in decreasing order by La Ferrassie (10), the La Chapelle Aux Saint (8), the Kabwe/Dali/Zkd 10/Ngadong11/Sangiran 17 (7), the Ceprano and Steinheim (6), the Arago/Saccapastor/Amud/ Sambrumenchan (5), Shanidar1/Mt Carmel (4), ER3733/OH9/Zkd11, 12 /Swascombe/Ehrndorf (3), Skhul (2), and Cro-Magnon (1). But, the Petralona and other European forms are now grouped under Neanderthals and show only local evolution in Europe (Martinez & Arsuaga, 1997). Also, both partial cranium as well as the clavicle of Narmada show clear separations from African *H. erectus*/ergaster. Overall, it may be noted that Narmada skullcap is unique, which could be classified as the so-called "archaic" *H. sapiens* or the *H. heidelbergensis*, if we follow a grade concept and conceive worldwide distribution of such a hominin species. Alternatively on cladistic considerations, it may be more befitting to regard the skullcap belonging to a different species/clade.

**The Postcranial Fossils**

The significance of the postcranial fossils is to understand the body dimensions of the Narmada hominin, which the skullcap cannot tell, and therefore may reflect on hominin adaptations during middle Pleistocene in South Asia. For instance, the clavicle could yield a fair estimate of the upper chest breadth across, the antero posterior depth of the upper chest whereas the 9$^{th}$ rib reflects the lower maximum expanse of the thorax, thus revealing the shape and size of the trunk of the hominin. Moreover, in the absence of long bones, the clavicle length would also provide a fair estimation of the stature. In addition, the general morphology and the diaphyseal robusticity of the clavicle also reveal the body build and the life styles/occupations and ecological adaptations of the early hominins (Pearson, 2000).

To arrive at the shoulder width or the diameter across shoulders, which correspond to the biacromial diameter from the length of the clavicle, the author derived two regression equations from Parsons's data (1916). He got 30.6 cm shoulder width of the Narmada hominin from the 90 mm long right clavicle, which interestingly tallies closely with the biacromial diameter of the female Onges (Chatterjee, 1956) of the Andaman Islands, having a mean value of 31.2 ± 1.1 cm and a narrow range of 29–33.5 cm in a large sample of 29 females. Therefore, the Narmada hominin was similar to the Pygmy in width of its thorax. Similarly, a reasonable estimate of the stature of Narmada hominin was estimated. The regression equation worked out by Jit and Singh (1956) yielded a stature of 134.85 cm (4′ 4"). There were other estimates based on skeletal and contemporary populations of the Andamanese and the Onges. These samples have yielded six different estimates, ranging from 115 to 135 cm. These body proportions are not un-realistic because the early African *H. erectus* (Narioctome) had a modern thoracic morphology (Jellima *et al.*, 1993). This is certainly a surprise and recalls the tiny 100cm Indonesian "Hobbits", *H. floresiensis.*

Vrba (1979) and Churchill (1994) have observed relationship between the conoid index of the clavicle and the chest depth. The conoid indices of the Narmada hominin (81.7/78.4) fall in the range Pygmy (76.7 [78.4] 83.80) and also closely go with the mean value of modern humans (82.1), suggesting a modern type moderate chest depth and warm-humid tropical adaptation.

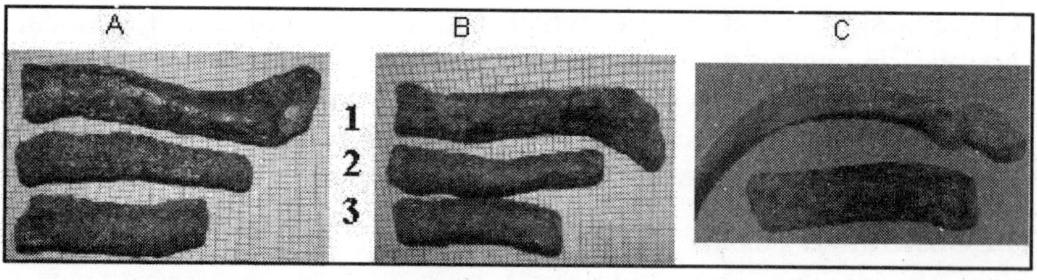


Figure 3: A Pygmy-sized Right Clavicle (1), a partial Left Clavicle (2) and a Left 9th Rib (3) in, dorsal (A) and ventral view (B), and Narmada Left Rib compared with modern human 9th rib (C) .

This contrasts from the western European Neanderthals (96) "hyper-polar" cold climatic adaptations (Franciscus and Churchill, 2002). The midshaft index (81.5/83.6) further attests the same, showing diaphyseal rounding touching the lower threshold of *H. sapiens* (80.0 [92.2] 110.1). It may also be observed that the midshaft index exhibits a general evolutionary trend- the flattened diaphyses (platycleidic) in early hominins (55-69.9) through the intermediate (mesocleidic) condition in some of them (70-84.9), and the rounded diaphyses (eurycleidic) in modern humans (85-above).

**Table 2**
**Select Morphometrics of Narmada and Modern Clavicles**

| | *Narmada (N=2)* | | *Andamanese (N=16)* | | | *Modern Other Modern Man* | | | *R/L. Difference Difference* | |
|---|---|---|---|---|---|---|---|---|---|---|
| *Measurement* | *Right* | *Left* | *Min* | *Mean* | *Max* | *Min* | *Mean* | *Max* | *Narm* | *Modm (N=30)* |
| Max. Clav L (CL) | 90 | 88 | 96 | 107 | 115 | 119 | 130.6 | 150.8 | 2 | -0.3 |
| Con L (COL) | 73.5 | 68 | 77.5 | 85.9 | 92 | 101.1 | 107.3 | 124.6 | 5 | 1 |
| Mid Dia AP (MDAP) | 13.5 | 13.4 | 8 | 8.8 | 10 | 9.9 | 11 | 14.2 | 0.1 | 0.3 |
| Mid Dia SI (MDSI) | 11 | 11.2 | 6.6 | 8 | 9 | 8 | 10.4 | 13 | -0.2 | 0.6 |
| Mid Dia Crf (MDCF) | 41 | 38 | 23.5 | 27.6 | 30 | 30 | 34.4 | 43 | 5 | 1.3 |
| St Epi AP (STAP) | 17.1 | 15.3 | 15.1 | 19.1 | 21.6 | 17 | 21 | 25.1 | 1.8 | 2 |
| St Epi SI (STSI) | 11 | 13 | 13.1 | 18.1 | 20.6 | 14.3 | 18.2 | 22.7 | -2 | -0.5 |
| Caliber Index | 45.6 | 43 | 22.6 | 26.1 | 30.2 | 23.2 | 26.4 | 30.1 | 2.8 | 1.2 |
| Inner-End Index | 28 | 28.3 | 31 | 37.4 | 41.6 | 33.4 | 39.1 | 47 | -0.2 | 2.2 |
| Conoid Index | 81.7 | 78.4 | 76.7 | 80.5 | 83.8 | 78.3 | 82.1 | 86.4 | 3.3 | 0.9 |
| Midshaft Index | 81.5 | 83.6 | 80 | 91.3 | 109.8 | 80 | 94.7 | 110.1 | -2.1 | 3.1 |
| Robusticity Index | 27.2 | 28 | 17.7 | 13.7 | 15.7 | 14 | 16.4 | 20.9 | -0.8 | 0.9 |

Figures in parentheses indicate reference points shown in the figure 4e. Linear measurements are in mm. AP=antero-posterior. SI=supero-inferior. CALI=MD CF./ CL.x100; INEI=STAP + MDSI; MIDI=MDSI / MDAP x 100; CONI=COL./ CLx100; ROBI=MDAP+MDSI/CL x 100.

**Table 3**
**Projections on the Stature, Biacromial Diameter, Head Circumference and Head Breadth of the Small Narmada Hominin Based on the Onge Data. S and BD in Parentheses Show Estimation from Stature and Biacromial Diameter Respectively**

| | | *From Stature* | | *From Biacromial Diameter* | | *From Head Circumference* | | *From Head Breadth* | |
|---|---|---|---|---|---|---|---|---|---|
| | *Sex* | *Onge* | *Narmada* | *Onge* | *Narmada* | *Onge* | *Narmada* | *Onge* | *Narmada* |
| Mean | M | 150.8 | - | 34.5 | 31.9(S) | 51.8 | 50.3 (BD) 51.6 (S) | 14.5(BD) | 14.4 |
| | F | 130.2 min 139.2 max (skeletal) | 115* Min 134.8 Max. (*Pb. S) | 30.0 | 29.6(S) | 48.5 | 48.0 (BD) 47.9 (S) | 13.7(BD) | 13.7(S) |
| SD | M | 4.0 | - | 1.6 | - | 1.7 | - | 0.5 | (S) |
| | F | 3.8 | - | 1.4 | - | 1.5 | - | 0.5 | - |
| N | M | 30 | - | 24 | - | 30 | - | 16 | - |
| | F | 22 | 1 | 16 | 1 | 22 | 1 | 9 | 1 |

The exceptionally high caliber and the robusticity indices of the Narmada clavicles attest very strongly developed nuchal and pectoral muscles, suggesting a uniquely very stout, robust and short and stocky archaic hominin, even shorter then the shortest extant female pygmy of the Andamans Islands- an "archaic or robust Pygmy" well adapted to South Asian equable climate. The calvaria on the other hand, belong to a unique pre-Neandertal European "archaic" hominin or the *H.*

*heidelbergensis* or an "archaic *H. sapiens* / *H. erectus* hybrid. The "small" hominin survived with its advanced Late Acheulian to Middle Palaeolithic projectile technology, whereas the "large" hominin with the massive Acheulian choppers, handaxes and cleavers. Whether the small (Pygmoid) hominins were among the ancestors of the Indonesian Hobbits- *Homo floresiensis* (Brown *et al.* (2003) is still an open and interesting question to explore (Sankhyan & Rao, 2007), though it may still be speculated that the archaic Pygmoid hominins from Narmada valley on their Southeast Asian migration if got insulated in the Flores Island, could easily become paedomorphic dwarfs, like the Hobbits as per the Island Rule (Heteren & J. de Vois, 2007).

**Table 4**
**Projections on the Stature, Biacromial Diameter, Head Circumference and Head Breadth of the Small Narmada Hominin based on the Onge Data. S and BD in Parentheses show Estimation from Stature and Biacromial Diameter respectively**

| *Species* | *N* | *Midshaft Index* |
|---|---|---|
| Narmada *Homo* (*Homo erectus / H. sapiens*) | 2 | 81.5/83.6 |
| Australopithecus *afarensis* (AL. 333 x -6 / 9) | 1 | 68. 6 |
| African *Homo erectus / H. ergaster* (WT - 15000) | 2 | 55 .8 / 61.7 |
| Olduvai *Homo* (OH - 48) | 1 | 70. 3 |
| Kenyan *Homo habilis* (E. R. - 1808) | 1 | 83. 3 |
| Chinese *Homo erectus* (Zhoukoudian) | 1 | 76. 3 |
| Neanderthal Man: Mix sample | 17 | 68. 4 ± 9.1 |
| Neanderthal Man:Regourdou-1 (France) | 1 | 60. 0 |
| Neanderthal Man: Atapuerca (Spain) | 4 | 66. 8 |
| Neanderthal Man:Shanindar1 left (Iraq) | 1 | 63. 0 |
| Modern *Homo sapiens:* Coimbra, Portugal | 160 | 89.0 ± 18.0 |
| Modern *Homo sapiens*: Andamanese | 16 | 80 (91.3) 109.8 |
| Modern *Homo sapiens*: Indian | 14 | 80 (94.7) 110.1 |
| Modern *Homo sapiens:* Pygmy+ Indian | 30 | 80 (92.2) 110.1 |

Data partly from Carretero *et al.* (1997).

## REFERENCES CITED

Brown, P., Sutikna, T., Morwood, M.J., Soejono, R.P., Jatmiko, Wayhu Saptomo, E., and Due, R.A. (2004), A New Small-bodied Hominin from the Late Pleistocene of Flores, Indonesia. *Nature 431*: 1055-1061.

Carretero, J.M. Arsuaga, J.L. and Lorenzo, C. (1997), Clavicles, Scapulae and Humeri from the Simo de los Huesos Site (Sierra de Atapuerca, Spain). *J. Human Evol. 33*: 357- 408.

Chatterjee, B.K. (1955), A Comparative Study of the Different Body Proportions of the Onges of Little Andamans. *The Anthropologist* 2(2): 12-21.

Cameron, D., Patnaik, R. and Sahni, A. (2004), The Phylogenetic Significance of the Middle Pleistocene Narmada Hominin Cranium from Central India. *Internat. J. Osteoarchaeol. 14* (6), 419-447.

Churchill, S.E. (1994), *Human Upper Body Evolution in the Eurasian Later Pleistocene.* Ph.D. Dissertation, University of New Mexico, New Mexico.

Dennel, R. and Roebroeks, W. (2005), An Asian Perspective on Early Human Dispersal from Africa. *Nature* (Review) *438*: 1099-1104.

Flower, W.H. (1880), On the Osteology and Affinities of the Natives of the Andaman Islands. *J. Anthropological Institute* (London) *9:* 10-135.

Franciscus, R. G. and Churchill, S.E. (2002), The Costal Skeleton of Shanidar 3 and a reappraisal of Neandertal Thoracic Morphology. *J. Human Evol.* *42*: 303-356.

Gabunia, L., de Lumley, M-A, Vekua, A., Lordkipanidze, D. and de Lumley, H., (2002), Decouverte dun nouvel hominide a Dmanissi (Transcaucasie), Georgia). *C. R. Palaevol.* *1:* 43-253.

Heteren, A.H. van, Vos, J. de (2007), Heterochrony as a Typical Island Adaptation in *Homo floresiensis*. In: Indriati, E. (ed.) *Recent Advances on Southeast Asian Paleoanthropology and archaeology*. Laboratory of Bioanthropology and Paleoanthropology Faculty of Medicne Gadjah Mada University, Yogyakarta, p. 95-106.

Jellema, L.M., Latimer, B. and Walker, A. (1993), The Rib Cage. In: Walker, A. and Leakey, R. (eds) *The Nariokotome* Homo Erectus *Skeleton,* pp. 295-325. Cambridge, Harvard University Press.

Jit. I. and Singh, S. (1956), Estimation of Stature from Clavicle. *Ind. J. Med. Res.* 44: 137-156.

Jit, I. and Singh, S. (1966), The Sexing of the Adult Clavicles. *Ind. J. Med. Res.* *54* (6), 551-571.

Kennedy, K.A.R. (1992), The Fossil Hominin from the Narmada Valley: Homo erectus or Homo Sapiens. In: Jarrige, C. (ed.) *South Asian Archeology 1989*, pp. 145-152. Prehistory Press, Madison.

Kennedy, K.A.R. (1999), The Paleoanthropology of South Asia. *Evolutionary Anthropol.* *8*: 157-194.

Kennedy, K.A.R. (2000), *God-Apes and Fossil Men: The Paleoanthropology of South Asia*. The University of Michigan Press, Michigan.

Kennedy, K.A.R., Sonakia, A., Chiment, J. and Verma, K.K. (1991), Is the Narmada Hominin an Indian *Homo Erectus*? *Am. J. Phys. Anthrop.* *86:* 475 - 496.

Lumley, M. -A. de and Sonakia, A. (1985), Premiere de coaverte d'un *Homo erectus* sur le continent Indien A. Hathnora, dans la Moyenne Vallee de la Narmada. *L'Anthropologie 89*: 13 - 61.

Parsons, F.G. (1916), On the Proportions and Characteristics of the Modern English Clavicle. *J. Anat, 51:* 71 – 93.

Pearson, O.M. (2000), Activity, Climate and Postcranial Robusticity: Implications for Modern Human Origins and Scenarios of Adaptive change. *Curr. Anthrop.* *41* (4): 569-605.

Rajendran. P. R. Bharath Kumar and E. Vijaya Bhanu (2003), Fossilized Hominid Baby Skull from the Ferricrete at Odai, Bommayarpalayam, Villupuram District, Tamil Nadu, South India. *Current Science* – 84 (6) : 754-756. Bangalore.

Sankhyan, A. R. (1997a), Fossil Clavicle of a Middle Pleistocene Hominin from the Central Narmada Valley, India. *J. Human Evol.* 32, 3-16.

Sankhyan, A. R. (1997b), A New Human Fossil find from the Central Narmada Basin and Its Chronology. *Curr. Sci* 73 (12), 1110 - 1111.

Sankhyan, A.R. (1999), The Place of Narmada Hominin in the Jigsaw Puzzle of Human Origins. In: M.P. Tiwari and D.M. Mohabey (eds.) *Quaternary of India*, pp. 335-345. Gondvana Geol. Magz. Spl. Publ. 4.

Sankhyan, A.R. (2005), New Fossils of Early Stone Age Man from Central Narmada Valley. *Curr. Sci. 88* (5): 704-707.

Sankhyan, A.R. (2007), Significance of Human Post-cranial Fossils from Narmada with Remarks on the Skullcap, In A.R. Sankhyan & V.R. Rao (eds) *Human Origins, Genome & People of India: Genomic, Palaeontological & Archaeological Perspectives*, pp. 193-217. Allied Publishers, Pvt. Ltd., New Delhi.

Shauffer, I.A. and Collins, W.V. (1966), The Deep Clavicular Rhomboid Fossa. *J. Am. Med. Assoc. 195*: 158-159.

Sonakia, A. (1984), The Skull Cap of Early Man and Associated Mammalian Fauna from Narmada Valley Alluvium, Hoshangabad area, M. P. (India). *Rec. Geol. Surv. India 113:* 159-172.

Trinkaus, E. (1983), *The Shanidar Neandertals*. Academic Press, New York.

Vandermeersch, B. and Trinkaus, E. (1995), The Postcranial Remains of the Regourdou 1 Neandertal: The shoulder and arm remains. *J. Human Evol. 28:* 439-476.

Vrba, E.S. (1979), A New Study of the Scapula of *Australopithecus*. *Am. J. Phys. Anthrop. 51*: 117-130.

Walker, A. C. and Leakey, R.E.F. (eds) (1993), The Nariokotome *Homo Erectus* Skeleton. Harvard University Press, Boston.

CHAPTER–6

# Cultural, Faunal and Stratigraphic Contexts of Narmada Hominins

*A.R. Sankhyan, Sheuli Chakraborty, L. N. Dewangan, Shashi Prabha, Suvendu Kundu & V.R. Rao*

## INTRODUCTION

The Central Narmada Valley is a trough basin between the Satpura and the Vindhyan hills, filled with the Lower and the Upper Group Quaternary Alluvium. The Central Narmada Valley Quaternary deposits between Jabalpur–Harda sectors have unique importance in the Quaternary history of South Asia because of the following findings:

1. Very rich mammalian fossils and associated Palaeolithic implements since a long history of of over 150 years (Theobold, 1860; Medlicot, deTerra and Patterson, 1939; Dassarma, 1979; Badam, 1979; Khatri, 1966; Biswas and Dassarma, 1986; Mishra and Rajaguru, 1993; Rajaguru *et al.*, 1984; Biswas, 1997; (Badam *et al*, 1986; Lumley and Sonakia, 1985; Bhattacharya and Sonakia, 1989; Biswas, 1997; Pappu, 2001, and references there in).
2. It has a unique distinction of having yielded earliest human fossils at Hathnora (77 ° 53′ N: 22 ° 52′E), hitherto unknown in South Asia (Sonakia, 1984; Sankhyan, 1997a & b, 1999 and 2005).
3. It contains a number of tephra ash beds as reported form Pawla and Guruwara areas (Basu *et al.*, 1987) as well as Hirapur (Sonakia *et al.*, 1990), which provide the radiometric dates on the Youngest Toba Ash (YTA) of ~75000 years BP (Westgate *et al.*, 1998; Chesner *et al.*, 1991; Acharyya and Basu, 1993). The petrography and geochemistry of these ash beds are well studied (Mukhopadhyay and Ramchandra, 1997 and Westgate *et al.*, 1998).

4. Of late, the Lower Datum (~0.73 Million years BP) is also from palaeomagnetic studies (Agrawal *et al*, 1988; Rao *et al.* 1997), when Tiwari & Bhai (1997) have worked out a detailed lithostratigraphy of the Central Narmada Quaternary.

Historically, Theobold (1860) had classified the Pleistocene Central Narmada Alluvium into the Lower Group and the Upper on both lithological characters including the fossil content. Later, de Terra and Patterson (1939) followed this stratigraphy. They included laterite below the Lower Group and inset Holocene sequence above the Upper Group. The Lower Group and Upper Group and equivalent formations were respectively assigned Middle Pleistocene and Upper Pleistocene ages by de Terra and Patterson (1937, 1939), remarking that both Lower and Upper Groups carry Middle Pleistocene mammalian faunal remains, the Lower Group represents true Acheulian and early Soan, and the Upper group contains the late Soan industry. Though, the Soanian industry has been subsequently ruled out, yet the later scholars more or less followed the same scheme with some modifications by assigning ages of the mammalian fossils or stone tools (Khatri (1961; Biswas *et al.* ,1989; Biswas and Dassarma, 1981).

## OBJECTIVES OF PRESENT STUDY

While we are conducting exhaustive explorations and selected trial excavations in Central Narmada valley, the present paper just aims to record our observations on a few stratigraphic formations and sections study at and around the hominin site, Hathnora (Fig. 1) and an overview of the mammalian fossils and Palaeolithic implements recovered wherefrom, especially the *in situ* findings.

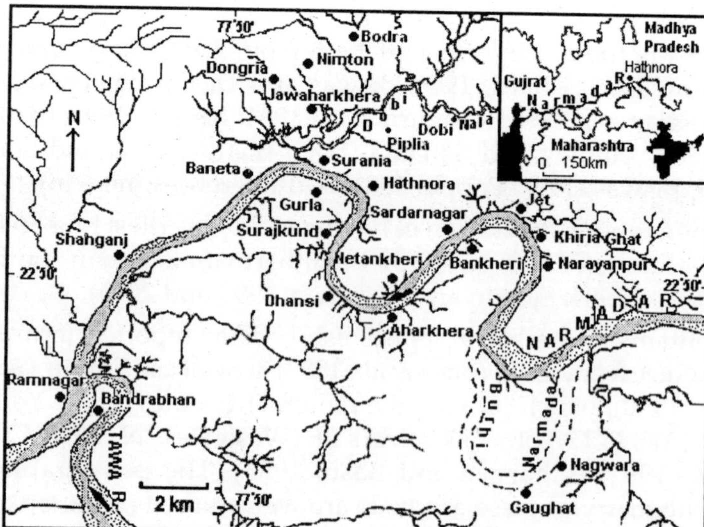


Figure 1: A Portion of Central Narmada Valley Around the Hominin Site, Hathnora

We are considering the stratigraphic scheme of seven formations by Tiwari and Bhai (1997) as a reference work for discussion and recording our own observations on various aspects. The seven formal lithostratigraphic formations are: *Pilikrar, Dhansi, Surajkund, Baneta, Hirdepur, Bauras,* and *Ramnagar*. Their major characteristics have been summarized in Table 1. In this paper we confine ourselves to the first three more ancient formations important.

**Table1**
**Quaternary Stratigraphic Succession of Narmada Valley Summarized by Sankhyan (2007) After Modification from Tiwari & Bhai (1997)**

| *Formation* | *Period* | *Date* | *Landform* | *Soil Type* | *Lithology* |
|---|---|---|---|---|---|
| Ramnagar | Late Holocene | < 4 ka | $T_0$ Inset terraces (15 m) | I | Dark gray, non-calcareous silts, sand and gravel |
| Bauras | Early Holocene | > 4-13 ka | $T_1$ Inset Terraces (20m); 15-30m vertical dissection and formation | II | Low to moderately calcified gray silts, sand and gravel |
| Hirdepur | Late Upper Pleistocene | 25-13 ka | $T_2$ Vertisol (30 m) | IV | Structureless gray sandy silt, fine sands, re-worked tephra, cross-bedded sand, calcareous sandstone, conglomerate |
| Baneta | Early Upper Pleistocene | 118-75 ka | $T_1$ Dissection and Aggradation (30 m) | V | Brown soil, brown calcareoussilt, volcanic ash, dark carbonaceous, clays, fine cross-bedded sand, calcareous sandstone, conglomerate |
| Surajkund | Middle Pleistocene | 500-200 ka | $T_1$ & $T_2$ Dissection & Aggradation (50 m) | VI | Yellow clayey soil, steel-gray and yellow clays, gray/brown silt; fine cross-bedded sand, gravels, calcareous congloformerate |
| Dhansi | Lower Pleistocene | >700 ka | Erosional unconformity (20m) | VII | Red soil, red to yellow /orange sand, brown silt, gray sand and silt. |
| Pilikarar | Lower Pleistocene | >1000 ka | T1 and T2 Laterite and latosol (>10 m) | VIII | Laterite gravels and coarse sand |

## Pilikarar Formation

According to Tiwari (2007) the Pilikarar Fm belongs to the Lower Pleistocene and *lacks fossils*. We are in general agreement with the description of the formation given by Tiwari *(op cit.)* as comprising of three types of ferricreted gravels, which are partially to totally weathered, showing "primary laterite profile" consisting of kaolinite zone, spongy and tubular laterite and ferricrete; the laterite clasts are cemented with iron oxide and form the ferricrete. One or the other types are seen bordering the alluvial plains. Within the alluvium the Baneta formation overlies it. Contact between this formation and the Dhansi and Surajkund formations have not been observed. It has been assigned Lower Pleistocene age due to its high degree of ferrugination, not observed in any other formation (Tiwari and Bhai, 1997).

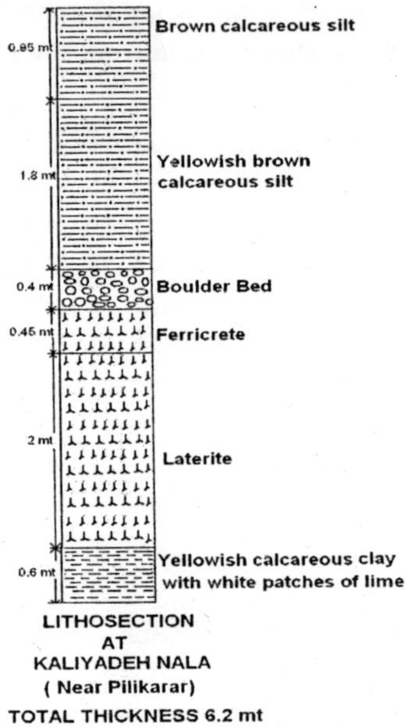


Figure 2: Lithosection near Pilikarar: The section near Devgaon (22*46'16"N, 77*37'51"E) at about 300m south from the new bridge reveals a 11.5m thick quaternary deposit. The exposed gravel bed is 2.9m thick and it is 1.1m thick in excavated portion. The overlying Baneta formation is 8.6m thick

We observed that the Pilikarar Formation disconformably overlays the laterite bed. It consists of clast-supported gravels/boulders containing the lithic fragments of laterite, quartzite, jasperoid, quartzite, banded hematite, limestone quartz and sandstone. This gravel bed or boulder bed is ranging from 0.2m to 4m. All the stone implements are found on this bed. The poorly sorted gravels and variable thickness of the gravel/ boulder bed represents an alluvial or colluvial fan originating from the foothills of Vindhyas, which form the northern valley margin, quite close by.

We studied two sections at the bank of Kaliyadeh Nala; one near to Pilikarar village on the left bank of the Nala, and the other on the right bank near Devgaon village. The exposed section is 6.2m thick and located one km northwest of the Pilikarar (22*46'N, 77*39' E) village.

From the base it shows 0.6m thick yellowish clay with white patches of lime, formed due to weathering of the overlying laterite bed. The laterite bed is 2m thick and overlain by 0.45m thick, hard and compact wide-spread ferricrete. The boulder bed, 0.4m in thickness, disconformably overlays the ferricrete, 1.8m thick yellowish brown calcareous silt, and 0.96m thick brown calcareous silt of the Baneta formation

Figure 3

Figure 4

Our excavation at Pilikarar in the Kaliyadeh Nala revealed the absence of mammalian both within the laterite deposit as well as in the disconformably overlying a colluvial layers/fan of the boulder-gravel and the overlaying alluvium of the Baneta formation. The laterite of secondary origins here comprises of three types of ferricreted gravels, which are partially to totally weathered, apparently of pre-Quaternary period. The colluvial boulder-gravel is very rich in Acheulian tools of various levels of size and refinement. The massive Choppers, flakes, cleavers and handaxes found in this thick deposition are confused to Early Acheulian by some workers (Patnaik *et al.*, 2009), which in our opinion are rather part and parcel of the Late Acheulian complex, represented by over 500 tools in our collection, none showing any inferior Early Acheulian technology in their manufacture. The massive sizes only indicate a different utility *not* technology.

**Dhansi Formation**

The top of the 15m thick Dhansi formation lying under the Surajkund Fm shows Matuyama Reverse Magnetic Polarity (Rao *et al.*, 1997), and therefore, older than 0.730 Mya (Agrawal *et al.*, 1988; Rao *et al*, 1997; Tiwari, 2007) falling in the Lower Pleistocene age, though fossils are not yet reported from this formation. According to Tiwari (2007), the Dhansi formation in the type section is 15m thick. It comprises red homogenous silty sand with calcareous reticulate veins. Matrix of the red silty sand is of iron oxide. It is recognized by a red soil at its top: consists coffee-coloured sandy clay with prismatic to massive structure in **Al** horizon; red indurated and massive silty sand with clay eluviations, iron oxide cementation, iron oxide concretion and greenish clayey reticulate mottling in B horizon. The colour of B-horizon changes, downwards in profile from red to orange, yellow and gray. Outside the Narmada valley, only comparable litho unit is Red silt formation of the Puma valley. Base of this formation is not exposed. It is overlain by the Surajkund formation in the type area. The sediments of this formation show reverse magnetic polarity. The contact between the Brunhes normal polarity and the Matuyama reverse polarity is located at the top of the Dhansi formation. Therefore the Dhansi formation is older than 0.7 Mya.

At Dhansi, the Dhansi formation is underlying below the Surajkund formation. The base of the Dhansi formation is not exposed at the Dhansi type-site. The yellowish orange sand layer of Dhansi is underlying below a thin pebbly layer. The Surajkund formation rests on this pebbly layer. We did not notice any cobble horizon or the presence of cobbles in Dhansi formation, which could have served as the raw material for manufacturing the stone tools. This observation is contrary to the recent claim of a solitary stone tool by Patnaik et al., 2009) attributed from Dhansi. Our observation is that the stone tool yielding horizon is located not within the Dhansi but above the Dhansi Formation and at the base of the Surajkund Formation. Our excavation at Burhi Narmada (See Figure 2) in February 2008 has confirmed the lack of stone tools in Dhansi Formation. We excavated a section measuring 6.3m thick of which 1.54m belongs to the Surajkund formation and the rest to the Dhansi. Hence, the reports of the stone tools from the Dhansi Formation are based on a misunderstanding.

The Dhansi formation at Burhi Narmada section is comprised of medium to fine-grained red concretionary sand, coarse-grained dark red sand with large concretions with iron patches, coarse grained hard compact dark brownish red sand with large bluish green concretions and iron nodules. In the excavated section we found only two stone implements - a small Middle Palaeolithic scraper and a flake recovered from the contact of Dhansi and Surajkund (layer 5), though a few stone tools including flakes, cleaver, discoid and scrapers were collected from Dhansi surface context at Burhi Narmada, which are very likely were drifted from the overlying Surajkund bed. These tools are made from large flakes detached from the boulders. These tools could have not been made from large flakes detached from the boulders rather than cobbles. This indicates that the tools are not *in situ* context in Dhansi Formation and could have been drifted from overlying Surajkund Formation.

Figure 5

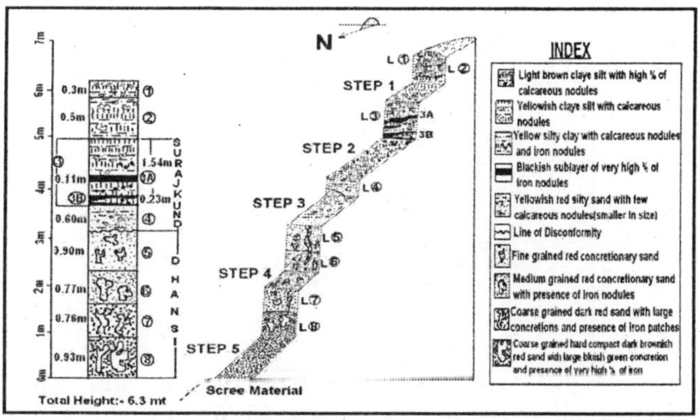


Figure 6: Excavated Sections at Burhi Narmada (Surajkund & Dhansi)

## Surajkund Formation

Surajkund formation is overlain by the Dhansi formation. They are separated by the Brunhes Normal Magnetic Polarity (Rao *et al.*, 1997). According to Tiwari (2007) the Surajkund Formation consists mostly of steel gray clays in the deeper part and conglomerate, gravel, fine sand, brown silty clay and yellowish clay in the peripheral part of the basin. In its type area, it is capped by a soil with pale clayey A 1 horizon with blocky structure followed by yellow clayey B-horizon with blocky structure and black *oxic* and stress *cutans* and iron oxide concretions. In the type area, it is underlain by the Dhansi Formation of Lower Pleistocene age and overlain by the Baneta Formation of the Early Upper Pleistocene age. It shows Brunhes normal magnetic polarity.

The type site the exposed section is 15.4m thick. From the base upwards it shows steel gray clay, (0.6m thick) yellow clay (1m thick) and cemented gravel (2.5m) beds of Surajkund formation. This is overlain by brown concretionary silt (2.4m), deep brown clay (2.7m). This in turn followed by light brown calcareous silt (2.6m), 3.1m yellowish brown calcareous silty clay and deep gray clay (0.3m).

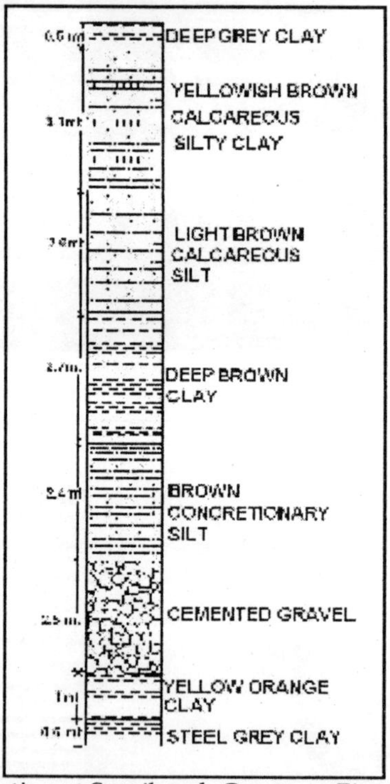


Figure 7: Lithosection Section at Surajkund: Course to Fine Sand adn Gravel Layer up to 1.3m. It is Overlain by Yellow Fine Burnt Sand (0.55m)

At *Hathnora* several exposed sections were examined. Two of them are illustrated here. The exposed section at the point C is further excavated. The exposed section is 11.2m thick where the excavated portion is 1.3m thick. From the base upwards it shows alteration of medium to coarse gray sand and the sheet deposition of gravels up to 70 cm. It is followed by the alteration of cross-bedded

Few burnt pebbles are also present in this layer. From the base up to this layer the lithofacies of Surajkund formation is noticed. The Baneta formation is disconformably overlying the Surajkund formation. The heterogeneous sandy pebbly concretionary layer (0.9m) represents the disconformity between these two formations. It is overlain by gray cross-bedded pebbly sand (1.1m) which is followed by the brown clayey silt with sand lenses (8m). The topmost layer is formed by the black soil (0.2m).

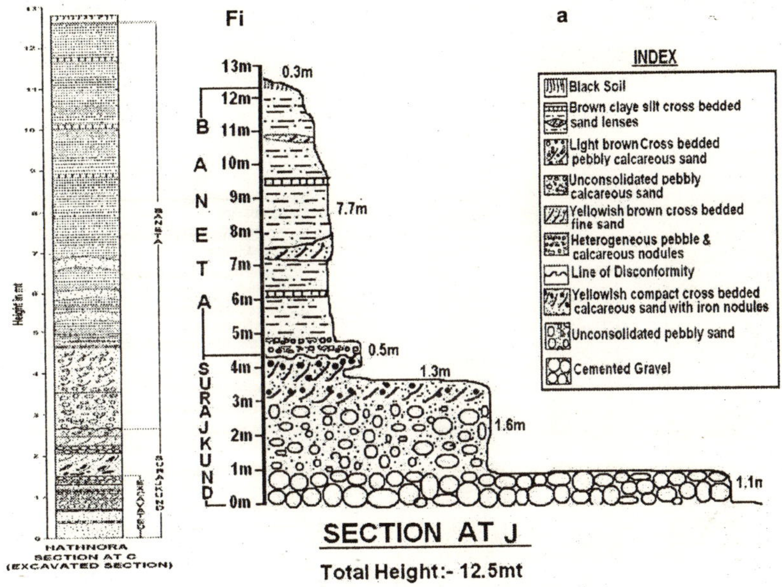


Figure 8: Lithosection at Hathnora

We did not find any burnt material in the exposed section at the *point J*. Here the unconsolidated pebbly sand consists of the pebbles of quartzite, jasper, chert, agate and sandstone. The cemented gravel layer also consists of the same material. We observed that the gravels are cemented by calcium carbonate. The degree of cementing or concretization is different in the sites around Hathnora. The cemented gravel bed of Sardarnagar represents higher degree of cementing than other sites around Hathnora.The cemented gravel bed of all the sites provided a large number of stone implements and fossils. From the cemented gravel bed in *Sardarnagar* we recovered a large number of Middle Palaeolithic stone implements including cleavers, hand axes, scrapers and small choppers. The cleavers recovered from this site are very fresh, fine and represent the homogeneity in their preparation. The stone implements are mainly made of quartzite. But at Hathnora we did not find such fine Middle Palaeolithic stone implements from the cemented gravel bed. Only few small choppers and some Upper.

## Khiriaghat

It is one of the richest fossiliferous sites of this area. We recovered many mammalian fossils from the cemented gravel bed at Khiriaghat. We observed the anticlinal and synclinal marks in Baneta formation on the exposed section of Khiriaghat which may indicates neotectonic movements having occurred during the Holocene time.

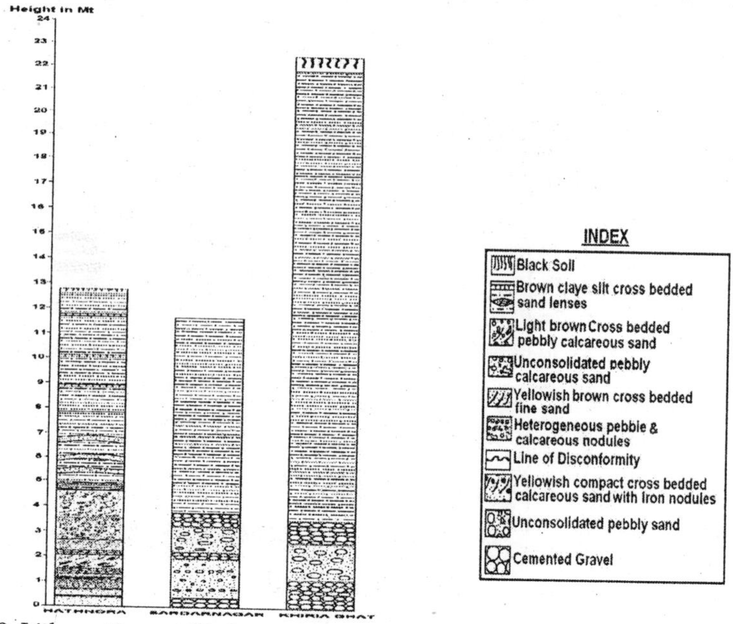


Figure 9: Lithosections at Hathnora, Khiriyaghat and Sardamagar Compared

## Netankheri

Here we observed that the cemented gravel bed is collapsed. The collapsed upper-cemented gravel bed contains the lithic fragments of sandstone, jasper, quartzite, chert, agate in plenty. The volcanic materials like chert, jasper, agate etc. are derived from the southern mountains, the Satpura Hills. It represents the aggradational cycle of Narmada. In the upper layers of Upper gravel ($U^3$) the marks of anticlines and synclines have been noticed indicating neotectonic movements as observed by us at Khiriaghat. Below the cemented gravel bed a yellowish calcareous sandy layer has been observed. It remains partly submerged in Narmada water. The Baneta formation disconformably overlays the $U^3$ gravel bed.

At Netankheri a 17.2m thick section is exposed. From the base upwards it shows yellowish calcareous sand (0.5m). It is overlain by cemented gravel bed (1.2m). The lithofacies of Baneta formation is disconformably overlying the cemented gravel layer. The disconformity is marked by a thin concretionary pebbly layer. A fine brown clayey-silt layer with presence of sand lenses (15.5m) of Baneta formation overlies on the pebbly layer.

**Table 2**
**Narmada Stone Collection 2006 to 2008 Classified**

| | *Pebble Tools* | | *Core Tools* | | *Flake Tools* | | *Blades* | | *Blade-lets* | | *Total* | |
|---|---|---|---|---|---|---|---|---|---|---|---|---|
| *SITE NAME* | *N* | *%* | *N* | *%* | *N* | *%* | *N* | *%* | *N* | *%* | *N* | *%* |
| ADAMGARH | | | 8 | 11.9 | 21 | 31.3 | 30 | 44.8 | 8 | 11.94 | 67 | 100 |
| AHARKHERA | | | 1 | 5 | 19 | 95 | | | | | 20 | 100 |
| AMKHERI | | | | | 246 | 93.2 | 16 | 6.06 | 2 | 0.76 | 264 | 100 |
| AJERA | | | 2 | 5 | 32 | 80 | 3 | 7.5 | 3 | 7.5 | 40 | 100 |
| AOLI GHAT | 1 | 5 | 4 | 20 | 15 | 75 | | | | | 20 | 100 |
| BARKHERA | | | 3 | 33.3 | 1 | 11.1 | 5 | 55.6 | | | 9 | 100 |
| BANETA | 1 | 5.9 | 1 | 5.88 | 15 | 88.2 | | | | | 17 | 100 |
| BABRI GHAT-I | 5 | 4.2 | 11 | 9.17 | 102 | 85 | 1 | 0.83 | 1 | 0.83 | 120 | 100 |
| BABRI GHAT-II | | | 11 | 11.6 | 84 | 88.4 | | | | | 95 | 100 |
| BARMAN GHAT | 11 | 9.3 | 14 | 11.9 | 93 | 78.8 | | | | | 118 | 100 |
| BARMAN KALAN BRIDGE | | | 1 | 25 | 3 | 75 | | | | | 4 | 100 |
| BANKHERI | | | 2 | 2.53 | 72 | 91.1 | 4 | 5.06 | 1 | 1.27 | 79 | 100 |
| BANDRABHAN | 11 | 4.1 | 18 | 6.77 | 237 | 89.1 | | | | | 266 | 100 |
| BUDHNI NALA | 2 | 6.9 | 9 | 31 | 18 | 62.1 | | | | | 29 | 100 |
| BUDHNI VILLAGE | | | | | 30 | 96.8 | | | 1 | 3.23 | 31 | 100 |
| BUDHNI RAIL BRIDGE | 12 | 8.6 | 35 | 25 | 91 | 65 | 2 | 1.43 | | | 140 | 100 |
| BHATERA | | | 13 | 9.15 | 124 | 87.3 | 5 | 3.52 | | | 142 | 100 |
| BHAUTI | | | | | 29 | 100 | | | | | 29 | 100 |
| BHEDAGHAT | 2 | 0.7 | 29 | 10.2 | 251 | 88.1 | 2 | 0.7 | 1 | 0.35 | 285 | 100 |
| BHILLARIA | 3 | 5.8 | 4 | 7.69 | 45 | 86.5 | | | | | 52 | 100 |
| BODARA | | | 8 | 15.1 | 29 | 54.7 | 2 | 3.77 | 14 | 26.42 | 53 | 100 |
| BORA RANI CAVE | | | 1 | 6.25 | 10 | 62.5 | 5 | 31.3 | | | 16 | 100 |
| CHINKI | 1 | 0.9 | 13 | 11.5 | 99 | 87.6 | | | | | 113 | 100 |
| DEVKACHHAR BARUREWA | | | | | 24 | 82.8 | 5 | 17.2 | | | 29 | 100 |
| DEWKACHHAR SHER | | | 10 | 30.3 | 21 | 63.6 | 2 | 6.06 | | | 33 | 100 |
| DHANA GHAT | | | 8 | 3.59 | 198 | 88.8 | 14 | 6.28 | 3 | 1.35 | 223 | 100 |
| DOBI NALA | | | | | 3 | 75 | 1 | 25 | | | 4 | 100 |

*Contd.*

| | Pebble Tools | | Core Tools | | Flake Tools | | Blades | | Blade-lets | | Total | |
|---|---|---|---|---|---|---|---|---|---|---|---|---|
| SITE NAME | N | % | N | % | N | % | N | % | N | % | N | % |
| DUGARIA | 2 | 1.4 | 23 | 16.2 | 117 | 82.4 | | | | | 142 | 100 |
| GANJAL RAIL BRIDGE | | | 4 | 19 | 17 | 81 | | | | | 21 | 100 |
| GOUGHAT | | | 3 | 60 | 2 | 40 | | | | | 5 | 100 |
| GURLA | 1 | 1.4 | 10 | 13.5 | 59 | 79.7 | 4 | 5.41 | | | 74 | 100 |
| GURARI NALA | | | | | 6 | 100 | | | | | 6 | 100 |
| GWARI GHAT | 1 | 5 | 6 | 30 | 13 | 65 | | | | | 20 | 100 |
| HATHNORA | | | 13 | 5.73 | 208 | 91.6 | 5 | 2.2 | 1 | 0.44 | 227 | 100 |
| HANDIA | 2 | 3.6 | 9 | 16.4 | 43 | 78.2 | | | 1 | 1.82 | 55 | 100 |
| HOSHANGABAD RAIL BRIDGE | 9 | 5.2 | 24 | 13.9 | 140 | 80.9 | | | | | 173 | 100 |
| ISHARPUR | | | 7 | 4.52 | 140 | 90.3 | 6 | 3.87 | 2 | 1.29 | 155 | 100 |
| JAWAHARKHERA | 1 | 0.9 | 16 | 14.8 | 86 | 79.6 | 3 | 2.78 | 2 | 1.85 | 108 | 100 |
| JHALSARGOND | | | 11 | 2.91 | 357 | 94.4 | 9 | 2.38 | 1 | 0.27 | 378 | 100 |
| KALIAYADEH NALA | 6 | 9.1 | 7 | 10.6 | 53 | 80.3 | | | | | 66 | 100 |
| KANDARWADA | | | 5 | 2.35 | 189 | 88.7 | 14 | 6.57 | 5 | 2.35 | 213 | 100 |
| KHIRIA GHAT | 3 | 12 | 2 | 7.69 | 21 | 80.8 | | | | | 26 | 100 |
| KOLHAR RIVER | 1 | 5.9 | 4 | 23.5 | 12 | 70.6 | | | | | 17 | 100 |
| LACHHORA | | | 1 | 20 | 3 | 60 | 1 | 20 | | | 5 | 100 |
| LADAIYA | | | | | 4 | 100 | | | | | 4 | 100 |
| MACHHA GHAT | | | 4 | 2.16 | 167 | 90.3 | 14 | 7.57 | | | 185 | 100 |
| MADANPUR | | | | | 49 | 100 | | | | | 49 | 100 |
| MAHADEO PIPARIA | 12 | 6.4 | 15 | 8.02 | 159 | 85 | 1 | 0.53 | | | 187 | 100 |
| MANGROL | | | 2 | 3.13 | 56 | 87.5 | 3 | 4.69 | 3 | 4.69 | 64 | 100 |
| MOR GHAT | | | 1 | 0.55 | 174 | 96.1 | 1 | 0.55 | 5 | 2.76 | 181 | 100 |
| NABAL GAON | 6 | 8.8 | 10 | 14.7 | 51 | 75 | 1 | 1.47 | | | 68 | 100 |
| NAGWADA (BURHI NARMADA) | | | 2 | 6.67 | 28 | 93.3 | | | | | 30 | 100 |
| NAKTI-TALAI | 1 | 1.2 | 22 | 25.6 | 59 | 68.6 | 2 | 2.33 | 2 | 2.33 | 86 | 100 |
| NETANKHERI | 15 | 2.2 | 37 | 5.36 | 591 | 85.7 | 33 | 4.78 | 14 | 2.03 | 690 | 100 |
| NIMABAR | 8 | 12 | 10 | 14.9 | 48 | 71.6 | 1 | 1.49 | | | 67 | 100 |
| NIMTONE | | | 9 | 17.3 | 43 | 82.7 | | | | | 52 | 100 |

*Contd.*

| | *Pebble Tools* | | *Core Tools* | | *Flake Tools* | | *Blades* | | *Blade-lets* | | *Total* | |
|---|---|---|---|---|---|---|---|---|---|---|---|---|
| *SITE NAME* | *N* | *%* | *N* | *%* | *N* | *%* | *N* | *%* | *N* | *%* | *N* | *%* |
| PAMLI | | | | | 22 | 100 | | | | | 22 | 100 |
| PARAMHANSH GHAT-I | 10 | 9.5 | 4 | 3.81 | 91 | 86.7 | | | | | 105 | 100 |
| PARAMHANSH GHAT-II | 5 | 2.1 | 21 | 8.64 | 207 | 85.2 | 8 | 3.29 | 2 | 0.823 | 243 | 100 |
| RAJIV GANDHI SETU | | | 13 | 5.24 | 223 | 89.9 | 12 | 4.84 | | | 248 | 100 |
| RAM NAGAR | 4 | 31 | 1 | 7.69 | 8 | 61.5 | | | | | 13 | 100 |
| RATIKARAR-I | | | 3 | 13 | 18 | 78.3 | 2 | 8.7 | | | 23 | 100 |
| RATIKARAR-II | | | | | 6 | 85.7 | 1 | 14.3 | | | 7 | 100 |
| REWA BANKHERI | | | 3 | 1.67 | 166 | 92.2 | 7 | 3.89 | 4 | 2.222 | 180 | 100 |
| SHAHAGANJ GUEST HOUSE | 2 | 2 | 3 | 3.03 | 88 | 88.9 | 6 | 6.06 | | | 99 | 100 |
| SATDHARA | 3 | 5 | 2 | 3.33 | 55 | 91.7 | | | | | 60 | 100 |
| SARDAR NAGAR | 15 | 14 | 14 | 12.7 | 79 | 71.8 | 2 | 1.82 | | | 110 | 100 |
| SURAJKUND | 3 | 1.1 | 8 | 2.85 | 257 | 91.5 | 12 | 4.27 | 1 | 0.356 | 281 | 100 |
| SURANIA | 1 | 2.8 | 6 | 16.7 | 29 | 80.6 | | | | | 36 | 100 |
| SANKLA | | | 7 | 7.61 | 84 | 91.3 | 1 | 1.09 | | | 92 | 100 |
| SITARAM GHAT | | | 1 | 1.01 | 93 | 93.9 | 2 | 2.02 | 3 | 3.03 | 99 | 100 |
| TALAIYA GHAT | 1 | 4.5 | | | 20 | 90.9 | 1 | 4.55 | | | 22 | 100 |
| UMARIA | | | 1 | 4 | 24 | 96 | | | | | 25 | 100 |
| TOTAL | 161 | 2.2 | 550 | 7.52 | 6277 | 85.8 | 249 | 3.4 | 80 | 1.093 | 7317 | 99.999 |

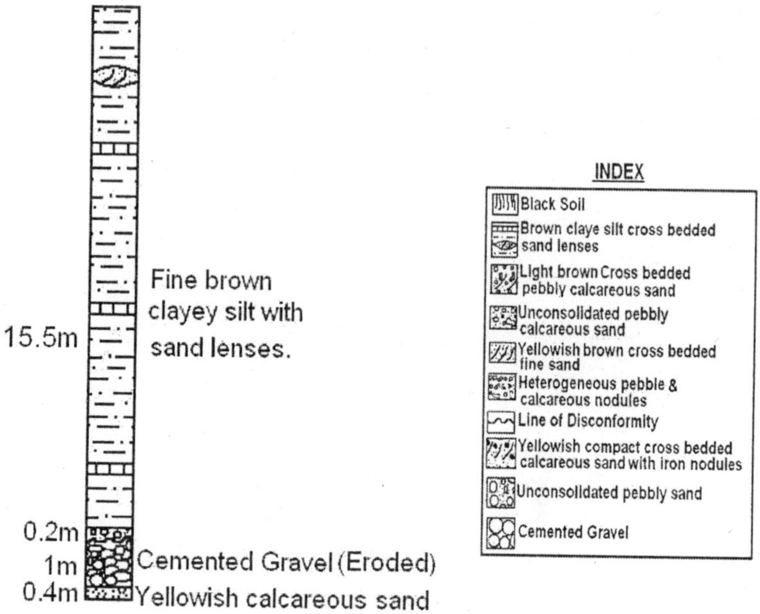


Figure 10: Litho-Section at Netankheri

## The Stratigraphic Context of the Hominin Fossils

As noted above the Surajkund formation is reported from several localities adjoining Hathnora. The Surajkund formation is the richest fossiliferous formation in the valley having yielded Middle to Late Pleistocene fossil assemblage consisting *Hippopotamus namadicus, Equus namadicus, Sus namadicus, Stegodon namadicus* and *Cuon alpinus* (Biswas, 1997; Badam, 1979, Badam *et al.*, 1986, 2001; Biswas, 1997; Sankhyan, 1997a and b).

Located in the west of village Hathnora village, on the right bank of Narmada, 22 km North-East of Hoshangabad town, the hominin site comprises of cemented gravels, erroneously called as "Boulder Conglomerate". Of course, it is overlain by the thick terrace of concretionary clays of the Baneta Formation, capped at the top by the Holocene Black Cotton Soil (vertisol)

Total section at Hathnora is about 18m thick, of which the lowermost 3 meters constitute the hominin-bearing sheet gravel, deposited fluvially on relict platforms and rock-cut terraces of the Vindhyan bed rock. The sheet gravel is distinguished into three units. The basal part/unit-I is about 1.5 meter thick forming a vast horizontal platform, and is partly/rather almost submerged in Narmada waters. During the summer of 2005 when water level fell down, the lower portion of the Unit-1 exposed the "Boulder Bed" that yielded a large mammalian fossils- also excavated *in situ* position, besides over 100 massive Acheulian tools- handaxes, cleavers, choppers and flakes and discoids (Sankhyan *et al.*, 2007). *Table* 2 below summarizes our total collection of *7317* stone tools made during 2006 through 2008.

Both the Skullcap (Sonakia, 1984) as well as the postcranial human fossils (Sankhyan, 1997a and b, 2005) from Hathnora come from the Lower part of the U-2 or the Upper part of the U-1 cemented gravel/ sheet deposit of the Surajkund Formation. Interestingly, it is the unit-I sheet gravel that has yielded most of the mammalian fossils. There is a regular recovery of largely complete crania, mandibles, dentition and bones of mammals like, *Bubalus palaeindicus, Equus namadicus, Hexaprotodon palaeindicus and Bos namadicus* from this bed at Hathnora further attest this (Kennedy *et al.*, 1991; Sankhyan, 1997a,b). Although, the stratigraphic context of the fossils remains unchanged, their post-fossilization fragmentation and

Figure 11

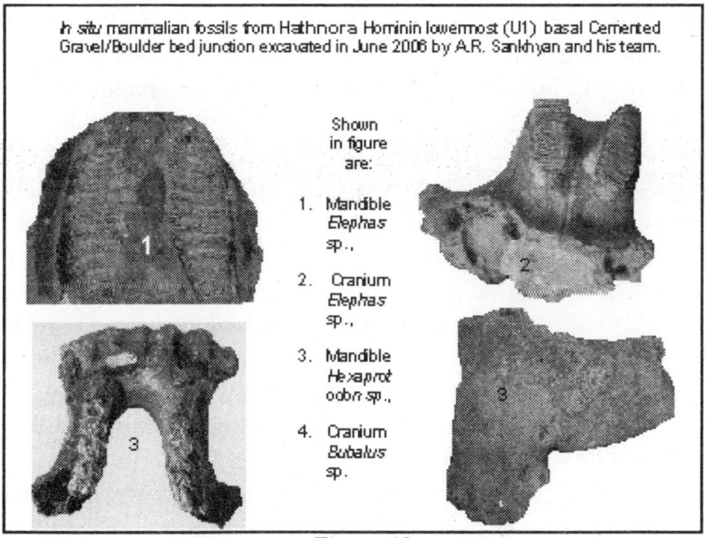


Figure 12

displacement has occurred primarily through secondary erosion and weathering, and through a recent change in the hydrological system (see Cameron *et al.*, 2004). The fauna of the unit-I are typical of Middle Pleistocene affinities (Badam *et al.*, 1986; Biswas, 1997; Sankhyan, 1997a and b) as do the middle to late Acheulian tools Lumley and Sonakia, 1985a; Bhattacharya and Sonakia, 1989; Sankhyan, 1997a,b), such that an upper chronological limit of *ca.* 500 could be assigned to the Hathnora hominin fossils. The lower temporal limit or a probable antiquity could be taken from a recent date of *ca.* 236 ka, suggested by the gamma spectrometric U-series of a bovid scapula recovered from the hominin site (see Cameron *et al.*, 2004). Indirectly also, a date of a *ca* 670 ka for the early Acheulian at Bori in South India (Mishra *et al.*, 1995) may support the inferred antiquity of the Hathnora hominin's middle to late Acheulian tool-kit.

Our work is under progress and the data under detailed analysis.

## REFERENCES CITED

Acharyya, S. K. and Basu, P. K. (19930, Toba Ash on the Indian Subcontinent and Its Implications for the Correlation of Late Pleistocene Alluvium. *Quat. Research 40:* 10-19.

Agrawal, D. P., Kotlia, B.S. and Kusumgar, S. (1988, Chronology and Significance of the Narmada Formations. *Proc. Ind. Nat. Sci. Acad. 54A*: 418 - 424.

Badam, G. L. (1979), *Pleistocene Fauna of India with Special Reference to the Siwaliks.* Poona: Deccan College.

Badam, G. L., Ganjoo, R. K., Salahuddin, R.K.G. and Rajaguru, S.N. (1986), Evolution of Fossil Hominin– The Maker of Late Acheulian Tools at Hathnora, Madhya Pradesh, India. *Curr. Sci. 55* (3): 143-145.

Badam, G. L. (2001), Palaeontological Excavations in Narsinghpur District, Central Narmada Valley, Madhya Pradesh, India. *Puratan 12:* 61-76.

Bhattacharya, D.K. and Sonakia, A. (1989), Cultural Remains from the Earliest Hominin Site on Narmada. In: Tiwari, S.C. (ed.), *Changing Perspectives of Anthropology in India*, pp. 313 - 320. Today and Tomorrow's Printers and Publishers, New Delhi.

Biswas, B. (1997), Fossil Mammalia of the Quaternary Sequence of the Narmada Valley: Their Affinity, Age and Ecology. In: *Quaternary Geology of the Narmada Valley,*, pp 91-104. Geol. Surv.Ind., Calcutta, Spl. Publn. No. 46.

Biswas, S., and D. C. Dassarma (1981), New Species of Stegodon from Narmada Valley In *Field Conference, Neogene Quaternary Boundary, India,* 1979: *Proceedings.* Calcutta: Geological Survey of India.

Brown, P., Sutikna, T., Morwood, M.J., Soejono, R.P., Jatmiko, Wayhu Saptomo, E., and Due, R.A. (2004), A New Small-bodied Hominin from the Late Pleistocene of Flores, Indonesia. *Nature 431*: 1055-1061.

Chesner, C.A., Rose, W.J., Drake, A.D.R. and Westgate, J. A. (1991), Eruptive History of Earth's Largest Quaternary Calderas (Toba, Indonesia) clarified. *Geology 19:* 200-203.

De Terra, H., and P. Teilhard De Chardin (1936), Observations on the Upper Siwalik Formation and Later Pleistocene Deposits in India. *Proc. Am. Philos. Soc. 76: 791-882.*

DeTerra, P. and Patterson, T.T. (1939), Studies on the Ice Ages in India and Associated Human Cultures. *Cong, Inst. Washington, Publ. 493*: 313-326.

Khan, A.A. and Sonakia, A. (1992), Quaternary Deposits of Narmada with Special Reference to the Hominid Fossils. *J. Geol. Soc. India 39*:175-154.

Khatri, A. P. (1961), Stone Age and Pleistocene Chronology of the Narmada Valley. *Anthropos 56*: 519-30.

Khatri,A.P. (1964), Rock Paintings of Adamgarh (Central India) and Their Age. *Anthropos 59*: 759-69.

Khatri, A. P. (1966), The Pleistocene Mammalian Fossil of the Narmada River Valley and Their Horizons. *Asian Persp. 9*: 113-33.

Khatri, A.P. (1966), Origin and Evolution of Hand-axe Culture in the Narmada Valley (Central India). In D. Sen and A.K. Ghosh (eds) *Studies in Prehistory (Robert Bruce Foote Memorial Volume)*, pp. 96-121. Calcutta: Firma K.L. Mukhopadhyay.

Lumley, H. de and Sonakia, A. (1985), Contexte Stratigraphique et Archaeologique de L'Homme de le Narmada, Hathnora, Madhya Pradesh, Inde. *L'Anthropologie 89*: 3-12.

Lumley, M.-A. de and Sonakia, A. (1985), Premiere de coaverte d'un *Homo erectus* sur le continent Indien A. Hathnora, dans la Moyenne Vallee de la Narmada. *L'Anthropologie 89*: 13-61.

Medlicot, H.B. (1873), A Note on a Celt found by Mr. Hacket in the Ossiferrous Deposits of the Narmada Valley on the Stage of Deposits. *Geol. Surv. Ind. Rec. 6*: 49-57.

Mishra, S., Venkatesan, T.R., Rajaguru, S.N. and Somayajulu, B.L.K. (1995), Earliest Acheulian Industry from Peninsular India. *Curr. Anthrop. 36* (5): 847-851.

Misra, V. N. (1974), The Acheulian Industry of the Rock Shelter IIF-23 at Bhimbetka, Central India: A Preliminary Analysis. Paper presented at the seminar on Indian prehistory held at Poona in june 1974.

Misra, V. N. (1975-76), The Acheulian Industry of the Rock Shelter IIIF-23 at Bhimbetka, Central India: A Preliminary Study. *Puratattva 8*: 13-36.

Misra, V. N. (1978), The Acheulian Industry of the Rock Shelter IIIF-23 at Bhimbetka, Central India. *Aust. Archaeology 8*: 63-106.

Misra, V. N. (1985), The Acheulian Succession at Bhimbetka, Central India. In V. N. Misra and P. Bellwoods *Recent Advances in Indo-Pacific Prehistory*, 35-47.New Delhi: Oxford-IBH.

Misra, V.N. (1989), Stone Age India: An Ecological Perspective. *Man and Environment* XIV: 17-64.

Misra, V. N. (1997), Early Man and his Environment in Central India. *Palaeont. Soc. India 42: 1-18.*

Misra, V. N., Y. Mathpal and M. Nagar (1977), *Bhimbetka: Prehistoric Man and His Art in Central India,* Poona: Exhibition Souvenir of the Archaeological Exhibition organized by the Department of Archaeology, Poona university, and Deccan college, Pune, at Bal Gandharba Rangamandir Art Gallery, pp. 26-29, May Poona: Sakal Press.

Misra, V. N., S. N. Rajaguru, G. L. Badam, R. K. Ranjoo, and R. Korisettar (1990), Further Research in the Prehistory and Quaternary Geology of the Narmada Valley. In N.C. Ghosh and S. Chakrabarti (eds) *Adaptation and Other Essays,* pp. 53-59. Santiniketan: Research Publications, Visva-Bharati.

Mohapatra, G.C. (1990), On the Track of Early Man in Western Sub-Himalayas, *Presidential Address at the 77th session of the Indian Science Congress, Anthropology and Archaeology Section*, Cochin.

Princep, J. (1832), Note on the Jabalpur Fossil Bones. *J. Royal Asiatic Soc. Bengal 1*: 456-58.

Princep, J. (1833 a), Note on the Fossil Bones Discovered Near Jabalpur. Read at the Meeting of 30th October 1833. *J. Royal Asiatic Soc. Bengal* 2(23): 583-88.

Princep, J. (1833 b), Note on the Fossil Human Bones. *J. Royal Asiatic Soc. Bengal* 2: 631-35.

Princep, J. (1834), Note on the Fossil Bones of the Nerubudda Valley Discovered by Dr. G.G. Spillsbury near Nershinhpur, etc. *J. Royal Asiatic Soc. Bengal 3,* Sec. 10, (34): 524-29.

Rao, K. V., Chakrabarti, S., Rao, K. J., Ramani, M. S. V., Marathe, S. D. and Borkar, B. T., (1997), Magneto-stratigraphy of the Quaternary Fluvial Sediments and Tephra of Narmada Valley, Central India. In Tiwari, M.P. and Bhai H.Y. (eds) *Quaternary Geology of the Narmada Valley,* pp. 65-78, Geol. Surv. India, Spl. Publn. No. 46.

Sankhyan, A. R. (1997a), Fossil Clavicle of a Middle Pleistocene Hominin from the Central Narmada Valley, India. *J. Human Evol.* 32, 3-16.

Sankhyan, A. R. (1997 b), A New Human Fossil Find from the Central Narmada Basin and Its Chronology. *Curr. Sci* 73 (12), 1110 - 1111.

Sankhyan, A.R. (2005), New Fossils of Early Stone Age Man from Central Narmada Valley. *Curr. Sci. 88* (5): 704-707.

Sankhyan, A.R., Halder, D.P., Chatterjee, R., Paul, J. Chakraborty, S., Dewangan, L.N. Chakravarty, R. and Rao, V.R. (2007), Narmada Project: A Brief Note on the Recent Stone Implements and Fossil Faunal Findings. In A.R. Sankhyan & V.R. Rao (eds) *Human Origins, Genome & People of India: Genomic, Palaeontological & Archaeological Perspectives*, pp.218-224.Allied Publishers, Pvt. Ltd., New Delhi.

Spillsbury, G. G. (1833), Account of the Fossil Bones Discovered in the Bed of the Omar Nadi Near Narsinhpur or Garawara in the valley of the Nerubudda. *J. Royal Asiatic Soc. Bengal* 2: 388-95.

Spillsbury, G. G. (1837), Notice of New Sites of Fossil Deposits in the Nerubudda Valley. *J. Royal Asiatic Soc. Bengal 6: 487-89.*

Spillsbury, G. G. (1841), Notes on Fossil Discoveries in the Valley of the Nerubudda. *J. Royal Asiatic Soc. Bengal 10(2): 626-28.*

Theobald, W. (1860), On Tertiary and Alluvial Deposits of the Central Portion of the Narbudda Valley. *Mem. Geol. Surv. India* 14 (1): 66-125.

Tiwari, M.P. (2007), Correlation of Lithostratigraphy and Chronology of the Narmada Valley Quaternary. In A.R. Sankhyan & V.R. Rao (eds) *Human Origins, Genome & People of India: Genomic, Palaeontological & Archaeological Perspectives*, pp. 165-174. Allied Publishers, Pvt. Ltd., New Delhi.

Tiwari, M.P. and Bhai H.Y. (1997), Quaternary Stratigraphy of the Narmada Valley. In Tiwari, M.P. and Bhai H.Y. (eds) *Quaternary Geology of the Narmada Valley*, 33-63. Geol. Surv. Ind. Spl. Pulb. No. 46.

Westgate, J.A., P.A.R. Shane, N.J.C. Pearce, W.T perkins, R. korisettar, C. A. Chesner, M.A.J. Williams and S.K. Acharyya (1998), All Toba tephra Occurrences Across Peninsular India belong to 75000 years B.P. eruptions. *Quaternary Research* 50: 107-112.

CHAPTER–7

# Evolutionary Trends in Narmada Fossil Fauna

*G.L. Badam & A.R. Sankhyan*

## INTRODUCTION

### Lithostratigraphy

The Narmada Valley is probably one of the most researched and talked about river valleys in India because of its anthropological, archaeological, geological, historical palaeontological, and religious significance. The river flows across the middle of the Indian subcontinent through a rift (known as Narmada rift) formed between the Vindhya and Satpura mountains and marks a traditional dividing line between the north and south of India. Originating in the Maikala Range in the eastern Madhya Pradesh, the river flows for a distance of around 1300 km through mainly Madhya Pradesh and Gujarat before emptying in the Gulf of Cambay, near Baruch, in Gujarat. At Bhedaghat, near Jabalpur, the Narmada flows over a fall of 10 m at what is known as Dhuandhar water falls and thereafter flows in the form of a saucer shaped basin unto Handia, near Hoshangabad. This basin has attracted the attention of numerous scholars from India and abroad for various reasons for the last 150 years or more, e.g., Princep (1832, 1833 a,b, 1834), Spillsbury (1833, 1837, 1841), followed by De Terra and Paterson (1939), and subsequently by several Indian scholars. Scholars have discovered numerous fossils belonging to mammals, reptiles, fish and amphibians (the last two in negligible percentage), molluscan shells and thousands of Stone Age tools, from Lower Palaeolithic right unto Mesolithic, manufactured by Early Man.

The previous works on different aspects of the valley are too numerous to be referred to here. These have already been given in detail by Badam (1979 a,b, 1984, 1996, 2001 and 2007a,b) and several authors (see Tiwari and Bhai, 1997; Tiwari and Mohabey,1999, and references therein). However, a word about the stratigraphy can be said here, which has been variously interpreted by various scholars. Different names have been used for different or sometimes the same horizon which has created some confusion about the schemes of classification being adopted. To avoid unwanted confusion the Geological Survey of India came up with a scheme of lithostratigraphic classification wherein age old terms like Older Alluvium and Younger Alluvium have been replaced by a new set of terms generally acceptable as a result of recent new bio and chrono stratigraphic data collected over the years by various scholars including the present authors. The new scheme of classification is given below in Table 1 with brief comments on the lithounits of the various formations.

**Table 1**
**The Recent Nomenclature of the Lithounit Formations of Narmada Quaternary (Adapted from Tiwari & Bhai, 1997)**

| | |
|---|---|
| Recent/Holocene | Ramnagar Formation<br>Bauras Formation |
| Upper Pleistocene | Hirdepur Formation<br>Baneta Formation |
| Middle Pleistocene | Surajkund Formation<br>Dhansi Formation |
| Lower Pleistocene | Pililkarar Formation |

The Pililkarar Formation is recognised as the basal unit of the Quaternary sequence in the Narmada Valley, which is comprised of lateritic gravels with ferricrete at the top, and the lithomarge red clay at the bottom. It is devoid of vertebrate remains. Overlying this is the Dhansi Formation, exposed near village Dhansi, comprising grey sand, brown silt, yellow and orange sand and red silty clay. It contains fossils, but less in frequency as compared to the overlying Surajkund Formation, exposed extensively as calcareous conglomerates, grey silty sands, brown to steel grey and yellow clays. It is the most richly fossiliferous lithounit of the Narmada Valley. The overlying Baneta Formation is comprised of calcareous conglomerate, grit, gravels, brown calcareous silts, sandy silt, carbonaceous clays towards the top, and volcanic ash at some places, having yielded a date of about 75,000 years B.P. This formation covers much of the Narmada alluvial plain and yields fossils of Upper Pleistocene affinity. Followed in succession comes another later Pleistocene lithounit, named as Hirdepur Formation, which comprises calcareous conglomerate, sand, sandstone, calcareous light grey silts and sands. It is relatively poor in fossil content. All the above Pleistocene formations have distinctive soils. The Baneta and the Hirdepur formations change from coarser lithofacies (near the Satpura fault) to finer lithofacies (away from the fault). The Holocene period is covered by two lithounits, the older of these is known as Baurus Formation consisting of calcareous gravels, sands and silts. The youngest or the topmost lithounit known as Ramnagar Formation comprises sands, silts and clays. These are largely devoid of fossils or contain sub-fossilised bones.

## OBSERVATIONS

### The Fauna

The updated faunal list of Siwaliks (Pinjor Formation) and Central Narmada Valley compiled from previous (Gentry, 1997) and recent

**Table 2**
**Upper Siwalik (Pinjor) and Narmada Valley Fauna**

| *Order/Family* | *Pinjor (Upper Siwaliks)* | *Narmada Valley* |
|---|---|---|
| Hominidae | ? | *Homo erectus* or "*archaic*"*Homo sapiens* |
| Carnivora | *Mellivora sivalensis* | *Ursus namadicus* |
| | *Panthera* cf. *P. cristata* | *Panthera* sp.. |
| | *Canis pinjorensis* | *Canis* sp. |
| | *Crocuta felina* | *Cuon alpinus* |
| | *Crocuta colivini* | *Holarctos namadicus* |
| Bovidae | *Bubalus palaeindicus* | *Bubalus palaeindicus* |
| | *Bubalus platyceros* | *Bubalus bubalis* = modern Indian buffalo |
| | *Bos acutifrons* (Pilgrim, 1939) | *Bos namadicus* |
| | – | *Bibos gaurus* |
| | *Bison sivalensis* | *Bison sp.* |
| | *Leptobos falconeri* | *Leptobos frazeri* (Pilgrim, 1905) = *Bos* |
| | - | *namadicus* (De Terra & Chardin, 1936; |
| | - | *De Terra & Paterson*, 1939). |
| | | *Boselephus tragocamelus,* |
| | | *Antilope cervicapra* |
| Elephantidae | *Elephas hysudricus* | *Palaeoloxodon namadicus* |
| | *Stegolophodon stegodontoides* | *Elephas namadicus* |
| | | *Elephas hysudricus* |
| | | *Elephas maximus* |
| | | *Stegodon insignis ganesa* |
| Cervidae | *Cervus punjabiensis* | *Cervus unicolor* [=sambar] |
| | | *Cervus duvauceli* [=barasingha] |
| | | *Axis axis* |
| Hippopotamidae | *Hexaprotodon sivalensis* | *Hexaprotodon namadicus* |
| | *Pentaprotodon sivalensis* | *Hexaprotodon palaeindicus* |
| Suidae | *Sus falconeri* | *Sus namadicus,* |
| | *Sus hysudricus* | *Sus palaeindicus* |
| Rhinocerotidae | *Rhinoceros palaeindicus* | *Rhinoceros unicornis* [=living species] |
| | *Rhinoceros sivalensis* | |
| Equidae | *Equus sivalensis* | *Equus namadicus* [zebrine] |
| | [caballine] | *Equus hemionus khur* [ zebrine] |
| | | *Equus asinus* [zebrine] |
| Rodentia | *Hystrix leucurus* | |
| | *Mus linnaeusi* | |
| | *Hadromysloujacobsi* | |
| | *Rhizomys pinjoricus* | *Rhizomys* sp.? |

published sources (e.g., Badam, 2007 a,b; Nanda & Sehgal, 2007; and other scholars) is given in *Table* 2.

In recent years several genera of micro-vertebrates have been collected for the first time from the Narmada Valley and also molluscan shells which are listed below in Table 3 As said above some amphibian and fish fossils have also been reported from the valley.

**Table 3**
**Aquatic Fauna from Narmada Valley**

| | |
|---|---|
| Crocodilidae & Gavialidae | *Crocodylus palaeindicus, Gavialis gangeticus* |
| Emydidae (Turtles/Tortoises) | *Pangsura tectum, Trionyx gangeticus, Emys sp., Clemmyx sp* |
| Mollusca by R. Patnaik (2007): *Millardia meltada, Bandicota bengalensis, Tatera indica* [?= *Tatera pinjoricus* (Siwaliks)], *Gerbillus* sp. | Mollusca by A. Deshpande - Mukerjee (2007): *Lamellidens* sp. , *Corbicula* sp., *Parreysia* sp., *Melania* sp., *Bellamya* sp. |

## Likely Faunal Evolutionary Linkages

In view of the recent multidisciplinary research in the Narmada Valley and surrounding areas the understanding of the fauna in proper perspective calls for some comments. The initial nomenclature of the species listed above has undergone some revisions over a period of time. As mentioned earlier some of the genera do exist at present. *Rhinoceros unicornis* is identical with the living species. Recently, and for the first time in India, three fossilized horn cores of *Rhinoceros unicornis* have been identified by Badam (in press) in a collection from the Narmada Valley made by late Dr. V. S. Wakankar about thirty years ago and now housed in the Archaeology Museum of the Vikram University, Ujjain, Madhya Pradesh.

*Bubalus palaeindicus*, *Cervus unicolor* and *Cervus duvauceli* are related to the modern Indian buffalo, sambar and the barasingha respectively. *Bos namadicus* is profusely represented in the Narmada Valley and had a possible ancestor in the *Bos acutifrons* of the Siwaliks (Pilgrim, 1939). *Bos namadicus* is supposed to have given rise to the present day Indian cattle *Bos indicus* (Badam, 1984).

The skull claimed to be of *Leptobos frazeri* (Pilgrim, 1905) may be nothing but a damaged skull of *Bos namadicus* (De Terra and Chardin, 1936; De Terra and Paterson, 1939). The latter authors opined that the tusk fragments assigned to *Stegodon* are too imperfect for precise identification. A few years back the author was tempted to assign one of the skulls he excavated from a Late Pleistocene horizon in the Ghod Valley near Inamgaon, in Maharashtra, as *Leptobos* but it was re-identified by Dr Caroline Grigson as that of *Bos namadicus*. Further, *Bos gaurus* is now named as *Bibos gaurus* (Badam and Grigson, 1990).

*Bubalus arnee* is a transitional form between *Bubalus palaeindicus* and *Bubalus bubalis*. It may have certain characters reflected in the process of domestication which are yet not very clear and thus the species is hard to identify unless the sample is large. Besides, at present we do not have any statistical or osteological data to support it.

Some of the elephant species like *Stegodon* spp. and *Elephas hysudricus* are survivals from the Siwaliks of NW India. *Elephas namadicus* (sometimes named as *Palaeoxodon namadicus*) is identical with *Elephas antiquus* of Europe and in some earlier publications it has been mentioned as *Elephas antiquus*. Similarly, *Elephas hysudricus* and *Hypelephas hysudricus* represent one and the same species and the first one gets the priority in usage.

It is possible that *Hexaprotodon namadicus* was also derived from a Siwalik ancestor, *Hexaprotodon sivalensis*. *Hexaprotodon namadicus* and *Hexaprotodon palaeindicus* are identified on the basis of shallow depth in the latter. Both the species have six incisors each and it is not correct to name the species as *Hippopotamus palaeindicus* as some scholars have been doing. It may be mentioned here that evolution in the genus is indicated by the gradual elimination of second incisors, one by one, and one of the specimens in this category has been described by Sahni and Khan (1961) from Siwaliks with five incisors instead of six, which may represent an evolutionary stage leading to the four- incisored Hippopotamus. This was named as *Pentaprotodon sivalensis*. The present day hippopotamus is the *Hippopotamus amphibius* which is not indigenous to India.

*Equus caballus* as identified by Supekar (1968) has been re-identified as *Equus namadicus* (Badam, 1979 a,b) which is regarded as ancestral to modern *Equus hemionus* (Hooijer, 1963).

*Cuon alpinus tripathii*, a new subspecies reported from the Narmada Valley may not warrant a separate status at present. *Cuon alpinus* is presently reported from South India but its fossil forms are not well established.

There appears some doubt about the identification of *Holarctus namadicus* as Colbert (1942) is the only scholar who has mentioned it. In fact, it has been listed without any diagnostic characters on which the species was established. This species is included in Notoungulates which has been divided into several Orders by Darwin while he was on the Beagle. However, what Darwin created was on the basis of living forms and not the fossilized ones. Sometimes the species is referred as Holarctic ungulate which makes its specific identification rather doubtful.

The reptiles like *Pangsura tectum* and *Gavialis gangeticus* are identical with the reptiles living in the Indian rivers today. In view of their long time span and slow evolutionary process their impact on chronology is not as pronounced as their use in palaeoecology.

The above remarks suggest that many species have been created on account of minor morphological variations without taking any account differences due to the genetic factors, sex, age, abnormalities, individual and geographical variations and animal's response to them.

Summing up the problem of nomenclature the authors suggest that changes in it are bound to occur as more and new fossil discoveries are made and hence it is necessary to follow the guidelines of the Commission for International Code of Zoological nomenclature, which meets periodically, to get acquainted with the latest information in this regard and the possibility of synonymizing of various genera/species.

As per our current understanding, the various Narmada Quaternary mammalian fauna can be assigned to the following genera and species as they appeared temporally (see Table 4).

**Table 4**
**Chronological Occurrences and Ranges of Fossil Mammals in Narmada Valley**

| *Temporal Span* | *Genera and Species* |
|---|---|
| Lower to Upper Pleistocene | *Elephas hysudricus, Stegodon insignis ganesa.* |
| Middle Pleistocene | *Elephas namadicus, Sus namadicus, Hexaprotodon namadicus* |
| Middle to Upper Pleistocene | *Elephas namadicus, Sus namadicus, Equus namadicus, Bos namadicus* |
| Upper Pleistocene | *Sus palaeindicus, Hexaprotodon palaeindicus* |
| Upper Pleistocene to Holocene | *Antilope cervicapra, Cervus unicolor, Cervus duvauceli, Axis axis, Boselaphus tragocamelus,Equus asinus, Elephas maximus* |

## Hominin Fossils

Hathnora stands unique in South Asia for having yielded the unequivocal Middle Pleistocene hominins crucial for understanding *Homo erectus*/*Homo sapiens* transition. The first discovery of the hominin partial skullcap (Sonakia, 1984) has filled up the gap in our knowledge of the hominin evolution in this part of the world and in South Asia as a whole, though there has been a difference of opinion about its nomenclature. On the basis of archaeological associations, this species fits in the description of "archaic" *Homo sapiens* (Badam *et al.*,1986), which was later also claimed by Kennedy *et al.* (1991) on the basis of craniometric and non-mensural characters. This was followed by important postcranial discoveries of hominin fossils from the same locality, e.g., two clavicles and one left 9th rib by Sankhyan (1997a, b, 1999, 2005).

The hominid discoveries have given Narmada Valley recognition worldwide. Work on the Narmada Valley is going on in right earnest from a multidisciplinary point of view and it is hoped that with patience and luck many more discoveries of the hominin fossils from the valley or other parts of the country would come to light one day. While the absolute dates for the hominin fossils remain unsettled, recently under the Narmada Project launched by the Anthropological Survey of India in June 2005, in *situ* collections of important fossil fauna have been made from the hominin bearing bed and from sections immediately below it (Sankhyan *et al.*, 2007). The fossil findings speak proxy for the age, ecology and the process of humanization in South Asia, further attested by the *in situ* collections of the lithic cultural artefacts, dealt with separately.

## DISCUSSION

The wide distribution in time and space of some fossils is on account of similar ecological niches, climatic conditions and geographical history prevalent in most parts of Central and South Indian regions. The animals seem to have had zonal distribution pattern in these parts without any definite ecological barriers between them. Most of the forms appear to be the late survivals from the Siwaliks, having migrated to other suitable areas in India (especially the Narmada-Godavari complex) when the conditions in northwest became unfavourable an account of glaciations.

The ice sheet as a result of Pleistocene glaciations pushed out repeatedly from the northwest. It acted as a physical and climate barrier to the movement of animals northwards and made the southward migration of

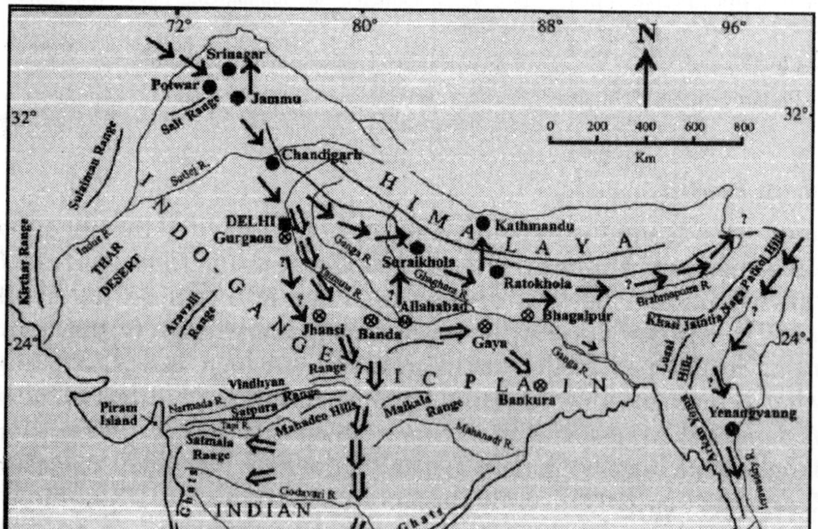


Figure 1: Probable Routes of Migration of the Quaternary Fauna in South Asia

most of the animals possible. Many of the species became extinct in course of such migrations due to adverse climatic conditions and allied factors like non-adaptability and hence are not represented in these deposits in such profusion or are totally absent. A few evolved into advanced forms in the Holocene.

The variability of the climatic conditions during the Pleistocene (at times more warm and humid and at other times much drier and cooler than today) gave rise to profusion of large and varied fauna. Nevertheless, this magnificent assemblage of animals was not totally indigenous to India. Progressive groups possibly of local origin were the primates, many giraffe-like forms, musk-deer, goats, buffaloes, bovids and pigs. The mammals which were shared by the contemporary fauna of Europe were the sabre-toothed cats, the hyena, wolves, rhinoceroses, horses of the genus *Equus*, various deer, antelopes and hippopotamii. The migratory routes lay east and west of the Himalayas (Pilgrim, 1925) and most of the larger animals migrated from Egypt, Arabia, Central Asia and North America through passes across Alaska, Siberia and Mongolia. Hippopotamii and elephants had their early origin in Central Africa from where they radiated out and entered India during the Tertiary period through Arabia and Iran. Rhinoceros, horse and camel, all originating in North America, evolved in some countries of central and western Asia before migrating to India. The elephant and horse have been a world traveller and reached to almost every country of the world.

It is well known that the migration of mammals chiefly occurred in the Tertiary, starting vigorously in the Lower Eocene and continuing with gaps till the Pleistocene. The Himalayan range began to be elevated as early as Eocene. In the Miocene it must have acted as a formidable barrier to the free migration of mammals between India and Central Asia. However, the migratory routes lay between Burma and China and through Baluchistan into Persia. Intercommunication also took place between India and North America and Mongolia.

Between India and Africa, interchange of faunas probably took place more easily. There is sufficient evidence for the existence of land-bridge across the straits at the entrance of the Persian Gulf. A corresponding bridge across Red Sea would have opened up ready means of communication between India and Africa through Arabia. Many species of European and Central Asian origin migrated to India during glacial periods and survived, directly or indirectly, until the modern times or became extinct.

Thus, based on the above discussion, the linkages of the Middle Pleistocene mega fauna of Narmada Valley *vis-à-vis* that of the Lower Pleistocene of the Siwaliks, and the Holocene India may be delineated as follows:

(1) *Stegodon insigns ganesa '! Elephas namadicus '! Elephas hysudricus*

(2) *Hexaprodaon namadicus '! Hexaprotodan palaeindicus*

(3) *Sus namadicus'!Sus palaeindicus*

(4) *Equus namadicus'!Equus asinus*

(5) *Bos acutifrons'! Bos namadicus*

(6) *Bubalus platyceros'! Bubalus palaeindicus*

(7) *Rhinoceros sivalensis'!Rhinoceros unicornis*

Three Narmada species clearly appear to have their predecessors among the *Bos acutifrons, Bubalus platyceros* and *Rhinoceros sivalensis,* respectively that inhabited the Pinjor Formation of the Upper Siwaliks of India.

## CONCLUSIONS

The Narmada Valley is one of the richest areas for fossils and cultural materials manufactured by Stone Age Man. This valley has yielded innumerable animal fossils and also a few hominin fossils, which have a direct bearing on the evolution of Man in South Asia. Besides, being a unique mid-continental place in the Old World, Narmada Valley has formed a traditional north and south dividing line. This has been an important path for transmission of the monsoons from southeast to northwest as well as for the faunal migrations from north to the south. That is why the Narmada Valley houses an admixture of Old and New World elements, initially migrated from outside. Thus, the Narmada fauna brings forth the evidence of endemic and immigrant species crucial for the study of linkages and evolution through the understanding of the dispersal of species within India and in- and out-migration from other geographical regions in time and place.

## REFERENCES CITED

Badam, G.L. (1979 a), Quaternary Palaeontology of The Central Narmada Valley and Its Implications in Prehistoric Studies. *Geol. Surv. India Misc.Publ.* 45: 311-20.

Badam, G.L. (1979 b), *Pleistocene Fauna of India,* Pune: Deccan College.

Badam, G.L. (1984), Pleistocene Faunal Succession of India. in: R. O. Whyte (ed.), *The Evolution of East Asian Environment,* pp. 746-755, Hongkong, University of Hongkong.

Badam, G.L. (1996), Taphonomy and Palaeoecology of the Fossil Vertebrates from the Central Narmada Valley, District Narsinghpur, Madhya Pradesh, India.*Mimeograph Project Report,* Indira Gandhi Rashtriya Manav Sangrahalaya, Bhopal.

Badam, G. L. (2001), Palaeontological Excavations in Narsinghpur Distt., Central Narmada Valley, Madhya Pradesh, India. *Puratan 12:* 61-76.

Badam, G.L. (2007 a), On the Biostratigraphy and Biochronology of The Central Narmada Valley Quaternary. in: A.R. Sankhyan & V.R. Rao (ed.), *Human Origins, Genome & People of India: Genomic, Palaeontological & Archaeological Perspectives,* pp.153-164.Allied Publishers (p) Ltd.,New Delhi.

Badam, G.L. (2007 b), The Central Narmada Valley (A Study in Quaternary Palaeontology and Allied Aspects). Indira Gandhi Rashtriya Manav Sangrahalaya, Bhopal and D.K. Printworld (P) Ltd. New Delhi.

Badam, G.L. (in press), A Catalouge of Fossil Mammals Housed in the Archaeological Museum of Vikram University, Ujjain.

Badam, G.L. and C. Grigson (1990), A Cranium of Gaur, *Bibos Gaurus* (Bovidae, Mammalia) from the Pleistocene of India. *Mod. Geol: 15*: 49-58.

Badam, G. L., Ganjoo, R. K., Salahuddin and Rajaguru, S.N. (1986), Evaluation of Fossil Hominid-The Maker of Late Acheulian Tools at Hathnora, Madhya Pradesh, India. *Curr. Sci. 55 (3)*: 143-145.

Colbert, E.H. (1942), The Geological Succession of the Proboscidea in India, In: Osborn., H.F., *Proboscidea, Amer. Mus. Nat. History vol.2,* pp.1421-1521.

Deshpande-Mukerjee, A. (2007), Molluscan Shells, in: G. L. Badam (ed.), *The Central Narmada Valley (A Study in Quaternary Palaeontology and Allied Aspects),* pp.173-180, Indira Gandhi Rashtriya Manav Sangrahalya, Bhopal and D. K. Printworld (P) Ltd., New Delhi.

De Terra, H., and P. Teilhard De Chardin (1936), Observations on the Upper Siwalik Formation and Later Pleistocene Deposits in India. *Proceedings of the American Philosophical Society 76:* 791-882.

De Terra and T.T. Patterson (1939), Studies on Ice Ages in India and Associated Human Culture. *Carn. Inst. Washington. Publ. 493:* 313-326.

Gentry, A.W. (1997), The London Collection of Narmada Fossil Mammals, In: *Quaternary Geology of the Narmada Valley,* pp. 105 – 115, GSI, spl. Publn. No. 46.

Hooijer D.A. (1963), Preliminary Identification of Some Fossil Mammals from Narmada Valley, India, *Rivista Di Science Prehistoric* 18(1-4),P.20

Kennedy, K.A.R., Sonakia, A., Chiment, J. and Verma, K.K. (1991), Is the Narmada Hominid an Indian *Homo Erectus*? *Am. J. Phys. Anthrop. 86:* 475 - 496.

Nanda A. C. & R. K. Sehgal (2007), Geology and Mammalian Faunas of the Siwalik Group of Northwestern Himalayas: Recent Investigations. in: A.R. Sankhyan & V.R. Rao (ed.), *Human Origins, Genome & People of India,* pp. 77-90, Allied Publishers (p) Ltd., New Delhi.

Patnaik, R. (2007), Microvertebrates, in: G.L.Badam (ed.)*The Central Narmada Valley (A Study in Quaternary Palaeontology and Allied Aspects),* pp. 147-172, Indira Gandhi Rashtriya Manav Sangrahalaya, Bhopal and D.K. Printworld (P) Ltd., New Delhi.

Pilgrim, G. E. (1905), On the Occurrences of *Elephas Antiquus (Namadicus)* in the Godavari Alluvium with Remarks on the Species, Its Distribution and the Age of the Associated Indian Deposits. *Rec. Geol. Surv. Ind.* 32 (3): 199-218.

Pilgrim, G. E. (1925), The Migration of Indian Mammals. *Presidential Address, Section of Geology,* Twelfeth Indian Science Congress.

Pilgrim, G. E. (1939), The Fossil Bovidae of India. *Mem. Geol. Surv. India, Palaeont. Indica. N. S.*, 26: 356.

Princep, J. (1832), Note on the Jabalpur Fossil Bones. *Journal of the Royal Asiatic Society of Bengal* 1:456-58.

Princep, J. (1833 a), Note on the Fossil Bones Discovered Near Jabalpur. *Journal of the Royal Asiatic Society of Bengal* 2(23):583-88.

Princep, J. (1833 b), Note on the Fossil Human Bones. *Journal of the Royal Asiatic Society of Bengal* 2:631-35.

Princep, J. (1834), Note on the Fossil Bones of the Nerubudda Valley Discovered by Dr. G.G. Spillsbury Near Nershinhpur, etc. *Journal of the Royal Asiatic Society of Bengal* 3, Sec. 10, (34): 524-29.

Sahni, M. R. and E. Khan (1961), On an Abnormal Dentition of *Hexaprotodon Sivalensis Falc. and Caut. Res. Bull. P. U. (N. S.), 12 (3-4)*, pp. 259-261.

Sankhyan, A. R. (1997 a), Fossil Clavicle of a Middle Pleistocene Hominid from the Central Narmada Valley, India. *J. Hum. Evol. 32*: 3-16.

Sankhyan, A. R. (1997 b), A New Human Fossil find from the Central Narmada Basin and Its Chronology. *Curr. Sci 73 (12):* 1110–1111.

Sankhyan, A. R. (1999), The Place of Narmada Hominin in the Jigsaw Puzzle of Human Origins in: M.P. Tiwari and D.M. Mohabey(ed), *Quaternary of India.* pp. 335-345 Gondvana Geological Magazine Spl. Publ.

Sankhyan, A. R. (2005), New Fossils of Early Stone Age Man from Central Narmada Valley. *Curr. Sci. 88 (5)*: 704-707.

Sankhyan, A.R., D. P. Halder, R. Chatterjee, J. Paul, R. Chakravarty & V.R. Rao (2007), Narmada Project: A Brief Note on the recent Stone Implements and Fossil Faunal Findings in: A.R. Sankhyan & V.R. Rao (ed) *Human Origins, Genome & People of India: Genomic, Palaeontological & Archaeological Perspectives*, pp.218-224. Allied Publishers (p) Ltd., New Delhi.

Sonakia, A. (1984), The Skullcap of Early Man and Associated Mammalian Fauna from Narmada Valley Alluvium, Hoshangabad Area, M. P. *Rec. Geol. Surv, India 113:* 159-172.

Spillsbury, G. G. (1833), Account of the Fossil Bones Discovered in the Bed of the Omar Nadi Near Narsinhpur or Garawara in the Valley of the Nerubudda. *Journal of the Asiatic Society of Bengal* 2:388-95.

Spillsbury, G. G. (1837), Notice of New Sites of Fossil Deposits in the Nerubudda Valley. *Journal of the Asiatic Society of Bengal 6 : 487-89.*

Spillsbury, G. G. (1841), Notes on Fossil Discoveries in the Valley of the Nerubudda. *Journal of the Asiatic Society of Bengal 10(2): 626-28.*

Supekar, S. G. (1968), *Pleistocene Stratigraphy and Prehistoric Archaeology of the Central Narmada Basin.* Unpublished Ph.D. Thesis. Deccan College Library: Pune.

Tiwari, M. P. & Bhai H. Y. (1997), Quaternary Stratigraphy of the Narmada Valley. In: *Quaternary Geology of the Narmada Valley, Geol. Surv. Ind. Spl. Pulb. No.* **46**: 33-63.

Tiwari, M. P. & D. M. Mohaby (ed.) (1999), *Quaternary of India.* Gondvana Geological Magazine Spl. Publ. 4.

CHAPTER–8

# Cranial Embryogeny and Hominin Phylogeny

*Anne Dambricourt Malassé*

## INTRODUCTION

After a long period focused on East Africa, the debate on the origins of Anatomically Modern Human, *Homo sapiens* sensu stricto, as well as that of the oldest species of the genus Homo, is again topical. This focus is due for the most part to the outstanding conditions for fossilisation and excavations of Plio-Pleistocene fossils and, on the other hand, to the increasing research programmes in those areas of the Old World. North Africa (Ain El Hanech, Algeria) and South East Asia (*Homo erectus* child from Modjokerto), also raised the question of the great age of *Homo* genus (1,8 Myr). But this is during the last decade that the geographic areas have expanded from the Arabic peninsula to Southern Europe, India and China (Majuangou, 1.66 Myr (Zhu *et al.* 2004, Huang and Zhang 2007)).

The four remarkably preserved skulls from Dmanissi in Georgia, dated around 1.8 Myrs belong to the same morphological pattern than their African contemporaries *Homo habilis* and *Homo erectus* (Lordkipanidze *et al.* 2006), but they show sufficient exocranial diversity to distinguish them as *Homo georgicus* (Lumley M.A. *et al.* 2004, Spoor *et al.* 2007). This variability, well dispersed in geographic space, is a small sample of what really was the anatomical diversity of the oldest known human species. This species has lived in East and South Africa, but quite certainly too in West Africa (Tchad, Niger, Mali, Mauritania (de Lumley *et al.* 2006)) as well as on the Indian peninsula, where the human presence is confirmed in the Potwar plateau by artefacts dated 1.8 myr in Riwat (Rendell *et al* 1989, Allchin 1995) and in Central India at Isampur (Blackwell *et al.* 2001). The Indus basin is one of the oldest migration paths between East Africa and Eurasia (Central Asia, Iran, western China), a geographical situation which can explain the sustainability of the Indian Soanian industries (mode 1) during the Pleistocene (Gaillard *et al.* 2002, Dambricourt Malassé 2008, Gaillard and Dambricourt Malassé 2008).

The oldest artefacts were recorded in East Africa at Kada Gona and Ounda Gona (2,6 – 2,5 Myrs), Omo (2,5 Mya), but also in the North of the Yiron Rift (Israël, 2,4 Mya) and in France (Saint Elbe, 2,4-2,2 Myrs). Such a geographical dispersal implies the great antiquity of the genus Homo around 3 Mya (Boeda 2005). The convergences of these discoveries call into question the African origins of Homo genus.

In the same time, better knowledge developed to understand what means an erected posture from the axial skeleton to the endocranial part of the clivus that can explain why Eurasian or Asian origins are possible without an Australopithecine ascendance (Deloison 2004). These new data have implications for the geographical and phylogenetical understanding of *Homo sapiens* emergence.

## EMBRYOGENY AND CONVERGENCES IN HOMINID LINEAGES

The oldest fossil showing the emergence of an upright position, well asserted up to the endocranium (i.e. the spheno-occipital flexure), is an isolated part of a cranial base (petrous, basi-occipital and mastoid process) discovered in Ethiopia and attributed to *Ardipithecus ramidus,* with an age of 4.4 Myrs (White et al. 1995). This fossil has been associated with like-pongid teeth belonging to an oldest geological layer far from 1 km, nevertheless such an association is not in accordance with the occluso-postural equilibrium well known in posturology (Bonnier 1997) nor with the embryogenesis of the cephalic tissue. Teeth and brain share the same neuroblastic steam cells. The Australopithecine as well as the Homo genus developed an embryonic differentiation completely changed when compared with Paninae and Ponginae, not only for the brain, the teeth and the occlusion, but also for the all cephalo-caudal axis (Dambricourt Malassé 1987, 1988, 1993, 2004, 2006, Caro 2004).

The great anatomical craniofacial resemblance between two south African fossils SK847 (Swartkrans) and STW53 (Sterkfontein) is such that to establish a taxonomic diagnosis, it becomes necessary to take into account the features acquired during embryonic development, such as the spatial organisation of the semi-circular canals (Spoor *et al* 1994). Each one of the canals occupies one of the three Euclidian planes; an angle separates the lateral (or horizontal) canal from the posterior that differs between Paninae and modern humans. This angle is closed in Paninae, whereas it is more open in modern humans as well as in *Homo habilis* (Spoor *et al. ib*). A Gorilla foetus or a new born Chimpanzee both have a 10° angle that does not change until the adult stage, whereas in modern humans, it measures 30° (Dambricourt Malassé *et al.* 2000).

Compared to Paninae and Ponginae, and whatever the post-natal development stage, the australopithecine skull, on one hand, and that of human on the other, are modified in the three spatial plans towards a straightening of the whole face with a less projecting profile. In the vertical plan one can clearly observe 1) the straightening of the anterior pillars of the middle face closer of the anterior cranial fossa (McCollum 2008), 2) the same changes for the mandible with the straightening of the symphysis. The combination causes a withdrawal of the dental row towards the pharyngeal sphere. In the transversal plane, a rotational motion re-organized the two deciduous dental arches towards the frontal plane. These re-adjustments are in accordance with those of the cranial base observed in the sagittal and transversal planes (Dambricourt Malassé 1987); the sphenoid shows an endocranial surface clearly vertically oriented compared with Paninae and Ponginae (fig.1).

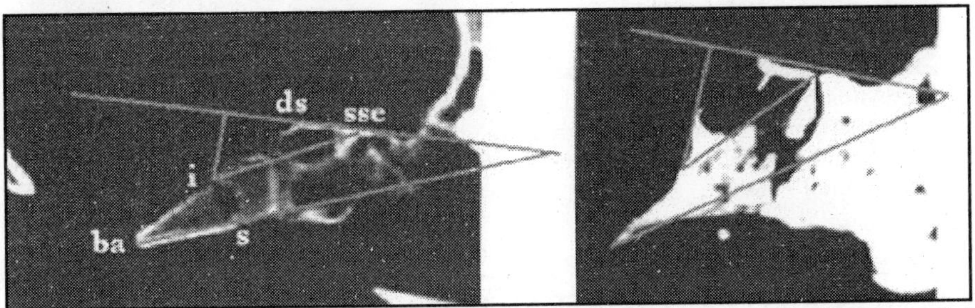


Figure 1: Midsagittal Scan of Basicranium: The Most Flexed Stage in Pan Ontogeny (left) and Adult Sterkfontein 5 (right): ba: Basion, ds: dorsum sellae, i: endocranial limit of the Spheno-occipital Synchondrosis, s: exo-cranial limit of the Spheno-occipital Synchondrosis, sse: location of spheno-ethmoïdal Synchondrosis (in Dambricourt Malassé 2005).

Correlation are observed between this endocranial verticality and 1) a forward motion of the petrous pyramids in the transversal plane (Dean 1986, Dean and Wood 1981), 2) a more curved temporo-mandibular joint and 3) a posterior cranial fossa in a lower position. Those reorganizations associated between the base and the faces are finding in orthopaedics, and considered as dynamics that underlies the cranio-facial growth (Björk and Skeller, 1984, Deshayes 1991, 2006a, b, Deshayes *et al.* 2002). The applied analyses to great anthropoids find the same principles (Deshayes and Dambricourt Malassé 1990).

The restructuration concerns not only the skull, but also all the cranio-sacral and endocranial architectonics. Nevertheless, unlike Homo, in Australopithecine there is no generalization of the verticality to the exocranial side of the clivus (fig.2), while the semicircular canals remain unchanged. In this respect, one of the two South African fossils, SK847, shows an open angle, it is therefore a *Homo habilis*, whereas the Sterkfontein fossil STW53 is like a Paninae, so this is an *Australopithecus*. The anatomical convergences of the two new organisms characterized by permanent bipedalism, come from an evolutionary process acting on the embryonic pattern shared by the Ponginae, Paninae and their common ancestors. This embryonic and dynamic pattern common to numerous fossil and living species, has been define as "fundamental ontogeny". (Dambricourt Malassé 1987, 1988, 1993, Dambricourt *et al.* 1998, Chaline 1999).

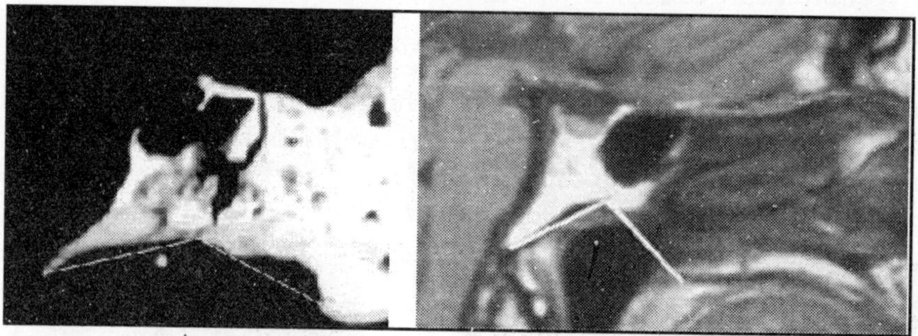

Figure 2: Midsagittal Scan and IRM of the Basi-spheno-ethmoïdal Complex: Sterkfontein 5 (left) and *Homo Sapiens* (right) The lines and the Angle Visualize the Exocranial Straightening of the Clivus and the Repositioning of the Palate below the Anterior Cranial Fossa

## EMBRYONIC ORIGIN OF THE POSTERIOR CRANIAL FOSSA POSITION AND FACIAL STRAIGHTENING

Many scholars have searched for the origins of the straightened clivus that characterizes the hominid lineage (i.e. the spheno-occipital flexure), making reference to the winding of the telencephalon and the cerebellum, more important than in any other primates. Thanks to the new medical imaging techniques and 3D reconstructions, Jeffery (2002), Jeffery and Spoor (2002, 2004) could study a series of human foetuses from the end of the embryonic stage until birth. The encephalon winding (cerebral hemispheres and cerebellum) follows an irregular pace, while the sphenoidal angle fluctuates without correlation. Authors conclude to the lack of physiological links between the flexion and the rolling up of the brain, putting in mind that the flexion marks the end of the embryonic period.

Orthodontists dealt with this issue in order to better correct the children malpositions of the two dental arches and the deficiencies in transversal growth. This medical field focuses on the flexion mechanisms located at the spheno-occipital synchondrosis, and bases the treatments on the morphogenic principles seen above. The success of extraoral forces reveal that during the growth, the midfacial morphogenesis is under the influence of the three dimensional dynamics of the spheno-occipital flexion and of the frontalization of the two petrous pyramids (fig.3). Correlations exist between the posterior cranial fossa and some angles of maxillae and mandible (like the symphyseal angle).

Our research works show that these relationships start very early in embryogenesis, between the 7th and 8th week (Dambricourt Malassé 1987, 1988, 1993, 2005, 2006a). On the 6th week the cartilaginous base of the skull, that is to say the chondrocranium or *planum basale*, is flat, formed with the basi-occipital, the postsphenoid and the presphenoïd aligned but separated by the spheno-occipital and the intersphenoïdal synchondrosis (fig.4,5). This organization is the ancestral mammal condition, that of all fossil species, Australopithecine, Omo Homo or any Dryopithecine.

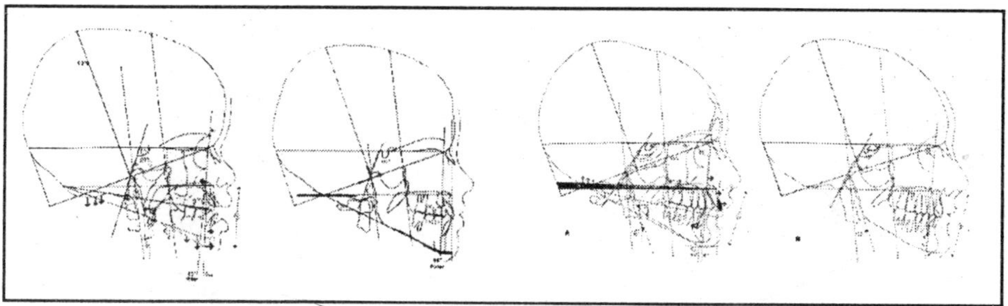

Figure 3: Delaire-Deshayes Architectural Analysis Before and After the Orthodontic Appliances. A Great Flexion (Dental-Skeletal Class III) and an Insufficient Flexion (Dental-Skeletal Class II) (Deshayes 1991).

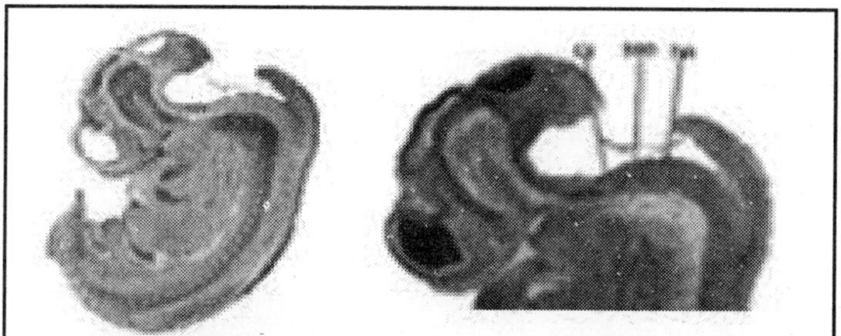

Figure 4: Magnetic Resonance Microscopy of Midsagittal Section of a 37-42 days Post-ovulation Human Embryo (Carnegie Stage16-17): cs: sphenoïdal corpus, sso: spheno-occipital synchondrosis, ba: basi-occipital

Right from the beginning of the 20th century, anatomists like Levi (1900) very accurately described the development stages of the human basi-cranium, while other naturalists compared primates such as Cercopithecus, Tarsier or other mammals. The most detailed description is Levi's, illustrated with high-quality drawings which had no equivalent until the recent perfecting of Magnetic Resonance Microscopy (MRM, fig. 4). From the 7th week, the sphenoid body rotates on its axis, followed shortly by a basi-occipital straightening. This dynamics causes the vertical dimension of the skull and the vertical orientation of the facial growth vectors (fig.5).

However, any cephalic details illustrate the morphological stages. In order to understand the cause of the spheno-occipital rotation, one must compare the whole of cephalic tissues without isolating them from the cephalo-caudal unit. Figure 6 synthesizes the result. Whatever the primate species, the future central nervous system, or neural plate, grows along the underlaying dorsal chord. By doing so, the plate invaginates to form the neural groove and progressively closes to give rise to the neural tube. Its cephalic end, formed by three vesicles (proselencephalon, mesencephalon, rhombencephalon), stretches in the anterior part of the chord, but instead of following a longitudinal direction, it begins to rotate antero-posteriorly centred on the end of the chord.

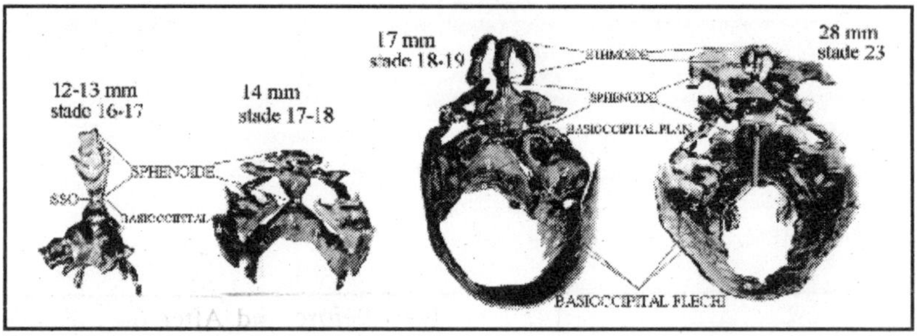


Figure 5: Four Stages of the Human Chondrocranial Morphogenesis, from the Flattened to the Flexed Conformation, Superior View (After Levi 1900)

The neural vesicles follow a front to back motion, in relation with the kinetics of some neuroblastic cytoskeletal fibers. The differences between the species appear as soon as the rotation goes beyond the vertical line, going through this chordal apex. For instance, there are no possible

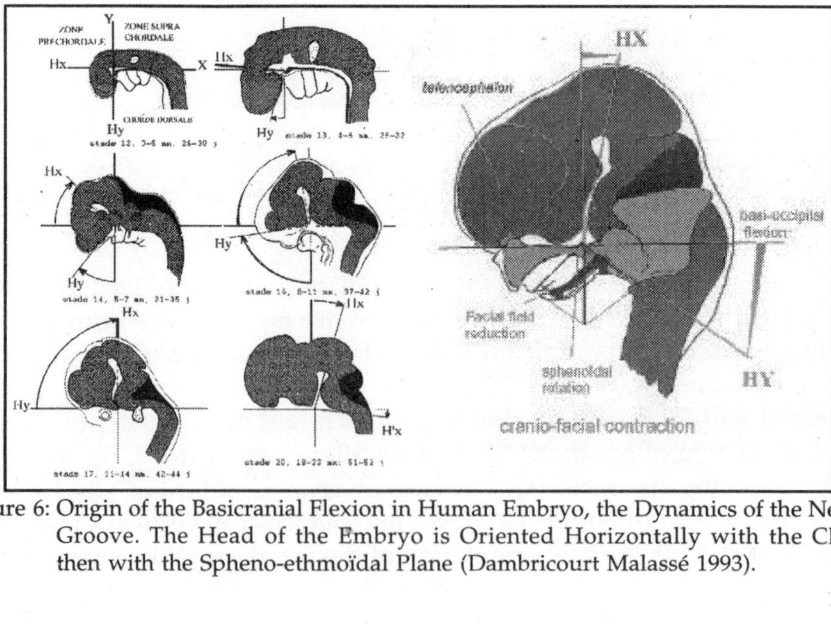


Figure 6: Origin of the Basicranial Flexion in Human Embryo, the Dynamics of the Neural Groove. The Head of the Embryo is Oriented Horizontally with the Chord then with the Spheno-ethmoïdal Plane (Dambricourt Malassé 1993).

confusions between homo genus, macaca and pan. in fact, the divergences are those of the consensual linnaean classification and phylogenetic distribution of extinct and living primates: prosimian, monkeys, great apes, homininae and homo (martin and pilbeam, the cambridge encyclopedia of human evolution, 1994).

The trajectories of *Macaca* and *Homo* for instance, are similar but the human rotation increases with simultaneous changes that occur in the underlaying sphenoidal synchondrosis, close to the apex of the chord. The basi-occipital, postshenoïd and presphenoïd are repositioned with a gain of verticality and a reduction of the antero-posterior length more important in Homo than in Macaca, where the three cranial fossae are less storied vertically, the mandibular cartilage longest and the *septum nasi* prognatic (fig. 7).

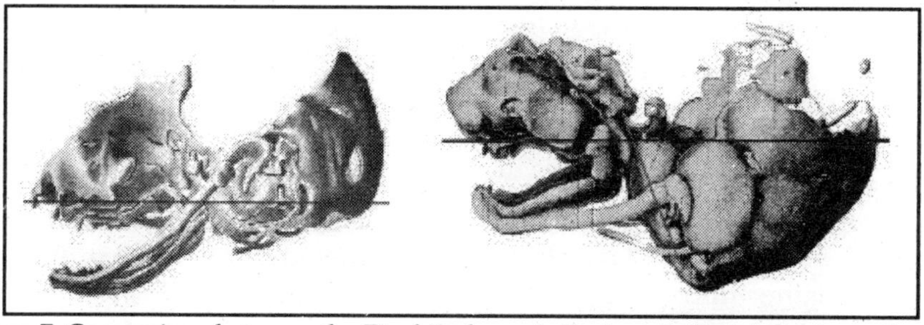

Figure 7: Comparison between the Final Embryonic Basicranio-Facial Conformation of a Cercopithecine and *Homo Sapiens* Showing the Important Changeover of the Posterior Cranial Fossa Downward and Forward

The differences in range mean that, right from the emergence of the neural plate, the neuroblastic tensional dynamics are different. Yet the straightening of the clival plane, the more downward and lowered position of the posterior cranial fossa, are dependant on this rotation, and not on the development of the most anterior vesicle, the telencephalon (future cerebral hemispheres).

The petrous pyramid do not exist at that stage, their counterparts are the two otic capsules located on each side of the basi-occipital. Their endocranial face connects them to it, while the exocranial is in connexion with to the cartilage of the first branchial arch; the Meckel's cartilaginous of the future mandible (figure 7). They therefore move downward and forward, inducing the repositioning of the mandibular cartilage, the temporo-mandibular joint (TMJ) and the straightening of the anterior part in the junction of the two right and left cartilaginous sticks. It straightens slightly in Macaca and very strongly in Homo, leaving a triangular space, the future ossified trigonum mentale that does not exist in any monkey nor great ape; only Australopithecines and Homo have it, in correlation with the low position of both basioccipital and TMJ. The facial tissues re-organize themselves according to the repositioning of the basal cartilaginous tissues, which confirms the clinical observations in infantile dento-maxillo-facial orthopaedics.

## PHYLOGENETIC ORIGINS OF THE POSTERIOR CRANIAL FOSSA LOWER POSITION AND FACIAL STRAIGHTENING IN AUSTRALOPITHECINES AND HOMO

All the extant primate species shared this dynamics, but the cranial bases differ in the range of their sphenoidal rotation. Non-primate mammals like Chiropters (bats) for example, have barely flexed cartilaginous base, the rotation of the three vesicles does not go further than the vertical line passing through the end of the chord. Later, during the fetal period, the cerebellum, pons and medulla (rhombencephalon), the tectum and tegmentum (mesencephalon), the cerebral hemispheres and the cerebellum (telencephalon), are lying on a flat base; the foramen magnum is not visible in inferior vie,. It cannot be seen either in fossil species like Plesiadapiforms.

When the medial sagittal section of the skull shows a long base and face, as in the oldest or extant prosimians (Adapiform, Lemuriform, Lorisiform), the mandibular body is low and the dental arches narrow. With fossil monkeys such as the Aegyptopithecus, the winding neural tube exceeded that of any prosimian species, fixing that of the oldest simiiforms: none of the Platyrrhine, Cercopithecidae or Hylobatidae has gone beyond the limit. It is no longer the case in extant Ponginae and Paninae, their sphenoidal flexion is clearly greater than that of a monkey; their mandibles, which illustrate this flexion, have the same conformation, whatever the ontogenetic stage (Dambricourt Malassé 1987).

Unfortunately there is no complete base of Proconsulidae, Dryopithecinae, neither Ramapithecinae nor Sivapithecinae, while the endocranial profile of *Sahelanthropus tchadensis* is still published. Nevertheless by comparing the numerous mandibles of fossil species (Dryopithecinae, Ramapithecinae, Proconsulidae), with the corresponding values from Ponginae and Paninae, it is possible to conclude that their posterior cranial fossae had the same growth vectors, a greater lowering than that of any monkey's fossil. The emergence of this embryonic flexion, yet observed within the living great apes, could therefore be dated around

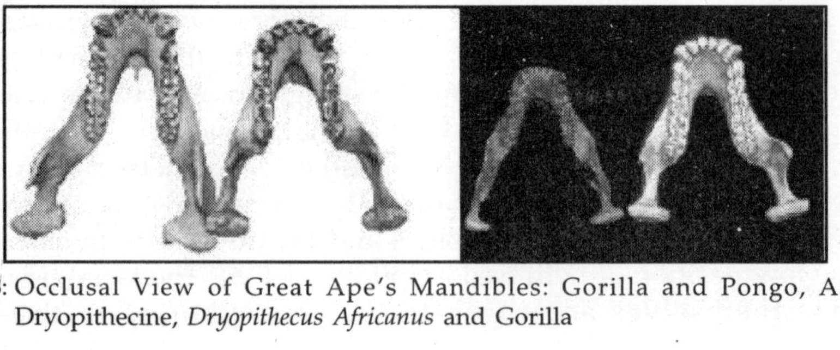

Figure 8: Occlusal View of Great Ape's Mandibles: Gorilla and Pongo, African Dryopithecine, *Dryopithecus Africanus* and Gorilla

20 millions years ago (*Proconsul africanus*) (fig. 8). However, by comparing external reconstructed profile of *Sahelanthropus tchadensis* (fig.9), the growth pathway of the occipital (membranous squama, cartilaginous basi-occipital) did not differ from that of Ponginae-Paninae pattern, the profile is that of their juvenile stages (Dambricourt Malassé 2004a, 2006a). Even the occlusion with the canine lock (the crown longest than premolar's), is in conformity with this juvenile conformation of the base. As known in occluso-posturology, this is not the size that is significant, but the type of occlusion. In the opposite, on Australopithecine and Homo, the inion is below the Frankfurt plane. The embryonic development of this fossil never exceeded the limits already common to Ponginae-Paninae pattern. The shape of the isolated mandibles can confirm this. Our occluso-postural and organogenetic analysis reaches to the same conclusion than Wolpoff, Pickford, Senut and Hawks (2002), adding an ontogenetic interpretation in the sense of heterochronies (Dambricourt Malassé 2006b).

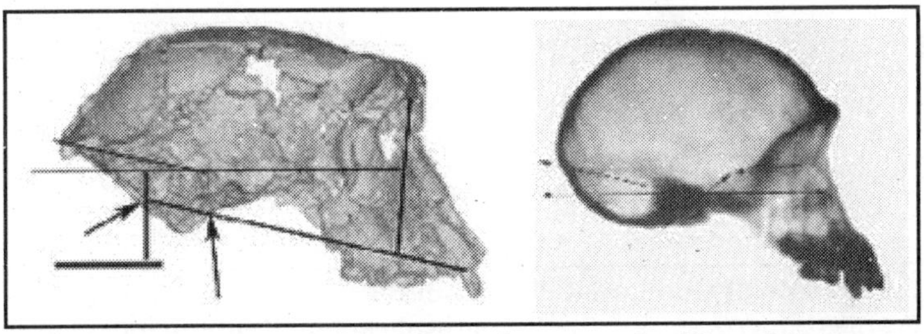

Figure 9: Comparison in the Frankfurt Plane between the Virtual Reconstructed Skull *Sahelanthropus Tchadensis* and a Young Chimpanzee. The Exo-inion is in a Young Pongid Position. The Opisthion Position is Changing (Dambricourt Malassé 2006b); the External Views do not give access to this point Contrary to the First Interpretation (Zollikӧfer et al. 2005).

The lower and upper faces are known with European, African, and Asian species (*Ouranopithecus macedoniensis* and *Greacopithecus freybergi* (Greece), *Proconsul africanus* (Kenya), *Sivapithecus indicus* (India), *Rudapithecus hungaricus* (*Dryopithecus brancoi*, Hungary) *Pierolapithecus catalaunicus, Dryopithecus laietanus* and *Dryopithecus major* (Spain). They show no contradiction with the morphogenetic data from the three living great apes. On the contrary, there are homologies in the variability of the intersphenoidal synchondrosis activity. In *Pongo pygmeus* the intersphenoidal synchondrosis fuses at birth while it remains active in Paninae. This stabilisation causes a change in the growth trajectories of the spheno-ethmoido-frontal complex that topples upward and backward (Deshayes 1991). Those differences cannot be seen with mandibles (fig. 8), but they can be observed on the upper face with the absence of frontal sinus and a pteriac suture that comes in contact with the sphenoid greater wing and the parietal bone, whereas that of the Paninae comes in contact with the frontal and temporal bones. Miocene Asian species, *Sivapithecus indicus* already established those circumnatal differences (fig. 10).

The human pteriac sutures are the same than in Pongo. Yet, in the oldest human species the lack of newborn does not enable to know the ontogenetic modalities of this synchondrosis, but the angular opening between the lateral and posterior semi-circular canals indicates a complete change in the neural tube dynamics, corroborated by the downward and forward expansion of the posterior cranial fossa. In other hand, in modern *Homo sapiens,* the intersphenoidal synchondrosis undergoes complete closure by 3 months of age. This was very probable acquired with the first human species. Now a question is to know if such ontogenetic changes are convergences between Asian fossils and Homo, or genetic inheritance between Asian Sivapithecinae and the oldest human species.

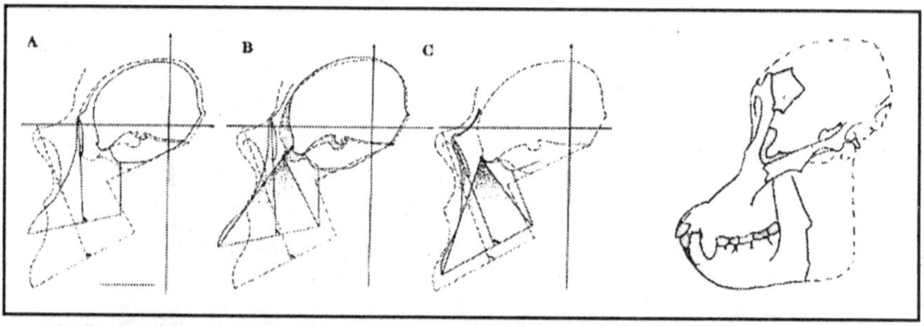


Figure 10: Comparison of Gorilla and Pongo Adult Profiles, in the Vestibular Repair. The Profiles Superpose in their Occipito-sphenoïdal Conformation, but they Differ After a Motion of the Spheno-ethmoïdo-frontal Unit (Delattre and Fenart 1960). Right: *Sivapithecus Indicus* (GSP 15 000, Siwaliks, Pilbeam 1984).

In first conclusion, an increase of the "rolling-up" kinetics in the range above the dorsal chord can explain why adult primate shows a flexed base in association with a facial shortening and a transversal enlargement compared to other species. The prolonged winding dynamics of the neural tissue goes with a fetal and post-natal encephalization such as the myelinization, particularly prolonged in *Homo sapiens* corresponding to the most recent evolutionary stasis.

The upright position of the Australopithecine and Homo species result of new tensional dynamics specific of the neural tube with their consequences on the sphenoidal rotation. Thus, unlike the common idea, ontogenetic encephalization was neither the prime mover of hominization nor the physical cause of the posterior cranial fossa repositioning. All the cranio-sacral organogenesis evolved and at the stage of hominids, the amplification of the three vesicles dynamics was sufficient to generate a vertical positioning of the basicranium. This is concomitant with axial skeleton remodelling.

This distinction between organogenesis and fetal growth enables to understand why Jeffery *et al.* did not find correlations between fetal telencephalization and the basal angle and then why there are difficulties to distinguish between an evolved *Homo erectus* and an early *Homo sapiens*. This is a matter of chronological distinctions, not from a gradual phylogenetic point of view, but from an understanding of the mode and tempo of ontogenetic evolutionary process.

The endocranial and facial closeness between species of Australopithecines and the oldest human species, reflects that of the mutations affecting the embryogenesis common to Ponginae, Paninae and to their ancestors. This is a first rate observation, for it means that the type of mutations may have occurred in African Dryopithecines as in Asian Ramapithecines

The second observation is the consensual phylogenesis showing an increasing contraction of the chondrocranium since 55 million years, occurring with long stasis punctuated by new embryonic patterns, moving the three cranial fossae upward with a shortening of the basi-cranio-facial complex. This evolution follows the punctuated equilibrium theory as defined by Gould and Eldredge: very long periods of stasis followed by anatomical discontinuities. Macro-evolutionary process and anatomical discontinuity are not in contradiction; 1) discontinuity is a natural process well observed in development genetics (Montandon *et al.* 2008) and 2) the transmission of a type of mutations with constant effects can explain the evolutionary continuity with integration of previous mutations. The emergence of a more complex central nervous system is necessary for the posture control (Dambricourt Malassé 1993, 2004, 2006a, Dambricourt Malassé *et al.* 1998, Chaline 1999, Chaline *et al.* 1996, 1999, 2000). The high degree of integration between the social tissues and the environment characterizes the Primates; ecological crises offer greater chances for these new organisms to survive, because of the reflexive abilities, which increase. Those parameters including palaeo-embryogenetic data enable to reconsider the relationships between Australopithecines and Homo.

## ECOLOGICAL CONDITIONS OF PHYLOGENETIC CONVERGENCES

Among many palaeontologists, P.V. Tobias (1999) gave up the savannah paradigm which prevailed to the emergence of Australopithecines. The reason is the discovery in South Africa, of the Australopithecine Stw573 skeleton dated of 3.3 millions years. The animal died in a wooded environment and its anatomy was adapted to arboricolism (Clarke, 1999). It is therefore no longer surprising, as soon as one understands the embryonic origin of the erected postures. The two Australopithecine and Human embryogeneses might have therefore emerged separately in the same ecological conditions, the tropical habitats of the Afro-Eurasia supercontinent, recorded in deposits that extended now from Spain to Southeast Asia.

A global warming took place from 5 Myrs ago with the drying up of the Mediterranean sea, the European great anthropoids became extinct (Spain, France, Greece, Hungary), in Africa *Ardipithecus kadabba* (5,5 Myrs) survived in wooded conditions (teeth of *Ardipithecus ramidus,* Aramis 4,4 Myrs) whereas some populations engendered the first Australopithecines (isolated fragmented base, Aramis 4,4 Myrs). They may have formed a monophyletic group with the extinct Paranthropus. In Asia, *Sivapithecus indicus, Sivapithecus sivalensis, Sivapithecus parvada, Ramapithecus punjabicus, Indopithecus (Gigantopithecus bilaspurensis)* which lived in sub-Himalayas disappeared during the late Miocene (Patnaik *et al.* 2005, Pillans *et al.* 2005), as the Chinese *Lufengpithecus lufengensis* and Ramapithecines (Rukang and Oxnard 1983, Gaur 1987, Zhao and Zhang 2008), whereas *Gigantopithecus blacki* survived until the Pleistocene. Other species in Thaïland engendered Pongo (Chaimanee, Y. *et al.* 2003). However, where the oldest Homo species emerged 3 millions years ago? On the geological scale, the both erected postures nearly occurred at the same time. The main question remains to know why these convergent genetic mutations–dependant on the same past mutations–occurred 15 millions years after the great ape pattern (Chaline *et al.* 1999). Palaeontology cannot solve this evolutionary process, but it is possible to take into account the palaeo-environnemental circumstances favourable for parturition and longer learning phases. There is no reason for them to be different from the ones of the great anthropoids. This can be a clue to look for the oldest human species within the Pliocene layers, known for holding a wide variety of great anthropoid species. Reconsidering the ancient human ascendance rooted in pliocene Asian habitats, seems as interesting as prospecting in the East-African deposits.

### Distinction between a *Homo Erectus* Sensu Largo and a *Homo Sapiens*: The Posterior Cranial Fossa Conformation before the Dermal Bones of the Vault

It is therefore necessary to make the difference, on an adult skull, between the basicraniofacial conformation, established during embryogenesis, and the neurocranium, differentiated with the cerebral hemispheres whatever their shape, volume and dimensions. The boundary between the territories formed in accordance with the embryonic "rolling-up" and those induced by fetal brain development, is complex to delimitate in external view, probably the pteriac and asteriac sutures mark those limits. However, more details are necessary on the endocranial side of the bones in the clivo-petrous limits and temporo-exo-occipital sutures. Such investigation needs well preserved skulls and CT scan explorations.

One of the best cases that give strong support for this deduction is the fossilized skull of *Homo floresiensis* in Southeast Asia. The sagittal section is sufficient to deduce that this skeleton belongs to a late subspecies of *Homo erectus*: no chin, high position of the posterior cranial fossa, lesser rolling up of the cerebellum and of the occipital lobe. The bones of the wrist confirmed those embryonic and fetal conformations as the comparison of the scapular girdle (Broom *et al.* 2006, Tocheri *et al.* 2007, Larson *et al.* 2007).

In the middle Pleistocene, any human fossil shows a development of the neocortex, visible with greater high of the temporal and parietal squama. However, this encephalization occurred without the downward and forward remodelling of the posterior cerebral fossa, in a highest position than in *Homo sapiens* (fig. 11). The neuroblastic tensions of the neural plate did not evolved, the embryonic pattern is the one shared by the oldest species and remained unchanged.

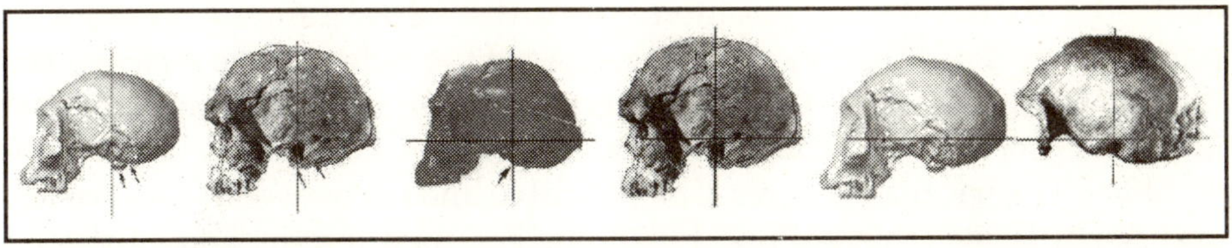

Figure 11: *Homo Georgicus* D 2700 and Herto-*Homo sapiens* with the Forward Position of the Occipital Condyle, the lowering of the Posterior Cranial Fossa Relatively to the Condyle, the Closure of the External Flexion and the Motion of the Alveolo-dental Arch. Middle: *Homo Floresiensis* and Herto-Homo Sapiens. Low: *Homo Georgicus and* Hathnora

In Europe, the encephalization increased during upper Pleistocene with the Neanderthal lineage, but the posterior cranial fossa stayed as high as in *Homo ergaster* with a specific evolutionary trend. The occipito-spheno-ethmoidal complex was expanding, like shown by 1) the formation of a third malar sinus (Heim 1989), 2) the overall pneumatization of the frontal sinuses with continuous supra-orbital ridge between the two arcades, 3) the retro-molar space between the anterior border of the mandibular ascending ramus and the last dental alveole, since youngest ontogenetic stage, 4) a lateral semicircular canal less lowered than in the oldest species (Hublin *et al.* 1996). In Asia, the lower Pleistocene fossils like Sangiran 17 (*Homo erectus*) also fluctuate toward extension (Dambricourt Malassé 2002) although they were less cephalized than the late Neanderthals. The neocorticalisation is a polycentric and gradual evolutionary trend, independent of the basicranial dynamics that lead its own evolutionary parameters, without never gone beyond the limit of the oldest species.

There are no *Homo sapiens* before 160 kyr, the oldest skulls come from Africa with Herto and in Near East with Kafzeh (95 kyr), the posterior cranial fossa is clearly in a more forward and downward position and the frontal cephalic curvature is more expressed, but it follows, chronologically, the new sphenoidal rotation. The tensional dynamics of the neural plate must have evolved under the influences of the previous genetic mutations effects of which amplifie the increasing complexity of neocorticalisation and vascularization. Therefore, the basicraniofacial complex evolved with a decreasing longitudinal growth of the face, the two dental arches still in « end to end» occlusion and the exocranial features still robust, but the chin is clearly saillant. With Neolithic skulls, the occlusion changes again, with an alveolo-dental mandibular retrognathie and a general gracilization of the exocranial table.

The encephalization was gradual but this trend did not lead gradually to *Homo sapiens*, this neo-corticalisation should not to be confused with the transition to *Homo sapiens*, which is a punctuated equilibrium. In this respect, the Narmada skull alternately interpreted as a *Homo erectus* or *Homo sapiens* (Lumley and Sonakia 1985, Kennedy et al. 1991, Sonakia and Biswas, 1998), is not sapiens (Fig. 11). Since all the populations have evolved with the neocorticalisation, how to distinguish, among non-sapiens populations, those that were the ancestors of the oldest *Homo sapiens*? Did the late forms of Asian *Homo erectus* contribute to the emergence of *Homo sapiens*? Discrete traits enable to observe phyletic continuity. Among the significant exocranial features for a plausible lineage between *Homo sapiens* and Asian *Homo erectus* (Pope 1992), one can mention the shovel-shaped incisors, the presence of three roots on the first inferior molar, and the bony exocranial superstructures such as the supramastoïd crest and the torus angularis. This eminence is a thickening of the cortical bone next to the asteriac suture.

The frequency and geographical dispersion of the torus angularis is an interesting data as shown by the comparison of 50 well-preserved skulls or *os parietalis* from lower Pleistocene until the first "modern" *Homo sapiens* (Herto, Kafzeh, Omo Kibish 1). In Europe and Near East (n=21), the torus angularis is already present in Dmanissi on one skull, then on 4 late lower Pleistocene skulls (Ceprano, Tautavel, Castel di Guido, Reilingen), but it is never visible on middle Pleistocene and Neanderthals skulls including the Near Eastern fossils (n= 17). On African skulls (11 adults, 1 sub-adult) it is never visible (OH 9 has a pseudo-torus), one exception is the late middle Pleistocene skull of Kabwe (ca 200 ky). On the opposite on Asian *Homo erectus* (13 skulls), there is a highest frequency (n=9): in India with Hathnora, in China with Dali, Sinanthropus III and X, in Indonesia with Ngawi and Sangiran 17, then Ngandong 1, 5 and 6 (upper Pleistocene). The Kabwe skull shows a significant encephalisation, but it keeps the *Homo erectus* basicranial pattern, this is also the only known African fossil with a torus angularis that may attest to genetic flows, or migrations, from India. The torus angularis lack on the oldest African *Homo sapiens* (Herto, Omo Kisbish 1) and the Near-East Kafzeh. However, we could observe a well-developed torus angularis on an Indian Neolithic skull from Tekka Lakota (Karnataka).

Its presence on *Homo sapiens* skull is therefore independent from the lowering of the posterior cranial fossa. Taking into account its phylogenetic frequency, only the more recent Asian *Homo erectus* could transmit this discrete character. If *Homo sapiens* emerged only in Africa, the hypothesis of interbreeding between Asian *Homo erectus* and African *Homo sapiens* is very unlikely for two reasons; the first comes from the punctuated mutations we observe now, with the type of genes coding for cephalocaudal embryogenesis. This is not any more the same genetic program. The second because Asian *Homo erectus* have derived from the oldest human species at least since 2 millions years without embryonic change; the genetic barrier with extreme East populations should be established long time ago. It is therefore undeniable that Neolithic Indians from Tekka Lakota were remote descendants of Indian *Homo erectus* such as Hathnora. The embryonic approach of human origins gives strong support to this hypothesis (Sankhyan and Rao, 2007).

If, in the coming years, discoveries will confirm the Asian ape roots of the human lineage, it will be necessary to solve the origins of the oldest *Homo sapiens* of East Africa and the Near East. One hypothesis is that genetic flows occurred in the Middle Pleistocene, within *Homo erectus* populations living between the Indus delta and the shores East Africa; Kabwe supports this model. In fine, the origin of *Homo sapiens* could have been more like a kind of « fertile crescent » spreading through the eastern shores of the Arabian Peninsula, as well as through the great migration paths that are the major river valleys like the Indus and its tributaries, the Tiber, the Euphrates and the Nile.

## REFERENCES CITED

Allchin B. (1995), Early Human Occupation in the Northern Punjab, Pakistan: An Overview of the Potwar Project of the British Archaeological Mission to Pakistan (1981-1991). In Wadia, S., Korisettar R. and Kale V. S. (Eds.) Quaternary Environments and Geoarchaeology of India. Bangalore: Geological Society of India, 150-167.

Bjork, A. Skeiller V. (1984), La croissance du maxillaire dans les trois dimensions, comme lle révèle radiographiquement la méthode des implants, *Revue d'Ortho.Dento-Maxillo-Faciale*. 18, 11 : 281-298.

Blackwell B.A.B, Fevrier S., Blickstein J.I.B, Paddayya K., Petraglia M, Jhaldiyal R., Skinner A.R. (2001), ESR Dating of an Acheulean Quarry Site at Isampur, India, Indian *Journal of Human Evolution*, 40: A3.

Boëda E. (2005), Paléotechnologie ou anthropologie des techniques? Arob@se, Ed. Université de Rouen, vol.1, pp : 46-64.

Bonnier L. (1997), La modification de l´occlusion a-t-elle une répercussion immédiate sur le système postural fin? In Lacour M., Gagey P.M., Weber B. (Eds) *Posture et Environnement*. Sauramps: 77-86.

Caro P. (2004), Développement embryonnaire et évolution. Entretien avec Anne Dambricourt Malassé. *La Lettre de l'Académie des Sciences*, Paléontologie, 13 : 14-15.

Chaimanee Y, Jolly D, Benammi M, Tafforeau P, Duzer D, Moussa I, Jaeger JJ (2003), A Middle Miocene Hominoid from Thailand and Orang-utan origins. *Nature* 422: 61–65.

Chaline J. (1999), Origines de l'homme *Encyclopaedia Universalis*, Ed. Albin Michel.

Chaline J., Durand A., Marchand D., Dambricourt Malassé A., Deshayes M.J. (1996), Chromosomes and the Origins of Apes and Australopithecines, *Human Evolution*, 11, 43-60.

Chaline J., Dambricourt Malassé A., Did, B., Magniez-Jannin, F., Marchand D., Courant F. Millet J.J. (1999), Quantification de l'évolution morphologique du crâne des hominidés et hétérochronies. *Comptes Rendus de l'Académie des Sciences de la Terre et des Planètes*, 326 : 291-298.

Chaline J., durand A., Dambricourt Malassé A. David B., Magnez-Jannin F., Marchand D. (2000), Were Climatic Changes a Driving Force in Hominid evolution? In: Climates: Past and Present. M.B. Hart (Ed.). *Geological Society*, London, Special Publication, 181: 185-198.

Clarke, R.J. (1999), Discovery of Complete Arm and Hand of the 3.3 million-years Old Australopithecus Skeleton from Sterkfontein. *South African Journal of Science*, 95, 477-480.

Dambricourt Malassé A (1987), Ontogenèses, Paléontologenèses et Phylogenèse du corps mandibulaire catarhinien. Ph.D. National Museum of Natural History, Paris.

Dambricourt Malassé A (1988), Hominisation et Foetalisation, *Comptes Rendus de l'Académie des Sciences*, 307, II : 199-204.

Dambricourt Malassé A. (1993), Continuity and Discontinuity During Modalities of Hominization. In: "Modes and Tempos in Evolution in the Quaternary" *Quaternary International*, 19: 85-100.

Dambricourt Malassé A. (2002), Nouvelles Approches de l'évolution crânienne des Homo erectus de Java. In : " *Origin of settlements and chronology of Palaeolithic cultures in Southeast Asia*" (in French). Eds F. Sémah, C. Falguères, D. Grimaud Hervé, A.M. Sémah, Artcom, Paris.: 377-396.

Dambricourt Malassé A. (2005), Un nouvel angle de la base pour une meilleure compréhension de la morphogenèse basi-crânienne des hominidés et des modalités évolutives. *Biométrie Humaine et Anthropologie*, 23 : 1-2.

Dambricourt Malassé A. (2006 a), Evolution du chondrocrâne et de la face des grands anthropoïdes miocènes jusqu'à Homo sapiens, continuités et discontinuités. *Paléovol* Proceedings of the French Academy of Sciences. Tome 5 : 109-117.

Dambricourt Malassé A. (2006 b), La question des origines de la lignée humaine : les modèles évolutionnistes confrontés aux fossiles, implications en orthopédie et posturologie. Centre d'Etude d'Ostéopathie, de Posturologie et Sciences Annexes (Eds). Actes du 4ème Symposium, Toulouse.

Dambricourt Malassé A. (2008), Le peuplement humain en Eurasie : la Haute Asie et les piémonts sous-himalayens du Plio-Pléistocène à l'Holocène, origines, évolution humaine et migrations. *L'Anthropologie*, Asie, vol. 111, n°3.

Dambricourt Malassé, A. Deshayes M.J. (1992), Modeling of the Craniofacial Architecture During Ontogenesis and Phylogenesis. A. Berthoz, P.P. Vidal, W. Graf (Eds), The Head-Neck Sensori-Motor System. New York-Oxford, Oxford University Pres: 37-46.

Dambricourt Malassé A., Deshayes M.J., Magnies-Jannin F. Chaline, J., Marchand D. (1998), A Solution to Human Paradox: Fundamental Ontogenies and Heterochronies. *Human Evolution*, 14-4: 277-300.

Dambricourt Malassé A., Martin J.P., De Kerviler E. (2000), Neural Tube, Spheno-Occipital Flexion and Semi-circular Canals in Fossil and Modern Hominids. *Acta Anthropologica Sinica*, suppl. to Vol. 19: 82-89.

Dean M.C. (1986), Homo and Paranthropus Similarities in the Cranial Base and Developing Dentition, in : B. Wood, L. Martin, P. Andrews (Ed) Major Topics in Primate and Human Evolution. Camb.. Univ. Press () 249-265.

Dean M.C., Wood B.A. (1981), Metrical Analysis of the Basicranium of Extant Hominoïds and Australopithecus, *Am. J. Phys. Anthropol.* 59, 53-71.

Delattre A., Fenart R. (1960), L'hominisation du crâne étudiée par la méthode vestibulaire, Ed. CNRS, Paris.

Deloison Y. (2004), La Préhistoire du piéton, Plon.

Deshayes M.J. (1991), Reconsideration of Craniofacial Growth During Development and Evolution. Orthodontic Consequences *Rev Orthop Dento Faciale.* 25(3):353-65.

Deshayes M.J. (2006 a), Cranial Asymmetries and their Dento-facial and Occlusal Effects, *Orthod Fr.* 77(1): 87-99.

Deshayes M.J. (2006 b), Growth of the Skull and Bony Kinetics Interfering with Facial Morphogenesis. Conceptual Bases of Success in Orthopaedic Treatments before the Age of 6 *Orthod Fr.* 77(1): 63-78.

Deshayes M.J., Dambricourt Malassé A. (1990), Analysis of Various Craniofacial Architectural Types Using the Ontogenic Approach of Humanization. *Rev Stomatol Chir Maxillofac.* 91(4): 249-258.

Deshayes MJ, M. Desvignes, B. Romaniuk, J. Robialle, M. Revenu, Deshayes B. (2002), Cranial Analysis for Early Treatment and the Biodynamic Concept of Cranio-facial Morphogenesis. *Orthod Fr.* 73(4):395-406.

Gaillard CL, Dambricourt Malassé A, Magraner, J. Maitrerobert A., Voisin J.L. Nasir A. (2002), Discovery of Recent Lithic Industries with Archaïc Features in the Hindu Kush Range (Chitral district, North Pakistan). *Bulletin of the Indo-Pacific Prehistory Association*, Vol. 6: 25-33.

Gaillard CL, Dambricourt Malassé A. (2002), Early Human Occupations in the Western Himalaya and Border Regions. Extended Abstract of the International Conference on Quaternary Climate, Tectonics and Environment of the Himalaya, Kuman University, Nainital, India: 78.

Gaillard CL. Dambricourt Malassé A. (2008), Les principales étapes de l'occupation humaine en bordure de l'Himalaya occidentale, *L'Anthropologie*, Asie, vol. 111, n°3.

Gaur R. (1987), Environment and Ecology of Early Man in Northwest India, B.R. Publishing Corporation, New Delhi.

Heim J.L. (1989), Une nouvelle reconstitution du crâne néandertalien de la Chapelle aux Saints. *Comptes Rendus de l'Académie des Sciences*, Paris, t. 308, série II n°6, 1187-1192.

Huang W., Zhang P. (2007), Les plus anciennes occupations humaines en Chine, *L'Anthropologie*, 111, 2: 166-181.

Hublin J.J. Spoor F, Braun M, Zonneveld F, Condemi S. (1996), A Late Neanderthal from Arcy-sur-Cure Associated with Upper Palaeolithic Artefacts. *Nature*, 381: 224–226.

Jeffery N. (2002), Differential Regional Brain Growth and Rotation of the Prenatal Human Tentorium Cerebelli, *J Anat*. 200, 135-44.

Jeffery N., Spoor F. (2002), Brain Size and the Human Cranial Base: A Prenatal Perspective, *Am J Phys Anthropol*, 118, 324-340.

Jeffery N., Spoor F. (2004), Prenatal Growth and Development of the Modern Human Labyrinth, *J Phys Anthropol*. 123, 78-90.

Kennedy, K. A. R., Sonakia A., Chiment J., Verma K. K. (1991), Is the Narmada Hominid an Indian Homo Erectus? *American Journal of Physical Anthropology*, 86: 475-496.

Larson, S G, W.L. Jungers, M.J. Morwood, T. Sutikna, E. Saptomo, E. R Due, Djubiantono, T. (2007), Homo Floresiensis and the Evolution of the Hominin Shoulder. *J.H.E, 53*, 6: 718-731.

Levi G., (1900), Beitrag zum studium der Entwicke ung des knorpelingen primordial craniums des Menschens, *Arch. Mikros. Anat. Entwick.* 55, 341-414.

Lordkipanidze D., Vekua A., Ferring R., Rightmire G.P., Zollikofer C., Ponce De León M., Agusti J., kiladze G. Mouskhelielishvili A., Nioradze M., Tappen M. (2006), A Fourth Hominin Skull from Dmanisi, Georgia. The Anatomical Record Volume 288A, 11 : 1146 – 1157.

Lumley DE M.A, Sonakia A. (1985), Premières découvertes d'un Homo erectus sur le continent indien à Hathnora, dans la moyenne vallée de la Narmada. *L'Anthropologie* (Paris), 89, 1: 13-61.

Lumley DE M.A., Gabounia L., Vekua A., Lordkipanidze D. (2004), Les restes humains du Pliocène final et du début du Pléistocène inférieur de Dmanissi, Géorgie (1991-2000) I- Les crânes 2280, D 2282, D 2700, *L'Anthropologie*, 110 : 1-110.

Martin R. D., D.R. Pilbeam (1994), The Cambridge Encyclopedia of Human Evolution. Ed S. Jones.

Mccollum M.A. Nasomaxillary Remodeling and Facial form in Robust Australopithecus: A Reassessment. Journal of Human Evolution, Vol. 54, 1: 2-14.

Montavon T., LE Garrec J.F., Kerszber G M. D. Duboule (2008), Modeling *Hox* gene Regulation in Digits: Reverse Collinearity and the Molecular Origin of Thumbness, *Genes Dev*. 2008 February 1; 22(3): 346–359.

Patnaik R., D. Cameron, J.C. Sharma, Hogarth J. (2005), Extinction of Siwalik Fossil Apes: A Review Based on a New Fossil Tooth and on Palaeoecological and Palaeoclimatological Evidence. *Anthropological Science*, Vol. 113, 1, pp. 65-72.

Pilbeam D. (1984), The Descent of Hominoids and Hominids. *Scientific American*, 250, 3: 84-96.

Pillans B., M. Wiliams, D. Cameron, R. Patnaik, J. Hogarth, A. Sahni, J. C. Sharma, F. Williams, Bernor R.L (2005), Revised Correlation of the Haritalyangar Magnetostratigraphy, Indian Siwaliks : Implications for the Age of the Miocene Hominids Indopithecus and Sivapithecus, with a Note on a New Hominid Tooth. Journal of Human Evolution, vol. 48, n°5, pp. 507-515

Pope G.P. (1992), Craniofacial Evidence for the Origin of Modern Humans in China. Yearbook of Physical Anthropology. 35: 243-298.

Rendell H.M. R.W. Dennel, Halim M.A. (1989), Pleistocene and Palaeolithic Investigations in the Soan Valley, Northern Pakistan. *British Archaeological Report*, International Series 544, 364p.

Rukang W., C.E. Oxnard (1983), Ramapithecines from China: Evidence from Tooth Dimensions. *Nature*, 306, 258 -260.

Sankhyan, A. R, Rao, V.R. (2007), *Human Origins, Genome and People of India: Genomic, Palaeontological and Archaeological Perspectives*. New Delhi (India): Allied Publishers.

Sonakia A., Biswas S. (1998), Antiquity of the Narmada *Homo Erectus*, The Early Man of India. *Current Science*, 75, 24: 391-393.

Spoor F., M. G. Leakey, P. N. Gathogo, F. H. Brown, S. C. Antón, I. Mcdougall, C. Kiarie, F. K. Manthi, Leakey L. N. (2007), Implications of New Early *Homo* Fossils from Ileret, East of Lake Turkana, Kenya, *Nature* 448, 688-691.

Tobias P.V. (1995), *Lecture*. University College London, November 14.

Tocheri M.W., C.M. Orr, S.G. Larson, T.H. Sutikna Jatmiko, Saptomo E., R. A. Due, T. Djubiantono, M.J. Morwood, W.L. Jungers (2007), The Primitive Wrist of *Homo Floresiensis* and Its Implications for Hominin Evolution. *Sciences*, 317, 5845: 1743–1745.

Wanpo H., R. Ciochon, G. Yumin, R. Larick, F. Qiren, H. Schwarcz, C. Yonge, J. De Vos, Rink W. (1995), Early Homo and Associated Artefacts from China. *Nature* 378: 275-278.

Wolpoff, M. H., B. Senut, M. Pickford, Hawks J. (2002), Palaeoanthropology-*Sahelanthropus* or *'Sahelpithecus'*? *Nature* 419, 581-582

Zollikofer C. P. E., M. S. Ponce De León, D.E. Lieberman, F. Guy, D. Pilbeam, A. Likius, H. T. Mackaye, P. Vignaud, Brunet M. (2005), Virtual Cranial Reconstruction of *Sahelanthropus tchadensis*, *Nature* 434, 755-759.

Zhao L, Q.L.W. Zhang (2008), Age at First Molar Emergence in Lufengpithecus lufengensis and Its Implications for Life-history Evoltuion. *Journal of Human Evolution*, Vol. 54, 2: 251-257.

Zhu R.X., Potts R., XIE F, Hoffman K.A, Deng C.L., C.D. Shi (2004), New Evidence on the Earliest Human Presence at High Northern Latitudes in Northeast Asia, *Nature* 431, pp. 559–562.

The research work is commonly supported by the Major Basic Research Projects (2006CB806400 and 2007FY110200) of MST of China, NSFC (No. 40172009), CAS fundation and fundation of French Embassy in Beijing. We thank Prof. AR Sankhyan for his invitation of encouraging this work and Miss Guangcai Liu for her management of some figures of the paper.

Chapter–9

# The Entombed Baby of Tamil Nadu

*P. Rajendran & Peter Koshy*

## INTRODUCTION

During an archaeological exploration in May 2000 in Villupuram district of Tamil Nadu rich Stone Age cultural evidence was discovered at Odai in Bommayarpalayam. Following the discovery of the prehistoric cultural evidence an excavation was conducted in October 2001 at the Odai site. At the site there are aeolian and fluvial deposits of sand and gravel intermittently down to 5.7 m depth. Mesolithic of the Holocene (10,000 c. B.C) and Upper Palaeolithic of the late Upper Pleistocene periods (40,000 c. B.P) were discovered from various depths during the excavation. Below 5.7 m depth ferricrete (laterite) begins and it continues downward. Away from the excavation site, at about 1.5 m depth within the ferricrete, a suspected fossil was spotted on 14 th October 2001 at 12: 45 p.m. Since the ferricrete at the site was quite hard, it was impossible to extricate the fossil from the matrix. Close examination of the fossil revealed that it would be detrimental to remove the surrounding ferricrete.

The normal palaeontological approach to this sort of problem is to extract the fossil in its entirety from the matrix. This can be done chemically, by dissolving the matrix away to leave the fossil or by dissolving the fossil away to leave a hole from which a latex cast can be made, or physically, by digging the fossil out with fine needles or drills. In this case, none of these approaches was particularly useful, and therefore, the entombed fossil was dug out along with the surrounding ferricrete for further study (Fig.1).

## METHODOLOGY

The next attempt was to find out the methodology in the study of the entombed fossil. Since no precedence was known to study such a specimen, it was decided to image the fossil inside the nodule using technologies developed for medical scanning. Even though geologists as well as medical doctors expressed their doubts of a fossil within the ferricrete, it was decided initially to utilize X-ray to identify whether there is any faunal remains within it. The images taken at different KV in the Kumar Hospital at Kollam have clearly proved, for the first time, the existence of a faunal fossil within the ferricrete (Fig.2).

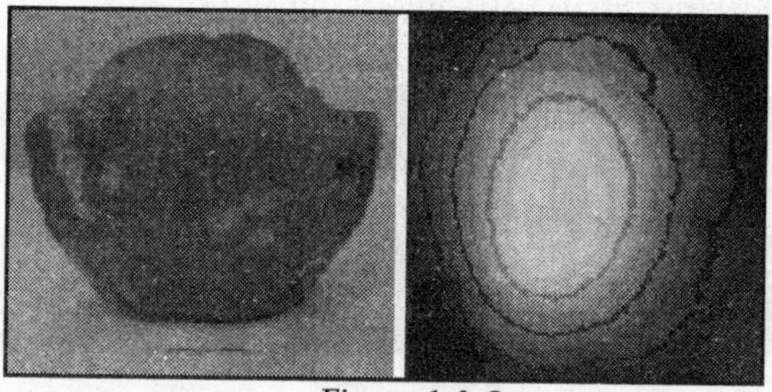

Figure 1 & 2

Success with X-ray led in the application of 2 D scanning by which AP Scanogram slice from above, AP Scanogram with image planes, Cross-sectional images, and Lateral scanogram viewed from the side are obtained (Fig.3). These analyses have proved it as a human skull and have shown several cranial features.

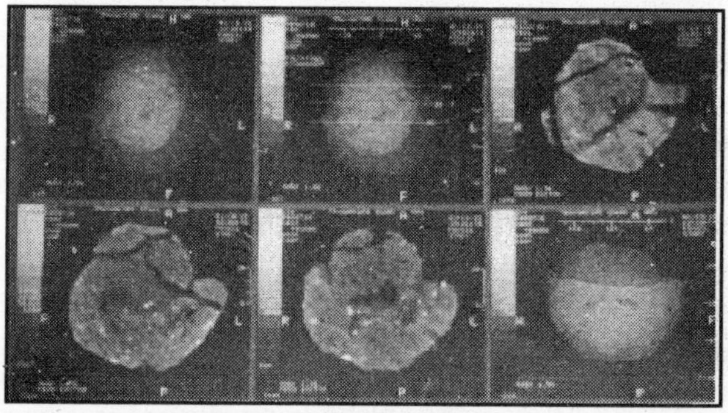

Figure 3

Since several points on its morphology and orientation remained inconclusive from the X-ray and axial images attempts continued to find out still better methodology. At that time a piece of recent literature regarding 3-D morphology reconstruction of Herefordshire fossil was obtained from the Internet (Briggs and Crowther 2001). According to it, theoretically it is possible to image the fossils inside their nodules using technologies developed for medical scanning. Some of these include Magnatic Resonance Imaging (MRI), X-ray Computed Tomography (CT), and 2-D, and 3-D scanning. MRI can work only with fluids and is thus of no use for the investigation of material like solid fossils. Since X-ray and 2-D analyses were already carried out only 3-D was then remaining.

3 D scanning was done by Dr. R. Bharath Kumar, Radiologist in the Upasana Hospital in Kollam, and it has resulted in the successful application of it, for the first time, in India in the study of an entombed fossil. It has revealed a hemi-spherical solid object with a spherical object within it, having a few lucent areas. Serial axial section shows the same hemispherical solid object with a central, slightly hypo-dense ovoid spherical object having air containing clefts within. The spherical object is covered by a fossilized structure measuring 1-2 mm, which has been identified as the fossilized part of the cranial bone.

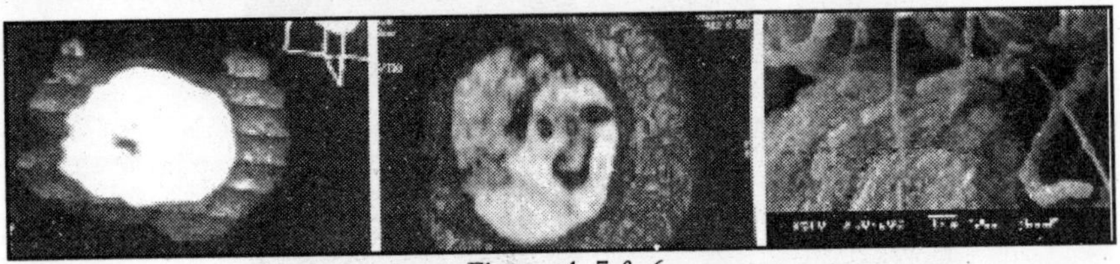

Figure 4, 5 & 6

In order to extract all the cranial features of the fossil the scanning in thin helical runs (3 mm x 4.5 mm) of the entire specimen on different planes was carried out and reconstructed hundreds of images at 2 mm interval. A few out of them include 3 D minimum intensity projection image showing the frontal bone, orbital cavity, nasal bone, maxilla, mandible, parietal bone, sphenoidal fontanella, and occipital bone (Fig.4); 3 D projection image showing the eye ball and nasal bone (Fig.5); axial 3 D minimum intensity projection image revealing ferricrete, cranial bone, and brain tissue; basal image having nasal bone, posterior nasal aperture, foramen ovale, zygomatic arch, carotid canal, foramen magnam, and foramen lacerum; 3 D minimum intensity projection of the cerebral axial image showing frontal pole, and longitudinal fissure; 3 D maximum intensity projection image indicating the cranial bone, brain tissue, and teeth within the maxilla and mandible; and plane axial section showing the coronal suture, anterior fontanella and sagital suture etc.(Rajendran 2003, Rajendran et al 2003).

Application of Photomicroscopy has revealed the complete picture of the skull besides identifying the first three cervical bones along with the skull. The nature of the fossilized cranial bones well confirmed that it is not possible to retrieve the fossil from within the ferricrete. It also proved my earlier observation from the 3 D images that it is not a detached skull and the remaining part of the body is still there within the matrix.

Based on Steiners analysis of the skull by Dr. Tijo Alex and Dr. C.S. Soonu it has been found that nasion, gonion and pogonion are almost in straight line indicating bimaxillary prognathism. This is one of the characteristics noted among the adults in the earlier human evolutionary stage and it has greater importance owing to their prominent nature even in its infancy.

In order to obtain the micro-characteristics of the fossil Scanning Electron Microscopy (SEM) was carried out at the Regional Research Laboratory at Pappanamcode in Trivandrum under the supervision of Dr. Peter Koshi, Scientist and Head in Electron Microscopy at R.R.L in Trivandrum and it was done under various magnifications ranging from x100 to x15,000 in 15 KV. Several images were taken and they have unraveled various vital factors which were not identified earlier in an entombed fossil within the ferricrete of the Middle Pleistocene. Images were studied by Dr. Santha Sadasivan, Assistant Professor in Pathology in Trivandrum Medical College and have identified fossilized human bone structure, RBC in dumbbell shape, blood vessels, membranous tissues, and brain tissues etc (Figs.6). For a comparative study a recent human foetus cranial sample was further studied under SEM which facilitated one to one comparison thereby proved beyond doubt that the Odai specimen belongs to a human baby fossil.

Since dating of the fossilized bone is difficult, attempt was made to find out the absolute age of the matrix in which it was found. The ferricrete which covers exactly over the cranium has been taken for Thermoluminescence dating. The TL date of 0.166 +/- 30

M of the ferricrete clearly shows its age to the Middle Pleistocene and the same chronology has been taken as the approximate age of the entombed human fossil (Rajendran *et al.* 2004).

## INFERENCES

Existence of a human fossil within the Middle Pleistocene ferricrete has been proved, for the first time, through radiological methodology. Anatomical inferences drawn from several images of the Odai specimen clearly prove that it is a well preserved, fossilized human baby. Even the fossilized brain tissues are seen in full as endocast in the brain case of 312 cc and the cranial bone measures 1-2 mm in thickness. Milk teeth, ten each, have been counted both within the maxilla and mandible. These signatures, along with the nature of the fontanella, indicate the age of the baby less than five months of post delivery age.

Pile of coins arrangement of the RBC and their clear revelation in dumbbell shape are unique. Presence of fossilized brain tissues, cranial bone structure and blood vessels appear extraordinary in a fossil of greater antiquity. Bimaxillary prognathism well confirm its greater antiquity and it has proved further by the TL date of 0.166 million for the ferricret in which the fossil is entombed. The TL date places the entombed fossil from Odai to the Middle Pleistocene and in the human evolution it belongs to the Homo sapiens (archaic) (Rajendran et al. 2006). This fossil discovery and its unique preservation within the ferricrete has created much attention, for the first time, among archaeologists, geologists and palaeoanthropologists to search for more fossils in such matrix. Above all this discovery enriches human fossil wealth from Asia.

## REFERENCES CITED

Rajendran. P, R. Bharath Kumar and E. Vijaya Bhanu (2003), Fossilized Hominid Baby Skull from the Ferricrete at Odai, Bommayarpalayam, Villupuram District, Tamil Nadu, South India. *Current Science*–84 (6): 754-756. Bangalore.

Rajendran. P. (2003), Unearthing India's Second Oldest Human Fossil. *News India* (Nature) 6:7. New Delhi.

Rajendran. P, M.P. Chougaonkar and C.S.P. Iyer (2004), Human Baby Skull within the Middle Pleistocene Ferricrete. *Puratattva*–34: 1-4. New Delhi.

Rajendran. P, Peter Koshy and Santha Sadasivan (2006), Homo Sapiens (Archaic) Baby Fossil of the Middle Pleistocene. Ancient Asia-1: 7-13. (Eds.) Vasant

Shinde, K.K. Bhan, Shweta Sinha Deshpande, Dilip Rajgor and Sanjay Deshpande. Mumbai.

Rajendran. P. (2006), (in press), Studies on a Human Skull Fossil Entombed within the Ferricrete. *UISPP XV Congress*, Lisbon.

CHAPTER–10

# The Oldest Palaeolithic of China

*Ya-Mei HOU & Lingxia ZHAO*

## INTRODUCTION

In discussing the issues of the initial expansion of hominids out of Africa, China is a critical part not only with some evidence from the past but also from recent increasing evidence, though it is literally at the end of Eurasia. It is proved that China is clearly involved in the sequence of human evolution.

After the important discoveries of Peking man site at Zhoukoudian in the early time of the twentieth century, more and more evidence of human evolution has continuously obtained from Lower, Middle and Late Pleistocene deposit in China. Among them many new early sites have been discovered throughout the country. In this paper we would like to focus on some main sites of them (Fig.1) and discuss some interesting questions.

## DISCOVERY OF THE EARLIEST PALEOLITHIC SITES IN CHINA

### Nihewan Basin Sites in the North

#### *Xiaochangliang Site*

In 1978 a new discovery in the Nihewang Basin became a big debate in Chinese academia. Archaeologists found some stone artifacts at Xiaochangliang from the Lower Pleistocene deposit of the Nihewan Basin, Yangyuan county of Hebei Province in north China (You et al., 1980). Because they look too much advanced even strange thing was not for the identification of the artifacts but for the recognition of the artifacts. Their appearance looked not like from Lower Pleistocene but like from later period. Prof. Pei doubted if they really belong to such an early geological time (Pei, 1980). However the Nihewan Basin is a standard geological and biological profile in north China to indicate the Lower Pleistocene. Prof. Jia thought it was from the Nihewan geological formation and showed stronger possibility of earlier man in China than ever known (Jia, 1980). The stone artifacts were made by fractured chert rock. Typology of them can be divided into cores, flakes and tools including various scrapers, points and borer etc. together with most chunks and debris (Fig.2). The characters of the industry were bipolar technique, small flakes, small tools and bone tools. Formal stone artifacts are only with number of several decades. This industry was defined as a pioneer cultural tradition before Zhoukoudian Loc.1. The main features appeared typical small tool tradition of north China. The site was dated as 1.35 Myr (Zhu *et al.*, 2001).

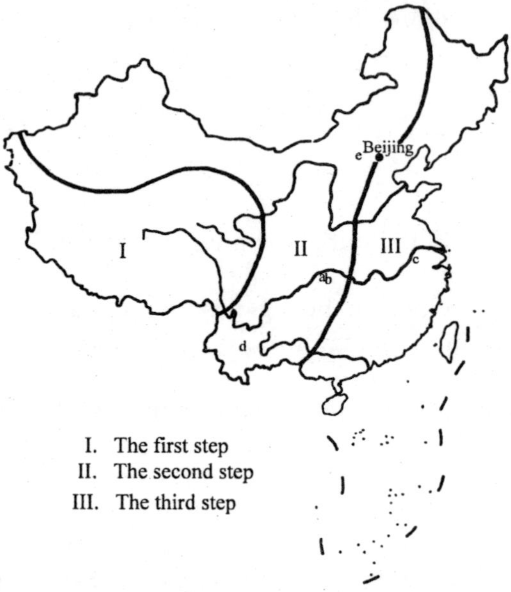


Figure 1: Location of the Introduced Sites in the Three-Step Geomorphology of China (Re-edited after Zheng, 2004)

*Dongggutuo Site*

In 1981 another early Pleistocene site was found at Donggutuo site in the Nihewan Basin (Wei *et al.*, 1985). From 5 trial excavated trenches more than one thousand stone artifacts were unearthed. Like the Xiaochanglian site raw materials of the artifacts are mostly from local bed rock source. But they don't share the same geological resource. The latter seems have better quality of raw materials. Both of them were located at bank of the ancient Nihewan Lake, whereas tool makers of these two sites were facing different climate condition. Xiaochanglian was under condition of more humid of deeper lake. Donggutuo period became drier and mixed with some fluvial formation. As similar as Xiaochangliang, the Donggutuo lithic industry also shows characters of bipolar technique, small flakes, small tools and bone tools (Fig.3). But they look more developed than the former one. In the early 1990s, Donggutuo was chosen to be worked by a collaborative project between Chinese and American for two years. In 1997 and 2000, some new excavations keep going at the site. More and more excavated materials are helping to have better understanding for Donggutuo site. In the new analysis on the Donggutuo industry a new

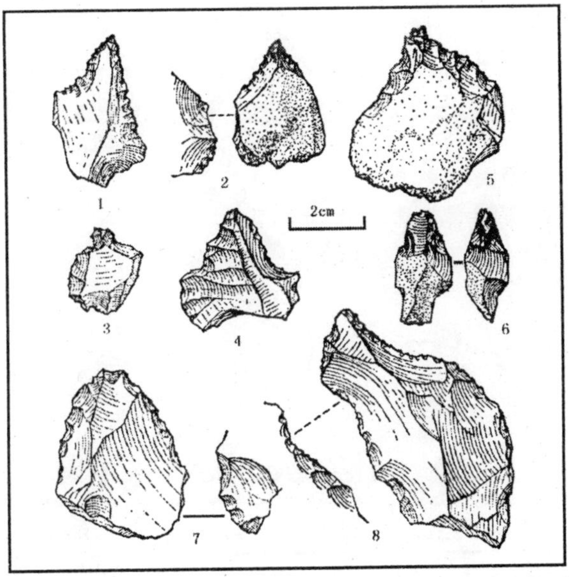


Figure 2: Stone Artifacts from Xiaochangliang Site of Nihewan Basin in North China (After Xie et al., 2006)

type of Donggutuuo lithic group was found and named "Donggutuo core" (Hou, 1999; Hou *et al.* 1999; Hou, 2000; Hou, 2003). The "Donggutuo core" presents a special idea to produce some small elongated flakes which are obviously different from other normal cores of producing normal flakes. The "Donggutuo core" may be a good indicator for understanding some particular needs of the ancient population here. Donggutuo site was dated as 1.1 Myr (Li and Wang, 1982; Wang *et al.*, 2005). Both sites above are associated with Nihewan fauna groups.

*Majuangou Site*

In 1992, the lower cultural layer than previous Xiaochangliang and Donggutuo was fund in the NHW Basin at Majuangou site and was estimated as not later than 1.8Myr by F. Brown through paleomagnetic method. In 2000 the other two lower cultural layer were fund below the first layer at same site. The three layers were named as MJG I, II and III. Each layer was yielding stone artifacts made by local siliceous stone (Xie et al., 2006). They are simple cores, flakes tools (most scrapers, some notches, small choppers) and hammer (Fig.4). In the cultural of MJG III, some pieces of refitting were also recovered. The unique phenomenon is many elephant bones and foot prints were discovered at MJG II and III, which shows relationship between human behavior and natural environment. The date for MJG II was proved as 1.64Myr (Zhu *et al.*, 2004). And MJG III can be thought as 1.66Myr by some researchers. Biostratigraphy study indicates that MJG III can be close to 1.8-2 Myr (Cai and Li, 2003).

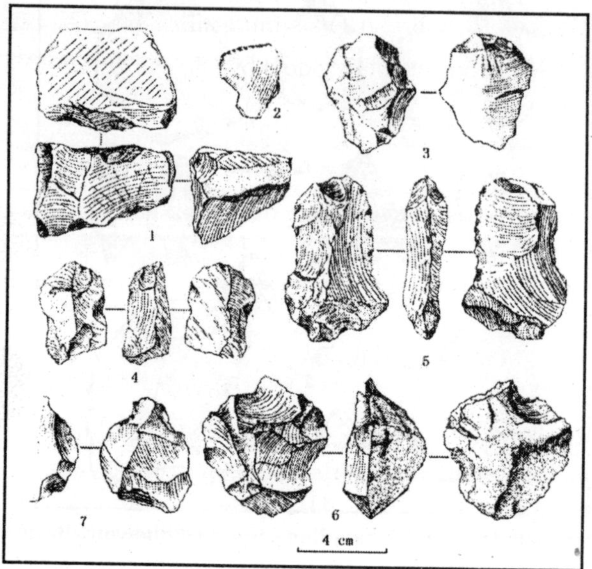


Figure 3: Stone Artifacts from Donggutuo Site of Nihewan Basin in North China (After Wei, 1985)

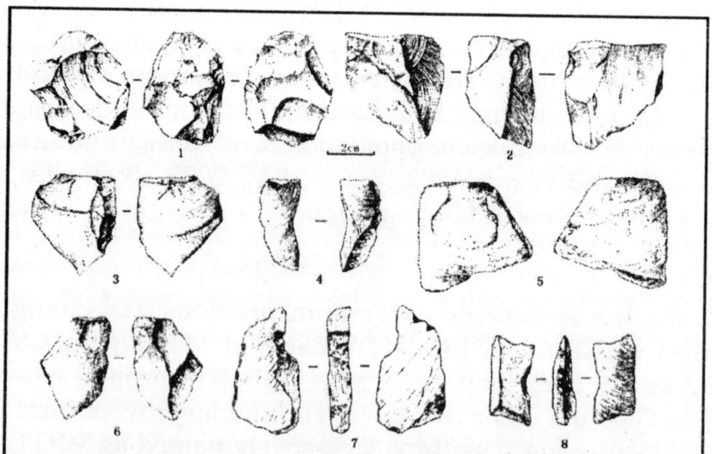

Figure 4: Stone Artifacts from Majuangou Site of Nihewan Basin in North China. 1, 2, Cores; 3-6, Flakes; 7, 8, Tools (After Xie et al., 2006)

## The Earliest Sites in the South

In 1965 three teeth of Yuanmou man was first discovered from Lower Pleistocene stratigraphy in Yuanmou of Yunnan province and named Yuanmouensis of *Homo erectus*. At the same place in 1973, three stone artifacts were first fund there (Fig.5; Wen, 1978). Later some more stone artifacts were also fund (Huang et al., 1985). They are cores, scrapers made on quartz showing lighty-duty tool and heavy-duty tool from different sites. It indicates the area is influenced by different culture from nabouring region. The Yuanmou site was dated as 1.7 Myr by different methods (Cheng et al., 1977; Qian, 1985; Qian, 1988).

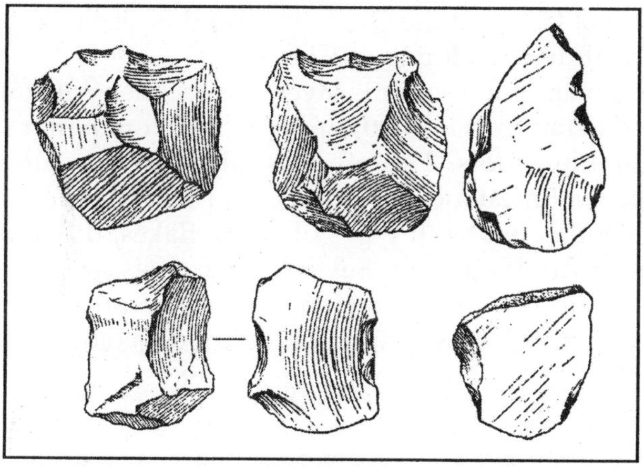

Figure 5: Stone Artifacts from Yuanmou Man Site (After Wen, 1978)

In recent twenty years some other early sites were successively fund in different provinces of south China. Three of them have become known in Chinese Paleolithic and Paleoanthropology field. Now they are presented here as following:

*Renzidong Site in Fanchang County of Anhui Province*

Located at 118°5′46"E and 31°5′23"N the Renzidong site were discovered in 1998 in Fanchang county of southern Yangtze River from late Cenozoic cave-fissure filling deposits. In two seasonal excavations, stone artifacts, bone artifacts, and a great variety of vertebrate fossils, including *Procynocephalus*, were all found *in situ*.

The vertebrate fossils from Renzidong with 67 mammal species show many primitive characters and consist mainly of extinct species. The mammalian fauna is very rich and rather old showing many transitional forms linking south and north China. Among them *Cervus* cf.*Philisi* can be compared with those of European Villafranchian faunas. 15 species are commonly shared by the faunas of Renzidong and Longgupo.. Compared with the other Early Pleistocene faunas from northern and southern China, the percentage of extinct genera and species is relatively higher. On the other hand, the appearance of *Equus* in the fauna shows that the fauna should be later than 2.6Ma. If 2.6 Ma can be considered as the lowest boundary of the Pleistocene recommended by many Chinese stratigraphers the geological age of the Renzidong fauna is very likely the early stage of the Lower Pleistocene. The much closer character of Renzidong fauna to those of northern China implies a cold period in China in the early stage of Lower Pleistocene and the changed climate caused the northern faunas to migrate southward and this geographic part of south Yangtze became a transitional zone between the Palaearctic and Oriental Regions (Jin *et al.*, 1999). The new discovery of Renzidong site is very helpful in zoogeography and paleoclimate of China in the Quaternary and is also a very important clue about early human evolution in China.

In a 1998 excavation in the same layer 59 specimens of stone artifacts were recognized (Zhang *et al.*, 2000). Iron ore is a dominant raw material by 52.5% for making tools. The other is siliceous mudstone, quartz-sandstone, siliceous limestone and gneiss. The artifacts are mostly small within several centimeters with types of cores, flakes, different scrapers, burins and the others (Figure 6). Several bone tools are also identified including one made on a piece of long bone and another made on a mandible of *Rhinoceros* sp. Biostratigraphic data and geological comparison conclude that the age of Renzidong site can be estimated to be Lower Pleistocene.

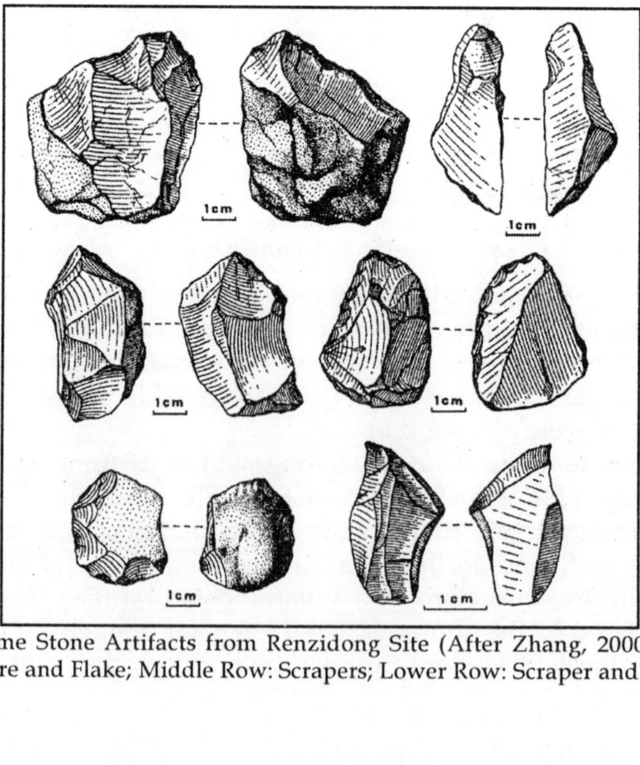


Figure 6: Some Stone Artifacts from Renzidong Site (After Zhang, 2000, Upper Row: Core and Flake; Middle Row: Scrapers; Lower Row: Scraper and Burin)

*Longgudong Site in Jianshi County of Hubei Province*

In southwest Hubei province, with an elevation of 794m a small hill (30°39′14.9″E, 110°04′29.1″N) of Jintang village in Gaoping town of Enshi city has long been known as Longgudong( dragon bone cave) or Juyuandong (giant ape cave) for its large number of mammalian bones and *Gigantopithecus* fossils. a very abundant mammalian fauna with 87 species were fund from here (Zheng, 2004). Weather microfauna or large mammals show strong Lower Pleistocene characteristics. And paleomagnetic work indicates that the age of Longgudong cave is correlated with the Matuyama epoch. The upper normal polarity is correlated to the Olduvai event, and the lower normal polarity corresponds to the Reunion Event (Zheng, 2004).

Several hundreds of stone artifacts were gotten from the cave in 1999-2000 excavation. The artifacts have been described as manuports, cores, flakes, tools, chunks and chips. Direct hammer percussion and bipolar techniques were used and adopted for core reduction and tool making. Most tools are small-sized. Tools can be classified into scarpers, points, burins and hammer stones (Li, 2004). Bone artifacts are identified as bone flakes, points and shovels. On some of them cut and chopper marks can be observed.

*Longgupo Site of Wushan County in Chongqing*

In the valley of Miaoyu a cave formation developed in Trassic Jialingjiang limestone became a sloping deposit after its collapse (Huang and Fang, 1991). It is the Longgupo site (109°4′50"E, 30°21′25"N) in Longping village of Miaoyu town in Wushan county. The deposits have been dated from 1-2.6 Ma by paleomagnetic and other different methods including ESR, Th, U and Amino Acid analyses (Huang *et al.* 1995). The cave has yielded lithic artifacts and the remains of *Gigantopithecus* and numerous other mammalian species confirming that these deposits were deposited during the Pliocene and Lower Pleistocene. But these deposits have also furnished a mandible fragment and several teeth that have been successively attributed to *Homo erectus wushanensis*, to *Homo habilis* or to *Homo ergaster* (Wood and Turner 1995), in the level estimated to date to 1.9 Ma (Huang *et al.* 1995). In addition, a Wushan fauna is composed of 92 species. Some species are very specific to the Lower Pleistocene such as *Gigantopithecus blacki*, *Ailuropoda microta*, *Pachycrocuta licenti*, and *Nestoritherium* sp., confirming the antiquity of the site.

Three stages of excavation were in 1985-86, 1997-98, and 2003-06. The earlier two stages were excavated according using a horizontal method by intervals of one meter divided into 20 levels. A total of 26 artifacts from four levels (5-8 levels) have been reported (Huang *et al.*,1995; Hou *et al.*, 1999; Hou *et al.*,2002; Hou *et al.* 2006). Limestones from the local area, including metamorphic and siliceous limestones are the main raw materials for making stone artifacts. The hard hammer percussion technique was used in the stone tools making. The tool blanks were procured by splitting the pebble in its long axis through bipolar technique. Most choppers were made from natural stones of pebbles or blocks except some retouched ones on large flakes. The artifacts include hammers, picks, choppers, proto-adze, proto-cleavers, knives and flakes (large and small sizes). Unifacial and alternative retouches were often used for making a tool edge into traversed, pointed, notched or convex shapes. Knives,, chisels and a habit of preparing a tool butt are particularly characteristic of this industry. The tool size are mostly large around 10-20cm. Some flakes are smaller than 10cm (Figure 7). The artifacts from this site show both the diversity and the particularity of tool typology among the early human artifacts in southern China 2 Ma ago. These stone tools indicate the level of development in material culture the early man in China had achieved in the early Pleistocene.

The third stage of field work here has being conducted by a Sino-Franco team co-lead by the first author, Eric Boëda and Huang Wanbo. In this period the archaeological excavation were made more careful based on geological sequence. Clearer archaeological layers were first time distinguished with lot of new information of the oldest human behaviour

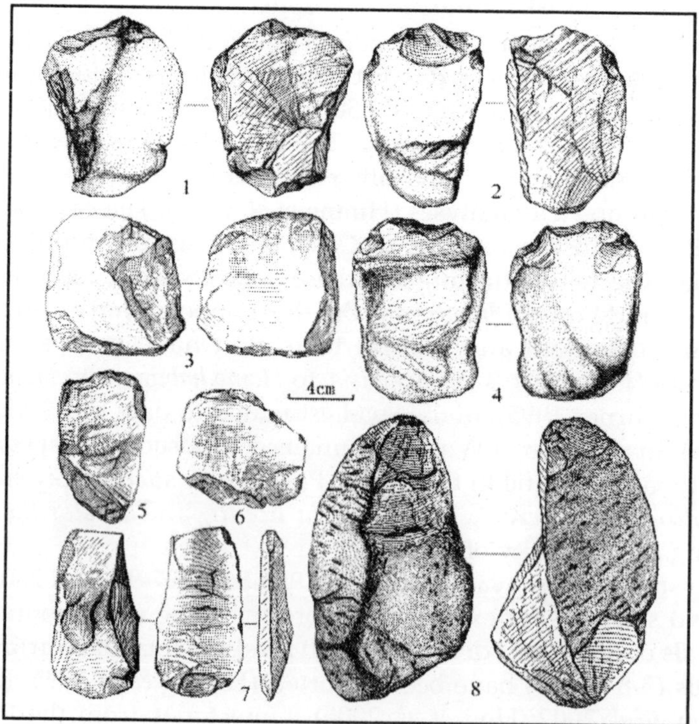


Figure7: Stone Artifacts from Longgupo Site (1-5.choppers; 6flake; 7.knife; 8. pick)

with more details than any previous excavation. The renewed excavations and further research work at Longgupo site offer great potential for providing us with more significant information for understanding the oldest human behavior in China.The results further confirm the paleonotological and archaeological interest of this site. New publications about this work are in preparation.

## COEXISTED HOMINOID EVIDENCE AND RELEVANT INFORMATION

With so many old archeological sites mentioned above from the Late Pliocene-Early Pleistocene in China, we would consider associated hominids with these materials. Up to now, no hominin fossils have been found in the Early Pleistocene sites in Nihewan basin, though plenty of stone artifacts and reliable paleomagnetic dating data are well documented in several sites, such as Donggutuo, Xiaolangliang and Majuangou (Wang *et al.* 2005, Zhu *et al.* 2001, Zhu *et al.* 2004).

However, in central and southern China there are a number of hominoid fossils that have often been linked to the archaeological materials there, including a mandible fragment from Longgudong in Wushan, 6 isolated teeth from Longgudong in Jianshi, and two incisors from Yuanmou.

Longgupo site is one of the most exciting and heavily debated early sites for its archeological evidence and questionable hominoid fossils. At least, two hominoid species have been discovered at this site *in situ*. The first is *Gigantopithecus blacki* known from more than 14 isolated teeth. A second taxon is known from a mandible. There are various opinions regarding the proper allocation of the mandible from Longgupo. Huang *et al.* (1991, 1995) thought that the mandible belongs to *Homo*, whereas Wu (2000) insisted that it belongs to an ape related to *Lufengpithecus*. The second author of this paper agrees with this assessment and thinks that the morphology of the mandible is very similar to that of *Lufengpithecus hudienensis* from Yuanmou). In fact the phylogeny of *Lufengpithecus* is still uncertain to be defined.

Longgudong in Jianshi is another important Lower Pleistocene site. Six hominin fossil teeth and More than 100 isolated teeth of *Gigantopithecus blacki* were discovered in the cave deposit along with six teeth assigned to another taxon.. Three teeth discovered in 1970s were suggested to belong to *Australopithecus* by Gao Jian *et al.* (1975) or *Homo erectus* by Zhang (1984), and the other three hominin teeth discovered in 1990s were assigned to *Meganhrpopus paleojavanicus* by Zhang (2004). Whatever species these teeth belong to, it has been belived by most Chinese scholars and some foreigners that they are hominins, not pongids. Up to now these isolated teeth did not attract much attention because of the lack of skulls and long bones which are more reliable for determining its phylogeny position.

*Gigantopithecus blacki* is an interesting taxon that needs to be discussed here because of its widespread occurance in Longgupo and Longgudong as well as several other Early Pleistocene cave deposit sites. Weidenrich (1946) proposed *Gigantopithecus blacki* as the forerunner of *Homo*, at that time only several isolated teeth were collected from drugstores. Based on three mandibles and nearly a thousand teeth of *Gigantopithecus blacki* from Liucheng in Guangxi, Woo(1962) suggested that it was an early extinct branch of hominid, not the direct forerunners of late hominids, the morphology of *Gigantopithecus* is between apes and hominids. However, most authorities, including the authors of this paper regard *Gigantopithecus* as a fossil pongine (Zhao, 2006). Until recently many authors have suggested that *Homo* (or some other hominin) and *Gigantopithecus blacki* coexisted in southern China in the Early and Middle Pleistocene, at sites such as Longgupo in Wushan, and Longgudong in Jianshi. However, the identity of this other hominoid, known from fragmentary remains has recently been called into question, and several authorituies now argue that it is not a hominin, but rather some sort of ape, a younger relative of *Lufengpithecus*.

*Lufengpithecus* is a fossil ape from Yunnan Province of China. Since the mid-1970s, large quantity of Late Miocene hominoid fossils have been found in Yunnan Province, including skulls, mandibles, maxillary, teeth and postcranial bones. Different opinions exist regarding the exact phylogenetic placement of *Lufengpithecus*. Some believe that *Lufengpithecus* is on the evolutionary line toward homininae (Gao, 1998, Gao et al., 2004, 2006), the others think that *Lufengpithecus* is a branch of the Ponginae related to the orangutan or a conservative hominid stock that preceded the split between Ponginae and Homininae. Based on enamel microstructure and dental development study the second author of this paper (Zhao et al., 2000, 2002, 2003, 2005, 2007), has suggested a potential relationship between *Lufengpithecus* and early hominins.

## CONCLUSION AND QUESTIONS

So far, the limited evidence in China could not provide definite new conclusions of human evolution in this region. However, they urge us to keep minds open in regarding early human evolution with wider possibilities. Asia is still a large area whose paleontology and archeology remains are still poorly known and understood. Many currently popular views must be tentative and the force of evidence is not enough to be adopted here and can only be considered as hypotheses. As well as noted by other scholars (Dennell, 2003; Dennell and Roebroeks, 2005) the necessity of considering Asia as a place of human origins needs to be taken more seriously and not be put aside. We put some questions for further discussion.

1. There is some hard evidence of hominins in Asia around 2 Ma in south China. Though they may be not enough to change any traditional theories or hypotheses about human origin, but they do offer suggestions of early human activity in the East.
2. Outside of China, there is additional old evidence from areas of Asia showing connections with .Africa, including Georgia in the north and Indonesia in the south. It needs to be made clear about how this evidence relates to that in China.
3. A very diverse environment could influence much for China to have a unusual early human evolution process. For example, the Qinghai-Tibetan Plateau has a long history of uplift and subsidence in the past 30 million years. "The Three Steps" geomorphology in east China can completely changed the climate in the whole area, including the new setting of monsoon system. It also made the loess plateau formed in north China and river system from the west to the east China. Such an enormous transformation influenced the local environment dramatically that led to the appearance of many new habitats and new species.
4. The new archaeological evidence of early human in China reveals a very different development of culture between the north and the south. In a recently reported site of Goudi-part of Majuangou site (Gao et al., 2005 ) a stone artifacts layer has been found at a similar or even earlier age than preciously reported site from the site of Majuangou(Zhu et al., 2004). The artifacts at both sites show clear "debitage" industry. However in the south, for example at Longgupo site the industry has strong character of "façonage"

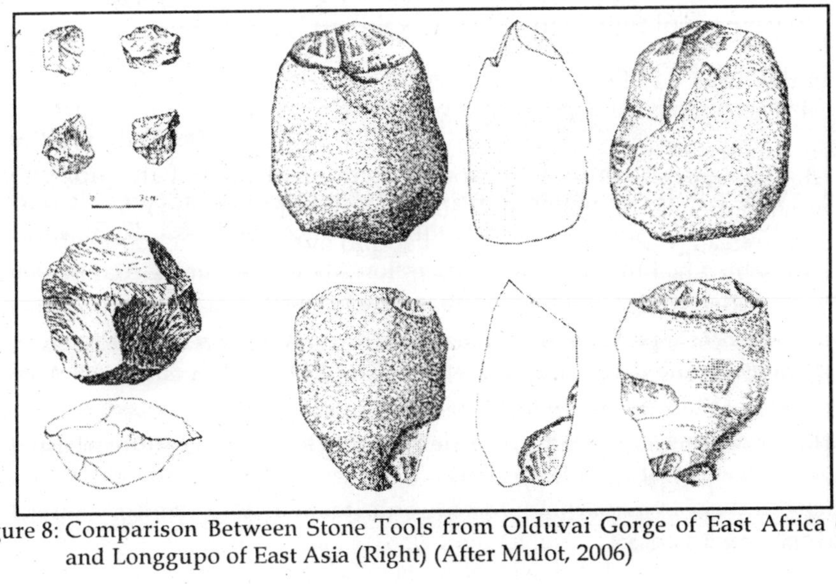

Figure 8: Comparison Between Stone Tools from Olduvai Gorge of East Africa (Left) and Longgupo of East Asia (Right) (After Mulot, 2006)

which belongs to consistent feature of later Chinese southern Paleolithic culture over a wide region. According to the distribution of distributed area of the Levallois phenomenon and the Acheulean phenomenon Boëda (2004) proposed a later developed handaxe culture in China as a local renovation. He believes that the early human culture developed convergently in the Eastern and Western parts of the world (Mulot, 2006). The study of the newly excavated materials from Longgupo site may reveal some new behavior of early humans here are different from that in E. Africa (Figure 8). Some scholar who have doubted the evidence from the Longgupo site (Gao et al., 2005) have become more positive after new observations for recently excavated stone artifacts (Wei Qi, personal communication). The artifacts from different layers of Longgupo site show very much diversity and a somewhat mature organization of technology. We doubt if it could be the earliest culture in the east. On the contrary the technology indicates some other earlier cultures were existent even before.

5. On the result of two instances of "Out of Africa" migration ( Templeton, 2002), Templeton (2005) has subsequently argued for three expansions of human evolution including the earliest time at 1.9 Ma which is close to the evidence for the earliest hominins in China. This implies that cosmopolitan gene flow has happened many times. The present record is only partly understood.. Dennell and Roebroeks (2005) go even farther based on some very recent evidence human evolution from different parts of Asia. They suggested the need for a new "Asian perspective" to fully understand early human evolution. The way of looking for the earliest tool maker in China is keeping long distance to explore.

## REFERENCES CITED

Boëda, E., Hou, X. (2004), Relationship Between East and West Asia in Paleolithic Age. Quaternary Sciences 3, 255-264.

Cai, B.Q., Li Q. (2004), Human Remains and the Environment of Early Pleistocene in the Nihewan Basin. Science in China (Earth Sciences).,Vol. 47 (5), 437-444.

Cheng, G.L., Li, S.L., Lin, J.L. (1977), Discussion About the Age of Yuanmou Man and the Early Matuyama Event. Geological Sciences (1) ,34-43.

Denell, R. (2003), Dispersal and Colonization, Long and short chronologies: how continuous is the Early Pleistocene record for hominids outside East Africa ? Journal of Human Evolution 45, 421-440.

Dennell, R., Roebroeks, W. (2005), An Asian Perspective on Early Human Dispersal from Africa. Nature 438,1099-1104.

Gao, J. (1975), Australopithecine Teeth Associated with *Gigantopithecus*. Vertebrata PalAsiatica 13, 81-88.

Gao, F. (1998), Phylogeny for the Large-bodied Hominoid of Yunnan (China) Its Significance in Human Origin. In: Chen, J., Jiang, Z., Ji, X., (Eds.), Collected Works for "The 30th Anniversary of Yuanmou Man Discovery and the International Conference on Palaeoanthropological Studies". Yunnan Science and Technology Press, Kunming, pp. 50-65.

Gao, F., Kelley, J., Zheng, L., Liu,W. (2004), An Infant Skull of Lufenpithecus from Yuanmou, Yunnan Province, China. American Journal of Physical Anthropology 38 (Suppl.), 98.

Gao, F., Kelley, J., Zheng, L., Liu, W. (2006), An Infant Skull of Lufengpithecus from Yuanmou, Yunnan Province, China. In: Yang, D., Yang, S., (Eds.), Collected Works for "The 40th Anniversary of Yuanmou Man Discovery and International Conference on Paleoanthropological Studies. Yunnan Science and Technology Press, Kunming, pp. 40-63, 251.

Gao, X., Wei, Q., Shen, C., Keates, S. (2005), New Light on the Earliest Hominid Occupation in East Asia. Current Anthropology (Suppl.) 46, 115-120.

Hou, Y. (1999), Expecting Two-million-year-old Human Remains in the Nihewan Basin, North China. Quaternary Research 1, 95.

Hou, Y. (2000), Donggutuo Lithic Industry of the Nihewan Basin, North China. PhD Dissertation of the Institute of Vertebrate Paloentology and Paleoanthropology, Chinese Academy of Sciences, 1–112.

Hou, Y. (2003), Naming and Preliminary Study on the Category of the "Donggutuo core". Acta Anthroplogica Sinica, 22(4), 279–291.

Hou, Y., Huang, W., Boëda, E., Zhao, L., Xu, Z., Daussy, A., Griggo, C., Rasse, M., Sarel, J., Li, Y., Lu, N., Bodin, E., Yuan, J. (2006), Le site de Longgupo et la naissance du genre humain en Asie. In:Chen, X., Bussotti, M. (Eds.), Sinologie Française. Zhonghua Shuju, Beijing, pp. 11, 7-22.

Hou, Y., Xu, Z. Huang, W. (1999), Some New Stone Artifacts Discovered in 1997 at Longgupo, Southern China. Longgupo Prehistoric Culture 1, 69-80.

Hou, Y., Xu, Z. Huang, W. (2002), Study on Stone Artefacts of Level 8 from 1998 Excavation at Longgupo, Southern China. Longgupo Prehistoric Culture 4, 1-10.

Hou, Y., Wei, Q., Lin,S.L., Feng, X.W. (1999), Excavation Report of 1997 at Donggutuo in the Nihewan Basin, North China. Quaternary Research 2, 139–148.

Huang, W.B. and Fang. Q.R. (1991), Wushan Hominid Site. Ocean Press. Beijing,1-230.

Huang, W.B., Ciochon, R., Gu, Y.M., Larick, R., Fang, Q.R., Schwartz, H., Yonge, C., de Vos, J., Rink, W. (1995), Early Homo and Associated Artifacts from Asia. Nature 378, 275-278.

Huang.W.W., Wei, Q., Zhang, X.Y. (1985), Paleolithic in Yuanmou Basin, Prehistory Research (4), 19-22,

Jin, C., Han, L., Wei, G. (1999), The Discovered Paleolithic Site of Renzidong in Fanchang County of Anhui Province. Acta Anthropologica Sinica.18 (1), 70-71.

Li, C. R. (2004), Stone Artifacts. In: Zheng, S. (Ed.), Jianshi Hominid site. Science Press, Beijing, pp. 37-66.

Li H., J. Wang (1982), Magnetostratigraphic Study of Several Typical Geologic Sections in North China. (in:) Quaternary Geology and Environment of China, China Ocean Press, Beijing, 33-38.

Mulot, R. (2006), Contre-enquête sure le berceau chinois. Science et Avenir Avril, 56-61.

Qian, F. (1985), On the Age of "Yuanmou Man–A Discussion with Liu Tungsheng et al. Acta Anthropolgica Sinica. Vol. 4(4): 324-331.

Qian, F. (1988), On the Dates and Natural Environments of China's Early Human Sites, In: Papers Collection on the Quaternary Galciers and Geology. Vol.5,. Geology Publishing House: Beijing.106-110.

Templeton, A.R. (2002), Out of Africa Again and Again. Nature 416, 45-51.

Templeton, A.R. (2005), Haplotype Trees and Modern Human Origins. Yearbook of Physical Anthropology 48, 33-59.

Wang, H., Deng, C., Zhu, R., Wei, Q., Hou,Y., Boëda, E. (2005), Magnetostratigraphic Dating of the Donggutuo and Maliang Paleolithic Sites in the Nihewan Basin, North China. Quaternary Research. 63 (3), 1-11.

Wei, Q. (1985), Palaeoliths from the Lower Pleistocene of the Nihewan Beds in the Donggutuo Site. Acta Anthropologica Sinica. Vol. 4 (4), 289-300.

Wei, Q., Meng, H., Cheng, S.Q. (1985), New Palaeolithic Site from the Nihewan Beds, Acta Anthropol.Sinica 4 (3), 223–232.

Weidenrich, F. (1946), *Apes, Giants and Man*. The University of Chicago Press, Chicago.

Wen, B. H. (1978), Paleolithic Discovered in Yuanmou Basin, Yunnan Province. In: Collected Papers of Paleoanthropology. Science Press, Beijing, 126-135.

Woo, J. (1962), The Mandibles and Dentition of Gigantopithecus. Palaeontologia Sinica, New Series D. 11, 1-94.

Wood, B., Turner, A. (1995), Out of Africa and into Asia. Nature 37, 239-240.

Wu, X. (2000), Longgupo Hominoid Mandible Belongs to Ape. Acta Anthropologica Sinica 19, 1-10.

Xie, F. Li, J. Liu, L.Q. (2006), Nihewan Paleolithic Culture. Huashan Literature Press, Shijiazhuang, 1-278.

You, Y., Tang,Y., Li, Y., (1980), Dicovery of the Paleoliths from the Nihewan Formation. Quaternaria Sinica, 5, 1–11.

Zhang, S., Han, L., Jin, C., Wei, G., Zheng, L., Xu, Q. (2000), On the Artifacts Unearthed from the Renzidong Paleolithic Site in 1998. Acta Anthropologica Sinica. 19 (3), 169-183.

Zhang, Y. (1984), The "Australopithecus" of West Hubei and Some Early Pleistocene Hominids of Indonesia. Acta Anthropologica Sinica. Vol.5 (3), 85-92.

Zhang, Y., Zhang, Z., Liu, W. (2004), Paleoanthropology of Jianshi Site. In: Zheng, S.,(Ed.), Jianshi Hominid Site, pp. 26-37

Zhao, L. (2006), Comprehensive Dental Study on Gigantopithecus. Ph.D. Dissertation, Graduate School of Chinese Academy of Sciences.

Zhao, L., He, Z. (2005), Dental Development and Ontogeny of Late Miocene large-bodied Hominoids from Yunnan, China. Anthropological Science 113(1), 79-83.

Zhao, L., Lu, Q., He, Z. (2002), Eruption Sequence of Lower Permanent Dentition of Lufengpithecus Lufengensis. Acta Anthropologica Sinica, 21(Suppl.) 14-18.

Zhao, L., Lu, Q., Xu, C. (2000), Enamel Microstructure of *Lufengpithecus lufengensis.* Acta Anthropologica Sinica, 19 (Suppl.), 77-82.

Zhao, L., Lu, Q., Zhang, W. (2007), Age at First Molar Emergence in Lufengpithecus Lufengensis and Its Implications for Life-history Evolution, Journal of Human Evolution, doi: 10.1016 j.jhevol.2007.09.019.

Zhao, L., Zheng, L., Gao, F., Jiang, C. (2003), Preliminary Study on Enamel Microstructure of Yuanmou Miocene Hominoids of China. Science in China (Series D) 46 (11), 1142-1150.

Zheng S. (Ed) (2004), *Jianshi Hominid site.* Science Press, Beijing. 1-412.

Zhu, R., Hoffman, K., Potts, R., Deng, C., Pan, Y., Guo, B., Shi, C., Guo, Z., Yuan, B., Hou, Y., Huang, W. (2001), Earliest Presence of Humans in Northeast Asia Nature 413, 413-417.

Zhu, R., Potts, R., Xie, F., Hoffman, K ., Deng C., Shi, C., Pan,Y., Wang, H., Shi, R., Wang, Y., Shi, G., Wu, N. (2004), New Evidence on the Earliest Human Presence at High Northern Latitudes in Northeast Asia. Nature 431, 560-562.

The research work is commonly supported by the Major Basic Research Projects (2006CB806400 and 2007FY110200) of MST of China, NSFC (No. 40172009), CAS fundation and fundation of French Embassy in Beijing. We thank Prof. AR Sankhyan for his invitation of encouraging this work and Miss Guangcai Liu for her management of some figures of the paper.

CHAPTER–11

# Vegetation and Climate of Narmada Hominins

*Poonam Verma, M. R. Rao & Rajeev Patnaik*

## INTRODUCTION

The Narmada River in central India flows along an East-West lineament and is bounded by the Vindhyan Hills in the north and Satpura Hills to the south. The central Narmada valley of India is well known for its rich records of vertebrate fossils and prehistoric sites and extensive Quaternary and Archaeological investigations have been done since 19th Century (De Terra and Paterson, 1939, Agarwal *et al.* 1988; Kennedy, 2003). Inspite of abundance of faunal and cultural material, the only fossil hominin evidence in the subcontinents referred as *Homo erectus*/archaic *Homo sapiens* is represented by calvaria, two clavicles and a partial rib from Hathnora in the central Narmada Valley (Sonakia, 1984; Kennedy and Chimant 1991, Sankhyan, 1997, 2005 and Cameron *et al.* 2004). Prehistoric hominin occupation in central Narmada Valley have taken place since early middle Pleistocene and this evidence was corroborated by the presence of stone artifact assemblages, ranging from the Lower Palaeolithic to the Chalcolithic periods.

Central India which possess approximately 26% of the total forest cover of the country has hitherto not received adequate attention to understand the antiquity of the tropical deciduous forests, the role of climate fluctuations on these forests and their impact on human inhabitation and behavior except some information available from north eastern part of Madhya Pradesh (Bera, 1990, 1994; Chauhan, 1994, 1996, 2000, 2002). The first exploratory palynological study from this region has been done by Nandi (1997) on the Quaternary alluvial deposits of the Narmada Basin but most of the litho units have not yielded spore-pollen except the thin layers of carbonaceous clay at the basal part of the Upper Pleistocene deposits proved to be productive.

In the present paper an attempt has been made to study hominin bearing Quaternary sediments of central Narmada Valley exposed at Hathnora and adjoining areas, Madhya Pradesh to reconstruct the palaeovegetational succession and palaeoclimatic scenario of the area on the basis of pollen / spores, invertebrate and vertebrate fossils and magnetic susceptibility evidences. These studies have been done through pollen analytical investigation of trench and core samples of Baneta formation and Kusumelli Dam respectively exposed at Hathnora and adjoining areas, Sehore district, Madhya Pradesh (Fig.1).

## GENERAL GEOLOGY

The Narmada River flows along E-W lineament, bounded by Vindhyan in the North and Satpura to the south, originates from Amarkantak in the east and flows for approximately 1300Km to the Gulf of Cambay in the west. The Precambrian Vindhyans and Cretaceous Deccan Traps form the basement of the extensively developed Quaternary deposits of the Narmada River Valley. These Quaternary deposits have been divided into seven formations, namely Pilikarar, Dhansi, Surajkund, Baneta, Hirdepur, Bauras and Ramangar based on the order of superposition, erosional unconformity, and nature of sediments, sedimentary structures, pedogenic characters and palaeomagnetic signatures (Tiwari and Bhai, 1997) ranging in age from Early Pleistocene to Holocene.

The present study is based on the Baneta Formation exposed at Hathnora village and the type section at the Baneta village at the right bank of Narmada River. At Hathnora 13m thick fluvial deposit exposure can be divided in to three horizons separated by unconformities. The lowermost ~ 4 m (Middle Pleistocene/early Upper Pleistocene) strata comprising of boulders/cobbles/pebbles deposits belonging to Surajkund Formation rests on the Cretaceous Deccan Traps and was deposited in a high energy channel environment. The red/orange coloration of the sandy-pebbly layers is separated locally by platy calcretized layers. This stratum is followed upwards by ~ 8 m of clay/silt layers (late Upper Pleistocene to early Holocene) deposited under floodplain condition belonging to the Baneta Formation. For Holocene climate studies, one perennial swampy lake (Kusumelli Dam) fed by subterranean water have been selected (Fig. 2).

## MATERIAL AND METHODS

Material for the investigation comprises both surface samples and sedimentary core. A total number of 34 samples of carbonaceous and sandy clay from 2m Baneta profile from cliff section and 14 samples from 1 m Kusumelli swamp profile each at the interval of 5 cm were collected for the palynological investigation. The conventional method of pollen analysis (Erdtman, 1943) using 10% aqueous KOH solution, 40% HF and acetolysis mixture (9:1, acetic anhydride and conc. $H_2SO_4$) was employed to extract the pollen/spores from the trench sediments. Radio carbon dating was done for the sample of Baneta Formation (BS 2643 date is 12460+/-224 Yr BP; BS 2633 date is 25340 +/- 440 Yr BP); another sample of Baneta Formation (BS 2278 date is 8740 +/ 450 yr BP ) and Kusumelli swamp (BS 2687 date is 4000 +/- 100 Yr BP) at the Radio Carbon Laboratory of the Birbal Sahni Institute of Palaeobotany, Lucknow. Based on pollen/ spore assemblage recovered by pollen analyses of the sediments of Baneta Formation (Late Pleistocene to Early Holocene) and Kusumelli Dam (Late Holocene), a broad inference of vegetation vis a vis climate change around this area could be drawn.

## POLLEN ANALYSIS AND INTERPRETATIONS

### Baneta Formation exposed at Hathnora (12460+/-224 to 25340 +/- 440 Yr BP)

In order to understand the sequential alternations in the vegetation and climate, the pollen diagram has been divided in to five distinct pollen zones from bottom to top, on the basis of fluctuations in the values of some prominent arboreals and non -arboreal taxa (Fig. 1). These pollen zones (BF I to BF V) are prefixed with initials 'BF ' after the name of the site of the investigation.

The pollen BF Zone-I exhibits the presence of Poaceae, Cyperaceae, Liguliflorae, Brassicaceae, Caryophyllaceae, *Artemesia*, Cheno/Ams in low frequencies, with a few trees like *Azadirachta, Holoptelea* and some shrubs suggesting the open grassland type vegetation flourished in cool and arid climatic conditions. The pollen BF Zone-II shows appearance of few more trees viz. *Syzygium,, Diospyros, Emblica* with increased percentage of *Acacia, Azadirachta, Holoptelea, Zyziphus* and *Symplocos,* with increased shrubs of Acanthaceae, Solanaceae, Faboideae. The frequency of Poaceae, Cyperaceae increased with decreased number of *Clerodendron,* Cheno/Ams, *Artemisia* are suggestive of moderately warmer and arid condition. The pollen BF Zone- III reveals the depletion in total vegetation. Trees were almost vanished except a few viz. *Diospyros, Emblica, Acacia, Zyziphus* and *Holoptelea.* Similarly shrubs and herbs are also showing fluctuating decreasing trends with decreased percentage of aquatics, ferns and algal fungal remains except a few herbs like *Artemisia* and Cheno/Ams, which are showing increased percentage. Such a vegetation mosaic shows that area was covered by open grassland and experiencing cool and dry conditions. The pollen BF Zone -IV exhibits that the arboreals *Syzygium, Symplocos, Salmalia, Alianthus, Azadirachta, Diospyros, Emblica, Acacia, Zyziphus and Holoptelea* are markedly increased. Pollen percentage of trees *with* fluctuating upgrading values of Acanthcaeae, Faboideae are indicative of moderately warm and humid climate. Percentage of grasses also increased with the new addition of *Lemna*, an aquatic element. The overall assemblage shows tree savannah type vegetation prevailed in the region. The pollen BF Zone- V exhibits more or less similar pollen assemblage as in pollen zone –IV with increased percentage of trees suggesting tree savannah type vegetation flourished in warm and humid climate (Fig. 3).

The pollen data obtained from the investigation of Baneta Formation exposed at Hathnora has provided some significant inferences concerning the vegetational development in the region during late Pleistocene period. On the basis of the pollen/spores recovered from the samples from the Baneta Formation exposed at Hathnora inferred between 12460 to 25340 yr BP, the area was covered with open vegetation constituting the grasses, Chenopodiaceae/Amaranthaceae, Asteraceae and *Artemisia* along with sparsely distributed trees viz., *Syzygium, Symplocos, Azadirachta, Diospyros, Emblica, Acacia and Holoptelea*. The record of marshy elements such as sedges (Cyperaceae) and *Polygonum* together with the aquatic elements *Potamogeton* and *Typha* and algal spores such as *Spirogyra* and *Zygnema* denotes the existence of water bodies/ponds /lakes in the close proximity of the site of investigation. The overall vegetation assemblage is suggestive of the prevalence of a cool and dry climate regime during the period of sediment deposition. A diverse microfossils that include, *Darwinula, Cypridopsis, Ilyocypris, Candona* (Ostrocods) pupilidae indet, *Gyraulus* (gastropods) and vertebrate assemblages like *Hippopotamus palaeindicus, Elephas hysudricus* have also been recorded from the Baneta Formation. The recorded data are indicating Early to Middle Upper Pleistocene in age and also indicate a warm climate, but the terminal part of the Upper Pleistocene may have become dryer as indicated by the presence of wild ass (*Equus hemionus khur*) and ostrich (*Struthio camelus*) (Patnaik, 2000). Bivalve shell from this layer have yielded a radiocarbon age of 35, 660 +/ - 2540 yr BP. From Magnetic susceptibility perspective, Baneta Formation at Hathnora section shows four magneto zones in which BMZ-III zone corroborate pollen BF Zone-III with high (c) values indicative of cooler and direr climate and BMZ-II corroborate with pollen BF Zone-II with low (c) values indicative of comparatively warmer climate. This vegetation scenario and corresponding climatic event is equivalent to the Last Glacial Maximum (LGM) episode which has been globally documented between 18, 000 to 22, 000 yr BP (Bradly, 1999).

## Baneta Formation at Type section, Baneta Village (8740+/-450 yr BP)

At Baneta, the location of the type section, a sample from the carbonaceous clay layer (BS 2278 yielded an age of 8740+/-450 yr BP. The palynological assemblage recorded include *Lemna, Artemisia, Terminalia, Mimosa, Pongamia, Holoptelea, Symplocos, Lagerstroemia, Poaceae, Cyperaceae,* aquatics, ferns and algal remains suggesting existence of tropical deciduous forest and warm and humid climate in the area.

**Kusumelli Swamp (4000 +/- 100 Yr BP)**

The study reveals that around 4000 yr. BP the tree-savannahs was covering the region which chiefly comprised grasses, members of Asteraceae, Chenopodiaceae/Amarantaceae and Malvaceae along with sparsely distributed tress viz. *Holoptelea, Symplocos, Terminalia.* This implies a cool and dry climatic condition with an amelioration trend. Subsequently in the later period the open mixed deciduous forest succeeded the tree-savannah with the sporadic invasion of moist tree taxa viz. *Lagerstroemia, Syzyzium, Mitragyna, Sapotaceae,* together with dry tree taxa such as *Holoptelea, Terminalia.* The representation of *Madhuca indica* and *Lagerstroemia* indicates that the forest was of moist deciduous type and climate was warm and moist type. Chronologically, this phase of the transformation of tree-savannah into mixed deciduous forest coincides with the period of climatic optimum (Benarde, 1996) which has been witnessed globally around 7000-4000 yr. BP. After this climatic optimum, the mixed deciduous forest got enriched with the arboreal taxa viz. Meliaceae, *Bombax, Madhuca indica, Diospyros, Lagerstroemia, Terminalia, Syzygium, Magnifera indica* and *Shorea robusta.* The record of Dipterocarpaceae (*Shorea robusta*) is the most important feature in this vegetational change. This proliferation of forest with increased diversity and immigration of Dipterocarpaceae signify the on set of a regime of south-west active monsoon and consequently moist climate with increased rainfall prevailed in the region. It is important to recognize that timely arrival monsoon contribute favorable conditions, especially for the germination of *Shorea* seeds immediately after their shedding (Meher-Homji, 1996). Since then, region experienced the expansion of the forest with increased number of moist tree types suggesting the active inception of south west monsoon. The whole vegetational assemblage suggests a warm and humid climate more or less similar to climatic condition prevailing today.

## CONCLUSIONS

Palaeovegetation dynamics and corresponding climatic events from pollen analytical investigation of different profiles of study area suggest the following conclusions:

Between Late Middle Pleistocene to Early Upper Pleistocene the area covered by sparse grassland under cool and dry climate. During Late Pleistocene time (~25 to 12 ka) area experienced Five phases of climate in which BF Zone-III, exhibits cool and dry climate, corresponds to Last Glacial Maximum (LGM) episode which has been globally documented to be between 22 to 18 ka (Bradley,1999). In Early Holocene time (~9 ka) the area may have been covered with dry deciduous forest represented by *Terminalia, Mimosa, Pongamia and Artemisia* under amelioration of climate when precipitation was higher than in the earlier formations. During late

Holocene (~4 ka) the valley experienced three climatic Phases in which second phase (Zone-II) exhibits the evidences of invigoration of SW monsoon and third phase (Zone-III) is more or less similar to present day climate conditions. The mammal assemblage from the Baneta Formation, comprising *Stegodon namadicus, Equus namadicus, Hippopotamus namadicus, Sus namadicus and Cuon alpinus*, suggests a warm climate with intermittent arid-humid phase in the Late Middle Pleistocene. Early to Middle Upper Pleistocene vertebrate assemblage including cyprinids fishes, crocodiles, *Hippopotamus palaeindicus, Elephas hysudricus* may indicate a warm climate, but the terminal part of the Upper Pleistocene may have become drier as indicated by the presence of wild ass (*Equus hemionus khur*) and Ostrich (*Struthio camelus*)

From Magnetic susceptibility perspective, Baneta Formation at Hathnora section shows four magnetozones in which BMZ-III zone corroborate pollen Phase-III with high ($\chi$) values indicative of cooler and drier climate and BMZ-II corroborate with pollen Phase-II with low ($\chi$) values indicative of comparatively warmer climate.

## REFERENCES CITED


Agrawal, D.P., Kotlia, B.S., Kusumgar, S. (1988), Chronology and Significance of the Narmada Formations. Proceedings of the Indian National Science Academy 54 (3), 418-424.

Benarde, M.A. (1996), Global Warming. John Wiley & Sons, New York, U.S.A.

Bera, S. K. (1990), Palynology of *Shorea Robusta* (Dipterocarpaceae) in relation to Pollen Production and Dispersal. *Grana* 29: 251-255.

Bera, S.K. (1994), Pollen Dispersal and Sedimentation in Tropical Sal Forest of Madhya Pradesh. *Geophytology* 23: 235-241.

Bradely, R.S. (1999), Palaeoclimatology: Reconstructing Climates of the Quaternary. Harcourt Academic Press, NewYork, USA

Cameron, D., Patnaik, R., Sahni, A. (2004), The Systematic Status of the Middle Pleistocene Narmada hominin from Central India with Comments regarding the Palaeoecology of the Locality. Int. J. Osteoarchaeol. 14(6), 419–447.

Chauhan, M. S. (1994), Modern Pollen/Vegetation Relationship in the Tropical Deciduous Sal (*Shorea robusta*) Forests in Madhya Pradesh. *Jour. Palynology* 30: 165-175.

Chauhan, M. S. (1996), Origin and History of Tropical Deciduous Sal (*Shorea robusta*) Forests in Madhya Pradesh, India *Palaeobotanist* 43: 89-101.

Chauhan, M. S. (2000), Pollen of Late-Quaternary Vegetation and Climate Change in Northeastern Madhya Pradesh, India. *Palaeobotanist* 49: 491-500.

Chauhan, M. S. (2002), Holocene Vegetation and Climate Changes in Southeastern Madhya Pradesh, India. *Current Science 83*: 1444-1445.

De Terra, H., Patterson, T.T., (1939), Studies on the Ice Age in India and Associated Human Culture. Carn. Inst. Washington, Pub.pp. 493.

Erdtman, G. (1943), An Introduction to Pollen Analysis, Waltham, Mass., U.S.A.

Kennedy, K.A.R. (2003), God-apes and Fossil Men: Palaeoanthropology of South Asia. Ann Arbor: University of Michigan Press.

Kennedy, K.A.R., Chiment, J. (1991), The Fossil Hominid from the Narmada Valley, India: *Homo Erectus* and *Homo Sapiens*? In *Indo-Pacific Prehistory 1990*, ed. P. Bellwood, 1:42-58. Canberra: Indo-Pacific Prehistory Association.

Meher-Homji, V. M. (1996), A Bioclimatologist Point of View. *Curr. Sci.* 352-357

Nandi, A. (1997), Palynological Studies on Quaternary Sediments of Central Narmada Valley, Madhya Pradesh. *G.S.I. sp. Pub. No. 46*, 87-90.

Patnaik, R. (2000), Palaeoenvironment of *Homo Erectus* Bearing Pleistocene Narmada Valley Deposits of India. *Bull. Oil Nat. Gas. Corp. Ltd*, 37, 247-249.

Sankhyan, A.R. (1997), A New Human Fossil from the Central Narmada Basin and Its Chronology. *Curr. Sci. 73*, 1110-1111.

Sankhyan, A.R. (2005), New Fossils of Early Stone Age Man from Central Narmada Valley. *Curr. Sci. 88 (5)*, 704-707.

.Sonakia, A. (1984), The Skull Cap of Early Man and Associated Mammalian Fauna from Narmada Valley Alluvium, Hoshangabad Area, Madhya Pradesh, India. *Rec. Geol. Surv. India, 113*, 159-172.

Tiwari, M.P., Bhai, H.Y. (1997), *Quaternary Stratigraphy of the Narmada Valley*. G.S.I. sp. Pub. No. 46, 33-63.

Chapter–12

# Jinniushan Hominin and Modern human Origins

*Karen Rosenberg & Lü Zuné*

## INTRODUCTON

Models of modern human origins have generally been tested in the western part of the Old World (Europe, the Levant and Africa) where the fossil and archaeological record is best known. Both replacement and multiregional models recognize that the evidence shows that modern humans evolved in Africa. They differ in whether modern humans evolved ONLY in Africa and then spread out to replace indigenous populations of archaic humans (Replacement or Out of Africa Model), or whether they evolved throughout the range of human habitation with gene flow between regions (Multiregional Evolution model). It follows, then, that to test these models, we should look outside the continent of Africa, especially at the geographic edges of the human range. In general, the attention of scholars investigating this issue has focused on the western edge of the human range in Europe, but these hypotheses can also be tested at the eastern edge, in East Asia. In this paper we discuss a human fossil at the other extreme edge of the Pleistocene range of human habitation in far northeastern China.

The Jinniushan specimen was discovered near the town of Yinkou, in Liaoning Province in far northeastern China in an isolated karst prominence in a fissure of a collapsed limestone cave (Lü, 1990, 2003). It was excavated in 1984 by a group from the Department of Archaeology at Beijing University led by Lü. The hominid specimen was discovered near the bottom of 15 meters of deposit, in the lower portion of what the excavators defined as Layer 7, which also contained the remains of Pleistocene fauna. Electron-spin resonance and uranium series dating of animal teeth from Layer 7 yield a date of about 260,000 years ago, consistent with the fauna (Chen *et al.*1994). Later dates have been previously reported for this specimen, but they represent an average of dates taken from several stratigraphic levels of the site, including several dates that were higher in the section than the human remains. We are comfortable with a date of approximately 260,000 years ago for Layer 7 and the hominid specimen that it contains.

The individual skeletal elements of the Jinniushan specimen were all found within an area of less than 2 square meters and consist of a cranium, with most of the maxillary dentition, one cervical and five thoracic vertebrae, two left ribs, a complete left ulna, a complete left innominate, a complete left patella and numerous articulated bones of both hands and both feet (*Figure 1*)

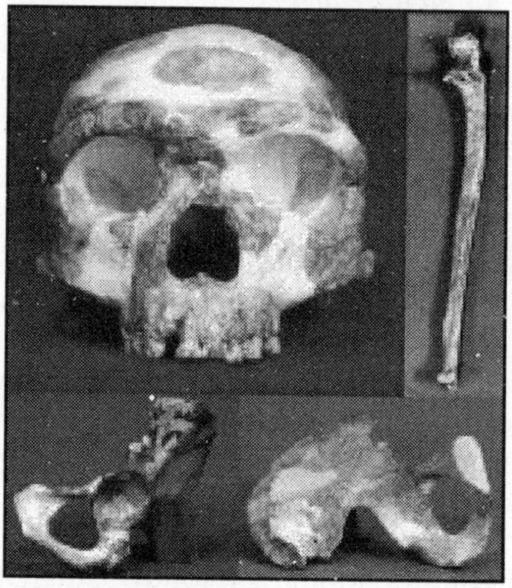

Figure 1: Elements from the Jinniuishan Skeleton.Cranium in Facial View, Left Ulna and Right Innominate (Rosenberg, Lü and Ruff, 2006)

There is no duplication of elements and the joint surfaces of adjacent bones articulate comfortably so that there is no reason to think that more than one individual is represented by these remains. It is one of the few specimens from China (and the only one from before the late Pleistocene) which includes many elements from a single individual.

The Jinniushan specimen is a young adult with some but relatively little wear on the molars. The specimen has been considered both male (Wu, 1988, Wu and Poirier, 1985) and female (Lü, 1995, 2003, Rosenberg, 1998, Rosenberg, Lü and Ruff, 2006, Wolpoff, 1999). The sex of the specimen is particularly important because our analysis involves estimation of stature and body mass which are ideally based on sex-specific regressions. The most reliable indicators of sex in humans such as those described by Phenice (1969) are found on the pelvis, specifically the pubis and they provide the most convincing evidence that the Jinniushan specimen is female. Because of damage to the medial portion of the pubis, it is not possible to evaluate whether there was a ventral arc present on the bone. However, a subpubic concavity is present and the medial aspect of the ischiopubic ramus is ridged rather than flat. According to Phenice (1969), these latter two features alone would classify the Jinniushan specimen as female. The sciatic notch which is generally wider in females than in males in all human populations is intermediate in breadth but shows variation between populations (Rosenberg, 2002). In general Neandertals have narrow sciatic notches (although males are still narrower than females within that sample). The Jinniushan specimen has a sciatic notch of intermediate width. Compared to the Kebara Neandertal specimen from the Levant, another (male) archaic human which preserves a complete innominate, the Jinniushan specimen is gracile in features like the iliac buttress and ischial tuberosity, features which reflect overall postcranial robusticity, again compatible with a sex determination of female. Based on the overall size of the innominate, some scholars have argued that the Jinniushan specimen is a male. However, based on the pelvic morphology, we are convinced of a female diagnosis for this specimen which is further supported by the cranial morphology.

The Jinniushan cranium is robust compared to modern Chinese specimens which was one of the things that led some researchers in the past to conclude that it was male (Wu and Poirier, 1985). However, when compared more appropriately with the Dali specimen, a cranium of similar geological (and developmental) age from Shanxi Province in northwestern China, the Jinniushan specimen is gracile, supporting a diagnosis of female. The Jinniushan cranium has similar outer dimensions to Dali, but has a thinner cranial vault, reflected in a larger estimated cranial capacity (Dali is 1120 cc and Jinniushan is 1280-1300). The Jinniushan supraorbitals are thinner than those of the Dali specimen and the differences between the two penecontemporaneous specimens seem to be well explained by sexual dimorphism.

Human postcranial remains from Chinese Pleistocene sites are extremely rare. In addition, because the morphology of the pelvis has been the center of a number of hypotheses relating to modern human origins and archaic human functional morphology in Europe and the Near East (Rak, 1990, 1991, 1993, Rak and Arensburg 1987, Rosenberg, 1988, 1998; Tague, 1992, Trinkaus, 1976, 1983, 1984), the Jinniushan specimen is particularly important as a comparison with specimens from those regions because it is not from the western Old World but from another extreme periphery of the range of human habitation. The preservation of associated cranial and postcranial elements in a single specimen provides a rare opportunity to estimate body size, pelvic shape, body shape, cranial capacity and finally encephalization for a single individual. Other estimates of these important variables from this time period are derived from sample means of isolated non-associated material from widely ranging specimens. the Jinniushan specimen represents the only known associated postcranial and cranial remains in the hominid fossil record between the earlier WT 15000 specimen from Kenya dated to 1.6 million years (Walker and Leakey 1993) and the later late Pleistocene Levantine material dated to about 122,000 years ago (Grün and Stringer 2000).

We estimated body size for the Jinniushan specimen in two different ways as outlined in Rosenberg, Lu and Ruff (2006). One estimate was based on a combination of stature and biiliac breadth and the other was based on estimated femoral head diameter (which was in turn based on acetabular breadth). These yielded estimates that were within 2.5% of each other and we have used the average of those as our estimate of body mass: 78.6 kg. This estimate makes the Jinniushan specimen the largest known female in the human fossil record, not surprising given the high latitude cold environment in which she lived.

Our estimate of stature was based on the only long bone preserved, the complete left ulna. We used a regression equation derived from a modern reference sample of Europeamerican females, given that the Jinniushan specimen also derives from a high altitude population. Reconstructed stature was 168.78 ± 4.3 cm (Rosenberg, Lü and Ruff, 2006).

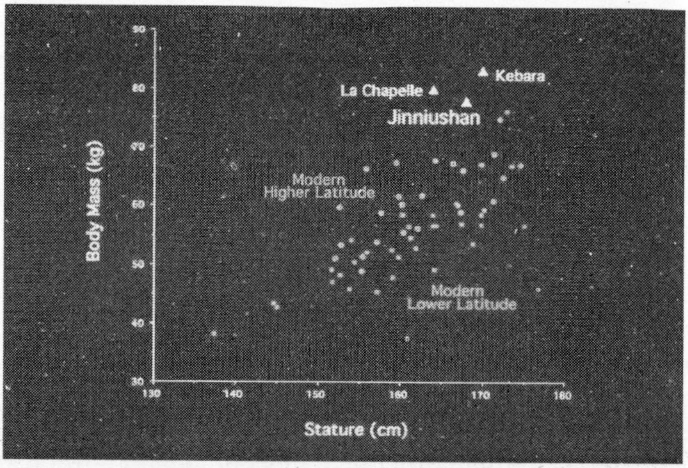


Figure 2: Estimated Body Mass Plotted on the Vertical Axis against Estimated Stature Plotted on the Horizontal Axis. Modern Higher Latitude Populations are Heavier Relative to Stature than Modern Lower Latitude Populations. The Two Neandertals (La Chapelle aux Saints and Kebara) and the Jinniushan Specimen fall Eell above the Modern High Latitude Populations. Data is from Ruff (2002).

Finally, we estimated trunk width based on the innominate bone based on techniques developed by Ruff (1995) and found that the Jinniushan individual had a bi-iliac breadth of about 344 mm (Rosenberg, Lü and Ruff, 2006). These estimates of body size, shape and proportions allow us to compare Jinniushan to the full range of modern humans from different climates. *Figure* 2 shows body mass plotted against stature for some modern populations showing that high latitude populations typically are heavier for a given height than low latitude populations (Ruff, 2002). Jinniushan falls above the modern high latitude populations quite close to the Neandertals who also lived in high latitude on the other side of the old world, consistent with ecogeographic principles (Bergmann's rule), namely a tendency among geographically widespread species to increase in body size in higher latitudes, probably as an adaptation to decrease surface area to body mass in colder climates.. Limb proportions also vary with climate following Allen's rule. *Figure 3* show that populations from regions that are warm today have relatively longer long bones (in this case, the ulna) relative to trunk width than populations from regions that are cold. Like archaic humans from Europe, Jinniushan falls above the modern Inupiats/ Aleuts, also suggesting adaptation to cold climate. In sum, Jinniushan's geographic location in far northern China suggests a cold-adapted population. This is consistent with her morphology, namely a large overall size, a wide trunk and relatively short limb length.

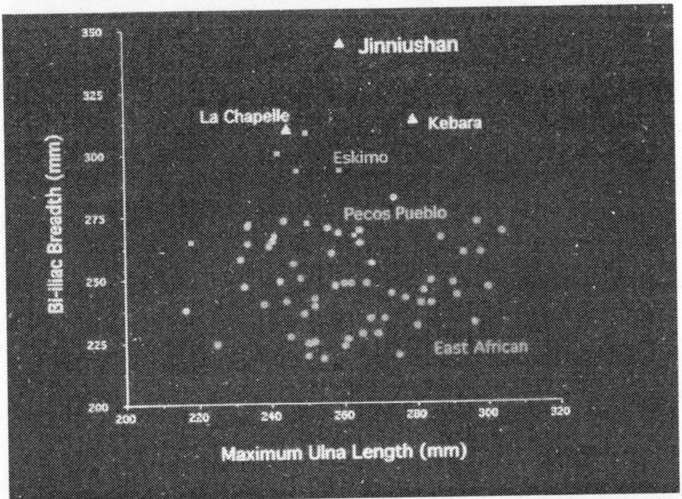


Figure 3: Estimated Bi-iliac Breadth on the Vertical Axis Plotted against Maximum Ulna Length on the Horizontal Axis. Modern individuals from Populations from Colder Regions (in this case Eskimos) have Relatively Wider Trunks (or relatively shorter ulnas) than individuals from Populations from Warmer Regions (in this case East Africa) with individuals from Geographically Intermediate Regions (in this case Pecos Pueblo from the American Southwest) Intermediate. The Neandertals (La Chapelle aux Saints and Kebara) and Jinniushan fall above the Modern Eskimo (Data from Ruff, 2002).

Cranially, the Jinniushan specimen has unusually think cranial walls, a gabled cranial contour, a broad frontal bone, central supraorbital thinning, and gracility of the nuchal plane, all modern features at a very early date in this region of the world that is as far as humans extended from Africa. The supraorbitals in this specimen project far forward and the nuchal torus extends across the entire occipital bone with a distinct straight upper border. All of this means that like the Dali specimen, dating from approximately the same time period in China, Jinniushan has a mosaic or combination of archaic and more modern features a point also made by Etler (1996), Lü (2003) and Wolpoff (1999) and consistent with its middle Pleistocene date.

The cranial capacity of the Jinniushan specimen is about 1300 cc, slightly larger than the 1120 cc size of the male from Dali. The fact that the Jinniushan specimen is the largest female in the human fossil record suggests that this large brain may be related to her large body size. The encephalization quotient of 4.09 based on this associated individual places it comfortably between previous estimates based on sample means from

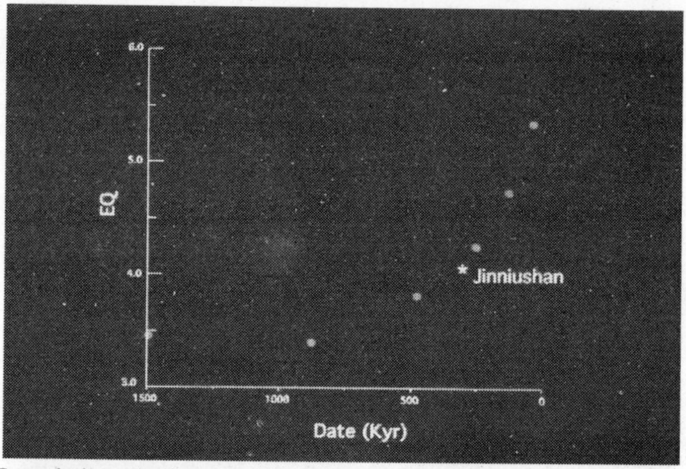


Figure 4: Encephalization Quotient from 1.5 million years ago to present. The Blue Dots are based on Sample Means of Unassociated Specimens, While the Jinniushan Specimen is based on Skeletal Elements from a Single Individual Data from Ruff, Trinkaus and Holiday (1997)

unassociated specimens from else where in the world of 3.82 for middle Pleistocene *Homo* and 4.26 for late middle Pleistocene *Homo* (Figure 4) (Rosenberg, Lü and Ruff, 2006, Ruff, Trinkaus and Holliday, 1997).

Finally, turning to the pelvis, the ilium is large and compared to modern Chinese populations quite robust. An interesting and relevant comparison is with the male Neandertal specimen from Kebara (Rak, 1990, 1991, Rak and Arensburg, 1987). The Kebara specimen is more robust than Jinniushan though it is slightly smaller in both overall dimensions and specifically in the dimensions of the acetabulum. The iliac crest in Kebara is much more sharply curved and sinuous than in Jinniushan and the iliac pillar is stronger, especially near the iliac crest. On both specimens, the iliac pillar is placed far anteriorly on the iliac blade, compared to modern humans, a trait which has been described as typically Neandertal. The ischial tuberosity on the Kebara specimen is much more robust than on Jinniushan and shows the morphology that Rak described as typical of

Neandertals in which the groove for the obturator tendon crosses the surface of the ischial tuberosity. That morphology does not appear on Jinniushan. Most of the differences between Kebara and Jinnisuhan are consistent with sexual dimorphism, with Kebara being male and Jinniushan being female. The body size difference however is not consistent with that and may reflect climatic adaptation as suggested above.

A comparison with the innominate specimen from Arago (Arago XIV which has also been considered female) shows that for all aspects of the innominate that are preserved on both specimens these two specimens from opposite sides of the old world are extremely similar (deLumley and deLumley, 1974). Unfortunately Arago XIV does not preserve the anterior portion of the pelvis so it is not possible to compare the pubic morphology, long believed to be a region in which Neandertals exhibited a unique derived condition compared to other humans.

The complete human pelvis from the Middle Pleistocene of Spain, from Sima de los Huesos at Atapuerca dating to about 200,000 years ago provides an important comparison with the Jinniushan specimen. They are quite similar with almost identical bi-iliac breadths (Arsuaga *et al.* 1999). Like the Sima de los Huesos male specimen, the Jinniushan female shows a pelvic aperture with the same changing cross-sectional dimensions seen in modern humans, suggesting the presence of a rotational birth mechanism like that typical of our species today. This confirms what many scholars of the evolution of human birth have argued that rotational birth like that seen in modern humans probably evolved by the Middle Pleistocene. This suggests that these archaic humans probably benefitted from assistance during childbirth as humans do today.

We have shown elsewhere (Rosenberg 1998) that while the pubis in the female Jinniushan specimen seems to be long by modern standards, it is shorter than the male Kebara and La Ferrassie specimens (the only archaic humans with this anatomy present). This is consistent with the unusual pattern seen in Neandertals in which male pubic bones are actually longer than female pubic bones in absolute terms in contrast to the more typical human pattern in which the pubic bone in females is longer than in males. Like the Neandertals which were long thought to be distinctive (and specifically, uniquely derived) in their pubic morphology, Jinniushan is at the extreme edge of the distribution of modern pubic length, but also at the edge of the distribution of body size. To the extent that Neandertals may be slightly different form modern humans in the length and cross-sectional dimensions of their pubis, Jinniushan fits the same pattern, albeit in a very large individual (again, the largest known female in the human fossil record). This shows evidence of continuity in the morphology of the pelvis across the old world (from one periphery to the other) and suggests that the pelvis in Neandertals does not provide evidence of a uniquely derived condition in these archaic humans from Europe.

The Jinniushan specimen shows a mosaic of cranial and postcranial features, some archaic and others modern. It shows some continuities with other archaic specimens to the west, but clear adaptations to an extreme (cold) climate. The Jinniushan specimen at the extreme northwestern periphery of human habitation in the middle Pleistocene is consistent with a mosaic transition from archaic to modern *Homo sapiens* in China.

## REFERENCES CITED

Arsuaga, Juan-Luis, Carlos Lorenzo, José-Miguel Carretero, Ana Gracia, Ignacio Martinez, Nuria Garcia, José-Maria Bermudez de Castro and Eudald Carbonell (1999), A Complete Human Pelvis from the Middle Pleistocene of Spain. *Nature* 399: 255-258.

Chen, Tiemei, Yang Quan and Wu En (1994), Antiquity of *Homo sapiens* in China. *Nature* 368: 55-56.

deLumley, H. and M. A. deLumley (1974), Pre-Neanderthal Human Remains from Arago Cave in SouthWestern France. *Yearbook of Physical Anthropology* 17: 162-168.

Etler, Dennis A. (1996), The Fossil Evidence for Human Evolution in Asia. *Annual Review of Anthropology* 25: 275-301.

Grün, Rainer and Chris Stringer (2000), Tabun Revisited: Revised ESR Chronology and New ESR and U-series Analyses of Dental Material from Tabun C1. *Journal of Human Evolution* 39: 601-612.

Lü,Zuné (1990), La découverte de l'homme fossile de Jing-niushan: Premiere étude. *L'Anthropologie (Paris)* 94(4): 899-902.

Lü Zuné (1995), Study of the Hip Bone of Jinniushan Man. *Journal of Chinese Antiquity* 2: 1-10.

Lü Zuné (2003), The Jinniushan Hominid in Anatomical, Chronological and Cultural Context. In: *Current Research in Chinese Pleistocene Archaeology* ed. Chen Shen and Susan G. Keates. *British Archaeological Reports International* Series 1179, Oxford: Archaeopress, pp. 127-136.

Phenice, TD (1969), A Newly Developed Visual Method of Sexing the os pubis. *American Journal of Physical Anthropology* 30: 297-302.

Rak, Yoel (1990), On the Differences Between Two Pelvises of Mousterian Context from the Qafzeh and Kebara Caves, Israel. *American Journal of Physical Anthropology* 81: 323-332.

Rak, Yoel (1991), The Pelvis. In: *Le Squelette Moustérien de Kébara* 2. Cahiers de Paléontologie, Editions du CNRS, Paris. pp. 147-156.

Rak, Yoel (1993), Morphological Variation in *Homo Sapiens Neanderthalensis* and *Homo Sapiens* in the Levant: A Biogeographic Model. In *Species, Species Concepts and Primate Evolution* ed. W. H. Kimbel and L. B. Martin. New York: Plenum Press. 523-536.

Rak, Yoel and Baruch Arensburg (1987), Kebara 2 Neanderthal Pelvis: First Look at a Complete Inlet. *American Journal of Physical Anthropology* 73: 227-231.

Rosenberg, Karen R. (1988), The Functional Significance of Neandertal Pubic Length. *Current Anthropology* 29: 595-617.

Rosenberg, Karen R. (1998), Morphological Variation in West Asian Postcrania: Implications for Obstetric and Locomotor Behavior. In: *Neandertals and Modern Humans in Western Asia.* Ed. Takeru Akazawa, Kenichi Aoki and Ofer Bar-Yosef. Plenum Press: New York. 367-379.

Rosenberg, Karen R. (2002), A Late Pleistocene Human Skeleton from Liujiang, China Suggests Regional Population Variation in Sexual Dimorphism in the Human Pelvis. *Variability and Evolution* 10: 5-17.

Rosenberg, Karen R. Lü Zune and Christopher B. Ruff (2006), Body Size, Body Proportions, and Encephalization in a Middle Pleistocene Archaic Human from Northern China. *Proceedings of the National Academy of Sciences* 103: 3552-3556.

Ruff, Christopher B. (1995), Biomechanics of the Hip and Birth in Early *Homo. American Journal of Physical Anthropology* 98: 527-574.

Ruff, Christopher B. (2002), Variation in Human Body Size and Shape. *Annual Review of Anthropology* 31: 211-32.

Ruff, Christopher B., Erik Trinkaus and Trenton W. Holliday (1997), Body Mass and Encephalization in Pleistocene *Homo. Nature* 387: 173-176.

Tague, R. G. (1992), Sexual Dimorphism in the Human Bony Pelvis, with a Consideration of the Neandertal Pelvis from Kebara Cave, Israel. *American Journal of Physical Anthropology* 88: 1-21.

Trinkaus, E. (1976), The Morphology of European and Southwest Asian Neandertal Pubic Bones. *American Journal of Physical Anthropology* 44: 95-104.

Trinkaus, E. (1983), Neandertal Postcrania and Adaptive Shift to Modern Humans. In: *The Mousterian Legacy: Human Biocultural Change in the Upper Pleistocene.* Ed. E. Trinkaus. Oxford: British Archaeological Reports International Series 164. Pp. 165-200.

Trinkaus, E. (1984), Neandertal Pubic Morphology and Gestation Length. *Current Anthropology* 25: 509-514.

Walker, Alan and Richard Leakey (eds.) (1993), *The Nariokotome Homo Erectus Skeleton.* Harvard University Press, Cambridge, Mass.

Wolpoff, Milford H. (1999), *Paleoanthropology* 2nd Edition. McGraw Hill.

Wu, Rukang (1988), The Reconstruction of the Fossil Human Skull from Jinniushan, Yinkou, Liaoning Province and Its Main Features. *Acta Anthropologica Sinica* VII(2): 97-101.

Wu, X and Frank Poirier (1995), *Human Evolution in China: A Metric Description of the Fossils and a Review of the Sites.* Oxford University Press: New York

## CHAPTER–13

# Re-looking at Prehistoric Susunia, West Bengal

*A.R. Sankhyan, L.N. Dewangan, Sheuli Chakraborty, Shashi Prabha, Suvendu Kundu & V.R. Rao*

## INTRODUCTION

After Central Narmada valley, it is the Susunia Upland (86°58¢ 30$^{2}$: 23°25´-26'E) of District Bankura in West Bengal, which appears to be palaeoanthropologically promising area for its Palaeolithic industries found in association with the mammalian fossils. The area had attracted the attention of some notable prehistorians (e.g., Ghosh, 1961; Krishnaswamy, 1961; Sen *et al.*, 1963; Sengupta, 1966; Chakrabarti, 1993; Dutta, 2009) and palaeontologists (e.g., Sastry, 1968; Dutta, 1976; Dassharma *et al.*, 1982; Badam, 1984), and has yielded numerous lithic artefacts to Calcutta University (Bhattacharya, 1987). But it is pertinent to a comprehensive and comparative scientific approach. Of course, it is of great interest to compare Susunia findings with those of the Narmada Valley, where we are carrying out systematic palaeoanthropological explorations and excavations. To get a preliminary comparative idea we conducted a week's short exploratory survey sometimes back and briefly present here our findings and We explored the peneplain area along the western flank of the Susunia *Pahar* (hill) (Figure 1), the small streams-debauching to the bigger stream, Gandheshwary. We also extended our preliminary exploration to the Sali and in the vicinity of Amarkanan hillock in Gangajalghati. The upland West Bengal lies between western Plateau and high lands, bordering Chhotanagpur plateau and the Gangetic delta. The great Indian shield disappears under the Gangetic alluvium in the *rarh* region, 87°E. The peneplain area contains Pleistocene fluvial and aeolian sediments deposited directly on the Plateau bed rock.

## OBSERVATIONS

### Stratigraphic Context

Though, it was so short a visit, we were rewarded with some good mammalian fossils and about 150 lithic artefacts, Lower Palaeolithic to Mesolithic (Microlithic) cultural levels (Figures 2- 4). Invariably, we noticed the weathered quartz as the raw material observed by the senior author in Jharkhand region, whereas the quartzite, which dominates Narmada Palaeolithic, is infrequent. The lithic industry lay scattered in pockets along the hill slope, gullies and palaeochanels. In general, we found one meter thick or so, alluvial-colluvial debris of fragmented quartz, interspersed

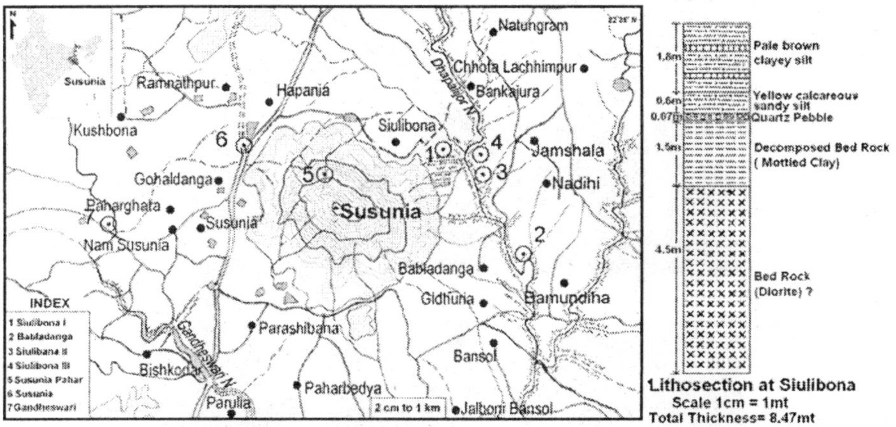


Figure 1: Map and the Site Stratigraphic Section of the Explored Susunia Prehistoric Area, District Bankura, West Bengal

with silt and clay sedimentation that embodies the lithic industry. Only at the *Jhor* bank, the sedimentation at the top horizon shows two meter thickness of the calcareous clay-sand deposition (Figure 1-2). This is in striking contrast to the central Narmada Basin, where we find very thick Quaternary alluvial deposits, invariably 20-30 meters, and going to even over 40 meters, and well sorted into different layers constituting seven distinct formations.

### The Lithic Industry

Our collection of the Palaeolithic tools is comprised of Acheulian handaxes, cleavers and scrapers (Figure 3-4 & Table 1). Typo-technologically these are comparable to the Late Acheulian of the Narmada Valley; we have over 5,000 in our collection at Kolkata. Of course, refinement and artistic skills which we see on the Narmada artefacts, is lacking on Susunia industry. The reason is the coarse quartz as the raw material, which is more friable and less durable. The microliths include almost all categories, but dominated by beautiful blades, lunates, points and scrapers.

Figure 2: Susunia Landscape and Quaternary Deposits Containing Fossils and Lithic Artefacts in Situ

Figure 3: Main Palaeolithic Implements (I-VII) from Susunia Recovered from the Sites Mentioned in the Area Map (Fig. 1)

**Table 1**
**Susunia Stone Tool Collection Classified**

| *Tool Typology* | *N* | *Percentage* | *Tool Typology* | *N* | *Percentage* |
|---|---|---|---|---|---|
| CHOPPER | 1 | 0.68 | CHOPPER | 1 | 0.68 |
| CHOPPING TOOL | 4 | 2.72 | CHOPPING TOOL | 4 | 2.72 |
| CLEAVER | 3 | 2.04 | CLEAVER | 3 | 2.04 |
| HANDAXE | 10 | 6.8 | HANDAXE | 10 | 6.8 |
| pyriform | 2 | *20* | SCRAPER | 76 | 51.7 |
| ovate | 2 | *20* | POINT | 14 | 9.53 |
| lanceolate | 1 | *10* | AWL | 1 | 0.68 |
| pointed | 1 | *10* | FLUTTED CORE | 2 | 1.36 |
| pear | 1 | *10* | KNIFE | 21 | 14.28 |
| elongated | 1 | *20* | BLADE | 6 | 4.08 |
| oblong | 1 | *10* | SPHEAR HEAD | 6 | 4.08 |
| *Total* | 10 | 6.8 | DENTICULATED | 2 | 1.36 |
| SCRAPER | 76 | 51.7 | UNFINISHED | 1 | 0.68 |
| biconvex | 6 | *7.89* | Grand Total | 147 | 100 |
| double sided | 2 | *2.63* | | | |

## The Fossil Collection

We observed that the fossils in general, are in very fragile condition and crumble if not handled with utmost care. Quite a few ones are well preserved, especially those which are trapped in the hard calcrete matrix. But, being covered with the hard matrix, these remain elusive to a non-palaeontologist collector. Again, it is quite a tedious and skillful task to remove the attached matrix to prepare the specimens for morphological observations and metric study.

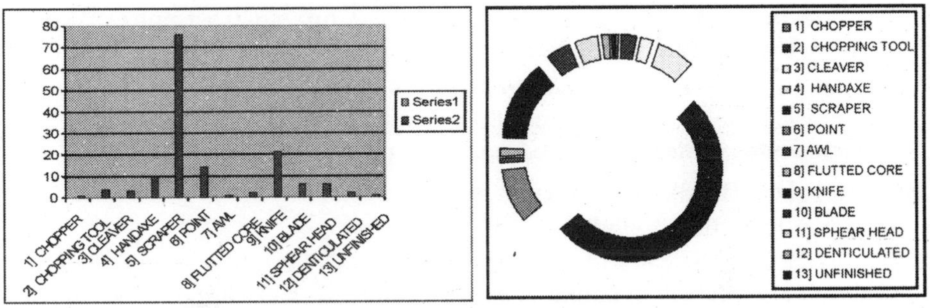


Figure 4: Pictorial Representation of the Main Tool-Types

The fossil collection consists of dentition and bone fragments, and at Susunia we visualize a parallel of the Late Middle Pleistocene to the early Late Pleistocene of the Narmada fauna. Our possession include the upper dentition of *Equus namadicus,* upper and lower dentition and an incisor of *Bos namadicus,* the fragment of an antler of a cervid, probably *Axix axix,* besides some mammalian bone fragments (Figure 5).

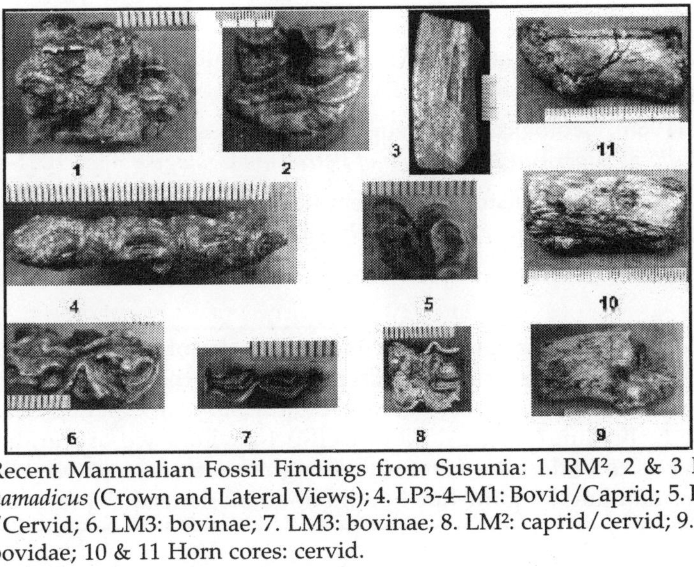


Figure 5: Recent Mammalian Fossil Findings from Susunia: 1. RM$^2$, 2 & 3 RM$^1$: *Equus namadicus* (Crown and Lateral Views); 4. LP3-4–M1: Bovid/Caprid; 5. LM$^1$: Caprid /Cervid; 6. LM3: bovinae; 7. LM3: bovinae; 8. LM$^2$: caprid/cervid; 9. Ulnar frag: bovidae; 10 & 11 Horn cores: cervid.

Pending any absolute dating, on the basis of stratigraphy, mammalian fossils and Palaeolithic industry, we tentatively believe that the earliest Susunia Palaeolithic is quite younger <200 Kya The prospects of human fossils cannot be ruled out, although we see only a small fossiliferous stretch in the area we examined. Next time we hope to extend our explorations to a wider area and may also decide where to excavate.

## REFERENCES CITED

Badam, G. L. (1984), Pleistocene Faunal Succession of India in R.O. Whyte (ed.) *The Evolution of the East Asian Environment Vol. 2*, pp. 746-775. Centre of Asian Studies, University of Hong Kong.

Bhattacharyya, M. (1987), Stages of Prehistoric Culture in *Rarh* Bengal (A Recent Exploration), in B.M. Pande, and B.D. Chattopadhyaa (eds) *Archaeology and history: Essays in Memory of A. Ghosh, Vol. I*, pp 47-52 , New Delhi.

Chakrabarti, D.K. (1993), *Archaeology of Eastern India: Chhotonagpur Plateau and West Bengal.* Munshiram Manoharlal, Delhi.

Dassharma D. C. S. Biswas and A. Nandi (1982), Fossil Vertebrates from the Late Quarternary Deposits of Bankura, Burdwan and Purulia Districts, West Bengal. *Mem. Geol. Surv. India (Pal. Indica).* XLIV (New Series): 1-65.

Dutta, A K. (1976), Occurrence of Fossil Lion and Spotted Hyaena from Pleistocene Deposits of Susunia, Bankura, West Bengal. *Journal Geological Society of India.* 17(3): 386-391.

Dutta, A K. (2009), Understanding Acheulian Culture in the Gandheswari River Valley, Bankura, West Bengal, India. In R. Ray & V. Jayaswal (eds) *Status of Prehistoric Studies in the Twenty-first Century in India*, pp.25-33. BAR International Series 1924, Archaeopress, England.

Ghosh, A. K. (1961), Prehistoric Studies in Eastern India. *Science and Culture* 27 (8): 369-375.

Sen, D., Ghosh, A. K. & Chatterjee, M. (1963), Palaeolithic Industry of Bankura, West Bengal. *Man in India.* 43 (2): 100-113.

Sengupta, S. (1966), Geological and Geophysical Studies in Western Part of Bengal Basin. *Bulletin American Association of Petroleum Geologist* 50(5) 1001-1017.

Sastry, M. V. A. (1968), Pleistocene Vertebrates from Susunia, Bankura District, West Bengal. *Indian Minerals* 20(2): 195-197.

We thank Mr. Abhijit Sengupta, the Secretary, Ministry of Culture, who desired us to present an urgent assessment report on the area in the light of a newspaper press release on Susunia by Professor M.B. Bhattacharya of Calcutta University and Dr. G. L. Badam (IGNCA, New Delhi) to whom we are grateful for encouraging us to undertake the study, though unfortunately, due to official compulsions and hurry a joint study could not materialized

CHAPTER–14

# Indian Palaeolithic Transitions

*A. R. Sankhyan & Indu Talwar*

## INTRODUCTION

An overview of the Palaeolithic diversity of the Old World may reveal five/six major cultural transitions. The earliest was the Oldowan/Early Acheulian transition, limited almost to the African continent and associated with *Homo habilis/Homo erectus* evolution. It could have been parallel to the Pre-Soanian/Soanian transition in the Potwar sub-Himalayan region of South Asia. It was followed by the Early/Late Acheulian transition recorded extensively in Africa, Asia and Europe with the spread of *Homo erectus*. Followed by in succession was the Late Acheulian/Middle Palaeolithic transition equally extensive in Africa, Europe and Asia, which serves a window to see the emergence and spread of archaic *Homo sapiens* and Neanderthals. But, the evolution and dispersion of anatomically modern *Homo sapiens* is witnessed during the subsequent Middle Palaeolithic/Upper Palaeolithic transition during late Pleistocene. The end of the Upper Palaeolithic is followed by the agro-pastoral Mesolithic and/or the Neolithic modern human populations that colonized the entire world during late Holocene.

Indian or South Asian Palaeolithic diversity is conspicuous in *three* typo-technological cultural complexes, viz., the sub-Himalayan Soanian, the peninsular Acheulian, and the north-eastern Hoabinhinian and Upper Annyathian (Sankhyan, 2009). The first two are the major Palaeolithic cultural complexes and debated on their evolutionary development-whether the Acheulian has evolved from the Soanian/ Chopper-Chopping complex or they coexisted or are supplementary or created by two different types of people or species. To appreciate the *Homo erectus-Homo sapiens* interface, it is necessary to understand these complexes.

## PRE-SOANIAN/SOANIAN TRANSITION

It is not conspicuous even though Soanian is reported from Lower Pleistocene of Potwar (Rendell & Dennell, 1985). The Soanian complexes are regarded creations of *Homo erectus*- a 'big game hunter' as documented by fossils of elephants, rhinos, hippos, equids, bovids and cervids. In fact, hominid fossil evidences associated with the pebble-cobble lithic cultures of south and Southeast Asia are scarce, documented in China and Indonesia only during Lower Pleistocene as the eastern group of the *Homo erectus* found at Lentien, Djetis, Trinil and Zoukoudian; the subspecies, "*Sinanthropus*" was the author of the Zoukoudian culture as was "*Pithecanthropus*" in Sangrian 2 and Trinil. The same hominins were presumably present in the Indian subcontinent (Pakistan, India, Nepal and Bangladesh) and from the adjoining regions (like Myanmar and Malaya) presumed.

Mohapatra (1981, 1990, and 2007) viewed a remarkable individuality of the Soanian unlike other pebble-cobble tool cultures, and noted that it flourished through three successive evolutionary stages- Early, Late and Evolved/Final Soan, spanning the period from Middle Pleistocene to Early Holocene. Soanian tools are typo-technologically distinctive non-biface or "pebble chopper/chopping", made on pre-planned/well-chosen handy rounded/oblong quartzite pebbles/cobbles flaked partially with the cortex retained on the butt. They portray independent evolution in three successive stages- 'Early, Late and Evolved/Final Soan' during Middle Pleistocene to Early Holocene, but are mostly restricted to the *duns* (Mohapatra, 2007) and occasionally in Frontal Range where we also find sporadic occurrences of the Acheulian in surface contexts.

## EARLY/LATE ACHEULIAN TRANSITION:

Unlike Soanian, Acheulian- a biface or "handaxe-cleaver" culture occurs predominantly in the peninsular region and also evolved independently into Late, Middle and Late developmental stages. The Acheulian man had splitted large tubular boulders for preparing cores modified into handaxes, cleavers, chopping tools, including discoids, spears, scrapers, etc. The handaxes are bifacial as they are flaked on both surfaces with a sharp cutting edge almost all-round, and generally larger (up to 13" long) than the Soanian cobble choppers, and vary in shapes from pear to pyriform and circular to ovate. The Handaxe could be used as a general purpose butchering-tool sometimes also thrown as a missile, and the cleavers used as cutting axes by hand for the flesh or wood or when tanged by hafting to a wooden stick.

Indian Acheulian in general shows some differences (Pappu, 2001, 2002), yet it is technologically similar to the Old World (African and European) Acheulian (McPherron, 2000; Noll and Petraglia, 2003). Early

Acheulian as distinguished by symmetrical and unrefined bifaces and cleavers, etc. is quite sparse in India, with only a few sites, such as Bori dated to 670 Kya (Mishra *et al.*, 1995) and Isampur dated to 1.27 Mya (Paddayya *et al.*, 2002) present stratified evidence suggesting the earliest human occupation of South Asia during Lower Pleistocene. Presence of Oldowan in the name of "Mahadevian" was visualised in Central Narmada valley by Khatri (1961), though not yet fully ascertained.

The Late Acheulian, marked by great refinement and symmetry of the bifaces, has been the most preponderant type in entire peninsular India/subcontinent during Middle and Upper Pleistocene, but mostly found in surface and variety of geomorphological or ecological contexts (Pappu, 2001). Some important reported examples are found in the studies of Khatri (1961, 1966), Armand (1985), Jacobson (1985), Misra (1985, 1989, 1995, 1998, 2001), Misra and Mate (1995), Paddayya *et al.* (2002), Clark (1998), Noll and Petraglia (2003), Chauhan (2003), etc.

Middle Acheulian is merely a 'transition' between Early and Late Acheulian (Jayaswal, 1978, 1982, 2009). Central Narmada Valley presents unique stratified context of the Late Acheulian (H. de Lumley & Sonakia, 1985, Bhattacharya & Sonakia, 1989, Badam *et al.*, 1986, Sankhyan, 1997 a, b, 2005). The Late Acheulian are found near sources of raw material, such as gravel or conglomerate beds and within sandy-pebbly gravel horizons; generally overlying the basal boulder gravels comprising Lower Palaeolithic artefacts (Guzder, 1980). The diminutive choppers and handaxes of the Middle Palaeolithic (Guzder, 1980; Tewari *et al.*, 2002; Corvinus, 2002) could be pointers of a divide between the 'light-duty' assemblages of the Middle Palaeolithic and the 'heavy-duty' assemblages of the Lower Palaeolithic. We may also visualise a local evolution of the former from the latter.

Unlike that of the pebble-cobble cultures, hominid affiliation of the Acheulian is much better documented. It was the culture of the *Homo erectus* of the fully developed form and diversity. Appearance of this culture is almost simultaneous in Africa and Europe. While its earlier form named *Homo ergaster* is associated with the beginning of this culture in Africa; in Europe it is named as *Homo antecessor* discovered from deposits dated to Lower Pleistocene and early Middle Pleistocene (1.6 to 1.3 my in Spain).

## THE LATE ACHEULIAN/MIDDLE PALAEOLITHIC TRANSITION:

But the main course of the Acheulian in the Old World is attributed to *Homo neanderthalensis*, though wide spread in Europe, had touched Africa and Asia as well. However this culture is found in very advanced form in several pockets in Asia during the Upper Pleistocene authored by the new hominid–an archaic form of *Homo sapiens*–morphologically close to modern man. This late Acheulian hominid affiliation as noted from Hathnora (Narmada valley, India), Mughared-es-Skhul (Mt Carmel) and Djbel

Kafzeh (Gailee) is likely to include the Siwalik Frontal Range Acheulian (hominid) whose tool outfit appears to be similarly late and advanced. The Late Acheulian tools were more refined, symmetrical and thinner since a soft-hammer or bone or antler was used to remove thinner and larger flakes in a regular way on both sides of the handaxes. The author and co-workers (Sankhyan *et al.*, 2007; Sankhyan, 2009) have found abundant symmetrical large ovate bifaces, U/V-shaped cleavers including large but thin chopping tools from the U1 cemented gravel stratum, whose upper part has yielded human fossils and is sandwiched by the U2 stratum having yielded Middle Palaeolithic tools. We see a gradual decrease in size turning into diminutive choppers, handaxes and tortoise cores, besides addition of the specialized tools like knives, scrapers, spear heads, etc., made on Levalloisian flakes and cores by prepared-core technique, plus inclusion of new raw material, such as the fine-grained chert, jasper, agate, quartz and chalcedony. Such simple Mousterian-like Levalloisian flake and core tools were used by Neanderthals in Europe and late archaic *Homo sapiens* in Africa and Southwest Asia 100 Kya as successful cultural adaptations to diverse environments around the world including the temperate and sub-arctic regions of the northern hemisphere with specialized big game hunting.

In fact, we find mixing of both Late Acheulian and the Middle Palaeolithic implements on the fossil hominin and other sites, also observed elsewhere (Jayaswal, 1974; 1978, Mishra, 1995). It is the evidence of transition and gradual local evolution as a result of distinct shift in land-use or it is due to immigration and replacement by early *Homo sapiens*. Similar transition has occurred at the Middle/Late Soan juncture in sub-Himalayas likely independent of the peninsular event. The Soanian and the Acheulian cultures appear separated by an imaginary Movius Line, but sometimes diffused due to overlap or exchanges or hybridization between the two peoples as is interpreted from the sporadic surface occurrences of the Acheulian in the Soanian region and the *vice versa*. This has happened during Holocene in the Frontal Range though not in the *duns*. However, occurrences of the chopper/chopping tools in the Acheulian Handaxe-cleaver Complex of Narmada valley and elsewhere could actually be mainly due to specific activities, and rarely due to exchanges/trading or capture/re-occupation of the sites by the non-Acheulian man and the tools technologically look part of the same culture. On the eastern end of India, we see a late arrival (35 Kya) of the Lower Palaeolithic in Tripura showing unique innovation of stone tools made on silicified fossil wood (Ramesh, 1986), yet typo-technologically they have Hoabinhinian and Upper Annyathian affinities of Burma and South East Asia (Sankhyan, 2007).

## THE MIDDLE/UPPER PALAEOLITHIC TRANSITION

Appearance of Upper Palaeolithic in archaeological record is viewed with the appearance of the anatomically modern *Homo sapiens*. This *Homo erectus-Homo sapiens* Interface is much debated and explained either by replacement due to inter-continental migrations out of Africa, or by regional continuity or parallel evolution. But, partial assimilation and hybridization could also be visualized in South China, Java, Narmada valley of India, etc. Located near the banks and mostly in surface contexts, the Upper Palaeolithic stone tool kit of Narmada valley is, like any other blade flake industry, abundant in diversified small blade tools types such as knives, side scrapers, projectile points/ spears and arrow-heads, borers/ drills, awls, and burins, made largely on igneous rock nodules of quartz, chert, agate, jasper, chalcedony and sometimes obsidian. They are on thin and nearly parallel-sided flakes, at least twice as long as wide triangular or trapezoidal in cross-section and of standardized shapes struck off from a prepared core usually by punch flaking by using indirect percussion. Compared to the earlier Middle Palaeolithic core and flake tools, the blade flakes were far more efficient due to long sharp cutting edges, and therefore related to higher selective behaviours for raw material curation and exploitation, other symbolic behaviours reflecting increased mental and cultural capabilities of the man.

## UPPER PALAEOLITHIC/MESOLITHIC/NEOLITHIC TRANSITION

The unusual feature in the lithic succession in the sub-Himalayas is the absence of the traditional Mesolithic– a transitional techno-cultural stage between the Palaeolithic hunting/food-gathering and the Neolithic food production. The Palaeolithic is directly succeeded by the Neolithic in the sub-Himalayan warm and moist periglacial terrain abundant in vegetation and animals. For instance in Tripura while the oldest terrace contains Palaeolithic implements, the younger terraces contain Neolithic tools are dated to ca.3500 to 1100 years B.P. (Ramesh, 1986). It is the other way round in the Peninsular India/South Asia, showing absence of Neolithic but wide occurrences of the Mesolithic or microlithic culture. We see a total absence of the Neolithic in the Vindhyan-Satpura confinements of Narmada valley abundant in Mesolithic culture.

In fact, the central Narmada valley alone provides unique encapsulated archaeological evidence from Lower Palaeolithic to Mesolithic, including the prehistoric rock art, and therefore was the region of intense human activity throughout the Stone Age. Evidences reveal that the Narmada valley had enjoyed a warm and equable climate during the Quaternary period, which, coupled with its strategic mid-continental place between East and West, made it one of the east-west passages of the prehistoric man during Middle to Late Pleistocene. In other words, the Vindhyan-

Satpura confinement of Narmada Valley served as a haven and refuge or a paradise to the prehistoric humans in South Asia.

## REFERENCE CITED


Armand, J. (1985), The Emergence of the Handaxe Tradition in Asia, with Special Reference to India. In *Recent Advances in Indo-Pacific Prehistory*. Edited by V.N. Misra and P. Bellwood, pp. 3-8. New Delhi: Oxford & IBH Publishing Co.

Badam, G. L., R.K. Ganjoo, R.K.G. Salahuddin, and S.N. Rajaguru (1986), Evolution of Fossil Hominin- The Maker of Late Acheulian Tools at Hathnora, Madhya Pradesh, India. *Current Science* 55 (3): 143-145.

Bhattacharya, D.K. and A. Sonakia (1989), Cultural Remains from the Earliest Hominid Site on Narmada. In *Changing Perspectives of Anthropology in India*. Edited by S.C. Tiwari, pp. 313 - 320. New Delhi: Today and Tomorrow's Printers and Publishers.

Chauhan, P.R. (2003), An Overview of the Siwalik Acheulian & Reconsidering Its Chronological Relationship with the Soanian–A Theoretical Perspective. *Assemblage* 7.

Clark, J.D. (1998), The Early Palaeolithic of the Eastern Region of the Old World in Comparison to the West. In *Early Human Behaviour in Global Context: The Rise and Diversity of the Lower Palaeolithic Record*. Edited by M. Petraglia and R. Korisettar, pp. 437-450. New York: Routledge Press.

Corvinus, G. (2002), Arjun 3, a Middle Palaeolithic Site, in the Deokhuri Valley, Western Nepal. *Man and Environment* XXVII (2), 31-44.

Dennell, R.W. (2003), Dispersal and Colonization, Long and Short Chronologies: How Continuous is the Early Pleistocene Record for Hominids Outside East Africa? *Journal of Human Evolution* 45, 421-440.

Guzder, S. (1980), Quaternary Environment and Stone Age Cultures of the Konkan (Coastal Maharashtra, India). Pune: Deccan College Postgraduate and Research Institute.

Jacobson, J. (1985), Acheulian Surface Sites in Central India." In *Recent Advances in Indo-Pacific Prehistory*. Edited by V.N. Misra and P. Bellwood, pp.49-57. New Delhi: Oxford & IBH Publishing Co.

Jayaswal, V. (1974), A Techno-typological Review of the Middle Palaeolithic Cultures of India. *Puratattva* 7, 12-16.

Jayaswal, V. (1978), *Palaeohistory of India–A Study of the Prepared Core Technique*. New Delhi: Agam Kala Prakashan.

Jayaswal, V. (1982), *Chopper-Chopping Component of Palaeolithic India*. Delhi: Agam Kala Prakashan.

Jayaswal, V. (2009), Prehistoric India: Assessment & Prospects in the Twenty-first Century, in R. Ray & V. Jayaswal (eds) *Status of Prehistoric Studies in the Twenty-first Century in India*, pp. 3-11. BAR International Series 1924, Archaeopress, England.

Kennedy, K.A.R. and J. Chiment (1991), The Fossil Hominid from the Narmada Valley, India: *Homo Erectus* or *Homo Sapiens*? In *Indo-Pacific Prehistory*. Edited by P. Bellwood, pp. 42-58. Canberra: Indo-Pacific Prehistory Association,.

Khatri, A. P. (1961), Stone Age and Pleistocene Chronology of the Narmada Valley. *Anthropos* 56: 519-30.

Khatri, A.P. (1966), Origin and Evolution of Hand-axe Culture in the Narmada Valley (Central India). In *Studies in Prehistory (Robert Bruce Foote Memorial Volume)*. Edited by D. Sen and A.K. Ghosh, pp. 96-121. Calcutta: Firma K.L. Mukhopadhyay.

Lumley, H. DE and A. Sonakia (1985), Contexte Stratigraphique et Archaeologique de L'Homme de le Narmada, Hathnora, Madhya Pradesh, Inde. *L'Anthropologie* 89: 3-12.

Lumley, M.-A. and A. Sonakia (1985), Premiere de coaverte d'un *Homo erectus* sur le continent Indien A. Hathnora, dans la Moyenne Vallee de la Narmada. *L'Anthropologie* 89: 13 - 61.

Mcpherron, S.P. (2000), Handaxes as a Measure of the Mental Capabilities of Early Hominids. *Journal of Archaeological Science* 27, 655–663.

Mishra, S. (1994), "The South Asian Lower Palaeolithic." *Man and Environment* XIX (1-2), 57-72.

Mishra, S. (1995), Chronology of the Indian Stone Age: The Impact of Recent Absolute and Relative Dating Attempts. *Man and Environment*, XX (2), 11-16.

Mishra, S., Venkatesan, T.R., & B.L.K. Somayajulu (1995), Earliest Acheulian Industry from Peninsular India. *Current Anthropology* 36 (5), 847-51.

Misra, V.N. (1985), The Acheulian Succession at Bhimbetka. In *Recent Advances in Indo-Pacific Prehistory*. Edited by V.N. Misra and P. Bellwood, pp. 35-47. Oxford & IBH Publishing Co.

Misra, V.N. (1989), "Stone Age India: An Ecological Perspective." *Man and Environment* XIV, 17-64.

Misra, V.N. (1995), Geoarchaeology of the Thar Desert, Northwest India. In *Quaternary Environments and Geoarchaeolgy of India*. Edited by S. Wadia, R. Korisettar and V.S. Kale, pp. 210-230. Bangalore: Geological Society of India.

Misra, V.N. (1998), Middle Pleistocene adaptations in India. In The *Pleistocene Old World- Regional Perspectives*. Edited by O. Soffer, pp. 99-119. New York: Plenum Press,

Misra, V.N. (2001), Prehistoric Human Colonization of India. *Journal of Bioscience* 26 (4), 491-531.

Misra, V.N. and M.S. Mate (Editors). (1995), *Indian Prehistory: 1964*. Pune: Deccan College Post-graduate and Research Institute.

Mohapatra, G.C. (1981), Acheulian Discoveries in the Siwalik Frontal Range. *Current Anthropology* 22 (4): 433-435.

Mohapatra, G.C., (1990), On the Track of Early Man in Western Sub-Himalayas, *Presidential Address at the 77th Session of the Indian Science Congress, Anthropology and Archaeology Section*, Cochin.

Mohapatra, G.C. (2007), Lithic Cultures of the Sub-Himalayas. In A.R. Sankhyan & V.R. Rao (eds) *Human Origins, Genome & People of India: Genomic,*

*Palaeontological & Archaeological Perspectives*, pp. 138-143. New Delhi: Allied Publishers.

Noll, M. and M.D. Petraglia (2003), Acheulean Bifaces and Early Human Behavioural Patterns in East Africa and South India. In *Multiple Approaches to the Study of Bifacial Technologies*. Edited by M. Soressi and Dibble, pp. 31-53. Philadelphia: University of Pennsylvania Press.

Paddayya, K. (1987), The Place of the Study of Site Formation Processes in Prehistoric Research in India. In *Natural Formation Processes and the Archaeological Record*. Edited by D.T. Nash and M.D. Petraglia, pp. 74-85. BAR International Series 352.

Paddayya, K. (1994), Investigation of Man-environment Relationships in Indian Archaeology: Some Theoretical Considerations. *Man and Environment*, 19 (1-2): 1-28.

Paddayya, K., B.A.B. Blackwell, R. Jhaldiyal, M.D. Petraglia, S. Fevrier, S., D.A. Chaderton II, J.I.B. Blickstein, and A.R. Skinner (2002), Recent Findings on the Acheulian of the Hunsgi and Baichbal Valleys, Karnataka, with Special Reference to the Isampur Excavation and Its Dating. *Current Science* 83 (5): 641–647.

Pappu, R.S. (2001), *Acheulian Culture in Peninsular India*. New Delhi: D.K. Printworld (P) Ltd.

Pappu, R.S. (2002), The Lower Palaeolithic Culture of India. In *Recent Studies in India Archaeology*. Edited by K. Paddayya, pp. 17-59. New Delhi: Munshiram Manoharlal Publishers Pvt. Ltd.

Ramesh, N.R. (1986), Discovery of Stone Age Tools from Tripura and Its Relevance to the Prehistory of South East Asia. Geosea V Proceedings, Vol. II, Geol. Soc. Malaysia, Bull. 20:289-310.

Rendell, H. and R.W. Dennell (1985), Dated Lower Palaeolithic Artifacts. *Current Anthropology*. 26 (3): 393.

Sankhyan, A. R. (1997a), Fossil Clavicle of a Middle Pleistocene Hominin from the Central Narmada Valley, India. *Journal of Human Evolution* (London) **32**: 3-16.

Sankhyan, A. R. (1997b), A New Human Fossil find from the Central Narmada Basin and Its Chronology. *Current Science* 73 (12): 1110-1111.

Sankhyan, A.R. (1999), The Place of Narmada Hominin in the Jigsaw Puzzle of Human Origins. In *Quaternary of India*. Edited by M.P. Tiwari and D.M. Mohabey, *pp. 335-345 Gondvana Geological Magazine Spl. Publ.*

Sankhyan, A.R. (2005), New Fossils of Early Stone Age Man from Central Narmada Valley. *Current Science* 88 (5): 704-707.

Sankhyan, A.R. (2009), Human Bio-Cultural Diversity in Prehistoric-to-Protohistoric India. In R. Ray & V. Jayaswal (eds) *Status of Prehistoric Studies in the Twenty-first Century in India*, pp.67-74. Proceedings of the Uisppxv Congress, held in September 2006 in Lisbon, Portugal. BAR International Series 1924, Archaeopress, England.

Sankhyan, A.R., D.P. Halder, R. Chatterjee, J. PAUL, R. Chakravarty & V.R. Rao (2007), Narmada Project: A Brief Note on the Recent Stone Implements and

Fossil Faunal Findings. In A.R. Sankhyan & V.R. Rao (eds) *Human Origins, Genome & People of India: Genomic, Palaeontological & Archaeological Perspectives*, pp. 218-224. New Delhi: Allied Publishers.

Sonakia, A. (1984), The Skull Cap of Early Man and Associated Mammalian Fauna from Narmada Valley Alluvium, Hoshangabad Area, M.P. (India). *Records Geological Survey of India 113*:159-172.

CHAPTER–15

# Hobbits and Pygmies: Trends in Evolution

*Anneke H. van Heteren & A. R. Sankhyan*

## INTRODUCTION

Evidence for a population of diminuative hominins, named *Homo floresiensis*, is yielded from excavations at Liang Bua, a large limestone cave on the island of Flores in eastern Indonesia (Brown et al., 2004; Morwood et al., 2005). *Homo floresiensis*, the holotype LB1, is a very strange creature compared to both *Homo sapiens* and *Homo erectus s.l.*. Its height is approximately 1 m, much smaller than both *Homo sapiens* and *Homo erectus s.l.*, and its cranial capacity is estimated to be between 380 and 430 cc (Brown et al., 2004; Falk et al., 2005; Jacob et al., 2006). The finds comprise the remains of several individuals, including one cranium and two mandibles. The remains share features with *Homo erectus s.l.*, but they also display features not seen in either *Homo erectus s.l.* or *Homo sapiens*.

There are several opinions about the origin of *Homo floresiensis*. One of the current hypotheses states that *Homo floresiensis* is a dwarfed descendent of *Homo erectus s.l.* (Brown et al., 2004; Morwood et al., 2005; van Heteren and de Vos, 2007). A second hypothesis states that LB1 is a pathological individual of *Homo sapiens* (Henneberg and Thorne, 2004; Jacob et al., 2006; Martin et al., 2006). According to a third hypothesis *Homo floresiensis* was descended from an early hominin, such as *Australopithecus* or *Homo habilis* (Morwood in Bower, 2005; Argue et al., 2006; Argue et al., 2007).

The original hypothesis of Brown et al. (2004) is intriguing and will be expanded upon.

## ISLAND ADAPTATIONS IN MAMMALS

Heterochrony is responsible for many of the physiological changes which island morphotypes underwent in relation to their ancestors as will be xplained below. Heterochrony refers to the timing or rate of one developmental process in the body changing during evolution relative to the rate of another developmental process (Ridley, 2003). Pedomorphosis is an example of heterochrony and occurs when an organism reproduces in the ancestral juvenile state. There are two heterochronic causes for pedomophosis (Ridley, 2003). The first is neoteny, where somatic development slows down in absolute time, whereas reproduction development proceeds at the same rate. The second is progenesis, where reproductive development accelerates, whereas somatic development proceeds at a constant rate.

Heterochrony is a feature which endemic island animals can display in respect to their ancestors. One of the potential effects of this heterochrony is dwarfing. In some cases pedomorphic features have been described in the literature for island species, such as for dwarfed elephants (Bromage et al., 2002; Palombo, 2001, 2003) and *Myotragus* (Bover and Alcover, 1999).

There are several changes in endemic island mammals compared to their ancestors which occur so frequently that they can be considered patterns. A change in size is the most obvious one and is described by Foster (1964). When mammals display gigantism on islands a possible mechanism is hypermorphosis (Caloi and Palombo, 1996), which is the exact opposite of progenesis and also a form of heterochrony. The most common change in large mammals is a reduction in size, as in Proboscidea (van den Bergh, 1999; van den Bergh et al., 2001).

When dwarfism occurs in endemic island animals the limbs often show relatively more shortening than the rest of the body, sometimes associated with an increase of the robusticity of the limbs, such as in *Myotragus* from Mallorca (Leinders and Sondaar, 1974; Spoor, 1988; Sondaar, 1994), Pleistocene cervids from Greece, Japan and the Philippines (de Vos, 2006) and *Candiacervus* from Crete (van der Geer et al., 2006). These adaptations can be recognized as pedomorphic features, since juveniles of any species tend to have short stubby limbs compared to adults (Lorenz, 1943). Furthermore, the femur of island species *Candiacervus ropalophorus* is relatively massive, just like the femora of mainland species *Cervus elaphus*, *Dama dama* and *Capreolus capreolus* at birth, whereas the adult specimens of the latter species have more slender bones (van der Geer et al., 2006); again a pedomorphic feature. The short snout of *Sus nanus* can also be called a pedomophic feature, because in general juveniles of mammals tend to have shorter snouts than the adults of the same species (Lorenz, 1943). Van Heteren and de Vos (2007) give more elaborate examples of island adaptations in vertebrates.

The pedomorphic features encountered in the adults of island species are caused by heterochrony. And because this is a general pattern the presence of pedomorphic features is an indication of island adaptations.

## ISLAND ADAPTATIONS IN *HOMO FLORESIENSIS*

Various measurements were taken on adults and juveniles of *Homo sapiens*, *Homo erectus s.l.* and *Pan troglodytes* to test the hypothesis that *Homo floresiensis* displays pedomorphosis as a mechanism of island dwarfing. *Homo floresiensis* is primarily compared with *Homo sapiens*. However, *Homo erectus s.l.*, the ancestor of *Homo floresiensis*, probably did not have exactly the same life history traits as *Homo sapiens*; therefore the other species are also included in the analyses to show a general pattern in hominin ontogeny.

In Table 1 the relevant measurements on a stereolithographic cast of the cranium and published measurements taken directly on the cranium of LB1 are presented, except for the mandibular angles, which are presented separately in Table 4. These measurements were chosen, because they vary over the lifetime of an individual and thus would reflect pedomorphosis, if it were occurring.

**Table 1**
**Measures Taken by Brown et al. (2004) and Measures Taken on the Cast of LB1**

| *Measures/Indices*<br>*Right* | *Measures from Brown et al. (2004)* | | *Left* |
|---|---|---|---|
| Cranial base length[1] | - | 71,5 mm | Not possible |
| Orbital breadth[2] | 32 mm | 32,0 mm | 31,7 mm |
| Orbital height[3] | 31 mm | Not possible | 30,7 mm |
| Orbital index[4] | 96.9 | - | 96,9 |

1. Cranial base length is the direct distance between the basion and the projected midpoints of the orbits on the medial border of the orbits.
2. According to Martin (1914). Because the sutura are invisible and the nose section is not entirely preserved, the position of the maxillofrontale is estimated on the cast.
3. According to Martin (1914).
4. Orbital index = orbital height * 100 / orbital breadth.

### Orbital Index

*Homo sapiens*, *Homo erectus s.l.* and *Pan troglodytes* do not differ significantly from each other in respect to the orbital index ($p>0.05$) and are therefore taken as one group for the statistical analyses of the orbital index. In general individuals of each dental stage are statistically similar in orbital index to the two preceding and two following dental stages, but statistically significantly different ($p<0.05$) from more remote dental stages. *Homo floresiensis* has a significantly different orbital index than the foetus with dental stage O, but a similar orbital index to all other juvenile groups (Table 2). The statistics indicate that *Homo floresiensis* is significantly different from all adult groups concerning the orbital index.

Because LB1 is similar to juveniles and different from adults, it is appropriate to group all juveniles and all adults together in just two age classes to make a stronger statistical case by creating a larger sample size. In Table 3 a comparison is made between the right orbital index of *Homo floresiensis* and the orbital indices of adults (N=62) and juveniles (N=99).

**Table 2**
**Group Statistics and T-test[1] of the Orbital index by Dental Stage**

| *Dent. Stage*[2] | *N* | *Mean* | *Std. Deviation* | *p H. Floresiensis* |
|---|---|---|---|---|
| O | 2 | 69,5585 | 0,50939 | 0,015[3] |
| I | 6 | 98,6016 | 2,73601 | 0,578[4] |
| II | 10 | 94,6744 | 4,70511 | 0,670[4] |
| III | 37 | 93,9230 | 6,99119 | 0,682[4] |
| IV | 31 | 90,1336 | 7,87801 | 0.408[4] |
| Va | 13 | 86,4169 | 4,9579 | 0,066[4] |
| Vb | 14 | 82,1621 | 5,01769 | 0,014[5] |
| VI | 46 | 84,6594 | 5,64399 | 0,038[5] |
| VII | 27 | 81,5001 | 7,31548 | 0,050[5] |
| Hf[6] | 1 | 96.8454 | - | - |

1. Independent sample T-test.
2. The dental stages are adopted and adapted (V is split in Va and Vb; O is added) from Hellman (1927), species included are *Homo sapiens, Homo erectus s.l.* and *Pan troglodytes.*
3. The orbital index of *H. floresiensis* differs significantly from dental stage O.
4. The orbital index of *H. floresiensis* does not differ significantly from juveniles with dental stages I, II III, IV and Va.
5. The orbital index of *H. floresiensis* differs significantly from adults with dental stages Vb, VI and VII.
6. *H. floresiensis* with dental stage VI.

Table 3 shows that from a statistical point of view the orbital index of adults is highly significantly different from that of juveniles ($p<0.000$) and that the orbital index of *Homo floresiensis* is significantly different from that of adults ($p<0.05$). So, based on these data adult *Homo floresiensis* (LB1) has a statistically indistinguishable orbital index from juveniles of *Homo sapiens, Homo erectus s.l.* and *Pan troglodytes.*

**Table 3**
**Group Statistics and T-test[1] of the Orbital Index by Age Class**

| *Age class*[2] | *N* | *Mean* | *Std. Deviation* | *p Child* | *p Homo Floresiensis* |
|---|---|---|---|---|---|
| adult | 62 | 83,0625 | 5,80619 | 0,000[3] | 0,022[3] |
| juvenile | 99 | 91,6180 | 7,90854 | - | 0,512[4] |
| *Homo floresiensis* | 1 | 96,8454 | - | - | - |

1. Independent sample T-test.
2. The age classes include *Homo sapiens, Homo erectus s.l.* and *Pan troglodytes.*
3. The orbital index of adults differs significantly from juveniles and *Homo floresiensis.*
4. The orbital index of *Homo floresiensis* does not differ significantly from the orbital index of juveniles.

## Mandibular Angle

The first author measured the mandibular angles on a cast of LB1 and from photographs of LB1 and LB6 (Figure 1). The mandibular angles range between 100° and 113° (Table 4). The right side of the mandible of LB1 is fractured so that it might not have its natural shape anymore, possibly changing the mandibular angle. The fact that angle α is more similar to angle γ, than angle γ, is a reason to consider angle a more reliable than angle γ, since mandibles tend to be symmetrical. Because of this reason angle β is considered to be invalid. Angles α and γ average out to a mandibular angle for LB1 of 111°, whereas LB6 has a mandibular angle of 112°.

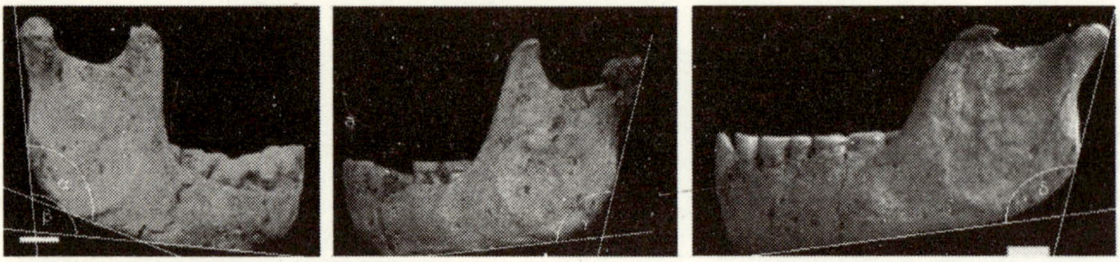

Figure 1: Top: Right Lateral View of the Mandible of LB1 Displaying the Two Possible Mandibular Angles, the Scale Bar represents 1 cm (modified from Brown *et al.*, 2004). Middle and Bottom: Left Lateral Views of the Mandibles of LB1 and LB6, Displaying the Mandibular Angle, the Scale Bar represents 1 cm (modified from Morwood et al., 2005). Angle a is more Similar to Angles d and g, than angleb.

The mandibular angle lies between 97° and 108° for adult *Homo erectus s.l.* (N=3) and between 107° and 113° for juvenile *Homo erectus s.l.* (N=5) (Table 5). The measured mandibular angles of LB1 and LB6 are most comparable to the mandibular angle of juvenile *Homo erectus s.l.*, rather than to the mandibular angle of adult *Homo erectus s.l.* and they are certainly not comparable to the mandibular angle of *Homo sapiens* regardless of age

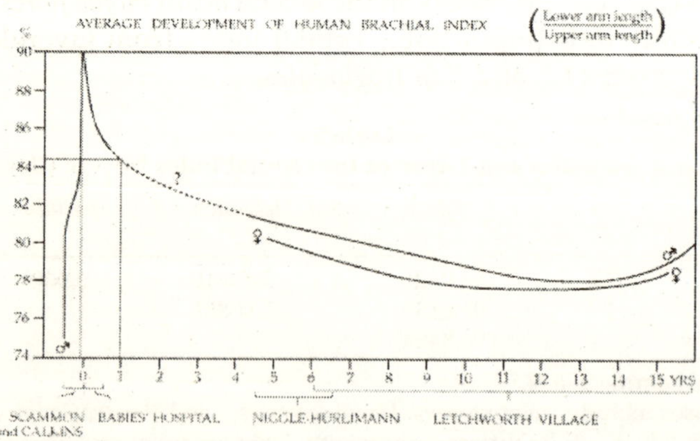


Figure 2: Development Curve of Brachial Index from Intrauterine Life to Puberty. Data have been taken from Various Sources as named. 0.5 to 5 years, Data Sparse. The Grey Lines Indicate the Brachial Index of LB1, which is Similar to the Brachial Index of Babies. Modified After Davenport (1934). Using the Data of Morwood *et al.* (2005) the Brachial Index of *Homo Floresiensis* can be Calculated by:

$$\frac{\text{Length ulna} * 100}{\text{Length humerus}} = \frac{205 * 100}{243} = 84.4.$$

(Tables 4 and 5). However, compared with *Pan troglodytes Homo floresiensis* does have a mandibular angle comparable to adults.

**Table 4**
**Mandibular Angles of LB1 and LB6**

| *Angle (in °)*[1] | *Measured from Cast* | *Measured from Photograph* |
|---|---|---|
| α (LB1) | 112 | 113 |
| β (LB1) | 100 | 100 |
| γ (LB1) | 110 | 109 |
| δ (LB6) | No cast available | 112 |

1. The positions of the different angles are indicated in Figure 1

**Table 5**
**The Ontogeny of the Mandibular Angle of *Homo Sapiens* and *Homo Erectus s.l.***

| *Age* | *Angle (in °) of Homo sapiens*[1] | *Angle (in °) of Pantroglodytes*[2] | *Angle (in°) of Homo erectus s.l.* |
|---|---|---|---|
| Early embryo | 130 | No data | No data |
| Birth | 140-145 | No data | No data |
| Juvenile | 128-133 | 121-129 | 107-113[3] |
| Adult | 120-127 | 108-120 | 97-108[4] |
| Old age | 117-124 | No data | No data |
| After loss of teeth | 124-131 | No data | No data |

1. Data from Moore and Lavelle (1974).
2. For reasons of sample size the individuals are only specified as juvenile or adult. The ranges indicate the 25th and the 75th percentile of the total sample (N=76).
3. *Sinanthropus* BI: 107°; *Sinanthropus* FI: 112° (Weidenreich, 1936), KNM-ER820: 111°; D2735: 110° (estimated from photographs) and KNM-WT15000: 113° (measured from photograph).
4. *Sinanthropus* GI: 97°; *Sinanthropus* HI: 108° (Weidenreich, 1936) and KNM-ER992: 108° (estimated from photograph).

## Membral Indices

According to Morwood *et al.* (2005) *Homo floresiensis* has relatively long arms compared to its legs. This is a feature typical for a juvenile morphology. Davenport (1934) gives a development curve of the intermembral index at successive ages up to 32 years old. And, Martin (1914) explains that during foetal life the arms are longer than the legs, at birth arms and legs have approximately the same length, between the sixth and the ninth year the legs become longer than the arms and during adulthood the relation between arms and legs is 4:5. So, following Martin (1914) LB1 has an intermembral index undoubtly within the range of juveniles only. And, although, following Davenport (1934) the intermembral index is inconclusive, it hints at juvenile morphology as well. Furthermore, since Morwood *et al.* (2005) already stated that the humerofemoral index is outside the range of (adult) *Homo sapiens*, it is likely that the interpretation following Martin (1914) is most appropriate.

Davenport (1934) also gives a development curve of the brachial index from intrauterine life to puberty. LB1 displays a brachial index of a child prior to birth or at about 1 year of age (Figure 2). So, *Homo floresiensis* has upper limb proportions comparable to juveniles.

**Torsions**

The right humerus of LB1 has a relatively limited degree of humeral torsion according to Morwood *et al.* (2005). The humeral torsion of LB1 is approximately 110°, which is less than in large bodied apes and modern humans (141-178°) and other known hominins (Evans and Krahl, 1945; Larson, 1988). This would imply that the humeral torsion only reflects phylogenetic information. However, humeral torsion is in part ontogenetic and a response to the dynamic forces exerted by shoulder rotators on the growing bone (Rhodes, 2006; Evans and Krahl, 1945). Jacob *et al.* (2006) conclude from this that the low humeral torsion of *Homo floresiensis* is caused by a lack of muscle development. However, the low humeral torsion of LB1 can also be viewed as a pedomorphic feature, because the humeral torsion of LB1 is comparable to the torsion of juveniles.

The tibial torsion of LB1 is approximately 14°. This is rather low for an adult individual. The normal tibial torsion for adults lies between 21° and 35° (Jacob *et al.*,1980; Reikerås and Høiseth, 1989; Strecker *et al.*,1997; Mullaji *et al.*,2008). For newborns this tibial torsion angle is approximately 0°[1]. The use of the legs in walking produces the tibial torsion mainly in the first four years of life (Kristiansen *et al.*,2001). So, the tibial torsion of LB1 is probably more comparable with the tibial torsion of juveniles than of adults.

**Facial Features**

It can be determined visually from fossils, casts and photographs that LB1 displays relatively little prognathism compared to adult *Homo erectus s.l.* and other more primitive hominins. Hominin juveniles always display less prognathism than adults of the same species, just like juvenile mammals in general have shorter snouts than adults (Lorenz, 1943), so the lack of prognathism in LB1 is also a pedomorphic feature.

**Endocast**

The endocast of *Homo floresiensis* has been compared with endocasts of adult *Homo erectus*, healthy adult *Homo sapiens*, microcephalic *Homo sapiens* and *Pan troglodytes* (Falk *et al.*,2005), and with the endocast of Mojokerto child (*Homo erectus* juvenile) described by Balzeau et al. (2005) (van Heteren, 2008).The endocast of LB1 looks most like the endocasts of *Homo erectus*. Note, however, that LB1 lacks the occipital expansion over the cerebellum of the adult *Homo erectus*, but in this respect looks more like juvenile *Homo erectus*, which also lacks this expansion, as seen in Mojokerto child.

**Body Size**

Dwarfism in vertebrates is a frequently observed process in endemic island species. Burness *et al.* (2001) have made estimations of the body mass of endothermic and ectothermic top herbivores and top carnivores based on island size. The top carnivore on Flores at the time of *Homo floresiensis* was the 70 kg ectothermic *Varanus komodoensis* (Komodo dragon). The top herbivore was the small endothermic *Stegodon florensis*. The possible body mass of *Homo floresiensis*, likely omnivorous, is not dealt with directly in this paper, however, it can be derived from their work by interpolation.

To determine the expected bodymass of *Homo floresiensis* it is assumed that *Homo floresiensis* is omnivorous and endothermic. The expected body mass of an endothermic top omnivore can logically be predicted to lie somewhere around the average of the values for endothermic top herbivores and endothermic top carnivores. The size of Flores as given by Burness *et al.* (2001) is 14154 km$^2$. Using this value in the regression equations of Burness *et al.* (2001), an endothermic omnivore such as *Homo floresiensis* is predicted to have a body weight of approximately 36 kg. Probably even slightly less, because the top niches on Flores are already occupied by *Varanus komodoensis* and *Stegodon florensis*. This value closely agrees with that estimated for LB1 (between 16 and 28.7 kg based on estimated stature, and 36 kg based on cross-sectional area of the femur) by Brown et al. (2004). Thus the body weight of LB1 is appropriate for an endothermic omnivore adapted to an island the size of Flores.

## DWARFING MODELS

Modern Pygmies are distributed all over the world mainly in tropical climates. Their short stature was thought to be an adaptation to the humid and warm conditions they live in (Cavalli-Sforza, 1986). But recently an alternative hypothesis has been postulated, which deals with life-history traits (Migliano *et al.*, 2007). Compared to normal-sized humans pygmy bodies are much reduced in size, but their heads are proportionally much less reduced, if not within the range of normal-sized humans.

The hominin fossils found in Narmada Valley (Sonakia, 1984; Sankhyan, 1997a, b; Sankhyan, 2005) might provide an indication that a similar situation was present in the Pleistocene. The morphological features of these fossils indicate that they might have belonged to some form of advanced *Homo erectus s.l.* (de Lumley and Sonakia, 1985; Cameron *et al.*, 2004). However, as the fossils are particularly small and comparable in size with modern pygmies (Figure 3) (Sankhyan, 2007b), they may have belonged to a pygmy advanced *Homo erectus s.l.*.

The distribution of this archaic pygmy need not necessarily be restricted to Narmada Valley or the Indian subcontinent; they may have been more widespread like their modern counterparts. The reasons for not having found any remains anywhere else (yet) may include the following. Firstly, the preservation potential of tropical pygmies is generally very low, because of the humid and warm environment in which they live. Secondly, large parts of South and Southeast Asia have not yet received enough palaeontological and archaeological attention and potential remains of archaic pygmies may still be hidden underneath the surface.

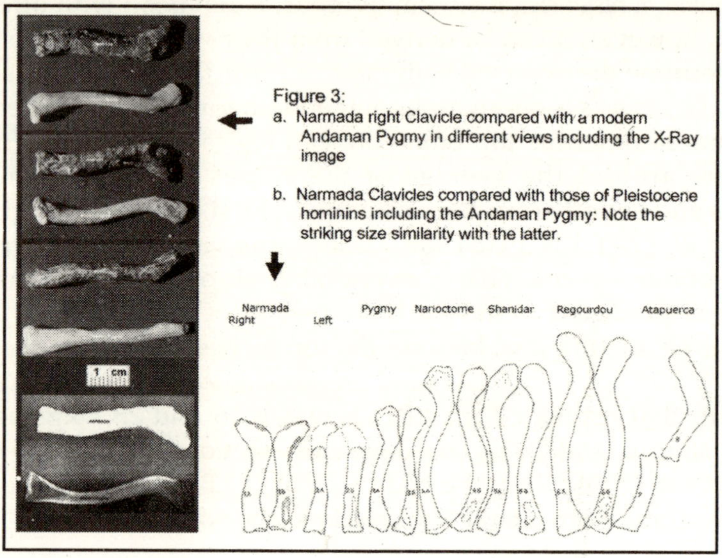


Figure 3:
a. Narmada right Clavicle compared with a modern Andaman Pygmy in different views including the X-Ray image

b. Narmada Clavicles compared with those of Pleistocene hominins including the Andaman Pygmy: Note the striking size similarity with the latter.

Figure 3

The hypothetically wide potential distribution of a morphotype so far only known from Narmada Valley opens up new possibilities regarding the ancestry of *Homo floresiensis*. As, according to this model, normal-sized *Homo erectus s.l.* might not have been the only morphotype present in Southeast Asia around 840 ka, when the ancestors of *Homo floresiensis* colonised Flores (Brumm *et al.*, 2006), there are now three potential ancestors of *Homo floresiensis*.

To account for the small stature of LB1, Richards (2006) has already suggested that *Homo floresiensis* could have had a "pygmy modification" of the growth hormone-insulin-like growth factor I axis (GH-IGF-I axis), which would consist of normal serum GH levels, but low serum IGF-I levels. The archaic pygmy hypothesised here is also expected to have displayed a similar modification. And if *Homo floresiensis* would then indeed be derived from this archaic pygmy, a magnification of the modification would be all that was needed to account for the short stature of this species.

Figure 4 displays in a schematic way the several hypotheses that have been postulated up until now concerning LB1 and *Homo floresiensis* as a species. However, with the information available at present it is impossible to determine whether normal-sized *Homo erectus s.l.* or an archaic pygmy would have been the most likely ancestor of *Homo floresiensis*. In contrast, primitive hominins, like Australopithecines or *Homo habilis* are unlikely to have been the ancestor of *Homo floresiensis*, as there is no indication for their presence outside Africa as opposed to *Homo erectus s.l.* and the pygmy advanced *Homo erectus s.l.*. The possibility of LB1 being a pathological individual of *Homo sapiens* and the arguments against that hypothesis have already been discussed extensively elsewhere (Falk *et al.*, 2007; van Heteren, 2008; Martinez and Hamsici, 2008)

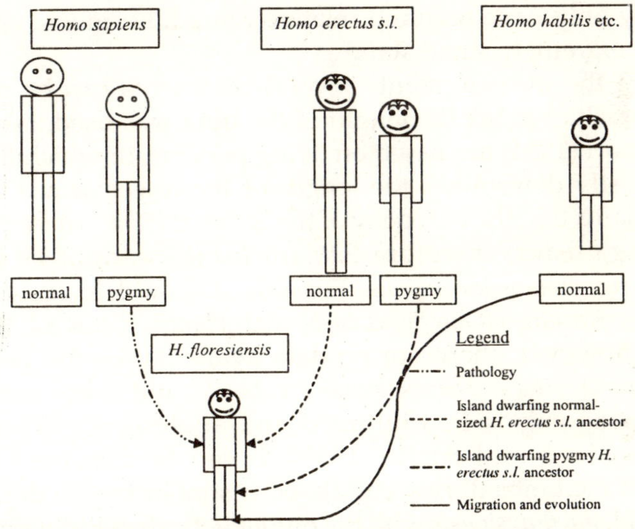


Figure 4: Schematic Representation of the Hypotheses Concerning LB1 and *Homo floresiensis*. Island Dwarfing with a Pygmy *H. erectus s.l.* as Ancestor is the New Hypothesis Postulated in this Chapter

## DISCUSSION

Several authors have provided evidence for close affinities between *Homo floresiensis* and *Homo erectus s.l.*. Zeitoun (2007) provides a cladogram in which LB1 belongs to a *Homo erectus*-clade, including the type specimen for *Homo erectus* (but see also Argue *et al.*, 2007). Tocheri *et al.* (2007) discusses the morphology of the wrist and supports the hypothesis of a new species; in the absence of *Homo erectus s.l.* reference material *Homo erectus s.l.* ancestry may not be unlikely. Gordon *et al.* (2008). An interpretation of the cranium of LB1 and postcranial remains in terms of size and scaling results in LB1 appearing to have been closely related to *Homo erectus s.l.* (van Heteren and de Vos, 2007; Gordon *et al.*, 2008).

Under the assumption that *Homo floresiensis* is a descendant of *Homo erectus s.l.* and has adapted to the island environment on Flores, the paedomorphic morphology of *Homo floresiensis* can be explained very well. The mechanism responsible for the island adaptations which are observed in *Homo floresiensis* is heterochrony.

The phenomenon of paedomorphic features occurring as a result of adaptation to an island environment is clearly not unique and is also expected to occur for a hominin in an island situation. Additionally, the expected weight of *Homo floresiensis* based on island size is in agreement with the estimated weight for LB1 based on postcranial elements.

Furthermore, the potential presence of archaic pygmies in Southeast Asia when Flores was colonised around 840 ka (Brumm *et al.*, 2006) ka provides an additional possibility for the ancestry of *Homo floresiensis*, and one which may only have required relatively small hormonal changes to account for its extremely small stature.

Concerning the measurements several comments can be made. To calculate the brachial index the length of the ulna was used, because the data of Davenport (1934) are based on living persons, in which the length of the ulna mostly determines the length of the lower arm. Davenport (1934) also explains that the ontogeny of the limbs of *Homo sapiens* is typical for bipedal organisms; therefore *Pan troglodytes* cannot be used for comparison with *Homo floresiensis*. Possibly it would have been more appropriate to compare *Homo floresiensis* with *Homo erectus s.l.* than with *Homo sapiens*; however, there are no data available for the postcranial remains of *Homo erectus s.l.*. Since *Homo erectus s.l.* and *Homo sapiens* have similar body proportions in adulthood and adolescence (Walker and Leakey, 1993; Clegg and Aiello, 1999), it can be assumed that the development of the limbs during childhood is similar too. In this case the comparison of *Homo floresiensis* with the ontogenetic development of *Homo sapiens* instead of the ontogenetic development of *Homo erectus s.l.* is valid.

## CONCLUSIONS

In this research, various metrical measures and indices documented to differ in juveniles and adults of *Homo sapiens*, *Homo erectus s.l.* and *Pan troglodytes* have been compared with those of *Homo floresiensis*. In the measures that can be taken upon the cast of LB1 or that are available from the literature, *Homo floresiensis* consistently groups with juveniles, not adults. Furthermore, *Homo floresiensis* also groups with juveniles according to non-metrical features.

In conclusion, *Homo floresiensis* has shown differences from adults concerning several features in ways that are strongly suggestive of heterochrony. Specifically, we suggest that *Homo floresiensis* shows features indicative of paedomorphosis. Further, the low body weight of *Homo floresiensis* is congruent with expectations based on an omnivorous endotherm adapted to an island the size of Flores. And, the hypothesised presence of an archaic pygmy in South and Southeast Asia adds another potential ancestor to the list of possibilities The data presented here support the hypothesis originally put forward by Brown *et al.* (2004) that the distinctive features of *Homo floresiensis* were caused by island dwarfing, whether it be with *Homo erectus s.l or* a Narmada-like archaic pygmy as ancestor.

## REFERENCES CITED


Argue, D., Donlon, D., Groves, C., Wright, R. (2006), *Homo Floresiensis*: Microcephalic, Pymoid, *Australopithicus*, or *Homo*? *Journal of Human Evolution* 51, 360-374.

Argue, D., Morwood, M., Sutikna, T., Jatmiko, Saptomo, W. (2007), *Homo Floresiensis*: What is it? Where Does it fit in the Human Story? In: Indriati, E. (ed.) *Recent Advances on Southeast Asian Paleoanthropology and Archaeology.* Laboratory of Bioanthropology and Paleoanthropology Faculty of Medicne Gadjah Mada University, Yogyakarta, p. 47-53.

Balzeau, A., Grimaud-Hervé, D., Jacob, T. (2005), Internal Cranial Features of the Mojokerto Child Fossil (East Java, Indonesia). *Journal of Human Evolution* 48, 535-553.

Bergh, G.D. van den (1999), The Late Neogene Elephantoid-bearing Faunas of Indonesia and their Palaeozoogeographic Implications. A Study of the Terrestrial Faunal Succession of Sulawesi, Flores and Java, including evidence for early hominid dispersal east of Wallace's Line. *Scripta Geologica* 117.

Bergh, G.D. van den, Vos, J. de, Aziz, F., Morwood, M.J. (2001), *Elephantoidea* in the Indonesian Region: New *Stegodon* Findings from Flores. In: Cavarretta, G., Gioia, P., Mussi, M., Palombo, M.R. (Eds). *The World of Elephants: Proceedings of the 1st International Congress.* Consiglio Nazionale delle Ricerche, Rome, pp. 623-627.

Brumm, A., Aziz, F., Bergh, G.D. van den, Morwood, M.J., Moore, M.W., Kurniawan, I., Hobbs, D.R., Fullagar, R. (2006), Early Stone Technology on Flores and Its Implications for *Homo Floresiensis*. *Nature* 441, 624-628.

Bover, P., Acover, J.A. (1999), Estimating Physical Characteristics of Neonate *Myotragus Balearicus* (*Artiodactyla, Caprinae*). *Deinsea* 7, 33-54.

Bower, B. (2005), Encore for Evolutionary Small-Timers: Tiny Human Cousins Get Younger with New Finds. *Science News* 168, 244-246.

Bromage, T.H., Dirks, W., Erdjument-Bromage, H., Huck, M., Kulmer, O., Öner, R., Sandrock, O., Schrenk, F. (2002), A Life History and Climate Change Solution to the Evolution and Extinction of Insular Dwarfs: A Cypriot Experience. In: Waldren, W.H., Ensenyat, J.A. (Eds.), *World Islands in Prehistory: International Insular Investigations* V Deia International Conference of Prehistory. Archeopress, Oxford, pp. 420-427.

Brown, P., Sutikna, T., Morwood, M.J., Soejono, R.P., Jatmiko, Wayhu Saptomo, E., Rokus Awe Due (2004), A New Small-bodied Hominin from the Late Pleistocene of Flores, Indonesia. *Nature* 431, 1055-1061.

Burness, G.P., Diamond, J., Falannery, T. (2001), Dinosaurs, Dragons, and Dwarfs: the Evolution of Maximal Body Size. *Proceedings of the National Academy of Sciences of the United States of America* 98, 14518-14523.

Caloi, L, Palombo, M.R. (1996), Functional Aspects and Ecological Implications in Hippopotami and Cervids of Crete. In: Reese, D.S. (Ed.), *Pleistocene and Holocene Fauna of Crete and Its First Settlers.* Prehistory Press, Madison, pp. 125-151.

Cameron, D., Patnaik, R., Shani, A. (2004), The Phylogenic Significance of the Middle Pleistocene Narmada Hominin Cranium from Central India. *International Journal of Osteoarchaeology* 14, 419-447.

Cavalli-Sforza, L.L. (1986), *African Pygmies.* Academic Press, Orlando FL, p. 461.

Clegg, M., Aiello, L.C. (1999), A Comparison of the Nariokotome *Homo Erectus* with Juveniles from a Modern Human Population. *American Journal of Physical Anthropology* 110, 81-93.

Davenport, C.B. (1934), Ontogeny and Phylogeny of Man's Appendages. *Proceedings of the National Academy of Sciences of the United States of America* 20, 359-364.

Day, M.H. (1986), *Guide to Fossil Man.* Londen, Cassell.

Evans J.D., Krahl, V.E. (1945), The Torsion of the Humerus: A Phylogenetic Survey from Fish to Man. *American Journal of Anatomy* 193, 303-337.

Falk, D., Hildebolt, C., Smith, K., Morwood, M.J., Sutikna, T., Brown, P., Jatmiko, Wayhu, Saptomo, E., Brunsden, B., Prior, F. (2005), The Brain of LB1, *Homo Floresiensis. Science* 308, 242-245.

Falk, D., Hildebolt, C., Smith, K., Morwood, M.J., Sutnika, T., Jatmiko, Saptomo, E.W., Imhof, H., Seidler, H., Prior, F. (2007), Brain Shape in Human Microcephalics and *Homo Floresiensis. Proceedings of the National Academy of Sciences of the United States of America* 104, 2513-2518.

Foster, J.B. (1964), Evolution of Mammals on Islands. *Nature* 202, 234-235.

Geer, A.A.E. van der, Dermitzakis, M.D., Vos, J. de (2006), Relative Growth of the Metapodals in a Juvenile Island Deer: *Candiacervus* (*Mammalia, Cervidae*) from the Pleistocene of Crete. *Hellenic Journal of Geosciences* 41, 119-125.

Gillberg, P., Olofsson, H., Mallmin, H., Blum, W.F., Ljunghall, S., Nilsson, A.G. (2002), Bone Mineral Density in Femoral Neck is Positively Correlated to Circulating Insulin-like Growth Factor (IGF)-I and IGF-binding Protein (IGFBP)-3 in Swedish Men. *Calcified Tissue International* 70, 22-29.

Gordon, A.D., Nevell, L., Wood, B. (2008), The *Homo Floresiensis* Cranium (LB1): Size, Scaling, and Early *Homo* Affinities. *Proceedings of the National Academy of Sciences of the United States of America* 105, 4650-465.

Hellman, M. (1927), Changes in the Human Face brought about by Development. *International Journal of Orthodontia, Oral Surgery and Radiography* 13, 475-516.

Henneberg, M., Thorne, A. (2004), Flores Human may be Pathological *Homo sapiens.* In: Barham, L., (Ed.). Some Initial Informal Reactions to Publication of the Discovery of *Homo floresiensis* and Replies from Brown & Morwood. Before Farming 4, 2-4.

Heteren, A.H. van (2008), *Homo Floresiensis* as an Island Form. *Palarch's Journal of Vertebrate Palaeontology* 5, 1-12.

Heteren, A.H. van, Vos, J. de (2007), Heterochrony as a Typical Island Adaptation in *Homo Floresiensis*. In: Indriati, E. (ed.) *Recent advances on Southeast Asian Paleoanthropology and archaeology*. Laboratory of Bioanthropology and Paleoanthropology Faculty of Medicne Gadjah Mada University, Yogyakarta, p. 95-106.

Jacob, R.P., Haertel, M., Stüssi, E. (1980), Tibial Torsion Calculated by Computerised Tomography Compared to Other Methods of Measurement. *The Journal of Joint and Bone Surgery* 62-B, 238-242.

Jacob, T., Soejono, R.P., Hsü, K., Frayer, D.W., Eckhardt, R.B., Kuperavage, A.J., Thorne, A., Henneberg, M. (2006), Pygmoid Australomelanesian *Homo Sapiens* Skeletal Remains from Liang Bua, Flores: Population Affinities and Pathological Abnormalties. *Proceedings of the National Academy of Sciences of the United States of America* 103, 13421-13426.

Kristiansen, L.P., Gunderson, R.B., Steen, H., Reikerås, O. (2001), The Normal Development of Tibial Torsion. *Skeletal Radiology* 30, 519-522.

Larson, S.G. (1988), Subscapularis Function in Gibbons and Chimpanzees: Implications for Interpretation of Humeral Head Torsion in Hominoids. *American Journal of Physical Anthropology* 76, 449-462.

Leinders, J.J.M., Sondaar, P.Y. (1974), On Functional Fusions in Footbones of Ungulates. Zeistschrift für Saugetierkunde 39, 109-115.

Lorenz, K. (1943), Die Angeborenen Formen möglichen Verhaltens. Zeitschrift für *Tierpsychologie* 5, 235-409.

Lumley, de, M.-A., Sonakia, A. (1985), Contexte Stratigraphique et Archaeologique de L'Homme de le Narmada, Hathnora, dans la Moyenne Valle de la Narmada. *L' Anthropologie* 89: 13-61.

Made, J. van der (1988), *Sus nanus nov. Sp.*, a Piocene dwarf pig from Capo Figari (Northeastern Sardinia). *Bollettino della Società Paleontologica Italiana* 27, 367-378.

Martin, R. (1914), *Lehrbuch der Anthropologie in systematischer darstellung*. Gustav Fischer, Jena.

Martin, R.D., MacLarnon, A.M., Phillips, J.L., Dussubieux, L., Williams, P.R., Dobyns, W.B. (2006), Comment on "The brain of LB1 *Homo floresiensis*". *Science* 312, 999.

Martinez, A.M., Hamsici, O.C. (2008), Who is LB1? Discriminant Analysis for the Classification of Specimens. *Pattern Recognition* 41, 3436-3441.

Migliano, A.B., Vinicius, L., Lahr, M.M. (2007), Life History Trade-offs Explain the Evolution of Human Pygmies. *Proceedings of the National Academy of Sciences of the United States of America* 104, 20216-20219.

Morwood, M.J., Brown, P., Jatmiko, Sutikna, T., Wahyu Saptomo, E., Westaway, K.E., Rokus Awe Due, Roberts, R.G., Maeda, T., Wasisto, S., Djubiantono, T. (2005), Further Evidence for Small-bodied Hominins from the Late Pleistocene of Flores, Indonesia. *Nature* 437, 1012-1017.

Mullaji, A.B., Sharma, A.K., Marawar, S.V., Kohli, A.F. (2008), Tibial Torsion in Non-arthritic Indian Adults: A Computer Tomography Study of 100 Limbs. *Indian Journal of Orthopaedics* 42, 309-313.

Palombo, M.R. (2001), Paedomorphic Features and Allometric Growth in the Skull of *Elephas falconeri* from Spinagallo (Middle Pleistocene, Sicily). In: Cavarretta, G., Gioia, P., Mussi, M., Palombo, M.R. (Eds.), *The World of Elephants, Proceedings of the 1st International Congress.* Consiglio Nazionale delle Ricerche, Rome, pp. 492-496.

Palombo, M.R. (2003), *Elephas? Mammuthus? Loxodonta?* The Question of the True Ancestor of the Smallest Dwarfed Elephant of Sicily. In: Reumer, J.W.F., de Vos, J., Mol, D. (Eds), *Advances in Mammoth Research. Proceedings of the Second International Mammoth Conference Rotterdam,* 16-20 May 1999.Deinsea 9, 273-291.

Reikerås, O., Høiseth, A. (1989), Torsion of the Leg determined by Computed Tomography. *Acta Orthopaedica* 60, 330-333.

Rhodes, J.A. (2006), Adaptation to Humeral Torsion in Medieval Britain. *Americal Journal of Physical Anthropology* 130, 160-166.

Richards, G.D. (2006), Genetic, Physiologic and Ecogeographic Factors Contributing to Variation in *Homo Sapiens*: *Homo Floresiensis* reconsidered. Journal of *Evolutionary Biology* 19, 1744-1767.

Ridley, M. (2003), Chapter 20 Evolutionary Developmental Biology. In: *Evolution 3rd edition.* Blackwell Publishing, Oxford, p. 572-589.

Rightmire, G.P., Lordkipanidze, D., Vekua, A. (2006), Anatomical Descriptions, Comparative Studies and Evolutionary Significance of the Hominin Skulls from Dmanisi, Republic of Georgia. *Journal of Human Evolution* 50, 115-141.

Sankhyan, A.R. (1997a), Fossil Clavicle of a Middle Pleistocene Hominin from the Central Narmada Valley, India. *Journal of Human Evolution* 32, 3-16.

Sankhyan, A.R. (1997b), A New Human Fossil Find from the Central Narmada basin and Its Chronology. *Current Science* 73, 1110-1111

Sankhyan, A.R. (2005), New Fossils of Early Stone Age Man from Central Narmada Valley. *Current Science* 88, 704-707.

Sankhyan, A.R. (2007a), Significance of Human Post-cranial Fossils from Narmada with Remarks on the Skullcap. In: Sankhyan, A.R., Rao, V.R. (eds.) *Human Origins, Genome & People of India.* Allied Publishers Private Limited, Kolkata, p. 193-217.

Sankhyan, A.R., Rao, V.R. (2007 b), Did Ancestors of the Pygmy of Hobbit Ever Live in Indian Heartland? In: Indriati, E. (ed.) *Recent advances on Southeast Asian Paleoanthropology and archaeology.* Laboratory of Bioanthropology and Paleoanthropology Faculty of Medicne Gadjah Mada University, Yogyakarta, p. 76-89.

Sonakia, A. (1984), The Skull Cap of Early Man and Associated Mammalian Fauna from Narmada Valley Alluvium, Hoshangabad Area, M.P. (India). *Records Geological Survey of India* 113, 159-172.

Sondaar, P.Y. (1994), Paleoecology and Evolutionary Patterns in Horses and Island Mammals. *Historical Biology* 8, 1-13.

Spoor, C.F. (1988), The Body Proportions in *Myotragus Balearicus* Bate, 1909. Koninklijke Nederlandse Akademie van Wetenschappen, *Proceedings B* 91, 295-309.

Strecker, W., Keppler, P., Gebhard, F., Kinzl, L. (1997), Length and Torsion of the Lower Limb. *The Journal of Bone and Joint Surgery* 79-B, 1019-1023.

Tocheri, M., Orr, C., Larson, S., Sutikna, T., Jatmiko, Saptomo, W., Awe Due, R., Djubiantono, T., Morwood, M., Jungers, W. (2007), The Primitive Wrist of *Homo floresiensis* and Its Implications for Hominin Evolution. *Science* 317, 1743-1747.

Vekua, A., Lordikipanidze, D., Rightmire, G.P., Agusti, J., Ferring, R., Maisuradze, G., Mouskhelishvili, A., Nioradze, M., Ponce de León, M., Tappen, M., Tvalchrelidze M., Zollikofer, C. (2002), A New Skull of Early *Homo* from Dmanisi, Georgia. *Science* 297, 85-89.

Vos, J. de (2006), Notes About the Parallels in Evolution of the Pleistocene Cervids from Greece (Crete, Kassos and Karpathos), Japan (the Ryukyu-islands) and Philippines (Masbate). Hellenic Journal of Geosciences 41, 127-140.

Walker, A.C., Leakey, R. (Eds.). The Nariokotome *Homo erectus* Skeleton. Harvard University Press, Cambridge.

Weidenreich, F. (1936), The Mandibles of *Sinanthropus Pekinensis*; A Comparative Study. *Palaeontologia Sinica,* D7 Fast 4, 1-162.

Zeitoun, V., Widianto, H., Djubiantono, T. (2007), The Phylogeny of the Flores Man: The Cladistic Answer. In: Indriati, E. (ed.) *Recent advances on Southeast Asian Paleoanthropology and archaeology.* Laboratory of Bioanthropology and Paleoanthropology Faculty of Medicne Gadjah Mada University, Yogyakarta, p. 54-60.

# PART III

# THE EARLY MODERN HUMANS

Chapter–16

# A New Sub-Himalayan Holocene Lithic Industry

*Vidwan Singh Soni & Anujot Singh Soni*

## INTRODUCTION

The Palaeolithic investigations in the northwestern sub-Himalayas have since been known by the Soanian industries first discovered by de-Terra and Paterson (1939) in the Potwar region of Pakistan. After independence, the research in this region was carried out mainly by Paterson & Drumond (1962) and later by Rendell et al (1989), Dennell et al (1991) and Salim (1994) in Pakistan, by Lal (1956), Sankalia, (1974,) Mohapatra (1990, 2007), Mohapatra& Singh (1979) Saroj (1974), Sankhyan (1983), Karir (1985), Joshi (1968), Singh & Karir (1998) and Gaillard et al (2008), and then recently by Chauhan (2004, 2007a, 2007b) and Soni & Soni (2005, 2007, 2008, 2009), in India. The lithic artefacts that have since been collected by most of the earlier investigators were claimed as belonging to the Mode-1 category and have generally followed the approach of de-Terra & Paterson though the recent finds (Chauhan 2004, Soni& Soni 2008,2009) scientifically deem to prove something entirely different. The earlier investigators (particularly in the Indian part of the sub-Himalayas) never found any lithic industry in stratigraphic or datable context and they had merely speculated (Mohapatra 2007) the Soanian to have existed probably from mid to late or terminal Pleistocene. Most of the earlier researchers had categorized Soanian either on the basis of now out-dated Alpine glaciations chronology (de-Terra & Paterson 1939) or the tool typology and other un-datable geological attributes. However, the present authors' discovery of Soanian artefacts along with terracotta pieces and some new tool types strongly demands that the stone-age research in the northwestern sub-Himalayas be reconsidered in light of these new revelations. In the following, three already reported and one new site are (Fig.1) being discussed which call for a change in the interpretation of the Soanian and its relation to the Holocene epoch geo-archaeology.

## EVIDENCE FROM JANDORI SITE-COMPLEX

### Site Jandori-6

As recently reported (Soni& Soni 2009), a huge assemblage of flakes with some cores and choppers was found in association with wheel-made pottery (plain red ware) in a buried state having been fabricated and utilized contemporaneously. The stone artefacts and potsherds recovered from the upper slope-wash sediment layer in the excavated trench have no $CaCO_3$ deposit on them while those excavated from the dense layer of artefacts below this bear intense depositions of this salt. This shows that the artefacts in the lower layer were collected there as creep deposit during some arid phase. They could not spread out in wider area due to slow fluvial drift and thus lot of $CaCO_3$ was retained in the sediment to be deposited on the artefacts. After that, when the arid phase came to an end, the heavy rains caused the remaining artefacts mixed with slope wash to cover the thick salty layer. The upper clayey layer (Soni& Soni 2009, Fig-2) and the sloping surface area around the trench containing artefacts without $CaCO_3$ are a testifier to it All the artefacts recovered from the trench and those found spread around it contained in general a large number of edge-ground specimens (a & c in Fig.2), many large size unifacial, Toth Type-1 (Toth 1985) flakes and generally the Soanian tools (see Fig.2). Definitely there is a Hoabinhian (Marwick 2007) element mixed with the Soanians and a connection between the two is therefore envisaged.

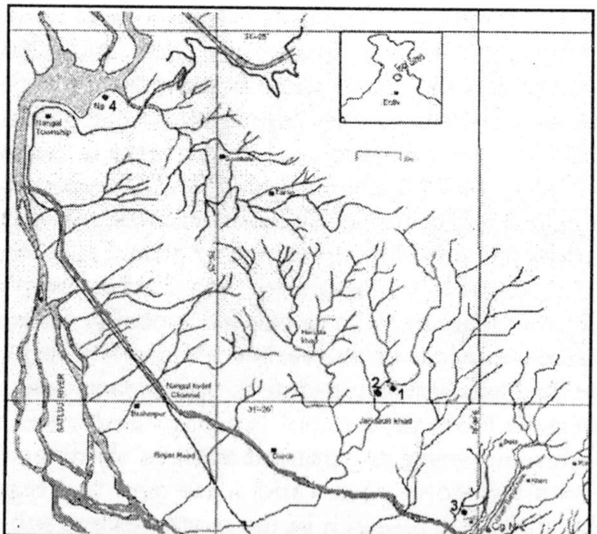


Figure 1: Map of the Region Showing 4 Sites (1) Jandori-6, (2) Jandori-3, (3) Bika-1, (4) Nangal.

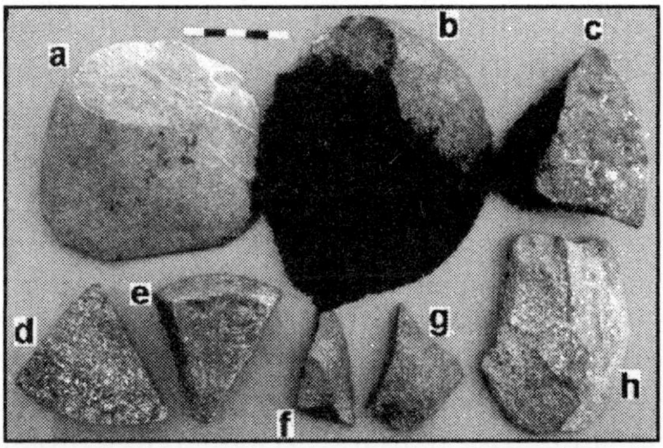


Figure 2: Artefacts from Jd-6 (a) Proto-cleaver on a type-1 flake having straight distal ground-edge & a proximal flake scar on dorsal surface. (b) Large type-2 flake having a smooth convex working edge. (c) Wedge-like core having a convex ground-edge. (d) Burin on a triangular type-3 flake, salt deposits are due to its deep burial. (e) A stone-punch of rectangular cross section having cortical platform. (f) A small pointed cutting tool with a sharp edge on type-3 flake. (g) Borer on a g-type-3 flake. (h) A cleaver on a type-3 flake.

## Site Jandori-3

Just about 1 Km down stream of Jd-6, there is another small site Jd-3 situated on the right bank of the Jandori stream. The site is a plane terrace of 40m length and 12m maximum width and has a mild longitudinal slope. Some lithic artefacts were seen exposed near the distal end of the slope and therefore a trial trench of 1.5 x 1m area was excavated there at. Total 386 lithic artefacts were recovered from this site out of which 40 came from the upper about 20 cm depth of the sediment and 257 were embedded in a dense c25 cm thick layer. The rest of the lithic artefacts were found

Figure 3: Artefacts from Jd-3 (a) A Sumatralith-like Uni-facially Flaked Sub-rectangular Core. (b) Stone-punch of Rectangular Cross Section with a Cortical Platform. (c) Ventral Surface of a Proto- cleaver from Excavation. (d) Retouched Type-2 Flake having a Tang. (e) Sumatralith- like Oval Unifacial on a Cobble. (f) Dorsal Surface of a Type-1 side Flake with Smoothly Ground Upper Edge

sporadically embedded in the clayey layer overlying a layer of gravel of boulders of local sand stone mixed with clayey sediment underlain by the middle Siwalik bedrock, and some were obtained from the adjoining shallow test pits. During the excavation of the larger trench which went up to 60 cm or so, burnt clay and weathered terracotta pieces were found even in the dense layer of the lithic artefacts. Ten stone artefacts were edge-ground and very large first-flakes akin to proto-cleavers were also present in the excavated assemblage (see Fig.3c). Two unifacials were almost similar to Sumatraliths (Fig.3a, e) of Hoabinhian culture and the presence of edge-ground elements along with them suggests that this assemblage has good similarity with the excavated assemblage of Jandori-6 site situated just a kilometer in the upstream of this stream. All the lithic

Figure 4: Artefacts from Bika-1 (a) Rectangular Cleaver on a Type-1 Flake Retouched on Both Surfaces. (b) Scraper on a Type-1 Side Flake with a Proximal Scar on Dorsal Surface. (c) Knife with Tang on a Type-3 Siret. (d) Elongate Type-5 Flake with Ground Convex Distal Edge.(e) Rectangular Flake with Retouches on One Side. (f) Rectangular Side & End Scraper on Type-4 Flake

specimen found in the thick layer deep in the trench were laden by $CaCO_3$ salt deposit and hence show that that layer was a result of the creep deposit during the arid phase hinted at in the discussion of Jd-6 site. A stone punch (Fig.3b) found in this excavation is a tool generally found in post-Pleistocene (Inizan et al 1999) prehistoric sites and so the presence of potsherds along with stone tools shows that the site belongs to the Holocene epoch and our finding of most of such stone tools from the terrace surfaces laid down during mid-Holocene (Soni & Soni 2008) or so (see also No. 3 in the following), also supports this inference. Lithic artefacts obtained from the excavation of this site are almost similar to those from the Jandori-6 site (Soni & Soni 2009) found in buried context and so belong to the same industry.

## THE EDGE-GROUND ELEMENTS OF BIKAPUR-CHOE SITE

Recently, we found another site having affinity with Hoabinhians as it contained edge-ground artefacts and also large and small utilized as well retouched flakes whose details are being presented in this section. The assemblage contains uni-facially flaked cobbles, choppers and cores/core-tools. The stone artefacts were found on a large area cusp terrace on the left bank of a short run stream 'Bikapur Choe', a tributary of River Satluj passing through the Indian Punjab region. The cusp terrace mentioned above is a 135m long and 60m wide lowest terrace of the main Bikapur stream. This terrace mainly consists of a 50-70 cm thick silt deposit overlying the middle Siwalik bedrock with occasional lenses of gravel at places over the bedrock. There was no agricultural activity visible on the terrace but many rectangular pits of size 1x 0.3x 0.3m had been dug out by the forest department uniformly spread over the terrace, and those pits had exposed several stone-tools apparently buried under the slope wash from the background hill range running parallel to the Bikapur stream. We did not need to excavate the site as these pits provided us with 63 representative artefacts yielding 3 to 6 specimens per pit. Some artefacts and weathered potsherds of plain red ware were also seen on some raised portions exposing middle Siwalik bedrock. The artefacts collected from this site (Fig. 5 & 6) being reported first in the present paper consisted of the following types;

Figure 5: Artefacts from Nangal Sites (a) Oval Cobble with Cupules on Both Surfaces and on Sides. (b) Thick Type-3 Flake with Abraded Distal Edge used for Battering. (c) Fan-like Cleaver on a Type-4 Flake. (d) Peripherally Retouched Type-1Side-flake Scraper. (e) Oval Scraper on a Type-4 Flake

As seen in Table-1, the only difference of this assemblages from that of the Jandori sites is that the Bika-1 artefacts are almost all retouched with majority of them having been used as scrapers. Here also flakes are quite abundant which make about 90% of the total assemblage with the presence of quite a good number of large cleavers (see Fig.4a). Edge-ground specimens (Fig.4d) are also found to have a large percentage (see Table-1). So the excavated and surface sites given in sections 2 and 3, possess a fair cultural similarity with each other.

**Table 1**

| *Artefact Type* | *Number* | *% of Total* | *Remarks* |
|---|---|---|---|
| Choppers | 1 | 1.59 | End chopper with 3 flake scars |
| Cores/Core scrapers | 4 | 6.35 | Nosed core-1, utilizes scrapers-1, simple core-1 |
| General Flakes | 10 | 15.87 | Mostly retouched & utilized |
| Flake scrapers | 23 | 36.51 | 5 are large & thick, rest are rounded & sub-peripheral |
| Cleavers/proto cleavers | 8 | 12.70 | – |
| Large (12.5 to13.3cm) | 4 | 6.35 | 2-with cortical dorsal & one partly cortical; utilized |
| Medium (6.8 to9.4cm) | 4 | 6.35 | Both with cortical & semi-cortical dorsal surfaces |
| Other Tools | 6 | 9.51 | – |
| Stone punch | 1 | 1.59 | With cortical head |
| Knives with tang | 2 | 3.17 | 1- with tang, 1 is knife cum scraper on flakes |
| Points | 2 | 3.17 | 1-on triangular first flake, 1-pointed blade on type-3 siret |
| Blade/flake | 1 | 1.59 | 1-on rectangular blade-flake |
| Edge-ground | 11 | 17.47 | – |
| Core tool | 1 | 1.59 | Small chopper-like with ground convex edge |
| Flake tools | 10 | 15.87 | On all Toth type flakes ; 5-on type-1 |
| Total | 63 | 100 | – |

## EVIDENCE FROM OTHER SITES

The present authors reported certain sites dated to early and mid Holocene times which also contain small and large size artefacts of the same typology sans edge-ground elements as were abundantly obtained from the above mentioned 3 sites. The Nangal sites (Soni & Soni 2008) have yielded large size flakes, proto-cleavers, and cobble tools and have been dated to around 6KaBP (see Fig.5). Some small cup-shaped valleys reported earlier (Soni & Soni 2007) do show some edge-ground flakes and very large-sized fresh and unrolled flakes or proto-cleavers are also not foreign to them. They apparently belong to the Holocene lithic industry being proposed in this presentation in all respects accept large percentages of edge-ground specimens. Finding very few or no edge-ground specimens from general open air sites may be because of the reason that the gloss of edge-grinding gets lost due to agricultural activities etc. Such element might be present in wide regions of sub-Himalayas but it could not have been recognized by the earlier workers mainly due to their meager and at times very selective collections made from unspecified site areas.

## INFERENCES

The Soanian chronology first defined by de-Terra & Paterson and subsequently followed by others has already been termed as outdated for want of dating and true geological relevance of the sites known to them. However, many recent finds by the present authors, especially from the dated sites and sites with known time-brackets, deem to provide new chronological and typo-technological evidence for its proper definition.

The discovery of quite a large number of edge-ground elements and identification of Sumatraliths in earlier and new Soanian assemblages points to a definite relationship of the Nepal (Corvinus 1994) and Southeast (Marwick 2007) Asian lithic industries of Hoabinhian or Bacsonian affiliation. Large amounts of all the so called early to late Soan tool types are present in numerous stone-age sites discovered by the present authors mainly from the lowest stream terraces dated to Holocene epoch. In addition to that, the finding of the Soanian artefacts and many new and known Meso/Neolithic type tools in association with potsherds in buried state and from some isolated open young terraces deem to propose it as a 'Holocene Lithic Industry'. The intrusion of the Hoabinhoidal element into the sub-Himalayas during mid or late mid-Holocene is a new phenomenon to be reckoned with as to when and in what context Hoabinhian/Bacsonian hominines entered the Soanian zone or interacted with them. The context in which the artefacts excavated from the Jandori sites are found in two types of sediments (with and without the deposition of $CaCO_3$) points to the possibility of some pottery using people having occupied the sites during some arid phase of Holocene epoch. High concentrations of stone artefacts abandoned by their fabricators got collected in natural pits, or at the distal ends of the hill slopes along with the creep wash (indicated by thick deposits of $CaCO_3$ on them, see Soni &Soni 2009) which were later covered by slope wash during a subsequent wet phase. There is a strong possibility that these sites were in fact occupied by the humans during early to late Harappan times who also used pottery along with the Soanian-types, Meso/Neolithic types, and many other stone-tool types (see fig.5) discovered for the first time by the present authors.

## REFERENCES CITED

Chauhan P.R. (2004), *Issues and Themes in Anthropology, Eds.* V.K. Srivastva and M.K. Singh, Dehli, pp: 293-342.

Chauhan P.R. (2007), Soanian Cores and Core-tools from Toka, Northern India: Towards a New Typo-technological Organization. *J.Anthropol. Archaeol*doi: 10.1016/j.jaa..01 .001

Chauhan, P. R. (2007), Soanian Lithic Occurrence and Raw Material Exploitation in the Siwalik Frontal Zone, Northern India: A Geoarchaeological Perspective *J Hum Evol,* doi:10. 1016/j, jhevol.2oo7.09.017.

Corvinus, G. (1994), Prehistoric Occupation Sites in the Dang-Deokhuri Valleys of Western Nepal, *Man and Environment.,* Vol. 19, pp: 73-89.

Dennell, R.W., and Rendell, H.M. (1991), De Terra & Paterson and the Soan Flake Industry: A New Perspective from the Soan Valley, Northern Pakistan. *Man and Environment,* 16(2), pp: 91-99.

De-Terra, H and Paterson, T.T. (1939), *Studies on the Ice Age in India and Associated Human Cultures.* Washington; Carnegie Institutes' Publication.

Gaillard, C., Singh, M., and K. K. Rishi (2008), Technological Analysis of the Acheulian Assemblage from Atbarpur in the Siwalik Range (Hohiarpur District, Punjab). *Man & Environment*, Vol. 33, **2**, pp:1-14.

Inizan, M.L., Ballinger, M.R., Roche, H., Tixier, J. (1999), *Technology and Terminology of Knapped Stones,* CREP, Nanterre, p: 32.

Joshi, R.V. (1968), Early Stone Age Discoveries in the Banganga-Beas Region, *Cultural Forum,* Ministry of Education, New Delhi, pp: 96-99.

Karir, B.S. (1985), *Geomorphology and Stone-Age Culture of North Western India,* Sundeep Prakashan, Delhi.

Lal, B.B. (1956. 2007), Palaeoliths from Beas & Banganga Valleys, Punjab. *Ancient India Vol.* 12::58-92.

Marwick, B. Approach to Flaked Stone Artefact Archaeology in Thailand: A Hstorical Review. *Silpakorn University International Journal,* **7**:49-88.

Mohapatra, G.C. (1990), *Soanian-Acheulian Relationship*. Bulletin Deccan College Pune, Vol-49: 251-259.

Mohaptra, G.C., Singh Mukesh (1979), Prehistoric Investigations in a Sub-Himalayan Valley India, *Current Anthropology,* **20:** 600-602.

Mohapatra, G.C. 2007. Lithic Cultures of the Sub-Himalayas in, *"Human Origins, Genome & People of India"*Ed. A.R. Sankhyan & V.R. Rao. Allied Publishers, New Delhi, pp: 138-141.

Paterson, T.T., & Drummond (1962), H.J.H. *Soan the Palaeolithic of Pakistan*. Govt. of Pakistan, Karachi, Memoir 2.

Rendell, H.M., Dennell, R.W. & Halim, M.A. (1989), *British Archaeological Reports, B.A.R. International Series 544*.Oxfird, pp: 202-204.

Salim, M. (1994), *Paleolithic Culture of Potwar with Special Reference to Lower Palaeolithic*. Ph.D. Thesis submitted to Shah Abdul Latif University, Khairpur Pakistan.

Sankhyan, A. R. (1983), First Record of Early Stone Age Tools from Ghumarwin area, Himachal Pradesh. *Curr. Sci.*, 1, 52:126–127.

Sankalia, H.D. (1974), *Prehistory and Protohistory of India & Pakistan* Pune.

Saroj, H.M. (1974), *Lithic Industries of Jammu*. Unpublished Ph.D. Thesis, P. U. Chandigarh. Singh, M., Karir, B.S.,. *Prehistoric and Quarternary Studies of the Roopnagar District of Punjab*. Dept. of cultural Affairs, Archaeology & Museums, Chandigarh, 1998.

Soni, A. S. and Soni, V. S. (2005), Palaeolithic Tools from the Surface of Optically Stimulated Luminescence dated Alluvial Fan Deposits of Pinjaur Dun in NW sub-Himalayas. *Curr. Sci.*, 88: 867–871.

Soni, Anujot Singh & Soni, Vidwan Singh (2007), Discovery of New Palaeolithic Sites in the Sub-Himalayas, in *Human Origins, Genome & People of India: Genomic, Palaeontological & Archaeological Perspectives,* A.R. Sankhyan & V. R. Rao*(eds)*, pp: 144-149. Allied Publishers, New Delhi,

Soni, Anujot Singh., Soni, Vidwan Singh., & D.S. Dhillon (2008), Large Assemblages of Flakes & Cores found on dated Young Terraces of River Satluj and Its Tributaries. *Curr. Sc.*, 94: 577-580.

Soni, Anujot Singh & Soni, Vidwan Singh (2009), A Flake-rich Assemblage in Buried State and in Primary Context in the NW Sub-Himalayas. *Curr. Sc.* 96: 1130-1133.

Toth, N. (1985), The Oldwan Reassessed: A Close Look at Early Stone Artifacts. *J. Archaeol. Sci.* 12: 101-120.

We are thankful to Dr. A. R. Sankhyan for kind invitation to contribute this paper, recommending for financial support for the Kunming Congress.

Chapter–17

# Archaeology of the Transhumance in Ladakh Himalayas

*S.B. Ota*

## INTRODUCTION

The archaeological research, particularly prehistoric investigations in the glacial zone of Himalayas, is very limited, as it was believed till 90s that Stone Age Man never occupied the valleys in the Trans-Himalayan region during the Pleistocene period due to adverse climatic conditions in the higher altitudes. It was assumed that snow clad mountains, rugged terrain with high desert plateaus as natural barriers and extreme cold climate of the region would have not been favoured by prehistoric man for habitation. It was argued that the Ladakh valley was explored by man for the first time during 10th century AD when Buddhism first reached the valley and the time when Indian sub-continent established cultural contact with Central Asia, particularly with Tibet and China, through the Great Himalayan passes. Therefore, no substantial effort was made till recent past to look into the evidences of prehistoric cultures of Ladakh. Hence, the area remained terra incognita as far as the Stone Age Man is concerned till 90s.

Recent evidences brought to light from the valley have changed the previous notions and given root to the fact that man did venture into the rugged terrain much before the historical period. The evidences renewed interest among the archaeologists to undertake investigations and probe the cultural system of Early Man in this part of the sub-continent.

Ladakh is the largest Tehsil of Jammu and Kashmir State with Leh as it's headquartered. It covers an area of nearly 100,000 sq km between two highest mountain ranges–the Himalayas in the south and the Karakoram in the north. It is one of the largest in the Trans-Himalayan region, is bound in NW-SE by Ladakh range on the right and Zanskar range parallel to Ladakh range on the left bank of Indus. The valley is surrounded by snow clad ranges and altitude of these high desert plateaus of Ladakh vary between 2500 m and 5000 m from mean sea level with sparse vegetational cover of scrub jungle. Ladakh is a 'U' shaped narrow-valley drained by Indus which meanders through deep gorges known as 'Indus suture' or 'Sindhu furrow'. Rivers Suru and Zanskar flow into Indus at Kargil and village Nimmo, respectively as its major tributaries. Though the valley is narrow, yet alluvial flats do occur in the form of a fan at higher reaches where the streams emerge from the mountains into the valley. Most of the villages are located on these alluvial fans because of the availability of fertile land for cultivation and suitable for habitation.

Climatologically, Ladakh forms a distinct region with character akin to the cold highland type. The climate of the region is extremely cold and dry. The average annual rainfall is about 8 cm. The area experiences an extreme temperature in shade and sunshine. Mean monthly temperature is lowest in January and highest in July. Average monthly temperature ranges between 7.9° and 17.8° below zero degrees Celsius with about five months experiencing the temperature below freezing point.

This portion of Great Himalaya in Ladakh region preserves a long geological history beginning from Archaean with evidences of dynamic structural deformations of Himalayan orogeny. The basement complex of the Himalayas comprises three elements (a) the metamorphosed sedimentary Archaean, (b) intrusive granite and gneisses, and schists of post-Archaean age, and (c) remnants of Archaean granites, gneisses and schists. The rocks of Dharwar consisting of slate, phyllite, schist, quartzite, crystalline limestone and dolomite are also found in the region. Of the Mesozoic Era, the Triassic is the best and fully preserved. Mostly the outcrops of Jurassic and Cretaceous are seen in Ladakh valley.

The Quaternary formations of the valley comprise alluvial cones, moraines, lacustrine deposits and terraces. Alluvial cones in the form of fan-shaped deposits are noticed at places where streams emerge from the mountains into the valleys. Morainic deposits are found at many places in Ladakh as a proof of ancient glaciers. Ancient lake sediments are also found at places in the valley.

The most significant Quaternary deposits of the valley are the terraces developed along upper Indus and its tributaries which provide a long alluvial history suggesting the ancient levels of valley floors and contemporary palaeoenvironmental conditions. Of all the terraces, 'cemented boulder gravel' (De Terra and Paterson 1939) or 'Indus Pleistocene Conglomerate' (Tripathi *et al.*,1988) is considered to be the earliest Indus terrace in the area. This conglomerate is eroded at many places, leaving behind a few patches at a comparatively higher elevation from the present river bed. The subsequent river terraces along the upper Indus system are extensively seen in the area at different elevations and sometimes juxtaposed. Unfortunately, the detailed study of these terrace succession, their chronology and contemporary environmental conditions are extremely limited. The study of these terraces is significant because the material evidences of prehistoric man are preserved in the terrace deposits and the sediments offer reliable clues to the interpretation of Quaternary environment.

## PREVIOUS RESEARCH

Research into Stone Age cultures in Ladakh Himalaya can be traced back to the beginning of the century. As early as 1903, A.H. Francke (1903, 1904) reported a variety of stone artifacts comprising pots, lamps, spindle-whorl, tobacco-holder, butter dish, cups, spoons, ringstones (a kind of blunt axe), edged stone axes and knives from the upper Indus region. These artefacts were considered to be of recent origin because of the fact that Francke's own remark on his findings that "...... the stone age was not quite a matter of the past in Ladakh..." (1903: 389) was accepted without any doubt.

Later, the provenance of the solitary stone implement found from Kargil terraces by Chr and J. Hawkes and H. de Terra (1934) was suspected by the discoverers themselves thinking that the artifacts could have been carried by some traveler from the Kashmir valley and left there. It is because of the pre-conceived notion among the scholars then that Stone Age Man only occupied the sub-Himalayan terrain having a peri-glacial landscape immediately below the Pleistocene snowline. It was so much so that that even subsequent researchers working in the area considered Ladakh as culturally vacuum as far as prehistoric cultures are concerned. Therefore, the area remained unexplored from the point of view of early human habitations by archaeologists for a long time.

Subsequently, following the discovery of a few stone artifacts by Sankalia (1971) from the glacio-fluvial deposits at Pahlgam, a team of geoarchaeologists (Joshi *et al.* 1974), in 1972-73 undertook the investigation in Liddar valley, Kashmir. The significance of the study at Pahlgam lies in the fact that, besides their observation, they recognized importance of Ladakh to be an ideal region for the study of Quaternary glacial sequence and for the first time provided an optimistic suggestion for the future investigation in the high altitude tracts of Ladakh for the evidences of prehistoric man (IAR 1972-73; 13-14).

Confirmed evidence of Early Man in Trans-Himalayan region was brought to light for the first time when a group of geologists (Tripathi et al. 1988), in 1985, while carrying out investigation on the problem of Neogene/Quaternary successions of upper Indus system in Ladakh Himalaya. They collected stone artifacts from stratified context found in association with Indus terraces located near the village Nurla, Khalsi, Pashkyum and around Kargil. The artifacts assemblage comprise choppers (both unifacial and bifacial variety), pick, scrapers, cores and flakes, fabricated on chert, quartzite, granite, sandstone, limestone and vitric tuff which are locally available in the form of pebbles. This assemblage is divided into three cultural phases of which the earliest phase is of Lower Palaeolithic culture, whereas the last two phases are assigned to Middle Palaeolithic culture. Though these discoveries are significant, yet the chronology assigned to these industries needs to be revised in light of recent geological investigations carried out in the area (Dennell and Rendell 1991, Ganjoo 1993).

The evidences of post-Pleistocene Stone Age cultures were first brought to light by the geologists from Wadia Institute of Himalayan Geology, Dehra Dun, who paved the way for future research in transhumance. In 1980, an evidence of fire place with four splinters of unidentified bones was discovered by them near village Gaik in Ladakh (Sharma et al. 1989). Most noteworthy contribution of this discovery is solitary radiocarbon date (6710 + 130 yr BC: BS- 200) obtained on the charcoal sample from the hearth. It is the earliest date so far obtained for any archaeological site belonging to Holocene period from high altitude.

## PRESENT INVESTIGATION

In light of critical assessment of earlier works and encouraged by the discoveries made in Tibetan Plateau (Zhimin et al. 1982, Bellezza 1999, 2000, 2003), two short investigations were undertaken with a view to assess the potentiality of evidence of prehistoric remains in Ladakh Himalayas.

The first investigation was carried out in September 1988 (IAR 1988-89: 28 , Ota 1993), when few stone artifacts were picked up from the surface of scree on the left bank of Indus at village Alchi (34 ° 13′ 19″ N: 77 ° 10′ 35″ E). The collection comprises a unifacial chopper, three bifacial handaxes and a retouched worked block. Handaxes are fabricated on fine grained brown quartizite, while the chopper and the retouched block are on breccia and schist, respectively. The rocks are all available locally. On the basis of typo-technological features of these artifacts one would tend to assign the assemblage to Lower Palaeolithic cultural phase. However, it would be premature to do so due to the lack of precise knowledge of its stratigraphical context and in view of the meager collection. In spite of the limitations, the significance of this discovery lies with the fact that this Stone Age site lies in far upstream of Indus at an altitude of more than 3,120 m. This further strengthens the potentiality of looking for Stone Age evidence in a stratified context at a still higher altitude.

Subsequently, another investigation (IAR 1989-90: 34, Ota 1992, 1993) was undertaken in August 1989 following the discovery at Gaik (Sharma et al. 1989) with a view to know more about the associated cultural remains and particularly about the cultural specifics during Holocene. To fulfill the purpose, a stretch of about 10 km along the banks of Indus, between the village Gaik and Kiari, was explored.

## ARCHAEOLOGICAL EVIDENCE OF TRANSHUMANCE: THE AREA

The investigation that was carried out in 1989 by the present author established for the first time the evidence of transhumance in Ladakh Himalayas. The present area of investigation lies about 100 km southeast of district headquarters, Leh. Here Indus flows through a narrow valley either in a gorge or sometimes cutting through its older terrace having steep banks unlike the valley at Leh which is very wide. The average altitude of the valley at this place is about 3,900 m from mean sea level. The area is almost devoid of vegetation cover except during the summer months, i.e. June to October, when grass and few bushes grow on the terrace and river banks. The human habitations are very sparse because of less availability of suitable land for cultivation. A few habitations are located on flat terrace surface. During summer months, nomadic pastoral communities from lower altitude visit this area with their cattle as the area provides pastures for grazing. The exploration in the area brought to light two sites, namely Gaik and Kiari.

### Kiari

The site at Kiari (33° 45′ N: 78° 05′ E) is located 2 km away from the present village on the left bank of Indus. It is associated with Holocene Indus terrace. At this locality, a major portion of the cultural debris has already been destroyed during construction of road. With a view to ascertain the nature of human activity, a trial digging was carried out at the spot. Evidence of fire places, a good amount of faunal remains, a few pot-sherds, a burnt clay ball and stone objects comprising saddle quern, pestle and burnisher are unearthed in the excavation.

Altogether four different fire places in the form of temporary hearths and oven belonging to three successive activity phases were exposed during excavation. From these hearths few pot-sherds and charred animal bones have been recovered. The preservation of the cultural material at the locality is excellent, so much so that the wood burnt as fuel were exposed almost in their undisturbed condition in the fire places. The big sized charcoal pieces are clear evidence to the use of branches of trees and/or trunks of large bushes as fuel wood. Consequently, it may also be assumed that the vegetation cover in the area during that period was certainly better than today.

Altogether three pot-sherds have been recovered from this small-scale excavation. These potteries are handmade red ware with light brown slip on the outer surface, medium fabric and well fired, of which only one sherd is of rim portion and determines the shape as a high -necked vase having featureless rim and concave at the neck portion. The potteries recovered from Period II of Neolithic Phase (IAR 1961-62: 19, Fig. 6: 27) at Burzahom (Kashmir valley) are the nearest parallel to the potteries from Kiari. Burnt mark on the pot-sherds suggests their use for cooking purpose.

The pottery was manufactured, probably, from locally available clay produced from weathered shale and sandy clay.

A large number of moderately to completely charred fragmentary animal bones have been recovered from the excavation mostly as kitchen refuse. The faunal assemblage constitute Bos sp., Capra, Capra /Ovis, Nemorhaedus goral, rodent and bones of small ruminants. Besides, a specimen each of both vertebral and long bone of higher primate and bird, respectively has also been collected. The morphological features of bones of Bos sp., Capra, Capra/Ovis and small ruminants are slightly different and comparatively larger in size than the species found in plains. It suggests that these animals are of high altitude variety.

The most noteworthy features of these faunal remains are that Bos sp., Capra sp. And Capra /Ovis are of domesticated variety. The faunal assemblage is suggestive of a pastoral based economy supported with partial hunting of small ruminants and gathering. Since charred fragments constitute 55.85% of the total faunal assemblage, it is clear that animal food formed a major part of their dietary pattern. Cut-marks notice on certain bones confirms this observation.

Apart from hearths exposed during excavations, remains of at least five more successive fire places in the form of isolated charcoal patches spread over a stretch of about 100 m in exposed terrace profile at the locality have been noticed. The successive hearths occurring at different heights in the terrace suggest a repeated occupation of the site by Early Man. Altogether six different phases of occupation has been noticed at this place that establishes these evidences being the archaeological remnants of transhumance in the valley.

### Gaik

The site at village Gaik (33° 30′ N; 78° 10′ E) is located about 5.25 km form Gaik TCP (Traffic Check Post) on the right bank of Indus. The cultural remains of the site at Gaik are also associated with Holocene Indus terrace exposed on Gaik-Kiari road as that of Kiari. The site is badly disturbed by road cutting, and hence trial digging at the site could only yield evidence of a hearth.

## CHRONOLOGY & CULTURAL SPECIFICS

As regards the dating of these cultural remains is concerned three radiocarbon dates have been obtained of the charcoal samples from Kiari. These dates 2890+160 BP (PRL-1400), 2830+120 BP (PRL -1401) and 2770+120 BP (PRL-1402) push the antiquity of the human activities at Kiari to about 900 BC. The noteworthy aspect of these dates is their consistency from bottom to top corroborating very well with successive human activity. Considering the solitary radiocarbon date available earlier from Gaik (Sharma et al 1989), a broader time bracket ranging from 4,700 BC to 900

BC may be ascribed to the cultural assemblage. It may be mentioned here that, stratigraphically the sites at Gaik and Kiari, which are located at a distance less than 10 km from each other, are associated with one and the same Holocene Indus terrace. The site at Kiari lies comparatively at a higher elevation than the site at Gaik in a stratigraphic column. The human occupation at Gaik, therefore, is bound to be older than Kiari which is further confirmed by radiocarbon dates.

Despite the quantitative limitation of cultural material, the nature of cultural assemblage clearly suggests it to be the evidence of prehistoric transhumance. The nature of various associated cultural material and chronology assign the culture to Neolithic Phase. Report of such cultural phase has also been made from Central Asia (Gupta 1979: Dikshit 1982; Ranov 1982). The investigations, if carried out in future, would provide better insight to the animal domestication, cultural movements and origin of Neolithic transhumance in Trans-Himalaya and sub-Himalaya zone and its relationship with Central Asia.

## INFERENCES

The communities to whom this cultural assemblage of Holocene is ascribed were certainly nomadic. The faunal analysis suggests that their economy was mainly based on pastoralism, besides hunting and gathering. Absence of permanent settlements and temporary nature of hearths further enhances the nomadic life pattern of the communities. It seems plausible that these settlements were seasonal camps, probably occupied during summer seasons when the high altitude areas become suitable for human movements and pastures for cattle are available. The camps were selected wherever a suitable flat land near the river banks was available in narrow valley. The suitable flat lands were repeatedly occupied as evidenced from the successive hearth remains. The present day pastoral communities in the area such as Bakarwal, Gujar and Gaddi also move towards the higher altitude along with their cattle during summer months and prepare temporary settlements and hearths. The present day evidences of transhumance are well reflected in the archaeological past of sites Gaik and Kiari. Therefore, the archaeological remains from the sites may be the earliest evidence of transhumance in Ladakh Himalayas. It may not be out of place to mention here the optimistic views of Sahni (1936) who could realize and evaluate the evidence then in a scientific manner and remarked ".... we have no reason to assume that the Himalayas or the Pir Panjal range were a barrier to the migration of Palaeolithic or even Neolithic man", which now comes true. Further he could foresee then the future mode of research and thus laments 'On the view here adopted northern India and China must have had direct contacts across the Himalayas since the dawn of human existence, and the passes over these mountains probably mark some of the most ancient routes trodden by man. If, therefore, signs of Stone Age man were even to be found, say, on the Zoji-La itself, such a discovery would only be in accordance with expectation'.

## REFERENCES CITED


Bellezza, J.V. (1999), A Preliminary Archaeological Survey of Da Rog mTsho, *The Tibet Journal,* Vol.XXIV (1): 55-91.

Bellezza, J.V. (2000), Pre-Buddhist Archaeological Sites in Northern Tibet: An Introductory Report on The Types of Monuments and Related Literary and Oral Historical Sources, *Kailash (A Journal of Himalayan Studies),* Vol. XIX (1-2): 1-142.

Bellezza, J.V. (2003), Ancient Tibet: Bringing to Light the Forgotten, *Athena Review,* Vol.3 (4): 16-26.

Dennell, R.W. and H.M., Rendell (1991), De Terra and Peterson and the Soan Flake Industry: A New Perspective from the Soan Valley, Northern Pakistan, *Man and Environment* XVI (2): 91-99.

De Terra, H. and T.T. Paterson (1939), *Studies on the Ice Age of India and Associated Human Cultures.* Washington: Carnegie Institute Publ. 493.

Dikshit, K.N. (1982), The Neolithic Cultural Frontiers of Kashmir, *Man and Environment* VI: 30-36.

Francke, A.H. (1903), Notes on a Collection of Stone Implements from Ladakh, *The Indian Antiquary* 32: 389-391.

Francke, A.H. (1904), Ladakhi Stone Implements, *The Indian Antiquary* 33: 216.

Ganjoo, R.K. (1993), Late Quaternary Climato-Tectonic History and Reassessment of the Chronology of Prehistoric Cultures of Jammu Sub-Himalayas, India. In *Current Advances in Indian Archaeology, Vol. 1,* Ganjoo, R.K. and S.B.Ota (Eds.). Nagpur: Dattsons, pp.111-127.

Gupta, S. P. (1979), *Archaeology of Soviet Central Asia and the India Border-lands. Vol. II.* Delhi: B.R. Publ. Corp.

Hawkes, Chr., J. Hawkes and H. De Terra (1934), Palaeolithic Human Industries in the Northwest Punjab and Kashmir and their Geological Significance, *Connecticut Academy of Arts and Science Memoir 8*: 1-14.

*Indian Archaeology*–A Review (1972-73), New Delhi: Archaeological Survey of India.

*Indian Archaeology–A Review* (1988-89), New Delhi: Archaeological Survey of India.

*Indian Archaeology–A Review* (1989-90), New Delhi: Archaeological Survey of India.

Joshi, R.V., S.N. Rajaguru, R.S. Pappu and B.P. Bopardikar (1974), Quarternary Glaciation and Palaeolithic Sites in the Liddar Valley (Jammu-Kashmir), *World Archaeology* 5(3): 369-379.

Ota, S.B. (1992), Ladakh: Evidence of Stone Age Culture, *Himalaya Today III* (3&4): 48- 51.

Ota, S.B. (1993), Evidence of Transhumance from Ladakh Himalayas, Jammu and Kashmir, India. In *Current Advances in Indian Archaeology, Vol. 1,* Ganjoo, R.K. and S.B.Ota (Eds.). Nagpur: Dattsons, pp.91-110.

Ranov, V.A. (1982), The Hissar Neolithic Culture of Soviet Central Asia, *Man and Environment VI*: 63-71.

Sahni, B. (1936), The Himalayan Uplift Since the Advent of Man: Its Culthistorical Significance, *Current Science 5*: 57-61.

Sankalia, H.D. (1971), New Evidence for Early Man in Kashmir, *Current Anthropology 12* (4-5): 558-562.

Sharma, K.K., G Rajagopalan and V.M. Choubey (1989), Radiocarban Dating of Charcoal from Pre-Indus Civilization Fireplace, Upper Indus Valley, Ladakh, *Current Science 58*(6): 306-308.

Tripathi, C., B. C. Verma and R.K. Arora (1988), Lower and Middle Palaeolithic Artefacts from the Quaternary Sediments of Upper Indus Valley, Ladakh Himalaya, J&K, India, *Bulletin of the Indian Geologists' Association 21* (1) : 81-88.

Zhimin, An and Others (1982), Palaeoliths and Microliths from Shenja and Shuanghu, Northern Tibet, *Current Anthropology* 23(5); 493-499.

CHAPTER–18

# Early Occupations of Coastal Sri Lanka

*Samanti Kulatilake*

## INTRODUCTION

Prehistoric human remains associated with stone implements and faunal remains were discovered in a salvage archaeology operation in the coastal village Miniethiliya of southern Sri Lanka. The associated archaeological remains from this site indicate this to be a mid-Holocene habitation. This paper will discuss coastal occupation of Sri Lanka during the Holocene, while focusing on the physical anthropology and behavioural ecology of the prehistoric inhabitants of Miniethiliya. Five individuals were identified during the field season of 2008.

## PREHISTORIC COASTAL OCCUPATION IN CONTEXT

There is general consensus that modern humans first appeared in Africa and then went on to populate Eurasia and Australasia. Based on molecular and fossil evidence supported by chronological data, after a local African origin, modern humans have dispersed to populate the world, and by early Holocene times vast areas of the globe have been occupied (Cann *et al* 1987; Lahr and Foley 1994, 1998)

The possible exit strategies that could have been used by early modern humans expanding out of Africa include a northern route towards central Eurasia and a southern route along coastal regions of Somalia, Eritrea and the Red Sea towards Australasia (Walter *et al* 2000, Stringer 2000; Mellars, 2006; Field *et al.* 2007). There is well-dated evidence for human adaptation to coastal marine environments in the latter regions, dating from 125,000 years ago (Walter *et al* 2000). It has been hypothesized that the widespread adaptive strategy of exploiting aquatic resources may have provided an impetus for modern humans to expand out of Africa along the coasts

(Stringer 2000). Modern humans could have traversed both the interior and coastlines using a number of routes, and colonized South Asia relatively rapidly (Field *et al* 2007). Archaeological research has indicated that humans took with them their stone tool technology when they left Africa, and that living and travelling along the coasts would have made expansion into new territory easier (Mellars 2006).

This research concentrates on "Multiple Dispersals of Modern Humans" - a hypothesis formulated and discussed by Lahr and Foley (1994), Templeton (2002), Mellars (2006) and others. In connection to this hypothesis, the dispersal of modern humans using the southern dispersal route out of Africa has been proposed. Data from paleoenvironmental reconstruction indicates that, both the coasts and the interior would have been attractive to mobile hunter-gatherers (Kingdon 1993; Field *et al* 2007).

There is archaeological and fossil evidence that the South Asian subcontinent has been occupied by modern humans from Late Pleistocene times (James 2007). It is a region that has been successively migrated into and has been a source of dispersals to other parts of Asia. Sri Lanka is centrally located in this inferred "southern route" taken by anatomically modern humans who went on to occupy regions of Island Southeast Asia and Australia.

Early modern human occupation has been documented from Sri Lanka, dating from the late Pleistocene. Sri Lanka's rainforests and grassland regions have been occupied by modern humans as early as *c.* 40,000 BP (Perera in Press). These sites have offered insights to the behavioural ecology of early peoples inhabiting late Pleistocene rainforest environments (Kourampas *et al* 2008). Many of the sites are located in caves and rockshelters scattered in the central and south-western parts of the island. Three key rockshelter sites, Kitulgala Beli-lena and Batadomba-lena, and Fa Hien's Cave have been dated to a period of *c.* 40,000–8,000 BP (Deraniyagala 1992). The geometric microliths and articles of personal ornamentation recovered from these sites are clear indicators of modern human behaviour. (Deraniyagala 1992; Wijeyapala 1997; Perera in Press). Human skeletal remains are fragmentary and relatively sparse in these locations. Several prehistoric coastal sites including open-air habitation sites have been discovered, they have yielded a significant proportion of human skeletal remains. Bellan bendi Pelessa in the south-eastern plains is such an open air site which has yielded remains of at least 16 individuals (Kennedy 2000).

## Coastal Sites in Sri Lanka

The prehistoric coastal sites encountered so far are concentrated in the arid and semi-arid coastal zones of the island. They are found in the coastal belt associated with shallow lagoons and deltas. Some of these sites are shell-midden sites. These are of significant interest to archaeologists and physical anthropologists, since the exploitation of aquatic resources – a hallmark of modernity - is evident. Shell midden sites in Sri Lanka may be the result of natural or artificial (human-made) processes. Many shell midden accumulations in coastal regions of Sri Lanka are attributed to natural processes such as intermittent lowering of the sea levels during the mid-Holocene (Katupotha 1995). However deposition sequences of some shell patches in Udamalala, Pallemalla, and Miniethiliya are attributed to human activity. From Pallemalla excavations, remains of at least seven human burials associated with stone implements, land mammal bones, and shell debris were recovered (Ranaweera 2002; Somadeva and Ranasinghe 2006).

Other sites of interest include from the north and north-west, Mandakal Aru lagoon and Aruvakkallu. Along the southern coastal belt, there are a number of shell midden sites from Tangalle to Kirinda. These include Pathirajawela, Henagahapugala, Ussangoda, Kalametiya, Veligaththa, Arabokka, and Udapothana (Katupotha 1995; Perera pers. comm.). Most sites, dated to the mid Holocene yield mollusc shells and remnants of the sea water or estuarine molluscs *Meretrix spp.* and *Cerithidia spp.* (Katupotha 1995). In sites where human remains are also found, there are seawater and freshwater mollusc remains (*Acavus spp.*) as well as other faunal remains. The faunal remains include bone fragments of elk, deer, wild boar, and water buffalo (Somadeva and Ranasinghe 2006; Perera in Press).

### The Site of Miniethiliya

The village of Miniethiliya is situated about four kilometres inland from the present coast of southern Sri Lanka. Fluctuating sea levels may have placed this site closer to the shoreline during the mid-Holocene. Miniethiliya is also referred to as Hatagala Temple Land, off Hungama.

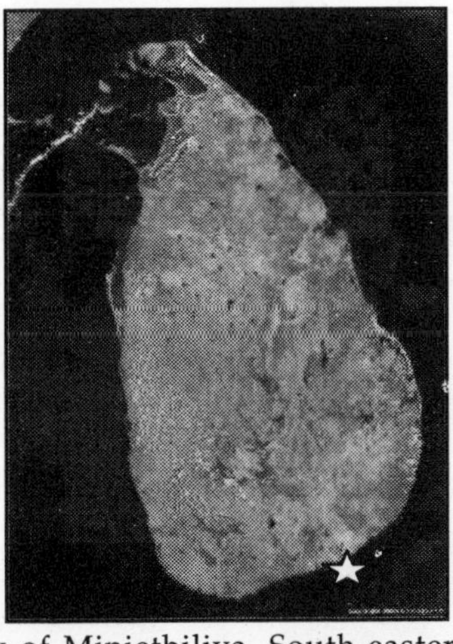

Figure 1: Satellite Imagery of Miniethiliya, South-eastern Coastal Belt of Sri Lanka
*http://eology.com/world/sri-lanka-satellite-image.shtml*

The term "Minie" refers to human corpses or bodies, and occasional human bones have been previously encountered in the paddy fields by villagers.

The villagers had been digging up a shell mound for commercial purposes. The economic value of shell middens has been of prime importance to recent people of these areas, while their archaeological significance has often been overlooked. In other regions of the world (e.g. Sumatra and coastal USA) shell middens have been mined from historic times for fertilizer, and more recently they have been tapped as a source of chicken-feed (Ceci 1984). In coastal Sri Lanka too, the extracted deposits along with any archaeological material and prehistoric human bones are crushed for the above purposes. At the Miniethiliya site, human remains buried alongside the prehistoric refuse were encountered. The excavation team from the National Archaeological Survey was able to salvage what could be recovered, before complete destruction of the site. The associated archaeological remains from this site are indicative of a mid-Holocene habitation.

## Subsistence Pattern and Symbolic Behaviour

Significant prehistoric human activity is associated with these particular shell midden deposits at Miniethiliya. Artifacts and ecofacts mixed with the shell debris are clear indicators that the shell middens were created artificially by humans who discarded remnants of their meals. In many coastal regions of the world, shell midden sites are associated with human activity (Ceci 1984). After a hearty meal of clams and oysters, people threw away the partially burnt shells as kitchen refuse. The term "kitchen middens" is also applied in certain instances to remnants of prehistoric meals. At Miniethiliya these shells would have accumulated in piles alongside the activity areas of the inhabitants. In the burial area, they would have piled up this refuse when they interred their dead.

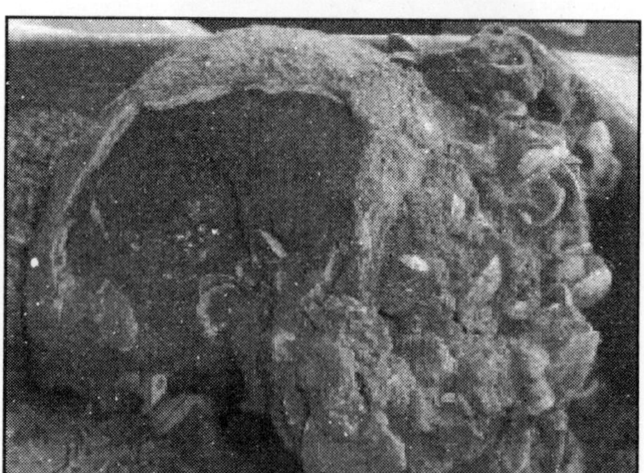

Figure 2: Cranium Encrusted with Shells in Pit 1

Ethnographic analogy suggests that prehistoric coastal peoples consumed shellfish as a major component of their diet, as even today people of these regions harvest and eat shellfish. It is often regarded as a delicacy. Based on abundant bivalve shells encountered in these prehistoric occupation sites, it is suggested that shell fish were delectable as well as a source of protein for these coastal populations. Preliminary results from the faunal analysis indicated the presence of land mammals such as deer, wild boar, and elk (Manamendra-Arachchi pers comm.). These people would have accessed coastal as well as inland resources, developing a solid subsistence base.

The human burials pattern encountered in Miniethiliya signifies modern human behaviour. The pattern discovered by the archaeologists show a cemetery-type layout. The burials are associated with the living areas and have been covered with heaps of shells. The human bones which are encrusted with bivalves (Fig. 2) exemplify these behavioural aspects of the mobile aquatic foragers of the mid Holocene.

Figure 3: Calotte from Pit A (Skeleton # 4)

Figure 4: Mixed Charred Bones from Pit 1

The burials have been greatly disturbed by recent activity, and much of the material was mixed. The human skeletal remains were easily recognizable. They were encrusted with calcite and mollusc fragments. They were associated with geometric microliths, hammerstones and grinders (Perera pers. comm.). Burnt and fragmented animal and human bones (Fig. 3) and some lithics were also recovered during the sorting process. Once the human remains had been sorted and cleaned, a preliminary examination and identification was conducted. Site details including maps, drawings and photographs of provenance and stratigraphy were used.

## Preliminary Description of Skeletal Remains

The study of the physical anthropology of the individuals allows for inferences on their biological adaptations. From the mixed burials, remains of five individuals were recognized. While skeleton numbers 1 to 4 had been buried in a "burial area" skeleton number 5 – which is of a child-had been buried alongside the hearth.

*Skeleton # 1* included an occipital bone fragment with a heavily developed nuchal crest suggesting that this could be an adult male. Fragmented long bones including a distal end of a femur and other fragmented cranial bones were also identified in association with this burial. *Skeleton* # 2 was recognized from a heavily distorted frontal bone has nasal bones, with parts of the zygomatic attached. The supraorbital ridges of the frontal are not pronounced. The right maxilla with teeth showing low attrition and the absence of a third molar indicated that this would belong to a sub-adult. Long bone fragments including a distal end of a radius were also associated with this burial. A fragmented mandible with several teeth showing high attrition belonged to *Skeleton # 3*. $M_3$ has only recently erupted, which indicated that this would be an adult. Careful cleaning and handling allowed the discovery of the hyoid attached to the matrix. This was a significant find for this individual. Several cervical vertebrae were also recovered. Fragments of the right humerus, fragments of a clavicle, radius, and a femur which appear to be relatively robust were also part of this skeleton.

*Skeleton # 4* included the calotte of an adult (a distorted frontal, occipital, parietals, and the right temporal). The maxilla and mandible were intact. No periodontal disease was observed. As no long bones have been excavated in association, it is possible that the rescue operation was unable to salvage them, or that they are fragmented and mixed with the other remains. Initial observations on the cranium show that this individual was dolichocranic. These four burials were located in a "burial area". Excavators observed that these individuals were buried in flexed positions (Perera pers. comm.).

*Skeleton # 5* was that of a child. Very thin and fragmentary cranial bones and fragments of a mandible and maxilla, mixed with charcoal from the associated hearth are among the remains. Based on tooth eruption, the estimated age is five to six years. This burial would have had special significance to the people who mourned the loss of a child, as it was laid to rest alongside the hearth of the habitation site, and not with the other burials. Insights to the mortuary practices and symbolic thought processes of these prehistoric aquatic foragers can be gleaned from these associations. *Skeleton # 6* from Miniethiliya was excavated separately. It has been placed in a plaster cast with the surrounding matrix, and awaits examination and analysis during the field season of 2009.

### Initial Observations and Directions for Further Studies

Modern humans of the Holocene who inhabited South Asia show a high degree of skeletal robusticity (Kennedy 2000; Kulatilake 2000). The people of Miniethiliya also possess features such as thick cranial bones and pronounced nuchal crests, which indicate robust muscular-skeletal structures. Further observations, measurements and comparative analyses will be required to assess the biological adaptations and affinities of these people.

Further study of the people from Miniethiliya will incorporate data already collected from circum-Indian Ocean populations (Kulatilake 2000; Stock *et al* 2007). The location of the site of Miniethiliya in coastal Sri Lanka is of significant interest in the discussion of modern human dispersals to South Asia, and Island Southeast Asia along coastal regions. It is anticipated that this study will serve as a precedent for further investigations related to the physical anthropology of people from other coastal sites. Through interdisciplinary collaboration, an examination of these peoples' subsistence, technology, symbolic expression, mortuary practices, and palaeopathology within the context of their palaeoenvironmental settings could provide more information in addressing questions about affinities and dispersal patterns of early modern humans of South Asia.

## REFERENCES CITED

Cann, R., M. Stoneking and A.Wilson (1987), Mitochondrial DNA and Human Evolution. *Nature* 325, 31–36.

Ceci, L. (1984), Shell Midden Deposits as Coastal Resources. *World Archaeology* 16 (1), Coastal Archaeology 62-74.

Deraniyagala, S.U. (1992), *The Prehistory of Sri Lanka: An Ecological Perspective.* Vol 1 & II. Department of Archaeology: Colombo.

Fields J.S., M.D. Petraglia, and M.M. Lahr (2007), The Southern Dispersal Hypothesis and the South Asian Archaeological Record: Examination of Dispersal Routes through GIS Analysis. *Journal of Anthropological Archaeology* 26, 88-108.

James, H.V.A. (2007), The Emergence of Modern Human Behaviour in South Asia: A Review of the Current Evidence and Discussion of the Possible Implications, in M.D. Petraglia & B. Allchin (ed.) *The Evolution and History of Human Populations in South Asia* (Interdisciplinary Studies in Archaeology, Biological Anthropology, Linguistics and Genetics) 201-227. Springer: Dordrecht

Katupotha, J. (1995), Evolution and Geological Significance of Holocene Emerged Shell Beds on the Southern Coastal Zone of Sri Lanka. *Journal of Coastal Research* 11(4): 1042-1061.

Kennedy, K.A.R., (2000), *God-apes and Fossil Men: Palaeoanthropology in South Asia.* The University of Michigan Press: AnnArbor.

Kingdon, J. (1993), *Self-Made Man and his Undoing.* Simon and Schuster: London.

Kourampas, N. I., I.A. Simpson, H.N. Perera, and S.U. Deraniyagala (2008), Late Pleistocene Hunter-gatherers in the South Asian Rainforest: Geoarchaeology of Inhabited Rockshelters in South-Western Sri Lanka. *Antiquity* 82, 316

Kulatilake, S.D. (2000), *Cranial Diversity and the Evolutionary History of South Asians.* Unpublished PhD Thesis. University of Cambridge: Cambridge

Lahr, M., and R. Foley (1994), Multiple Dispersals and Modern Human Origins. *Evolutionary Anthropology* 3, 48–60.

Lahr, M. and R. Foley (1998), Towards a Theory of Modern Human Origins: Geography, Demography, and Diversity in Recent Human Evolution. *Yearbook of Physical Anthropology* 41, 137–176.

Mellars, P. (2006), Going East: New Genetic and Archaeological Perspectives on the Modern Human Colonization of Eurasia. *Science* 313, 796–800.

Perera, H.N. (nd) *A Review of the Prehistory of Sri Lanka* (2nd edition). Department of Archaeological Survey: Colombo (in press)

Somadeva, R. and S. Ranasinghe (2006), An Excavation of a Shell Midden at Pallemalla in Southern Littoral Area of Sri Lanka. *Ancient Asia* 1, 14-24.

Ranaweera, R.M.S.L. (2002), *A Study of Human Skeletal Remains from Pallemalla Shell Midden in Southern Sri Lanka.* Unpublished BSc dissertation, University of

Sri Jayawardenapura Stock, J.T., M.M. Lahr and S.Kulatilake (2007), Cranial Diversity in South Asia Relative to Modern Human Dispersals and Global Patterns of Human Variation, in M.D. Petraglia & B. Allchin (ed.) *The Evolution and History of Human Populations in South Asia* (Interdisciplinary Studies in Archaeology, Biological Anthropology, Linguistics and Genetics): 246-268. Springer: Dordrecht

Stringer, C.B. (2000), Coasting Out of Africa. *Nature* 405 (6782), 24–27.

Walter, R.C., R.T. Buffler, J.H. Bruggemann, M.M.M. Guillaume, S.M. Berhe, B. Negassi, Y. Libsekal, H. Cheng, R.L. Edwards, R. von Cosel, D. Ne´raudeau, and M. Gagnon (2000), Early Human Occupation of the Red Sea Coast of Eritrea during the Last Interglacial. *Nature* 405, 65–69.

Wijeyapala, W.H. (1997), *New Light on the Prehistory of Sri Lanka in the Context of Recent Investigations of Cave Sites.* Unpublished PhD Thesis, University of Peradeniya.

I thank Dr. A.R. Sankhyan for inviting my paper and recommending me for the financial support making this possible.

CHAPTER–19

# Dental Evolution in Protohistoric Indians

*S.R. Walimbe*

## INTRODUCTION

Dentition is constructed of hard and dense material and therefore resists decay in the ground and often survives longer than bone. Our knowledge of many extinct pre-hominid and hominid fossils is based on dental evidence. The complexities of bio-cultural (or genetic-environmental) interaction in prehistoric human populations are well illustrated in dentition. Dental anthropology is a recently developed tool for physical anthropologists to describe a given population biologically. It has been realized that dental variations, both morphometric and pathological, provide valuable information for reconstructing phylogenetic relationships among different hominid species (ancient and living), the comparative study of different primate groups, evolutionary changes in dentition, or the impact of diet on dentition.

Investigations in the field of dental anthropology basically attempt to document and explain the changes observed in dental size and complexity during the course of human evolution. The mechanism of dental evolutionary process is not precisely known. Yet, it is fairly clear that during the course of human evolution tooth size has decreased and dental morphology has become simplified, and this change is proportionate to the technological advancement achieved by society (Brace 1962; Dahlberg 1945, 1962). It has been hypothesized that dental evolutionary status corresponds to the strong selective pressures posed by developing technology and increased efficiency of food preparation methods attained by any population. This evolutionary trend is well documented on the dental features of both ancient and present-day populations. For example, the coarse and uncooked diet of Mesolithic man probably resulted in large dental structures. The development and increased sophistication of man's technology during the food-producing Neolithic-Chalcolithic stage led to a relaxation of selection pressures resulting in dental reduction (Brace 1963, 1967; *quoted in* Lukacs 1984). The same evolutionary trend continues among the contemporary populations as well. Brace (1963, 1967) is of the opinion that the people with the smallest teeth in the world are those whose remote ancestors first developed a complex technology, adopted a sedentary life style based on agriculture subsistence, and made pottery for the effective boiling of foodstuffs. A general reduction in the size of jawbones, as a result of changed food habits and life styles, is yet another possible explanation for dental reduction (Robinson 1954), presuming the available space on the jaw being the main deciding factor for dental size.

In the initial stages dental anthropological research was confined to professional dentists. Studies were carried out only from a clinical point of view, mostly on patients, without any specific anthropological research design making the sample heterogeneous. After mid-1950's, the field of dental anthropology attracted many physical anthropologists. Gradually, measurement techniques were standardized and morphological features categorized. This facilitated meaningful comparisons of morphometric features for different ethnic groups. Now dental features are increasingly used for solving specific problems regarding human evolution and contemporary biological variations, the relationship between jaw size and dentition, occlusion accuracy, bilateral symmetry, sexual dimorphism, deciduous and permanent dental eruption patterns, and pathology. Further many physical anthropologists use this research tool for interpreting the nature of human adaptation in response to diet, occupation, sex and age, or towards the solving of forensic mysteries.

While ample dental data is available for many populations across the world, data on Indian populations, ancient and living, is extremely sporadic and incomplete. The field of dental anthropology had a slow start in India. Though for several decades the research orientations in physical anthropology remained focussed to establish '*racial*' or '*ethnic*' identity of different endogamous groups, the dental features were not used effectively. In recent years, however, serious attempts are being made to use dentition for interpreting facial evolutionary trends in relation to food habits. The paper provides summary of the dental anthropological studies carried out so far on the Indian skeletal populations, in two broad categories: morphometry and pathology.

## INDIAN SCENARIO

Though main aim of this paper is to discuss the studies on the Indian prehistoric dentition a brief mention of one study on contemporary populations is necessary (Walimbe and Kulkarni 1993). While most of the studies on contemporary populations are in taxonomic orientation, this study deserves special attention, as the results are relevant for the past populations as well.

Walimbe and Kulkarni (1993) have attempted to trace the dental evolutionary history in India, with special emphasis on dental size reduction tendencies. For better interpreting the archaeological dentition, vast dental data on four endogamous communities (viz. Maratha, Mahar, Mahadeo Koli and Gond) has been generated in this study. The main attempt is to evaluate the odontometric data in several perspectives. The dental reduction and simplification process is explained in relation to technological levels and food preparation methods. The study also takes into account the inter-group biological distances expressed in dental features, the nature of sexual dimorphism and bilateral symmetry expressed in dentition, and the correlation between facial measurements and dental size.

Walimbe-Kulkarni's (1993) work is based on a well-defined hypothesis with sociological dimensions. The theories propounded by social anthropologists and archaeologists trace the origin of Hinduism to the ancient agricultural societies, especially to the Indus Civilization of northwest India. The cult is supposed to have spread rapidly in India following the spread of agriculture. The intensified agricultural activities gradually involved several tribal isolates. The origin of the caste system in India is traced back to such a process of absorption (or '*Hinduization*') of tribal groups into the main stream of Hindu society (Kolenda 1978, Misra 2001). Probably in the initial stages these tribal people constituted the main labour force required for the agricultural activities, and consequently, they occupied a "low-caste" ranking in the social hierarchy, subordinate to the "high-ranking" Hindu populations. These newly converted groups gradually learnt farming activities thereby changing their subsistence pattern from nomadic hunting/gathering or pastoralism to sedentary agriculture. It seems that the tribal groups responded differentially to the process of *Hinduization*, some groups were quick enough in responding, a few others were rather slow, while some resisted the process of acculturization. Those who resisted continued to practice pastoralism or hunting/gathering subsistence life style, and because of their traditional system of local folk beliefs, were socially considered outside the Hindu caste system. Thus, the position of various groups in the Hindu social framework was decided according to the adoption of agriculture and Hindu beliefs. The process of *Hinduization* was very slow but well defined. As a result, in a cross-sectional segment three main groupings are evident, each with a distinctive pattern of technological capabilities: a. "high-caste" Hindus, who have been exposed longer to the agricultural practices, b. "low-caste" Hindus, who recently adopted agriculture as part of the *Hinduization* process, and, c. "non- caste" tribal groups who largely remained non-agricultural nomads even today with a functional but basic technology. The process of *Hinduization* still appears to be effective on the "non-caste" tribal groups. Many tribal groups are undergoing the process of acculturization and showing an inclination for settled agricultural life.

The four living endogamous groups selected for this study, Gond, Mahadeo Koli, Mahar and Maratha, represent populations experiencing different life styles and practicing different methods of food procurement and preparation. Morphometric assessment of the dental features of these four groups strongly supports the hypothesis of a direct relationship between technological achievement and food preparation methods, and dental reduction and simplification. The Gonds who are still hunter-gatherers have the largest and most complex dentition in the given series while the Marathas, a settled urban community, have the smallest and least complex dentition. The progress of dental reduction can be traced from the Gonds to the Marathas through the Mahadeo Kolis and Mahars (Table 1).

**Table 1**
**Total Crown Area (TCA) Among Selected Present-day Populations**
*(Figures in mm2)*

| *Population* | *Male* | *Female* | *F-M ratio* |
|---|---|---|---|
| Gond | 1204 | 1087 | 90.28 |
| Mahadeo Koli | 1138 | 1041 | 91.48 |
| Mahar | 1081 | 1016 | 93.99 |
| Maratha | 1040 | 986 | 94.81 |

This study states that the sociological hypothesis of *Hinduization* process cannot be tested in its entirety on the basis of biological parameters. Nevertheless, this study suggests that biological features, if they are related to occupation and food habits, can be used to support (if not to verify) sociological judgment. If the history of *Hinduization* is to be correlated with agricultural history, then the larger and more complex dentition in tribal groups, and, the smaller and simpler dentition in Hindu caste groups are justified. The Mahadeo Kolis who are undergoing rapid acculturization have smaller teeth than the Gonds, a tribal group. Mahars, a "low-caste" Hindu group, who have adopted agriculture only a few centuries ago, exhibit smaller teeth than the Mahadeo Kolis. The Marathas, representative of "high-caste" Hindu groups, who have been exposed to agricultural practices for a much longer period, have the smallest and least complex dentition in the given series.

The study further highlights the limitations of dental metric data in *'racial'* discrimination. The differences in dental size are largely attributed to occupational and dietary rather than taxonomical differences. Dental size is more susceptible to selective pressure than morphological or physiological features, and therefore changes in dental size are more gradual. Dental indices, however, are regarded to be of much more relevance in ethnic comparisons than absolute dimensions.

Dental size is also related to the space available in the jaw during the crown calcification process. It has been shown that the molar crown area is in direct proportion with the jaw size. Another study undertaken by the present author (Walimbe 1998) to investigate this association confirms that the change in subsistence strategies from hunting-gathering to agriculture and an accompanying decrease in work-demand placed on the masticatory apparatus resulted in changes in craniofacial morphology. Agricultural populations have less robust and smaller jaws than the pre-agricultural populations. The sequence of dental reduction thus appears to be in harmony with the craniofacial changes experienced during the agricultural transition.

The degree of sexual dimorphism as expressed in skeletal robusticity is of high intensity in the pre-agricultural phase. Differential work demands placed on males and females are reflected in bodily features. In hunting-gathering communities, males are presumed to have more laborious activities and therefore tend to be more robust. The females who are mostly engaged in domestic activities are rather gracile. On the other hand, in agricultural populations the workload on males and females is almost equal. As a result, males tend to be more gracile and females more robust in comparison with their counterparts in the pre-agricultural stage, thus reducing the robusticity gap. This fact is supported by archaeological skeletal evidence where a higher degree of sexual dimorphism is evident in Mesolithic populations than in the later farming communities (Walimbe 1998). In the four living groups studied, the Gonds, as expected, show a greater degree of sexual dimorphism in body measurements and dental size than the other groups whereas sexual dimorphism among the Marathas and Mahars is of much lower significance (Table 1). It is also possible that the differences in availability of food may be a contributory factor. Males consume proportionately more meat than females and this fact might be at least partially responsible for larger dentition in males.

## ARCHAEOLOGICAL DENTAL COLLECTIONS

In the first place not many skeletal collections have been subjected to rigorous anthropological scrutiny (Walimbe and Tavares 2002). Moreover, these skeletal reports seldom included dental data, and, occasionally when it appeared, remained limited to a casual comment on dental pathology (caries, alveolar resorption, dental abscess, attrition, etc.) and gross morphological features. Metric analyses were attempted only for molar teeth. Lack of awareness of the research potential of dental data on the part of the investigator was probably the main reason. The fragmentary nature of the material in some cases could have been a discouraging factor. In addition, heavy attrition precluded studies on occlusal morphological variation. Moreover, the evolutionary trends in metric features became evident only when greater recording accuracy was achieved with electronic or needlepoint dial callipers. As a result, reference to dental material had been very casual and incomplete. The features wherever reported have not been categorized using accepted standards, thereby further limiting the value of such research in comparative analysis. Nevertheless, some reports provided an inventory of the dental material.

Sewell and Guha (1929, 1931a/b) included dental analysis in their Makran, Mohenjo-daro (Marshall's series) and Nal osteological reports. These studies are noteworthy not only because for the first time dental material was studied but also many significant metric and pathological observations were made on the Indian sample. However, in the subsequent three decades such detailed treatment was rarely given to dental evidence.

Credit goes to Prof. Kenneth Kennedy and his student, Prof. John Lukacs, who not only set the trend for a systematic and thorough analysis of dental evidence in palaeoanthropological research in India but also encouraged many researchers to employ dental parameters in bio-cultural interpretations. The inclusion of a systematic anthropological analysis of prehistoric dental remains in osteological reports published by Kennedy in the mid-1960s (for example, the reports for Bellan Bandi Palassa, Langhnaj or Nevasa) showed the research potential of dental data while interpreting the bio-cultural adaptations. This attracted many scholars to use this new line of evidence in their skeletal analysis and subsequently reports for many sites incorporated data on dentition. Yet, for quite some time dental morphometry was studied primarily to answer the queries of the '*racial*' affiliations of these populations, and since the sample size in many being too small, no meaningful inferences could be derived. Nonetheless, recent studies on prehistoric human dentition are more focused on the specific research orientation of explaining the role of ecology and subsistence strategies in their evolution.

The works mentioned below include dental data at least marginally (reports with casual mention of dentition are not included).

*Mesolithic Sites:*

Bagor (Lukacs *et al.* 1982)

Batadomba Lena, Sri Lanka (Kennedy 1992; Kennedy *et al.* 1986a)

Beli Lena, Sri Lanka (Kennedy 1992; Kennedy *et al.* 1986a)

Bellan Bandi Palassa, Sri Lanka (Kennedy 1965)

Bhimbetka (Kennedy *et al.* 2002)

Damdama (Robbins 2000)

Langhnaj (Ehrhardt and Kennedy 1965)

Lekhahia (Lukacs 1997)

Mahadaha (Kennedy *et al.* 1992)

Sarai Nahar Rai (Kennedy *et al.* 1986b)

*Bronze Age Harappan Sites:*

Harappa (Bernhard *et al.* 1998; Dutta 1980, 1983a, 1983b; Hemphill *et al.* 1991; Lukacs 1982b, 1992a, 1998)

Rakhi Garhi (Walimbe in prep-a)

Rupar (Dutta *et al.* 1987)

*Neolithic-Chalcolithic Sites:*

Apegaon (Lukacs 1980)

Balathal (Robbins *et al.* 2007)

Balijapalle (Walimbe *et al.* 1993)

Banahalli (Walimbe in prep-b)

Budihal (Walimbe and Paddayya 1999)

Burzahom (Basu and Pal 1980)

Daimabad (Walimbe 1986a)

Hullikallu (Walimbe 1993a)

Ieej (Walimbe 1993b)

Inamgaon (Lukacs 1981a, 1985a, 1987: Lukacs and Walimbe 1984, 1986: Lukacs *et al.* 1983)

Kaothe (Walimbe 1990)

Mehrgarh, Pakistan (Lukacs 1983a, 1985b, 1988, 1989a)

Nevasa (Kennedy and Malhotra 1966; Walimbe and Mushrif 2006)

Piklihal (Malhotra 1967)

Tuljapur Garhi (Walimbe 1994, 1996a)

Walki (Mushrif and Walimbe 2000)

*Megalithic Sites:*

Agripalli (Walimbe *et al.* in press)

Borgaon (Walimbe 1986b)

Kanyathirthum (Walimbe *et al.* 1991)

Khairwada (Walimbe 1986b)

Kodumanal (Mushrif *et al.* in press-a)

Mahurjhari (Lukacs 1981b)

Pomparippu, Sri Lanka (Lukacs 1976; Lukacs and Kennedy 1981)

Raipur (Walimbe 1986b, 1992, 1993c)

S. Pappinayakkanpatti (Walimbe and Selvakumar 1998);

Sarai Khola, Pakistan (Lukacs 1983b, Lukacs and Hemphill 1990, 1991, Lukacs *et al.* 1985, 1989)

Timargarh, Pakistan (Lukacs 1983b, Lukacs and Hemphill 1990, 1991, Lukacs *et al.* 1985, 1989)

*Medieval-Early Historic-Historic Sites:*

Padri (Walimbe and Shinde 1995)

Kuntasi (Walimbe and Mushrif 1999).Kumhar Tekri (Gupta *et al.* 1970)

Jotsoma (Mushrif *et al.* in press-b)

Sanjan (Mushrif and Walimbe in press-c)

## DENTAL MORPHOMETRY

Most of these publications give data on two basic measurements, maximum crown length (mesio-distal diameter) and maximum crown breadth (bucco-lingual diameter), following the Moorrees' (1957) technique. Dental dimensions are used to compute three primary comparative standards, the measure of the cross-sectional area of the tooth (CA), the ratio of MD and BL diameter (CI), and the measure of crown bulk-module (CM), using Wolpoff (1971). Two composite figures are obtained to facilitate comparative study of dental adaptations in response to the subsistence pattern and the level of food processing technique, the total crown area (TCA), and the molar crown area (MCA). In addition, some studies provide basic data on three other indices for the maxillary and mandibular teeth, incisor breadth index, molarisation index and step index, without clearly highlighting the utility.

**Table 2**
**Molar Crown Area (MCA) for Selected Sites in Decreasing Order***

| *Culture* | *Site* | *MCA* |
|---|---|---|
| Mesolithic | Langhnaj | 756.01 |
| Chalcolithic | Daimabad | 726.23 |
| Mesolithic | Bellan Bandi Palassa | 702 46 |
| Neolithic | Mehrgarh | 697.74 |
| Mesolithic | Bagor | 695.10 |
| Megalithic | Mahurjhari | 675.54 |
| Chalcolithic | Inamgaon | 671.38 |
| Modern | Gond (M) | 661.23 |
| Chalcolithic Megalithic | Banahali | 654.74 |
| Chalcolithic | Nevasa | 642.91 |
| Megalithic | Timargarh | 642.45 |
| Megalithic | Pomparippu | 625.00 |
| Modern | Mahadev Koli (M) | 623.89 |
| Megalithic | Sarai Khola | 613.52 |
| Harappan | Harappa | 606.32 |
| Historic | Jotsoma | 606.25 |

*Contd.*

| *Culture* | *Site* | *MCA* |
|---|---|---|
| Megalithic | Kodumanal | 604.03 |
| Historic | Padri | 602.80 |
| Modern | Gond (F) | 597.07 |
| Modern | Mahar (M) | 597.24 |
| Medieval | Sanjan Dokhama | 593.12 |
| Megalithic | Hullikallu | 592.79 |
| Modern | Maratha (M) | 575.54 |
| Modern | Mahadev Koli (F) | 572.96 |
| Harappan | Rupar | 563.98 |
| Mesolithic | Sarai Nahar Rai | 563.76 |
| Modern | Mahar (F) | 561.20 |
| Neolithic | Burzahom | 559.99 |
| Modern | Maratha (F) | 546.60 |
| Historic | Kuntasi | 517.49 |

* Modified after Lukacs (1985a) and Walimbe-Kulkarni (1993).

Barring a few exceptions, one of the most significant features that emerges for maxillary teeth is the lager crown size of the mesial members of incisor, premolar and molar tooth class (I1s, Pm1s and M1s) than their respective distal members. These teeth are bigger in size, both length and breadth wise. Mandibular dentition too, shows such consistency in the molars, while the lateral incisors and second premolars are bigger than their respective mesial members. Usually maxillary and mandibular molars exhibit a progressive reduction of size in order of M1>M2>M3>. For deciduous dentition dm2s are larger than dm1s in both MD and BL dimensions, in both upper and lower jaws.

Among the populations listed in the Table 2, the highest MCA value is obtained for the Mesolithic Langhnaj and the lowest for the Historic Kuntasi. The Meso-lithic, Neolithic and Chalcolithic populations have MCA values of more than 640, except for that of Sarai Nahar Rai and Burzahom (563.76 and 559.99, respectively). The Harappan populations have molar size smaller than that of the Megalithic populations (MCA values 606.32 for Harappa and 563.98 for Rupar). The Daimabad specimen represents the Late Harappan phase of the Chalcolithic culture. This phase has not yielded much evidence of agriculture (Sali 1986). The subsistence was probably on both hunting and gathering with agricultural supplementation. The larger crown area of Daimabad specimen could be attributed to such mixed economy. No explanation can however be given for the smaller molar size area of the Mesolithic Sarai Nahar Rai or Neolithic Burzahom. Sarai Nahar Rai skeletons are characterized by large and muscular robust cranial and post-cranial features and tall stature (Kennedy *et al.* 1986). The discrepancy in dental size and body size is difficult to explain. At Burzahom also hunting and gathering way of life could be established on the basis of cultural antiquity. There is no evidence of agriculture or even for the domestication of animals. The smallest (in the series) dental size of Burzahom specimen does not fit in this context. The Harappan culture is essentially an urban culture. The smaller dental size in Harappans could be interpreted as urban adaptation of the population for the soft and processed food. High incidence of caries among Harappans supports the hypothesis of food economy consisting of more carbo-hydrate food than meat. The MCA of the Sanjan dokhama series, 593.12 $mm^2$, is based on large sample. So is not the case with the Sarai Nahar Rai, Burzahom or Rupar. The deviation from the normal trend seen in these populations can be to some extent attributable to smaller sample. By and large the Sanjan dentition (1500 AD) compares well with the modern population (where also sample size is large and therefore more reliable). The Sanjan MCA values stand between those given for the present day Gonds and Mahadeo Kolis. The Gonds are stated to have adapted agriculture very lately, and still obtain large component of their food from wild sources. The Mahadeo Kolis, scheduled tribe, though turned to farming probably a century ago, still have 'mixed' food economy. The Sanjan dentition can better be understood in this context. They were urban population, affluent, probably engaged in trade. The main component of their food economy must have been derived from domesticated varieties of flora and fauna. Masticatory stress, therefore, must have been less than that for the early agro-pastoral or Iron Age populations.

Of course, the inferences drawn from these comparisons are not to be stretched too far. For most of the populations, sample being small in size, data for male and female individuals is pooled. Furthermore, the sites are widely separated occupying diverse geographical areas and have evidenced racial differences in the skeletal morphology, etc. Lastly, different scholars have studied dental sample, and therefore personal error is possibly reflected in recording. To summarize the discussion, the 'pooled' MCA values for different cultural phases are given in table 3.

**Table 3**
**Culture-wise Pooled TCA/MCA Values**

| *Culture* | *TCA* | *MCA* |
|---|---|---|
| Mesolithic | 1258 | 673 |
| Neolithic | 1203 | 668 |
| Bronze Age | 1234 | 645 |
| Chalcolithic | 1218 | 699 |
| Megalithic | 1167 | 639 |
| Modern | 1101 | 597 |

The dentition of the Mesolithic skeletal series of Damdama has been studied in histological perspective for deriving a standard for age estimation (Robbins 2000). Pastor (1989) has studied dental microwear pattern and attrition for some Mesolithic, Chalcolithic and Bronze Age series. The present author does not have access to this doctoral dissertation;

but the scholar has subsequently published some of the results (Pastor 1992).

Of the list provided above more recent studies have used the reference plaster plaques prepared by the ASU Dental Anthropology System (Turner II *et al.* 1991) for making specific observations of occlusal morphology. While commenting on dental morphological studies, special mention must be made of the contribution of Diane Hawkey (2002). By using certain dental morphological traits she examined the relationships between the South Asian populations with other Late Pleistocene/Holocene world populations, and commented on the role of South Asian populations in the process of the peopling of the world. Usage of the dental morphometric features in explaining the biological origins, affinities, and probable migrations during the prehistoric times has been accepted by the archaeological community in India, though recently some doubts have been raised by historians for extending biological data for such purpose (Ratnagar 1998). Nonetheless, it would be worthwhile to mention few of the Hawkey's main inferences.

While putting one of the important conclusions Hawkey writes, both the Indus and the Deccan farming/herding communities share similarities with Indian Mesolithic hunter-gatherers, reflecting a common origin for the protohistoric communities. According to this study, the inhabitants of the Indus Civilization appear most likely the descendants of the indigenous hunter-gather populations of South Asia, rather than intrusive (and genetically distinct) populations from the West. In other words, this inference implies genetic continuity in the sub-continent for the last 20,000 years. While underlying genetic homogeneity of the Indus people, the study concludes that there is no biological support to the argument that the Indus civilization belongs exclusively to the Dravidians. "The confusing of a linguistically-defined population ('Dravidian') with a biological population (Indus) has plagued Indian population affinity research for many years" (Hawkey, 2002:194). The peoples of the Indus Civilization are dentally similar not only to modern Dravidian-speakers (of South India, Sri Lankan Tamil), but also to the Indo-European (Afghanistan/Pakistan, Bengal, Sri Lankan Sinhalese), and Austro-Asiatic (East India) groups as well. The dental data thus supports the hypothesis that the Indus population was multi-linguistic, and probably ethnically diverse (Hawkey, 2002:155). It may be noted that, even on the basis of craniometry it has now been appreciated that the Harappans do not exhibit any significant phenotypic type (Kennedy, 1984b). Though the skeletal material at Harappa is coming from three different deposits, the population belongs to a single morphometrically homogenous series. "The variations in cranial size and form are very much in the acceptable range and can be understood as a normal range of physical variability present in most urban populations, past and present" (Kennedy, 1982:217).

Hawkey further opines that there is no substantial amount of gene flow between the Indus and the Deccan farming/herding communities. In other words, the Deccan Neolithic-Chalcolithic groups are stated to have evolved directly from the hunting-gathering Mesolithic communities. In this case, few similarities seen between the Indus sample and contemporaneous peoples of the Deccan farming-herding cultures are due to cultural contacts (influencing food habits) rather than biological in nature. It may be noted that evidence for contact between the two groups, based on economic/trade exchange has been observed in the archaeological record (Possehl, 1976; Kennedy and Possehl, 1979).

Hawkey's dental morphological data further indicates that there is little evidence to support an external origin for the Iron Age / Megalithic populations. The data rather suggest the origins of the Iron Age populations within central and southern peninsular India, and not from north-western regions.

One more study deserves special mention while summarizing the comment on morphology, the study on the Sanjan dental series. A crude estimate of the size of the dental inventory of the excavation amounts to approx. 3600 to 4000. Only a part of this collection has been studies as yet. By any scale this is the largest dental collection representing a specific ethnic group, the Parsis, which is a very rare thing to happen in the archaeological record. The Parsis are Zoroastrian refugees from Iran, who made their landing near the present town of Sanjan on the coast of western India around 750 A.D. Though the Parsis have no formal written history prior to the advent of the British, right from their arrival on the Indian mainland about 1300 years ago, over the years they have adapted themselves to the local ecosettings, yet they have culturally secluded themselves from the indigenous population. Endogamy is very strictly followed. Because of reproductive isolation and the smaller population size, evolutionary changes appear to have accumulated more rapidly, which are seen in the form of more common occurrence of rare genetic dental morphological traits. One of the aims of this study is to compare the Sanjan skeletal population with the prehistoric and contemporary Iranian populations and the present-day Indian Parsi inhabitants.

## DENTAL PALAEOPATHOLOGY

Earlier studies on dental pathologies of Indian archaeological populations largely remained confined to caries, attrition, malocclusion, dental crowding, etc. Descriptions occurred only sporadically, but the approach was superficial and lacked an interpretive framework. Pathological recording was (is) normally based gross macroscopic observations, sometime at the most using 10-X magnifying lens. Recent studies (for example, series of Jotsoma, Kodumanal, Nevasa, Sanjan) have used radiography technique for confirming the diagnosis taking stringent precautionary measures. Main references used while describing the pathologies and anomalies are Larsen (1997), Ortner and Putschar (1981), Roberts and Manchester (1995) and Lukacs (1989b).

The foremost publication for dental palaeopathology is by Pal (1981), who commented on the incidence of specific dental diseases in some prehistoric skeletal series. However, the study to set the trend of interpreting pathologies in bio-cultural perspective for the Indian sites is probably the one on the Iron Age Megalithic skeletal series of Mahurjhari in Central India (1981b). Later Lukacs used dental palaeopathological evidence from the Indian sub-continent to redefine methodological concepts in the subject (Lukacs 1989b, 1995), and extended this approach to other sites, for example, to the Early Neolithic site of Mehrgarh in Baluchistan (1985b, also Lukacs and Hemphill 1990; Lukacs and Minderman 1992; Lukacs and Pastor 1988; Lukacs *et al.* 1985), sites of the Indus valley (Lukacs 1982b, 1991, 1992), Sarai Khola and Timargarh (Lukacs 1983b, Lukacs and Hemphill 1990, 1991, Lukacs *et al.* 1985, 1989) in North Pakistan. Besides caries and attrition, several dental and gnathic pathologies have been reported including enamel deficiencies, alveolar resorption, tarter accumulation, enamel coloration (flourosis) and ante-mortem tooth loss. Macroscopic dental pathology of the Gangetic Mesolithic series (Kennedy *et al.* 1986, 1992, Lukacs and Pal 1993), Deccan Chalcolithic skeletal series–Apegaon (Lukacs 1980), Inamgaon (Lukacs 1978; Lukacs and Walimbe 1998, 2000; Walimbe and Lukacs 1992), Daimabad (Walimbe 1986a), Kaothe (Walimbe 1990)–have been interpreted along with the dietary customs of these populations. It has been noted that pathologies like enamel micro-defects, caries and alveolar resorption occur more frequently in agricultural populations than they did in hunter-gatherer Mesolithic populations. On the other hand, attrition induced pathologies are more frequent in the Mesolithic populations consuming hard and unprocessed food. Studies on enamel defects on primary anterior teeth have proved useful in verifying archaeological hypotheses about cultural decline of Deccan Chalcolithic phase (Lukacs and Walimbe 1998). Special mention must be made of the dental studies on the Mahadaha collection, a Gangatic Mesolithic site (Kennedy *et al.* 1992; Lukacs 1990; Lukacs and Hemphill 1992; Lukacs and Pal 1993; Pastor 1992). The dental evidence recovered from this site proved to be the luckiest for having received the best laboratory attention. Each tooth has been described for its odontometric, morphological and macro/microscopic pathological lesions, thus providing an example of an excellent model study. This model has been used more recent studies carried out under the supervision of the present author (Mushrif *et al.*, in press a/b; Mushrif and Walimbe, in press). However, it needs to be mentioned that lack of adequate funding precludes dental microwear or histological analysis.

## COMMENTS

The subject of dental anthropology has a wide research potential in India to understand the nature of biological evolution in response to the ecological, technological and regional context. Archaeological and living Indian populations provide unparalleled laboratory conditions to test the hypotheses of dental evolution in broader perspectives. The continent provides a well defined range of archaeological sites covering a wide cultural span from the Mesolithic through to Early Historic levels. Many of these sites yield ample human skeletal and dental elements. More fascinating is the diversity seen in living populations. The range manifested in the variety of subsistence patterns, food preparation techniques, etc., among westernized urbanities, rural village farmers, nomadic pastoralists, tribal hunter-gatherers is the only one of its kind in the world. The studies on this kind of stratified sample are anthropologically profitable as many of the groups rigidly follow the endogamous practices since ancient times. The hypothesis of correlation between tooth size, complexity and technology levels could therefore be thoroughly studied on such prehistoric or living samples. A careful approach in this direction is necessary.

## REFERENCES CITED


Basu, A. and A. Pal (1980), *Human Remains from Burzahom*. Kolkata: Anthropological Survey of India. Memoir 56.

Bernhard, W., J.R. Lukacs and K.A.R. Kennedy (1998), Two Previously Undescribed Human Skeletons from Prehistoric Harappa, Pakistan, *Homo* 49(1):21-54.

Brace, C.L. (1962), Cultural Factors in the Evolution of the Human Dentition, in *Culture and the Evolution of Man* (M.F. Ashley Ed.), pp. 343-354. New York: Oxford University Press.

Brace, C.L. (1963), Structural Reduction in Evolution, *American Naturalist* 97: 39-49.

Brace, C.L. (1964), The Probable Mutation Effect, *American Naturalist* 98: 453-455.

Brace, C.L. (1967), *The Stages of Human Evolution*. Englewood Cliffs, New Jersey: Prentice-Hall.

Dahlberg, A.A. (1945), The Changing Dentition of Man, *Journal of the American Dental Association* 32:676-690.

Dahlberg, A.A. (1962), On the Teeth of Early Sapiens, in *Evolution and Hominization* (G. Kurth Ed.), pp. 205-11. Stuttgart: Fischer Verlag.

Dutta, P.C. (1980), Molar Crown Characteristics of the Bronze Age Harappans and Natural Selection, *Proceedings of the Symposium on Three Decades of Development in Paleontology and Stratigraphy in India*, Hyderabad: 85.

Dutta, P.C. (1983 a), A Study of the Molar Teeth of the Bronze Age Harappans in the Context of Evolutionary Biology, *Anthropologie* 21(2): 97-102.

Dutta, P.C. (1983 b), *The Bronze Age Harappans: A Bio-Anthropological Study of the Skeletons Discovered at Harappa*. New Delhi: Anthropological Survey of India.

Dutta, P.C., A. Pal, P. Gupta and B.C. Dutta (1987), *Ancient Human Remains from Rupar*. Kolkata: Anthropological Survey of India.

Ehrhardt, S. and K.A.R. Kennedy (1965), *Excavations at Langhnaj: 1944-1963: Part III: The Human Remains*. Pune: Deccan College Research Institute.

Gupta, P.A., Basu and P. C. Dutta (1970), *Ancient Human Remains*. Kolkata: Anthropological Survey of India.

Hawkey, D.E. (2002), The Peopling of South Asia: Evidence for Affinities and Microevolution of Prehistoric Populations from India/Sri Lanka. *Spolia Zeylanica* 39, 1-300.

Hemphill, B.E., J.R. Lukacs and K.A.R. Kennedy (1991), Biological Adaptations and Affinities of Bronze Age Harappans, in *Harappa Excavations 1986-1990: a Multidisciplinary Approach to Third Millennium Urbanization* (R.H. Meadow Ed.), pp. 137-182. Madison: Prehistory Press.

Kennedy, K.A.R. (1965), Human Skeletal Material from Ceylon, with an Analysis of the Island's Prehistoric and Contemporary Populations, *Bulletin of the British Museum, Geology* II-4:135-213.

Kennedy, K.A.R. (1982), Palaeodemographic Perspectives of Social Structural Change in Harappan Society, in *Archaeology of Pakistan: Recent Socio-cultural and Archaeological Perspective* (S. Pastner and L. Flam, Eds), pp.211-18. Ithaca: Cornell University South Asia Program.

Kennedy, K.A.R. (1984 b), A Reassessment of The Theories of Racial Origins of the People of the Indus Valley Civilization from Recent Anthropological Data, in *Studies in the Archaeology and Palaeoanthropology of South Asia* (K.A.R. Kennedy and G.L. Possehl Eds) , pp. 99-107. New Delhi: Oxford-IBH Publishing.

Kennedy, K.A.R. (1992), Tooth Size Variation of the Veddas and Prehistoric Sri Lankans, in *Culture, Ecology and Dental Anthropology* (J.R. Lukacs Ed.), pp. 171-182. New Delhi: Kamala Raj Enterprises.

Kennedy, K.A.R., T. Disotell, W.J. Roertgen, and J. Sherry (1986 a), Biological Anthropology of Upper Pleistocene Hominids from Sri Lanka: Batadomba Lena and Beli Lena Caves, *Ancient Ceylon* 6.

Kennedy, K.A.R., N.C. Lovell and C.B. Burrow (1986 b), *Mesolithic Human Remains from the Sarai Nahar Rai*. Ithaca, N.Y.: Cornell University, South Asia Programme.

Kennedy, K.A.R., J.R. Lukacs, R.F. Paster, T.L. Johnston, N.C. Lovell, J.N. Pal, B.E. Hemphill and C.B. Burrow (1992), *Human Skeletal Remains from Mahadaha: a Gangetic Mesolithic Site*. Ithaca, N.Y.: Cornell University, South Asia Programme.

Kennedy, K.A.R., J.R. Lukacs and V.N. Misra (2002), *The Biological Anthropology of Human Skeletal Remains from Bhimbetka, Central India*. Pune: ISPQS.

Kennedy, K.A.R. and K.C. Malhotra (1965), *Human Skeletal Remains from Chalcolithic and Indo-Roman Levels from Nevasa: An Anthro-pometric and Comparative Analysis*. Pune: Deccan College Research Institute.

Kolenda, P. (1978), *Caste in Contemporary India: Beyond Organic Solidarity*. Mento Park: Cummins.

Larsen, C.S. (1997), *Bioarchaeology: Interpreting Behaviour from Human Skeleton*. United Kingdom: Cambridge University Press.

Lukacs, J.R. (1976), Dental Anthropology and Biological Affinities of an Iron Age Population from Pomparripu, Sri Lanka, in *Ecological Backgrounds of South Asian Prehistory* (K.A.R. Kennedy and G.L. Possehl Eds.), pp. 197-215. Ithaca, NY: Cornell University, South Asia Program.

Lukacs, J.R. (1978), Biocultural Interaction in Prehistoric India: Culture, Ecology and the Pattern of Dental Disease in Neolithic-Chalcolithic Populations, in *American Studies in the Anthropology of India* (S. Vatuk Ed.), pp. 425-444. Delhi: Manohar.

Lukacs, J.R. (1980), The Apegaon Mandible: Morphology and Pathology, *Bulletin Deccan College Research Institute* 40:88-95.

Lukacs, J.R. (1981 a), Crown Dimensions of Deciduous Teeth from Prehistoric India, *American Journal of Physical Anthropology* 55: 261-266.

Lukacs, J.R. (1981 b), Dental Pathology and Nutritional Patterns of South Asian Megalithic Builders: the Evidence from Iron Age Mahurjhari, *Proceedings of American Philosophical Society* 125(3):220-237.

Lukacs, J.R. (1982 b), Dental Disease, Dietary Patterns and Subsistence at Harappa and Mohenjo-daro, in *Harappan Civilization* (G.L. Possehl Ed.), pp. 301-307. New Delhi: Oxford and IBH Publishing Co.

Lukacs, J.R. (1983 a), Human Dental Remains from Early Neolithic Levels at Mehrgarh, Baluchistan, *Current Anthropology* 24(3):390-392.

Lukacs, J.R. (1983 b), Dental Anthropology and the Origins of Two Iron Age Populations from Northern Pakistan, *Homo* 34:1-15.

Lukacs, J.R. (1984), Dental Anthropology of South Asian Populations. A Review, in The People of South Asia: The Biological Anthropology of India, Pakistan and Nepal (J.R. Lukacs Ed.), pp. 133-158. New York: Plenum Press.

Lukacs, J.R. (1985 a), Tooth Size Variation in Prehistoric India, *American Anthropologist* 87(4):811-825.

Lukacs, J.R. (1985 b), Dental Pathology and Tooth Size at Early Neolithic Mehrgarh: an Anthropological Assessment, in *South Asian Archaeology 1983* (J. Schotsman and M. Taddei Eds.), pp. 121-150. Naples: Istituto Universitario Orientale.

Lukacs, J.R. (1987), Biological Relationships Derived from Morphology of Permanent Teeth: Recent Evidence from Prehistoric India, *Anthropologischer Anzeiger* 45(2):97-116.

Lukacs, J.R. (1988), Dental Morphology and Odontometrics of Early Agriculturalists from Neolithic Mehrgarh, in *Teeth Revisited* (D.E. Russell, J.P. Santoro and D. Sigogneau-Russell Eds.), pp. 53:287-305. Paris: Memoires du Musee d' Histoire Naturelle.

Lukacs, J.R. (1989 a), Biological Relationships from Dental Morphology: The Evidence from Neolithic Mehrgarh, in *Old Problems and New Perspectives in the Archaeology of South Asia* (J.M.Kenoyer Ed.), pp. 75-88. Madison: Wisconsin Archaeological Reports.

Lukacs, J.R. (1989 b), Dental Paleopathology: Methods of Reconstructing Dietary Patterns, in *Reconstruction of Life from the Skeleton* (M.Y. Iscan and K.A.R. Kennedy Eds.), pp. 261-286. New York: AR Liss.

Lukacs, J.R. (1990), On Hunter-Gatherers and their Neighbours in Prehistoric India: Context and Pathology, *Current Anthropology* 31:183-186.

Lukacs, J.R. (1991), Localized Enamel Hypoplasia of Human Deciduous Canine Teeth: Prevalence and Pattern of Expression in Rural Pakistan, *Human Biology* 63:513-522.

Lukacs, J.R. (1992 a), Dental Paleopathology and Agricultural Intensification in South Asia: New Evidence from Bronze Age Harappa, *American Journal of Physical Anthropology* 87:133-150.

Lukacs, J.R. (1992 b) (Ed.) *Culture, Ecology and Dental Anthropology*. New Delhi: Indian Society for Human Genetics.

Lukacs, J.R. (1995), The Caries-correction-Factor: A New Method of Calibration Dental Caries Rates to Compensate for Antemortem Loss of Teeth, *International Journal of Osteoarchaeology* 5(2)151-156.

Lukacs, J.R. (1996), Sex Differences in Dental Caries Rates with the Origin of Agriculture in South Asia, *Current Anthropology* 37(1):147-153.

Lukacs, J.R. (1997), The People of Lekhahia: A Bio-cultural Portrait of Mesolithic Hunter-gatherers of North India, in *South Asian Archaeology 1995* (F.R. Allchin and B. Allchin Eds.), pp. 927-937. New Delhi-Oxford-IBH.

Lukacs, J.R. (1998), Canine Transportation in Prehistoric Pakistan: Bronze Age Case Reports, *Angle Orthodontist* 68(5):475-480.

Lukacs, J.R. and B.E. Hemphill (1990), Traumatic Injuries of Prehistoric Teeth: New Evidence from Baluchistan and Punjab Provinces, Pakistan, *Anthropologischer Anzeiger* 48(4):351-363.

Lukacs, J.R. and B.E. Hemphill (1991), Dental Anthropology of Prehistoric Baluchistan and the Peopling of South Asia, in *Advances in Dental Anthropology* (M.A. Kelley and C.S. Larsen Eds.), pp. 77-119. New York: Wiley-Liss, Inc.

Lukacs, J.R., M.R. Joshi and P. Makhija (1983), Crown Dimensions of Deciduous Teeth of Prehistoric and Living Populations of Western India, *American Journal of Physical Anthropology* 61(3):383-87.

Lukacs, J.R. and K.A.R. Kennedy (1981), Biological Anthropology of Human Remains from Pomparippu, *Ancient Ceylon* 4:97-142.

Lukacs, J.R. and L.L. Minderman (1992), Dental Pathology and Agricultural Intensification from Neolithic to Chalcolithic Periods at Mehrgarh (Muchistan, Pakistan) in *South Asian Archaeology 1989* (C. Jarriage Ed.), pp. 167-179. Madison: Prehistory Press.

Lukacs, J.R., V.N. Misra and K.A.R. Kennedy (1982), *Bagor and Tilwara: Late Mesolithic Cultures of North-west India: Vol.I. The Human Skeletal Remains*. Pune: Deccan College Research Institute.

Lukacs, J.R. and J.N. Pal (1993), Mesolithic Subsistence in North India: Inferences from Dental Attributes, *Current Anthropology* 34(5):745-765.

Lukacs, J.R. and R.F. Pastor (1988), Activity Induced Patterns of Dental Abrasion in Prehistoric Pakistan: Evidence from Mehrgarh and Harappa, *American Journal of Physical Anthropology* 76(3):377-398.

Lukacs, J.R., H. Retief and J.F. Jarrige (1985), Dental Disease in Prehistoric Baluchistan, *National Geographic Research* 1:184-197.

Lukacs, J.R., M. Schultz and B.E. Hemphill (1989), Dental Pathology and Dietary Patterns in *Iron Age Northern Pakistan, in South Asian Archaeology 1985* (K. Frifelt and P. Sorensen Eds.), pp. 475-496. London: Curzon Press.

Lukacs, J.R. and S.R. Walimbe (1984), Deciduous Dental Morphology and the Biological Affinities of a Late Chalcolithic Skeletal Series from Western India, *American Journal of Physical Anthropology* 65:23-30.

Lukacs, J.R..and S.R. Walimbe (1986), *Excavations at Inamgaon, Vol. II. Physical Anthropology of Human Skeletal Remains.* Pune: Deccan College Research Institute.

Lukacs, J.R. and S.R. Walimbe (1998), Physiological Stress in Prehistoric India: New Data on Localized Hypoplasia of Primary Canines Linked to Climate and Subsistence Change, *Journal of Archaeological Science* 25(6):571-585.

Lukacs, J.R. and S.R. Walimbe (2000), Health, Climate, and Culture in Prehistoric India: Conflicting Conclusions from Archaeology and Anthropology. *South Asian Archaeology 1997* (M. Taddei Ed.) pp. 333-381.

Malhotra, K.C. (1967), Further Observations on the Human Skeletal Remains from Neolithic Piklihal, *The Anthropologist* 14:99-111.

Misra, V. N. (2001), Prehistoric Human Colonization of India, *J. Bioscie* 26(4), 491–531. Indian Academy of Sciences.

Moorrees, C.F.A. (1957), Mesiodistal Crown Diameters of the Deciduous and Permanent Teeth in Individuals, *Journal of Dental Research* 36: 39-47.

Mushrif, Veena and S.R. Walimbe (2000), A Fresh Look at the Human Skeletal Remains from Chalcolithic Walki (Maharashtra), *Man and Environment* XXX(2):19-34.

Mushrif, Veena and S.R. Walimbe (2006), *Human Skeletal Remains from Chalcolithic Nevasa: Osteobiographic Analysis.* London: BAR International Series 1476.

Mushrif, Veena, K. Rajan and S.R. Walimbe. In press-a. *Human Skeletal Remains from Kodumanal.* Pune: Society of South Asian Archaeologists.

Mushrif, Veena , J. Tosi, D. Vasa, and S.R. Walimbe. In Press–b. *Human Skeletal Remains from Jotsoma, Nagaland.* Kolkata: CASTE

Mushrif, Veena and S.R. Walimbe. In press–c. *Human Skeletal Remains from Sanjan.* Mumbai: World Zoroastrian Foundation.

Pal, A. (1981), Dental Health in Ancient India, *Journal of Indian Anthropological Association* 16:171-177.

Pastor, R.F. (1992), Dietary Adaptations and Dental Microwear on Mesolithic and Chalcolithic South Asia, in *Culture, Ecology and Dental Anthropology* (J.R. Lukacs Ed.), pp. 215-228. New Delhi: Kamala Raj Enterprises.

Ratnagar, Shereen (1998), Back to Bones, *Man and Environment* XXIII(2):101-105.

Robbins, Gwen (2000), *Dental Histology and Age Estimation at Damdama: An Indian Mesolithic Site*. M.S. Dissertation. University of Oregon, Eugene, OR, USA.

Robbins, Gwen, V. Mushrif, V.N. Misra , R.K. Mohanty and V.S. Shinde (2007), Human Skeletal Remains from Balathal: a Full Report and Inventory, *Man and Environment* XXXII(2): 1-26.

Roberts, C. and K. Manchester (1995), *The Archaeology of Disease*. Ithaca, NY: Cornell University Press.

Robinson, J.T. (1954), *The Dentition of the Australopithecinae*. Pretoria: Transvaal Museum Memoir, 9.

Sali, S.A. (1986), *Daimabad 1976-79*. New Delhi: Archaeological Survey of India.

Sewell, R.B.S. and B.S. Guba (1929), Report on the Bones Excavated at Nal, *Memoirs of the Archaeological Survey of India* 35:56-89.

Sewell, R.B.S. and B.S. Guha (1931 a), Human Remains, in *Mohenjo-Daro and the Indus Civilization*, Volume 2 (J. Marshall Ed.), pp. 599-648. London: Arthur Probsthain.

Sewell, R.B.S. and B.S. Guha (1931 b), Report on a Collection of Bones Made by Sir Aurel Stein in Makran, *Memoirs of the Archaeological Survey of India* 43:191-200.

Turner, C.J. II, C.R. Nichol and C.R. Scott (1991), Scoring Procedure for Key Morphological Traits of the Permanent Dentition: The Arizona State University Dental Anthropology System, in *Advances in Dental Anthropology* (M.A. Kelley and C.S. Larsen, Eds.), pp., 13-31, New York: Wiley Liss. Inc. Publishers.

Walimbe, S.R. (1986 a), Palaeodemography of Protohistoric Daimabad, in *Daimabad 1976-79* (S.A. Sali Ed.) pp. 641-740. New Delhi: Archaeological Survey of India.

Walimbe, S.R. (1986 b), Human Skeletal Remains from Megalithic Vidarbha, *Puratattva* 18: 61-71.

Walimbe, S.R. (1990), Human Skeletal Remains, in *Excavations at Kaothe* (M.K. Dhavalikar, V.S. Shinde and Shubhangana Atre Eds.), pp. 111-231. Pune: Deccan College Research Institute.

Walimbe, S.R. (1992), Human Skeletal Remains, in *Megalithic Raipur* (1985-1990) (G.B. Degiurkar and Gouri Lad Eds.), pp. 125-132. Pune: Deccan College Research Institute.

Walimbe, S.R. (1993 a), An Anthropometric and Comparative Analysis of the Human Skeletal Remains from the Chalcolithic Levels of Hullikallu (A.P.) *Bulletin Andhra Pradesh Archaeology Department*, Hyderabad.

Walimbe, S.R. (1993 b), A Report on Adult Human Skeleton from Neolithic leej (A.P.), *Bulletin of the Andhra Pradesh Archaeology Department*, Hyderabad.

Walimbe, S.R. (1993 c), Human Skeletal Evidence from Megalithic Raipur, *Bulletin of the Deccan College Research Institute* 51/52: 667-678.

Walimbe, S.R. (1994), A Note on Child Burial from Chalcolithic Tuljapur Garhi, *Bulletin of the Deccan College Research Institute* 53: 397-400

Walimbe, S.R. (1996 a), Human Skeletal Evidence from Chalcolithic Tuljapur Garhi, in *Excavations at Tuljapur Garhi: 1984-85* (B.P.Bopardikar, Ed.), pp.43-46. New Delhi: Archaeological Survey of India.

Walimbe, S.R. (1996 b), Dental Pathology: A Valuable Indicator for Assessment of Physiological Stress in Ancient Populations, *Journal of Indian Anthropological Society* 28: 165-183

Walimbe, S.R. (1998), Bio-cultural Adaptations in Cranial Morphology Among the Early Farming Chalcolithic Populations of the Deccan Plateau, in *Contemporary Studies in Human Ecology: Human Factor, Resource Management and Development* (M.K. Bhasin and S.L. Malik, Eds.), pp. 25-40. Delhi: Indian Society for Human Ecology.

Walimbe, S.R., P. C. Caldwell-Ott and K. A. R. Kennedy. In press. Hitherto Undescribed Megalithic Burials from South Asia: the Skeletal Record. *Man and Environment.*

Walimbe, S.R., P.B. Gambhir and P.C. Venkatasubbaiah (1991), A Note on Megalithic Human Skeletal Remains from Kanyathirthum, Cuddapah District, Andhra Pradesh, *Man and Environment* XVI(1): 99-101.

Walimbe, S.R., P.B. Gambhir and P.C. Venkatasubbaiah (1993), Human Skeletal Remains from Neolithic Balijapalle in the Central Pennar Basin, Cuddapah District (A.P.), *Bulletin Deccan College Research Institute* 51/52:679-684.

Walimbe, S.R. and J.R. Lukacs (1992), Dental Pathology at the Origin of Agriculture: a Case Study on Deccan Chalcolithic Population, in *Culture, Ecology and Dental Anthropology* (J.R. Lukacs Ed.), pp. 117-132. New Delhi: Kamala Raj Enterprises.

Walimbe, S.R. and S.S. Kulkarni (1993), *Biological Adaptations in Human Dentition: an Odontometric Study on Living and Archaeological Populations in India.* Pune: Deccan College Research Institute.

Walimbe, S.R. and Mushrif-Tripathy V. (1999), Human Skeletal Remains of the Historical Period at Kuntasi, District Rajkot, Gujarat (Jointly with Veena Mushrif) *Bulletin Deccan College Research Institute*, 58-59: 117-139.

Walimbe, S.R. and K. Paddayya (1999), Human Skeletal Remains from the Neolithic Ashmound Site at Budihal, Gulbarga district, Karnataka, *Bulletin Deccan College Research Institute*, 58-59: 11-47.

Walimbe, S.R. and V. Selvakumar (1998), Anthropological Investigations on an Iron Age Adult Male Skeleton from S.Pappinayakkanpatti, Madurai district, Tamil Nadu, *Journal of Human Evolu*tion 9(1):19-34.

Walimbe, S.R. and V.S. Shinde (1995), Anthropometric Data on the Adult Skeleton from Medieval Padri, Man and Environment XX(2):43-55.

Walimbe, S.R. and A. Tavares (2002), Human Skeletal Biology: Scope, Development and Present Status of Research in India, in *Recent Studies in Indian Archaeology* (K.Paddayya Ed.). pp. 367-402. Indian Council of Historical Research, Monograph Series 6. New Delhi: Munshiram Manoharlal.

Walimbe, S.R. in Prep-a. *Human Skeletal Remains from Harappan Rakhi Garhi.*

Walimbe, S.R. in Prep-b. *Human Skeletal Remains from Neolithic Banahalli.*

Wolpoff, M.H. (1971), *Metric Trends in Hominid Dental Evolution.* Case Western Reserve University, Studies in Anthropology.

CHAPTER–20

# Continuum in the Rock Art of Eastern India

*A. K. Prasad*

## INTRODUCTION

Rock Art is our ancestors' earliest signatures drawn on the bare surfaces of rocks in rock shelters/caves in form of petrographs (rock paintings) and petroglyphs (engravings, cupules, etc.).It is the most exciting and extremely important means of understanding their thought process and the environment they lived in. With its antiquity ranging from the Palaeolithic period down to the historic era,it constitutes the earliest written and visual documents left for us by our ancestors. It is found all over the world barring for a few countries.

India is one of the three countries (besides South Africa) that has the richest and most varied treasure of rock art in the world. However, the famous ancient Magadha region,in eastern India ,so much known for its great historical and cultural heritage hardly figured on the Rock Art map of India till I made original discovery of about 100 painted rock shelters/ caves/open rock surfaces in the winter season of 1993-94 and there after.(Prasad, A.K.2003-4) This rock art site contains a large number of rock paintings, ancient inscriptions, Buddhist antiquities, as well as Stone Age tools and other archaeological evidences. These are located in the extremely remote, inaccessible and most dangerous forested hills of Nawada, Jamui, and Giridih and Kodarma districts (the latter two now form part of the newly carved out Jharkhand State).

This rock art region, while sharing some common features with other Indian rock art sites, contains several unique and special features .It represents entirely different trends from the Central Indian rock paintings in especially in case of subject matter,style and motivation. This different stylistic was also noticed by Neumayer in the rock paintings oh the neighbouring Hazaribagh district of Jharkhand.(Neumayer,E.1904-95). In contrast with the Central Indian paintings there is predominance of symbols/geometric designs over the human and animal figures. We also observe that motivation for paintings mainly remain ritualistic from beginning to the end. Stylistically also it differs as the figures are generally simple and static and not so dynamic and vigourous as fond in the Central Indian paintings. Other special features of this region's rock art are selecting only one rock shelter out of the entire cluster of shelters for painting, predominance of symbols/geometric designs, depiction of Garuda-dhwaj, snakes and other reptiles, phallic human and animal figures, engraved figures of humped bulls, presence of blue colour painting and a large number of ancient inscriptions including Kharoshti and Kharoshti-Brahmi .(Prasad, A.K.2006). Presence of more than 13 Stone Age tool factories,4 megalith sites, potsherds right from late Mesolithic/early Neolithic to early historic period and clay tablets depicting Buddha and other archaeological evidences suggest that this important rock art region must have been a major play ground not only for the Primitive Man but also his successors right from the Lower Palaeolithic period down to the early historic era. Here a complete sequence of cultural evolution of man can be observed and studied in most reliable and comprehensive manner. It has potentiality of bridging history with prehistory and throws light on many of the living tribal rituals and symbols (Bhattacharya, D.K.).

Based on the subject matter, colour, style, encrustation and superimposition the rock art of this region can be placed in four broad stages of development as follows-

1. *Stage I*– The earliest phase of the rock art of the hunters and gatherers roughly corresponding to the Upper Palaeolithic period containing mainly symbolic/ pre figurative.
2. *Stage II*– Rock art of the hunters and gatherers depicting hunting and dancing scenes besides symbols and intricate/geometric designs corresponding to the Mesolithic period.
3. *Stage III*– Rock art of the settled agriculturist and animal keepers using pottery corresponding to the Neolithic/Chalcolithic period.
4. *Stage IV*– Rock art of the People of the early historic period.

   The above four broad stages have been further sub divided. These are described in detail as follows-

## STAGE- I

The earliest paintings corresponding to the Upper Palaeolithic period are are executed mainly in dark red colour found generally under thick patination. These are further sub divide in Stage I a. and Stage I b.as under-

**Stage I a**

The human figures are drawn in symbolic form and also sometimes shown mingling with tree roots or reptiles. They appear to be ritualistic figures meant for certain rituals. Unlike the dynamic & vigorous early paintings of Central India, these figures are mainly static. The head is represented by some sort of dot or in semi circular form. The figures are drawn in outline or silhouette (II.A.1, II. B.1, X.A.1, II.D.2, etc). These are found associated with various types of symbols/intricate designs. Such intricate or geometric patterns covering large virgin space of the rock surface in the rock shelters/caves in this region (RS. II. D.2, I. A.8, XI. B.1, II. A.1, XIII.A.1 etc).

In context of the Central India rock paintings it is generally believed that the 'S' twist figures representing dynamism and vigour are earliest rock paintings. But it may not necessarily be always right. In this regard S.K. Pandey's observation is worth considering when he points out that in the developmental process the static figures will come first and the dynamic figures will follow then. The 'S' twist form of dynamic group was evolved from the stick- shaped form for some definite purpose (Pande, S.K. 1993)

As mentioned earlier the early paintings are generally accompanied by symbols in form of intricate designs/ geometric form of various types such as dots, grids, zigzags, chevrons, curves, rectangles etc. The rock paintings representing purely geometrical patterns are prefigurative or non-ionic art forms and succeeding figurative or iconic depictions painted either in red or green, animated human and animal figures need to be considered seriously as the earliest depictions belonging to the Upper Palaeolithic period (Sonawane, V.H. 1997). Also in the European rock art and rock art of other parts of the world these geometric designs are among the most puzzling elements of Upper Palaeolithic art (Leaky, R. 1996).

**Stage I b**

During the latter phase of the Upper Palaeolithic period the figures become comparatively flexible, dynamic and mainly in dancing pose either individually or in a group of two or three. They are shown in red slip or in thick lines. Besides dancing, some figures are also shown hunting individually or in group of two or three with bows of their own size. These dancers and hunters are generally adorned with animal head masks. The dancers and hunters are depicted performing ritualistic dance or ritualistic hunting. (II.A.1, I. A. 8, X.A.1, X.B.1etc). As mentioned earlier though there are stick figures with moderate dynamism and vigour, we don't find the Central Indian 'S' twist figures in this rock art region.

**STAGE- II**

With the advancement in the tool making technology life might have become easier and safer enabling the primitive to devote more time in artistic activities. The scope of rock art the Mesolithic paintings increased not only in respect of subject matter but also in use colour, style and motivation. Hunting scenes with bow and arrow, dancing individually or in small group were depicted in black and white colours besides the red. Though the symbols/geometric forms and stick human figures naturalism stared in depiction of animal figures.The paintings of the Mesolithic period placed in Stage II have further been sub divided in Stage II.a, II.b and II c. representing its early, middle and late phases respectively as under-

### Stage II a

It represents the early phase of the Mesolithic period. In this style the dynamic humans have been depicted as masked dancers and archers. The masks are in form of animals or birds. The archers are having long bows of their own size or even bigger. The dancers are shown dancing around the killed animals or near some symbols. The hunting scenes are ritualistic and not the actual hunt. The animals are shown in naturalistic outline generally without decoration. The archers are in a small group of 2 to 4 or sometimes even alone. The animals depicted are tiger, antelope, bear, boar, sambar, etc (RS. V. B.1, II. A.1, X. B.1 etc).

### Stage II b

It represents the middle phase of the Mesolithic period. It is also the most dynamic phase of the Mesolithic period. Naturalistic outline in depicting animals was retained but body decoration also started. Beautiful geographical designs of ritualistic character were also drawn. The archers are with slender body as well as heavily built. Bows are of the archer's height or some times smaller also. Humans are shown standing behind animals with upraised arms/hands as mark of triumph (RS. X. B.1, I. A.8, II C.2. etc).

### Stage II c

It represents late phase of the Mesolithic period. Slight stylization in depiction of humans and animals is found. Some times these are executed in double outlines. Body decoration increased. Human sized bows continued. Hunters and dancers are depicted individually or in larges groups. Besides bow and arrows big maces are also depicted. Geometrical designs continued to be depicted sometimes even independently. Besides doing hunting and dancing, the humans are occasionally also shown with a long string tied to the head or mouth of animals (RS. XI.A. 1, I. A.8, XI. B.1, II. A. 2, II. C.4 etc).

### STAGE III

At the end of the Mesolithic Period there was a remarkable change in the life style with start of settled life, domestication of wild animals and crops.

The new ground/polished tools were quite useful in clearing the forest land for cultivation. He also started making crude potteries which reached its zenith subsequently during the Chalcolithic period .Limited use of metal such as and copper, bronze and later on iron However, the tradition of making rock paintings continued even in this important change in life style. The Stage III representing the Neolithic / Chalcolithic period has been further sub divided in two phases as follows

**Stage III a**

Depiction of wild animals continued but there is obvious qualitative degeneration. Abstraction increased both in human and animal forms. Bodies of animals became more geometrical and crude. Animals depicted are mainly deer, wild boar, and antelope. Their bodies are shown too large and legs extremely small. Human figures are shown in stick form or in outline as well as having triangular body with long neck and hands in double lines. The human figures are generally small in size in comparison to animal figures (RS.III. C.5, XVI. A.7 etc).

**Stage III b**

It is very surprising that cattle and other domesticated animals have hardly been depicted in the rock paintings of this region discovered so far. However, there is a panel of engravings on a huge granite boulder which contains engraved figures of Harappan type Humped Bulls very prominently in the Rajabar Protected Forest. There are engraved figures of some other domesticated as well as wild animals also. Depiction of cattle's hoof in RS XVI. A.7 has also been included in this style. Unlike the Central Indian Chalcolithic paintings chariots have not been depicted in any painted rock shelter of this region discovered so far. Use of white colour is quite frequent in the paintings of this period.

**STAGE IV**

With rapid advancement in science and technology and literary activities people lived in big villages and cities away from hills and forest Inspite of this the creation 0f rock paintings continued by the tribals and also the non forest dwellers up to the Early historical period and in some areas till late medieval period Rock paintings of the early historical period have been placed under Stage IV. These have further been sub divided as Stage IV a, IV. b and IV c. representing the early, middle and late phases of early historical period. These paintings are mainly creation of the outsiders i.e. the non-forest dwellers. This category of people includes the traders and travelers especially from the North-West region of the Indian subcontinent and also the followers of Buddhism/Hinduism. A very large number of Kharoshti, Kharoshti- Brahmi, Brahmi and Shankh rock inscriptions have been found on the walls/ceilings of various rock shelters/caves of this region. In some of the Kharoshti and Kharoshti-Brahmi inscriptions names of certain traders from Kandhar region are mentioned who had performed some tribal/local rituals for sake of gaining wealth or destroying their enemies.(Mukherjee,B.N.1997). Most probably these painted rock shelters/ caves were located on the same forest trade route from Patliputra to the ancient port of Tamralipti used by emperor Ashok (to bid farewell to his daughter Sanghamitra leaving for Ceylon) during the 3rd century BC and I Chiang in the 7th century AD (Takakusu, J 1963).

**Stage IV a**

It represents the rock paintings of the Mauryan period (300 BC to 100AD). Depiction of stylized human and animal figures continued but animals have generally been drawn in naturalistic way. These are in ochre red as well as white outlines and also in slip quite often superimposed over the Mesolithic or Neolithic/Chalcolithic paintings. Brahmi and Kharoshti scripts and horse figures were introduced for the first time. The figures of this style are generally associated with the Mauryan symbols (moon-on-the-hill), other symbols, cross, elaborate designs in red or white outlines and Brahmi/ Kharoshti inscriptions (RS. III.A.2, I.A. 8, IV. A.1, VI. A. 1, etc).

**Stage IV b**

It represents the Kushan period (100 century AD to 300 AD). Horse riders/ warriors/other persons in scythian or Yueh Chin dress are depicted in dark red or white outline or wash. Humans and animals are also drawn in geometrical pattern with triangular or rectangular bodies respectively. These are superimposed over Mesolithic or Neolithic paintings and also drawn independently. Sometimes the figures are associated with Kharoshti, Kharoshti-Brahmi, Brahmi and Shankh inscriptions (RS. I.B.2, II. A.1, I. A. 8 etc).

**Stage IV c**

It represents painting of the Gupta and Post Gupta period. Beautiful realistic figures of horses, dogs, small wild animals (rabbits, monkey etc) birds, various types of circles/chakras, trees, flowers etc have been depicted on the walls/ceilings of the rock shelters/caves. The figures are generally painted in wash and sometimes in outlines. Painted as well as engraved figures of elephant, deer, peacock (RS. XV. A.3, XV. A.4, XV. A.3-b etc) and ceiling decoration comprising the red & white strips in RS.VI.A.1 and VI.B.1 are also placed in this group of paintings. Brahmi, Kharoshti, Kharoshti-Brahmi and Shankh inscriptions are found generally associated with these figures. Rocks shelters/caves with such paintings are located on the ancient Pataliputra-Tamralipti trade route (RS. III. A.1, I. A.8, III. A.2, II. A. 2 etc) or in the vicinity of some ancient city/monastery (RS. VI. A.1, XII.A.1 VI. A.2, VI. B.1).

It appears that the painted rock shelters/caves were completely abandoned around the end of the10th century AD even for performing rituals and other religious activities. It is difficult to ascertain exact reasons for this. Most probably it happened due to two main reasons. Firstly, this ancient forest trade route, connecting Pataliputra/Bodh Gaya with the ancient sea port of Tamralipti, near which most of the painted rock shelters lie, fell in disuse by this time due to various reasons. Secondly, these rock shelters/caves were gradually occupied by dreaded bears and other wild animals such as tigers, leopards, boars and also dangerous reptiles like king cobras, pythons, cobras and kraits etc. Visiting these shelters/caves must have become extremely unsafe and dangerous. Even the local tribes do not venture into these places. It happened some times during the exploration of this area that I had to drive out bears/leopards and wild boars out of the caves before entering them.

## CHRONOLOGICAL CLASSIFICATION

Direct dating of this regions rock paintings have not been done so far. As such I have attempted to provide a tentative chronological classification based on my observations regarding the subject matter, superimposition, encrustation, use of colours and the various styles adopted in this regions rock art as follows-

*Hunting Gathering Stage*– This stage of hunting wild animals and collecting forest products as means of livelihood has further been sub divided as under-

(a) Upper Palaeolithic Period (25000 B.C.to 10000 B.C.) having early and late phases represented by Stage I a. and Stage I b.

(b) Mesolithic Period (10000 B.C.to 4000 B.C.) having three phases - early, middle and late phases represented by Stage II a.,II b. and II c. respectively.

*Neolithic /Chalcolithic Period* from Hunting Gathering stage to the stage of settled Agriculture and domestication of animals (4000B.C. to 600 B.C) represented by stage III a. and Stage III b.

*Early Historical Period* (600 B.C.to1000 A.D.) with three phases as under

(a) Mauryan (300 B.C. to 100 A.D. ) represented by Stage IV a.

(b) Kushan (100 A.D. to 300 A.D.) represented by Stage IV b.

(c) Gupta/Post Gupta (300 A.D. to 1000 A.D.) represented by Stage IV c.

## CONCLUSIONS

This was a short description of the way rock art of this region probably developed from the Upper Palaeolithic period down to the early historical era. Initially the human figures associated with symbols/geometric designs were drawn in simple and static manner unlike the central Indian paintings. Gradually richness in content, colour and style is noticed which reached its peak during the middle phase of the Mesolithic period. Qualitative degeneration is observed in the rock paintings of this region like other rock art sites in India and abroad. Beautiful paintings were made during the early historical period but the hunting and dancing scenes are replaced by the events of the contemporary environment. It appears that the long process of making paintings/engravings on the bare surfaces of rock in rock shelters/caves ceased towards the end of the 10th century in this part of eastern India but fortunately the tradition of rock painting continues even today in form of *Kohwar* made during the marriages in many parts of Bihar,U.P.,M.P.,Jharkhand and Chattisgarh.

## REFERENCES CITED

Leakey, Richard (1996), *Origin of Humankind,* Phoenix, London, pp. 113-14.

Mukherjee, B.N. (1997), Discovery of Kharoshti and Kharoshti-Brahmi Inscriptions in Bihar, *Journal of the Asiatic Society,* Vol, XXXIX, No. 3-4, pp. 122,123.

Neumayer, E. (1994-95), Rock Paintings from Hazaribagh, Bihar, *Puratatva,* No. 25, pp. 82-83.

Pande, S.K. (1993), *Indian Rock Art,* Aryan Books International, New Delhi, p. 151.

Prasad, A.K. (2003-04), Important Discoveries of Prehistoric Rock Paintings, Ancient Inscriptions and Stone Age Tool in Southern Bihar and Adjoining Jharkhand, *Puratattava,* No. 34, pp. 68-90.

Sonawane, V.H. (1997), Upper Palaeolithic Art of India– A Fresh Look, *Purakala,* Vol.8 (1-2), pp. 12, 13.

Takakusu, J. (1966), *Mahavansa* (Reprint), Delhi, p. XXXI.8. Wakankar, V.S. and Brooks, R.R.R. 1976, *Stone Age Paintings of India,* D.B. Taraporevala Sons & Co., Bambay, pp. 12, 13.

Wakankar, V.S. and Brooks, R.R.R. (1976), *Stone Age Paintings of India,* D.B. Taraporevala Sons & Co., Bambay, pp. 12, 13.

CHAPTER–21

# Continuum in the Rock Art of Central & Eastern India

*Somnath Chakraverty*

## PREAMBLE

For emergence and capacity to create visual representations or art, certain neuro -biological competence is essential. Earliest manifestation of art is evidently connected to the evolved subspecies of *Homo sapiens sapiens*. Generally, the emergence of non - iconic and iconic art is evident during final phase of Pleistocene. Ability for abstraction of ideas and a suitable expressive means for representation were basic requirements for emergence of visual art among ethnic entities of Upper Palaeolithic period. In south Asia, particularly in India, cultural evidences suggest the successive presence of hominids from mid - Pleistocene onwards. Although, the direct fossil evidences are rare in this subcontinent, but gradual techno - typological advancements in successive chrono - cultural phases indirectly explain different corresponding levels of biological adaptability and changes. In Indian context determination of absolute chronology for rock art is a challenging area for which a number of workers are already engaged. In recent times, Rock Art Society of India in collaboration with a group of international experts from International Federation of Rock Art Organizations, Australia with support from Archaeological Survey of India, Government of India had initiated a long term project titled as - EIP ( Early Indian Petroglyph ) project. The objective of EIP project is to explore some potential sites with petroglyph as an evidence of origin and development of art in humankind. The basic hypothesis and scheme for this search was that even earlier periods such as Middle Palaeolithic and Lower Palaeolithic, nascent form of art, i.e. 'pre - art' or 'art - like' cupule marks were deliberately attempted by some of our predecessors such as archaic *Homo sapiens*, Neanderthals, *Homo erectus* or similar other hominids in Asia. Between the year 2001 and 2005 a total number of three sites were extensively explored and excavation continued in phases yielding no such outstanding results excepting confirmation of cupule marks in association with 'Lower and Middle Palaeolithic' assemblages. The major corpus of rock art in Australia is considered as Middle Palaeolithic in origin and the incidence of Lower Palaeolithic art in Australia is "very rare" (Kumar, Robert G Bednarik *et al.* 2005). It is also considered that the groups of Middle Palaeolithic sea farers from South Asia had reached Australia about 60,000 years ago and they were instrumental for diffusion of rock art from South Asia to Australia (Bednarik 1993). Therefore, the objective of the EIP project was to explore for evidences and towards a more dependable chronology for the origin of art in humankind and particularly in south Asian context.

In EIP project a reassessment on several cupule marks and an irregularly arranged meandering line located in the auditorium cave of Bhimbetka, Madhya Pradesh. Members of the international team had studied micro-erosional aspects for ascertaining chronology of the cupule marks and one meandering line that they believed to be of early anthropic origin and was possibly preserved in the Acheulian strata. The other site is Daraki Chattan in Mandsaur district of Madhya Pradesh where several cupule marks are distributed on the rock wall and in other surfaces within a narrow fissure in the rock. Excavation in the location has justified the site as habitation for Palaeolithic tool users. But by using optical dating method the cupules in Daraki Chattan in general have indicated "that the dated portion of this deposit is probably early to mid Holocene in age" (Kumar, Giriraj, Robert G. Bednarik, Alan Watchman and Richard G. Roberts, 2005: 63 ). The same team had also estimated dates of five different samples of paint including four white and one red by the using C14 Accelerator Mass Spectometry. Two samples containing white pigments of gypsum-bassanite paint applied to the imagery of a white quadruped zoomorph in Bhimbetka (Rock shelter AS – 144 ) had been dated as respectively -1100+_ 60 years BP and 5190+_ 310 BP. In another site, Jamori ( site : J-52) two dates from white paint collected from the inner part of the imagery of another zoomorph resulted 1720+_ 310 years BP and 4810+_ 370 years BP. Whereas the red paint applied on the body contour of the same zoomorph was analyzed and have been dated as – 2780 +_ 40 years BP ( Kumar, Giriraj , Robert G. Bednarik, Alan Watchman and Richard G. Roberts, 2005). Therefore, the hypothesis ( Bednarik, 1993, 2001 ) for indicating the series of non-iconic evidences, mostly the cup marks as the earliest form of human cognitive expression for 'pre-art' level, need to be verified further. When the art in its representational, iconic or figurative form supposedly had evolved from cupules, the intermediate forms showing the stages of transformation from simple cup marks to gradually modified figurative expressions of visual imagery must have been developed. But from hundreds of rock art sites available in all parts of Indian subcontinent, any single evidence of intermediate assortment is not reported so far.

## GENERAL ROCK ART IMAGERY

Indian rock art scholars like Gordon (1939-40); Wakankar (1976); Pandey (1990, 1993) etc; had suggested chrono-cultural evolution of rock art on the basis of certain morphic criteria such as style, use of colour and superimposition. But the stylistic development can hardly be traced uniformly in actual situation within the entire region. So, for the present purpose priority is given on the quantitative classification of the motifs prevalent in the region. This approach is to trace the thematic priority areas and its range of variables. Depending on the frequency analysis and classification of thematic content, colour-scheme, technique and style of art, the priority area of the artist, and identification of the possible source for thematic inspiration is attempted. Sometimes the repetition of the thematic content reflects the mental obsession of the artist attached to a particular aspect. In preliterate egalitarian societies, artist's perception is generally less individualistic and represents the interpretation of the society.

In the rock art sites of Central India, such as Bhimbetka, Adamgarh as well as in Pachmarhi, the earliest layer of paintings mostly represent larger figures of wild animals either depicted in red ocher, white or grey in colour. In Bhimbetka, within estimated total number of 6214 motifs, a maximum

Figure 1: Images of Zoomorphs in India, (1) Painted zoomorphs; District: Sundargarh; Orissa. (2) A carnivore attacking a deer within the forest habitat. Site: Pachmarhi; Madhya Pradesh (3) Engraved figures of animal footmarks. District: Sundargarh. Orissa (4) Predator attacking a deer. Site: Pachmarhi; Madhya Pradesh (5) Figure of a bovid. Site: Pachmarhi; Madhya Pradesh (6) X–Ray figure of a bovid. Site: Pachmarhi; Madhya Pradesh (7) Figure of a bovid Mahadeo Hills; Madhya Pradesh (8) Figure of two quadrupeds. Mahadeo Hills; Madhya Pradesh

number of 1983 figures or 27.08% of the total number of figures represent different animal species (Mathpal 1984). Numerically, the human figures rather in association with animal figures, with artifacts or single comprise the majority in the sites. Thus thematically, in central Indian plateau region, the artists were more anthropocentric.

It is also significant that within the total enumerated zoomorphs, a maximum number of 561 figures (33.33%) are of horses. On the contrary, the figures of horse-riders are 510(89.95%) within the category of anthropomorph in association with zoomorph. No doubt that in a particular time or for certain generations, the horse and horse-riders had influenced much on mental imagery of the artists. Figures of the archers and armed men are 377 in number, i.e. 54.40% of the anthropomorphic figures are with artifacts. In the battle scenes, individual warriors and other compositions represent group-conflict, violence and inter-ethnic or intra-ethnic struggle. Such idealize figures are thematically predominant in the Central India region.

Similar battle-scenes are rarely present in the rock art of northern region, eastern region or in the south. From a recently discovered site in Nilgiri hills, Tamilnadu of South India, portrayal of warriors and similar battle scenes are common. The maximum presence of a particular cultural element within a specific eco-cultural area suggests that the context, significance and functional use of the rock art vary from one region to the other. It follows the concept and principles of cultural-area. Either the artists had direct historical experiences about the battle or they indirectly learned about the episode through folklore and other modes of oral tradition.

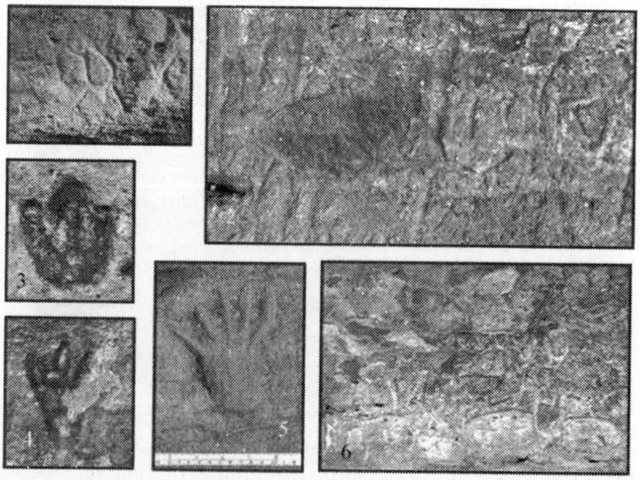

Figure 2: (1) Engraved Foot–marks and Other Non–figurative Motifs. District: Sambalpur; Orissa (2) Engraving motif of a fish. District: Sambalpur; Orissa (3, 4 & 5) Foot marks of different wild animals. District: Sambalpur; Orissa (6) A quadruped with long neck. District: Sambalpur; Orissa.

The figures of horse or horse-riders are prevalent in tribal and folk art of central and western parts of India. Various votive figurines representing horse or horse-riders are integral part of rituals, belief and practices among the tribal societies like Gond, Muria, Bison-horn Maria, Korku and Baigas living in the almost similar eco-cultural areas within the state. Among those tribal societies, horse is considered as the most suitable seat for an honourable person and so it is the symbol of might, authority, power and prestige.

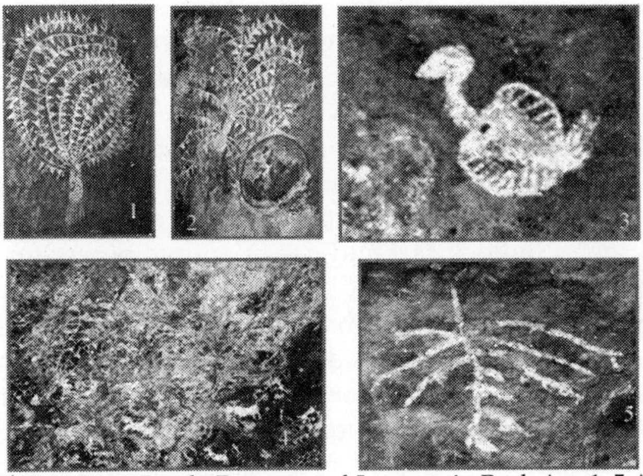

Figure 3: Phytomorphs–A Rarely Represented Imagery in Rock Art, 1–5 All Images found in Different Sites of Mahadeo Hills; Madhya Pradesh.

Korku tribe, living in Chhindwara and Hoshangabad districts of Madhya Pradesh is practicing a custom of erecting funerary pillar or '*gatha*' under a sacred tree. The tribal craftsmen prepare the commemorative wooden tablet by carving in its both sides. The carvings usually depict the occupation or other identifying characters of the deceased person. The figure of an archer is essential for the '*gatha*' of someone who was a successful hunter during his lifetime. Man or woman holding agricultural tools in hand are quite commonly represented on the memorial plaque. The '*gatha*' of any village leader is usually decorated with a figure of a horse-riding hero. The memorial tablets for woman are usually embellished with dancing motifs, figure with sickle or pots in hand. Both stylistically and in content, the motifs depicted on the memorial tablets are analogous to rock art. But the essential feature of any of the Korku memorial tablets is the symbolic presence of the figures of both sun and moon on the top. Sun and moon both are considered as supreme deities to the Korku tribe. But such celestial figures are entirely absent in the rock art sites of the region.

The economy as represented in the rock art of the region has two overlapping stages. The greater number of depictions is of hunter-gatherers. The facets of life-opportunities among the food gatherers were elaborately represented but the glimpses on the warriors do not contain any further details. There are two possibilities, either the warriors were alien, invaders, mythical characters or the semi-nomadic group and due to historical factor joined in any battle as hired force. But nowhere in the rock art within the entire region one can find the technologically superior type of weapons, particularly use of any fire arms or presence of warriors in association to any household scenes. But in several cases, the depiction of umbrellas is associated to both dance-scenes, rituals and cover the head of the horse-riding warriors. The economy of the society was possibly in transition. Besides food gathering, they reared selected types of domesticates such as cow, water-buffalo, goat or sheep etc. In majority of the rock art sites, no direct pictorial evidence for settled agriculture or use of plough exists. Fowling, collection of honey and seasonal fishing were their other sources for subsistence as evident in the rock paintings. In Chambal river valley and also in selected few sites of Betwa source region, the representation of bullock cart and use of animal power for ploughing is manifested in rock art.

Individual and group-hunting both were practiced simultaneously. Snares and nets were frequently used for hunting. Large mammals were attempted for planned group hunting. A clear division of labour is represented where the womenfolk were principally engaged in household activities. Responsibilities allocated to womenfolk included-grinding of fruit and cereals, cooking, nourishment of children, keeping of household utensils and other personal belonging etc. Figurines are rarely represented as carrying pots or with heavy head load of goods. Women are often shown as dressed in a short skirt but with projected breasts with a view to identify them discretely. Breast-feeding scenes are also frequent.

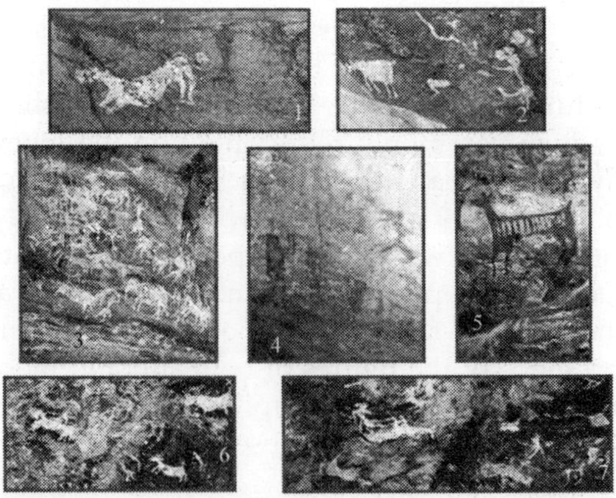

Figure 4: (1–3) Hunting of Animals. Pachmarhi; Madhya Pradesh (4) Hunting with Harpoon. Kaimur Range; Bihar (5) Wounded Animal Bleeding. Site: Budhni. Madhya Pradesh. (6) Hunting Scene. Pachmarhi; Madhya Pradesh (7) Hunted Animals being Processed. Pachmarhi; Madhya Pradesh.

In hair style, both male and female figurines are more or less identical. Men had long hair and they arranged their hair either in a bun or a knot of hair at a nape of one's neck. Mostly all warriors had similar hair style.

The rock art is a unique source for studying the material culture of the society in its ecological background. The bow and arrows were indispensable for every household. The baskets were of different types. Clay pots, club, four kinds of axes, including hunting axes and water containers. Rock shelters were their usual dwellings. Sometimes they also constructed lean-to type semi-permanent huts. Variety of musical instruments including horns, pipes, different types of drums and other percussion instruments were popular to them. Horns and pipes are frequently associated to battle scenes.

Figure 5: (1) A Man Playing a Harp being Surrounded by Tools and Weapons. Women are also represented here. Pachmarhi; Madhya Pradesh. (2) Use of wheel and other objects. The hair style is noteworthy. Pachmarhi; Madhya Pradesh (3) Household scene showing women and children gathered within a tent or a narrow rock shelter. The household utensils are hanging there. A dog or a wild carnivore watching from outside. Pachmarhi; Madhya Pradesh (4 & 7) Honeycomb and the monkeys. The other household scenes are also conspicuous. Pachmarhi; Madhya Pradesh (5) Combat scene. Pachmarhi; Madhya Pradesh (6) Community dance. Pachmarhi; Madhya Pradesh.

The horse and elephant-riding figures point out political hierarchy existed in the society. But above all, hunter-gatherers and animal-rearing groups were possibly more egalitarian in type in their socio-political structure. Their group-solidarity is evident in the religious practices of the community. Scenes represent group dances during rituals, magic and other supernatural performances. It is interesting to note that their dance-style was more or less similar to the Gond-speaking tribal groups inhabiting the region. In Mahadeo area of Pachmarhi, descriptive account of certain rituals in rock paintings has identical phases similar to the performances of local tribal communities. This annual autumn festival is related to the belief in fertility cult associated to the breeding and maintenance of domesticates.

Similar belief in fertility cult is not rare in the rock art, where x-ray paintings of cubs are delineated within the womb of quadrupeds. In rock art, palm prints, thumb impressions, hand stencils and finger markings are plenty. Such symbolic representations are also common to the local tribal households that are believed to protect themselves form evil eye, sorcery, witchcraft and similar other malevolent supernatural forces.

Figure 6: Elaborately Painted Rock Shelter Portraying Battle Scene or an Intra-group Feud. Pachmarhi; Madhya Pradesh

The other features present in the rock art point out the presence of animistic type of religion. Head hunting was practiced in the society. Head-hunting scenes are depicted in the Rajat Parbat rock shelters of Pachmarhi (Neumayer 1985). The personal adornment and hair style of victims as well as the assailant are similar. Possibly it portrays in-group feud or rivalry. Representation of two vultures on the tree depicts their presence as birds of prey who would exploit the carcass. They were waiting for the carcass as source of food within the battlefield. The composition signifies the artist's level of perception and a definite motive for transmitting the inevitable consequence of a battle.

Sometimes, the attitude of the artist towards a particular motif is reflected in their nature of execution. Sometimes, in the compositions of the rock painting, the dimensions of certain motifs are consciously exaggerated. The disproportionate motif, mostly larger than its other associated parts point out the purposeful attempt for attracting its viewers.

In central India, the early rock art represent a community which was closely similar to contemporary tribal societies, especially the marginal cultivators. Both similarities and differences are important for reconstruction of the early society and understanding their art as an integral cultural element. The basic similarity between the art of two different chronological periods may be explained in terms of common economic pursuits, social organization and material culture. The cultural continuity of certain elements is prevalent in the cultural-area under consideration.

In India, the early artist did not paint all available rock shelters within a locale. They had intentionally selected very few but suitable rock shelters which were more accessible for communication and display to the viewers. The visual language of the early society had gradually transformed into pictorial narratives for self identification.

On the basis of superimposition and techno-stylistic consideration, it is confirmed that the rock art of the region had developed through successive chrono-cultural periods. On the contrary, in the same region, the tribal art tradition is significantly present (Elwin 1951). The analogy between the two sets point to either relationship or a connection between the two art forms. It may be mentioned that the similarities are often observed between the rock art and tribal art with regard to forms, styles and motifs. In addition to the same, there is a coeval on the distribution pattern between the two sets. Based on the above argument, it may be hypothesized that the tribal art is a continuity of the total tradition of rock art.

It is indeed essential to make attempt for establishing the continuity between the two sets on the basis of various forms of data information with the methodological standardization and application of rigorous analysis.

Figure 7: (1) A Drummer and a Person holding an Axe, the Dress and Ornaments are Similar Pachmarhi; Madhya Pradesh (2) Drummers in ritual performance under a tree. Similar rites and rituals are common to the local tribal communities in Mahadeo Hills; Madhya Pradesh (3 & 5) Technique of fishing by employing trap. Pachmarhi; Madhya Pradesh (4) The attire and hair style of a man. Pachmarhi; Madhya Pradesh. (6) Comminity dance displaying battle axes raised in hand. Pachmarhi; Madhya Pradesh.

## COMPARATIVE ASSESSMENT: CASES FROM CENTRAL & EASTERN INDIA

In rock art of Pachmarhi, the majority of the figurative representations are solid-bodied (79.67%), stick figure or line drawing (14.49%) and outline or contour (3.79%). The figurative motifs are mostly naturalistic (90.63%) with the exception of few (0.67%) figures of zoomorph and anthropomorph which have been identified as more stylized. Within naturalistic figures an anthropomorph is rarely shown with traces of projected nose, distinct eyes and in general all human and animal figures are devoid of such recognizable facial details. On the contrary, several human figures, mostly depicted within battle-scenes are provided with distinct dress, other forms of personal adornment including ornaments and hairstyle. In both sectors it is observed that the initial drawings of anthropomorph and zoomorphic figures constitute arrangements of triangles to form the required figure.

In Korku society, horse-riding figures signify possession of wealth, power, prestige, higher status and overall dominance of the man in the society. Such figures as well as armed man in battle-scenes are frequent in Central Indian rock art sites. Such representations are quite common in Bhimbetka and other neighbouring rock art sites of Betwa source region and in Adamgarh hillock located in the southern bank of Narmada River.

In both sectors of art, technique of figural representations are mostly standardized and idealized, and repetitive forms are frequent. In both categories of art, the artist's creative impulses have seldom been expressed. The activity and experience of the ethnic group have largely been represented rather then the expression of individual perception.

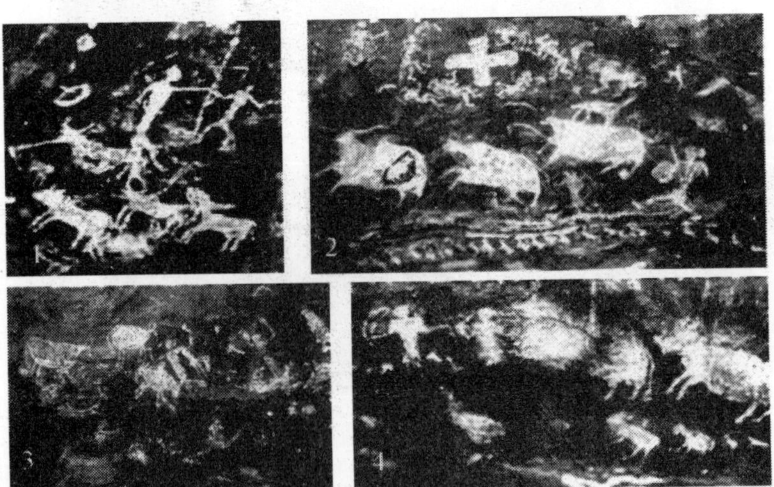

Figure 8: (1, 3 & 4) Life Activities of Pastoralists represented in Rock Art (2) Herd of bovines with their calves. X-ray figurine of one with calf in its womb is to symbolize the concept of fertility

A total number of 31 common elements of morphic types were found in both rock art and tribal art of Pachmarhi. It comprises 4 types of zoomorphs including depictions of unidentified quadruped mammals, deer, horse and cow. Within anthropomorphs, two morphic types are respectively group dance and man guiding horse-rider. In the category of anthropomorph with zoomorph and material trait, a total number of three types of pictorial elements are common which are - horse rider holding artifact, hunting with bow and arrow and scene of animal husbandry. In the category of anthropomorph with material trait, a maximum number of 11 motif-types in both sectors are identical. Such type of figures include man holding knife and dagger, holding umbrella, drummer, holding stick or club, musicians playing flute or horn, holding bow and arrow, holding only arrow, holding only bow, and figurative drawing of man and woman shown under a shelter. In material trait, identical items are respectively; - umbrella, sword, knife or dagger, pot or basket, rock shelter or trait for habitation, drum, bow and arrow, club or stick and flute or horn. One generalized figure of a plant in the category of phytomorph and one solitary motif of floral-like design under the category of non-figurative motif is identical in nature.

As the comparative study reveals, in both sectors, the pictorial glimpses on the pattern of life, activities and material culture are mostly indistinguishable. 31.96% of the total motif-elements identified in the rock art are thematically identical to those of tribal art. Therefore it is not unlikely that the Korku art tradition had been influenced by the rock art persisting in the same eco-culture region.

Among preliterate tribal Communities, the oral tradition including myths and legends is the major source for reconstruction of ethno-history. In order to understand the culture continuum, the comparison between rock art and ethnographic account of relevant tribal societies from the same region is necessary. In addition to the study of tribal art, different aspects of material culture could be a useful source to trace the ethnic milieu of rock art.

## REFERENCES CITED

Anati, Emmanuel. (1994), World Rock Art - *The Primordial Language.* Studi Camuni. 12. Italy

Anand, Mulkraj, V.S. Wakankar And S.K. Pandey (1974), *Marg* : Bhimbetka number. Bombay :Tata Press.

Anderson, C.W. (1918), The Rock Paintings of Singanpur. *Journal of The Bihar and Orissa Research Society.* 4 (3) : 298-306.

Bajpai, K.D. (1984), 'Rock-Shetters, Literary and Epigraphical Evidence. In *Rock Art of India.* Edited by K.K. Chakravarty. New Delhi; Arnold Heinemann: 72-78.

Bednarik , R.G. (1990), 'An Acheulian Haematite Pebble with Seriations.' *Rock Art Research.* 7: 75.2

Bednarik, Robert G. (1991), Asian Palaeoart and Eurocentric Science. *Purakala.* 2 (2): 71-76.

Bednarik, R.G. (1992), Developments in Rock Art Dating. *Acta Archaeologica.* 63 : 141-155.

Bednarik, R.G. (1993), Palaeolithic Art in India. *Man and Environment.* 18 (2): 33-38.

Bednarik, Robert. G. (1996), The Cupules on Chief's Rock, Auditorium Cave, Bhimbetka. *The Artefact.*19 : 63-72.

Bednarik, Robert. G. (2001), Cupules : The Oldest Surviving Rock Art. International Newsletter on Rock Art 30: 18 – 23.

Bednarik, Robert. G., G.Kumar, A.Watchman and R.G.Roberts.2005. Preliminary Results of the EIP Project. Rock Art Research 22(2): 147-197.

Bednarik, Robert. G., G.Kumar, A.Watchman and R.G.Roberts.2005. The EIP Project in 2005 : A Progress Peport. Purakala 14–15: 13-68.

Brooks, R.R.R. (1973), India's Rock Shelter Paintings. *Asia.* 31 : 44.

Brown, P. (1923), "Notes on the Prehistoric Cave Paintings at Raigarh." In *Prehistoric India.* Edited by P. Mitra, PP : 245-255. Calcutta : Calcutta University.

Bruil, H. (1952), *Four Hundred Centuries of Cave Art.* Montignac.

Chandramouli, N. (1994), Rock Art of Andhra Pradesh, South India. *Purakala.* 5 (1- 2) : 41-51.

Chandramouli, N. (1995), Petroglyphs from Naidupalli, Andhra Pradesh. *Purakala.* 6 (1-2) : 29 - 34.

Carllyle A.C.I. (1883), 'Notes on Lately Discovered Sepulchral Mounds, Cairns, Caves, Cave Paintings and Stone Implements'. Proceeding of the Asiatic Society of Bengal. 19 : 49.

Carllyle, A.C. (1885), Report on Tours in Gorakhpur and Ghazipur. *Report of the Archaeological Survey of India.*

Chakraverty, Somnath. (1995), "Isco : Rock Art Site in Hazaribag", In *Recent perspectives on Prehistoric Art in India and Allied Subjects.* Edited by R.K. Sharma and K. K. Tripathi, PP. 74 - 99. New Delhi : Aryan Books International.

Chakraverty, Somnath (1998), 'Rock Art in Central India : Its Role and Functional Significance'. In *History and Archaeology of Eastern India.* Edited by Asok Datta: 134-147. Books and Books, New Delhi.

Chakraverty, Somnath (1999), Primeval Rock Art and Ethnographic Analogy in India. *Bollettino del Centro Camuno di Studi Preistorici.* (31-32) : 213 - 222.

Chakraverty, Somnath (2003), *Rock Art Studies in India.* The Asiatic Society. Kolkata.

Chakraverty, Somnath and Asok K. Ghosh (1996), 'Standardization of Rock Art : an Approach for Unification. *Purakala.* 7 (1-2) : 23-28.

Clottes, J. (1996), Thematic Changes in Upper Palaeolithic Art : A View from the Grotte Chauvat. *Antiquity.* 70 : 276 – 288.

Clottes, J. (1997), Art or the Light and Art of the Depths. In Conkey, M.Softer, O. Stratmann, D & N.G. Jablonski (eds.). Beyond Art : Pleistocene Image and Symbol, *Memoirs of the California Academy of Sciences.* 23 : 203–216.

Clottes, J. & J. Courtin (1996), *The Cave Beneath the Sea. Palaeolithic Images at Cosquer.* New York, Harry N. Abrams.

Clottes, J. & D. Lewis–Williams (1998), *The Shamans of Prehistory. Trance and Magic in the Painted Caves.* New York, Harry N. Abrams.

Cockburn, J. (1883), On the Recent Existence of Rhinoceros indicus in the North Western Provinces and a Description of a Tracing of an Archaic Rock Painting from Mirzapur Representing the Hunting of this Animal. *Journal of the Asiatic Society of Bengal.* 52(2) : 56-64.

Cockburn, John (1884), On the Durability of Haematite Drawings on Sandstone Rocks. *Journal of the Asiatic Society of Bengal.* Proceedings (?). 20 (?) : 141-145.

Cockburn, John (1898), 'Cave Drawings in the Kaimur Range, North-West Provinces'. *Royal Asiatic Society of Great Britain.* 30: 89-97.

Corvinus, G. (1968), An Acheution Occupation Floor at Chirki-on-Pravara, India. *Current Anthropology.* 9 : 216-218.

Dubey, Meenakshi (1992), 'Rock Paintings of Pachmarhi Hills'. In Rock Art in the Old World. Edited by Michel Lorblanchet, PP: 131 - 145. New Delhi. Indira Gandhi National Centre for the Arts.

Fabri, C.L. (1936), The Vikramkhol Rock Inscription. Editorial remark. *Annual Report, Archaeological Survey of India,* 1930-34. 1 : 230.

Francke, (REV) A.H. (1902), Notes on Rock Carvings from Lower Ladakh. *The Indian Antiquary.* 31 : 398-401.

Franche, A.H. (1903), Some More Rock Carvings from Lower Ladakh. *The Indian Antiquary.* 32 : 361-363.

Francfort, Henri-Paul, Daniel Klodzinski and Georges Mascle (1992), Archaic Petroglyphs of Ladakh and Zanskar. In *Rock Art in the old World.* Edited by Michel Lorblanchet, PP. 147-192. New Delhi : India Gandhi National Centre for the Arts.

Ghosh, Asok K. (1984), 'Significance of Rock Art in the Light of Ethnographic Parallels'. In *Rock Art of India.* Edited by K.K. Chakravarty. New Delhi ; Arnold Heinemann : 106-111.

Ghosh, A.K. and Somnath Chakraverty (1995), "Rock Arts of Eastern India and their Bearing with Local Tribal Arts : a Cross-Sectional Study on Continuity in India at the Down of History. *In India At the Down of History* Edited by Asok Datta, Asok K. Ghosh and C. Margabandhu. Delhi : Agam Kala Prakashan.

Gordon, D.H. (1939 b), Indian Rock Paintings-II; the Rock Paintings of Kabra Pahar, Raigarh State. *Science and Culture.* 5(5) : 269-275.

Gordon, D.H. (1940 b), Animals and Demons in Indian Cave Art. *Science and Culture.* 5(11) : 662-667.

Gordon, D.H. (1940 a), Warfare in Indian Cave Art. *Science and Culture.* 5(10) : 662-667.

Gordon, D.H. (1958), *Prehistoric Background of Indian Culture.* Bombay: N.M. Tripathi Publication.

Gordon, D.H. amd F.R. Allchin (1955), Rock Paintings and Engravings in Raichur, Hyderabad. *Man.* 5(55) : 97-99.

Gordon, D.H. and Gordon. M.E. (1939-40), The Artistic Sequence of the Rock Paintings of the Mahadeo Hills. *Science and Culture.* 5(6-7) : 387-392.

Gupta, S.S. and K.D. Banerjee (1984), 'A Note on Dating of the Rock-Shelter Paintings at Jhinjhari'. In Rock Art of India. Edited by K.K. Chakravarty. New Delhi ; Arnold-Heinemann : 79-81.

Gupta S.P. (1979-80). 'The Alleged Upper Palaeolithic Bone Mother Goddess from Belan'. *Puratattva.* 11: 116.

Hunter, G.R. (1935), Interim Report, Dorothy Deep Excavation. *Nagpur University Journal.* 1(1) : 28-51.

Hunter, G.R. (1936), Final Report on the Excavation in the Mahadeo Hills. *Nagpur University Journal.* 2 : 127-144.

Joshi, R.V. (1975), *Stone Age Cultures of Central India : Report of The Excavations of the Rock Shelter at Adamgarh,* M.P. Deccan College, Pune.

Kenoyer J.M., J.D. clark, J.M Pal. & G.B. Sharma (1983), An Upper Palaeolithic Shrine in India. *Antiquity.* 57. : 88-94.

Khare, M.D. (1980), *Painted Rock Shelters.* Bhopal : Archaeology and Museums.

Khare, M.D. (1984), 'Excavated Remains from the Rock-Shelters in Madhya Pradesh'. In *Rock Art of India.* Edited by K.K. Chakravarty. New Delhi; Arnold-Heinemann : 129-136.

Khatri, A.P. (1961), Rock Shelters, Pachmarhi Hills, District Hoshangabad, *Indian Archaeology- A Review* : 960-961.

Khatri, A.P. (1964), Rock Paintings of Adamgarh (Central India) and their Age. *Anthropos.* 59 : 758-769.

Kumar, Giriraj (1996), 'Recording Standards and their Ratings: A Model for Conducting Study and Research in Purakala Vigyan'. In *Recent Perspectives on Prehistoric Art in India and Allied Subjects.* Edited by R.K. Sharma and K.K. Tripathi. New Delhi : Aryan Books International : 100-104.

Kumar, Giriraj (1998), Morajhari: A Uniquw Cupule Site in Ajmer District, Rajasthan. Purakala. 9 ( 1-2) : 61-64.

Laming, A. (1959), *Lascaux.* Harmondsworth.

Leroi Gourhan, A. (1982), *The Dawn of European Art.* Cambridge.

Mathpal, Yashodhar (1992), "Rock Art Studies in India", In *Rock Art in the Old World.* Edited by Michel Lorblanchet, PP : 207-214. New Delhi : Indira Gandhi National Centre for the Arts.

Mathpal, Y. (1975), "Prehistoric Art of Bhimbetka: A Preliminary Study". *Journal of the Puna University.* 95-108.

Mathpal, Y.N. (1976), Rock Art of India. *Journal of Indian History.* 54(1) : 27-51.

Mathpal, Y. (1979), "Rock Art of Bhimbetka Region, Central India". *Man and Environment.* 3 : 27-33.

Mathpal, Y. N. (1981), Prehistoric Art of India. *The Eastern Anthropologist.* 34(1) : 1-26.

Mathpal, Y.N. (1984), *Prehistoric Rock Paintings of Bhimbetka, Central India.* New Delhi: Abhinav Publications.

Mathpal, Yashodhar (1995), *Rock Art in Kumaon Himalaya.* New Delhi: Indira Gandhi National Centre for the Arts.

Mathpal, Yashodhar (1996), 'Painted Motifs of the Bhonrawali Hill (Central India). In *Recent Perspectives on Prehistoric Art in India and Allied Subjects.* Edited by R.K. Sharma and K.K. Tripathi. New Belhi; Aryan Books International : 36-40.

Mathpal, Yashodhar (1997), Rock Art of India : Its Past, Present and Future. *Purakala.* 8(1-2) : 37-44.

Mathpal, Yashodhar (1998), Rock Paintings of Bhonrawali Hill in Central India : Documentation and Study. *Purakala.* 9 ( 1-2 ): 5 - 52.

Mehta R.N., R.C. Agarwal, V.H. Sonawane, Parekh V.S. 1980. *Chandravati.* Boroda.

Mehta R.N. and V.H. Sonawane (1981), A Prehistoric Engraving. *Man and Environment.* 5 : 91.

Mills, J.P. and J.H. Hutton (1929), Ancient Monoliths of North Cachar. *Journal of the Asiatic Society of Bengal.* (N.S.) 25 : 285-300.

Misra, V.N. (1977), *Some Aspects of Indian Archaeology.* Allahabad: Prabhat Prakashan.

Misra, V.N. (1977), "Prehistoric Culture Sequence of Bhimbetka", In *Bhimbetka : Prehistoric Man and his Art in Central India.* Edited by V.N. Misra, Y. Mathpal and M. Nagar, Pune: Department of Archaeology, Poona University and Decean College: 10-22.

Misra, V.N. (1977), 'Bhimbetka: Reflexion of Life in Cave Art'. *Science Age.* 4(6) : 17-26.

Misra, V.N. and Y. Mathpal (1976), *Bhimbetka Excavations.* Pune: Deccan College.

Misra, V.N. and Y. Mathpal (1979), Rock Art of Bhimbetka Region, Central India. *Man and Environment.* 3 : 27-33.

Mitra, Panchanan (1927), *Prehistoric India.* Calcutta: University of Calcutta.

Morris, D. (1962), *The Biology of Art.* London.

Nagar, Malti (1977), "Living Prehistory Around Bhimbetka", in *Bhimbetka Prehistoric Man and his Art in Central India.* Edited by V.N.Misra, Y.Mathpal and M.Nagar, PP. 23-26. Pune : Department of Archaeology, Poona University and Deccan College.

Neumayer, E. (1983), *Prehistoric Indian Rock Paintings.* New Delhi : Oxford University Press.

Neumayer, E. (1985), The Rock Paintings of the Mahadeo Hills, India. *Bulletino del Centro Camuno di Studi Pretstorici.* 22 : 67-82.

Neumayer, E. (1991-92), Rock Pictures in Orissa. *Puratattva.* 22 : 13-24.

Neumayer, Erwin (1992), "Rock Art in India", In *Rock Art in the Old World.* Edited by Michel Lorblanchet, New Delhi : Indira Gandhi National Centre for the Arts. PP : 215-247.

Neumayer, E. (1993), *Lines on Stone- The Prehistoric Rock Art of India.* New Delhi: Manohar.

Pande, B. M. (1971), Neolithic Hunting Seene on a Stone Slab from Burzahom, Kashmir. *Asian Perspective.* 14 : 194-198.

Pande B.M. (1972), 'A Neolithic Tectiform from Burzahom, Dist :Srinagar'. *Journal of Indian Anthropological Society.* 7 : 175-177.

Pandey, S.K. (1993), *Indian Rock Art.* New Delhi : Aryan Books International.

Pandey, Nirmala (1996), 'Rock Art of Naryaoli (Dist. Sagar)'. In *Recent Perspectives on Prehistoric Art in India and Allied Subjects.* Edited by R.K. Sharma and K. K. Tripathi. New Delhi: Aryan Books International : 123-138.

Pradhan, S. (1995), Rock Art of Orissa: A Study of Regional Style. *Purakala.* 6(1-2): 5-15.

Ramabrahmam, V. (1996), Megalithic Art in Southern Andhra Pradesh: Recent Discoveries. *Purakala.* 7(1-2) : 47-50.

Reddy, K.T. and S.K. Rao (1996), 'Beliefs and Art– An Ethnoarchaeological View'. In *Recent Perspectives on Prehistoric Art in India and Allied Subjects.* Edited by R.K. Sharma and K.K. Tripathi. New Delhi; Aryan Books International. : 46-50.

Rivett-Carnac, H. (1877), 'Rough Notes on Some Ancient Sculpturings on Rocks in Kumaon, Similar to those Found on Monoliths and Rocks in Europe.' *Journal of the Asiatic Society of Bengal.* 46(1) : 1-15.

Rivett-Carnac, H. (1879), Prehistoric Remains in Central India (Abstract). *Journal of the Asiatic Society of Bengal; Proceeding.* : 9-11.

Rivett-Carnac, J.H. (1879), Prehistoric Remains in Central India. *Journal of the Asiatic Society of Bengal.* 48(1) : 1-16.

Sandars, N.K. (1968), *Prehistoric Art in Europe.* Yale University Press. New Haven & London.

Sen, D. (1949), Pachmarhi and Its Painted Caves and Rock Shelters. *Calcutta Geographical Review* : 35-43.

Sieveking, P. (1979), *The Cave Artists.* London.

Singh Deo, J.P. (1976), Prehistoric Cave Painting of Jogimath Danger. Orissa *Historical Research Journal.* 22(2) : 21-22.

Sharma, A.K. (1996), Excavation of the Painted Rock Shelters at Jhiri : A Preliminary Report. *Purakala.* 7 (1–2) : 39–46

Sharma, Madhuri (1996), 'Rock Paintings of Sehore District (M.P.)', In *Recent Perspectives on Prehistorie Art in India and Allied Subjects.* Edited by R.K. Sharma and K.K. Tripathi. New Delhi; Aryan Books International : 160–162.

Shukla, Pradeep Kumar (1996), 'Rock Engravings from North Raisen Region (M.P.).' In *Recent Perspectives on Prehistoric Art in India and Allied Subjects.* Edited by R.K. Sharma and K.K. Tripathi. New Delhi; Aryan Books International : 163-174.

Singh Deo, J.P. (1976), Prehistoric Cave Painting of Joginath Donger. *Orissa Historical Research Journal.* 22 (2) : 22.

Smith, Vincent A. (1906), Pygmy Flints. *The Indian Antiquary.* 35 : 185-195.

Sonawane, V.H. (1984), 'An Important Evidence to Date Rock-Paintings of Mesolithic Period.' In *Rock Art of India.* Edited by K.K. Chakavarty, New Delhi; Arnold Heinemam : 61-63.

Snawane Vishwarao (1992), 'Significance of the Chandravati Engraved Core in the light of Prehistoric Art in India'. In *Rock Art in the Old World.* Edited by Michel Lorblanchet, PP : 273-283. New Delhi : Indira Gandhi National Centre for the Arts.

Sonawane, V.H. (1997), Upper Palaeolithic Art of India: A Fresh Look. *Purokala.* 8 (1-2) : 5-16.

Soundara Rajan, K.V. (1997), Rock Art Legacy in India. *Purakala* : 8 (1-2) : 49-52.

Sundara, A. (1968), Rock Shelter, Hire Benakal Hills, Raichur. *Indian Archaeology 1967-68-A Review*, P. 67.

Sundara. A. (1974), Further Notice of Rock Paintings in Hire Benkal. *Journal of Indian History* 52 (1) : 21-32.

Sundara, A. (1984), 'Some Select Rock-Paintings from North Karnataka.' In *Rock Art of India.* Edited by K.K. Chakravarty. New Delhi; Arnold-Heinemann : 137-148.

Sundara, A. (1987), 'Some Noteworthy Rock-Paintings in Chick-Ramapura.' *Journal of Karnataka University* (Social Science) 23:

Sundara, A. (1996), 'An Engraved Geometrical Design from Gudnapura : from Harappa to Sonda (16th-17th Cent.) Period.' In *Recent Perspectives on Prehistoric Art in India and Allied Subjects.* Edited by R.K. Sharma and K.K. Tripathi. New Delhi; Aryan Books International : 41-45.

Tiwari, Shankar (1984), 'Excavation at Bhimbetka: A Reassessment.' In *Rock Art in India.* Edited by K.K. Charavarty, New Delhi : Arnold-Heinemann. : 149-153.

Tiwari, Shankar (1984), 'Twenty Five Years of Rock Paintings Exploration in the Betwa Source Region: A Reappraisal.' in *Rock Art in India.* Edited by K.K. Chakravarty. Arnold-Heinemann : New Delhi. : 228-238.

Verma, R.K. (1984), 'The Rock Art of Southern Uttar Pradesh with Special Reference to Mirzapur.' In *Rock Art in India.* Edited by K.K. Chakravarty, New Delhi: Arnold-Heinemann: 206-213.

Wakankar, V.S. (1962), Painted Rock Shelters of India. *Rivista de Science Prehistoriche.* 17 (1-4) : 237-253.

Wakankar, V.S. (1973), Bhimbetka Excavation. *Journal of Indian History* : 25-32.

Wakankar, V.S. (1975), Prehistoric Cave Paintings. *Marg.* 28 (4) : 17-34.

Wakankar, V.S. (1975), 'Bhimbetka the Prehistoric Paradise'. *Prachya Pratibha* 3 (2): 7–29

Wakankar, V.S. (1978), *The Dawn of Indian Art.* Ujjain : Bharati Kala Bhawan.

Wakankar, V.S. (1984), 'Bhimbetka and Dating of Indian Rock-Paintings.' In *Rock Art of India.* Edited by K.K. Chakravarty. New Delhi ; Arnold-Heinimann. : 44–56.

Wakankar Vishnu S. (1992), 'Rock Painting in India', in *Rock Art in the Old World.* Edited by Michel Lorblanchet. New Delhi : Indira Gandhi National Centre for the Arts. : 319-336.

Wakankar, V.S. and R.R.R. Brooks (1976), *Stone Age Paintings in India.* Bombay: D.P. Taraporevala Sons & Co.

CHAPTER–22

# Modern Adaptations of the Andaman Pygmy

*Umesh Kumar*

## INTRODUCTION

Hunting and gathering is the most ancient of human subsistence and in some cases it has still remained important to some human populations in the tropical rainforest. Human hunting and gathering behaviour has raised important questions regarding the subsistence mode of economy (Lee, 1968; Sahalins, 1972; Harris, 1985; Farb and Armelagos, 1980). The ecological conditions of their habitat have been studied in detail. In these studies attention to the availability, seasonality and density of resources has been significant (Yellen, 1971; Keene, 1981; Winterhalder and Smith, 1981). In recent years several articles have appeared on hunter-gatherers inhabiting the tropical forest. The description of hunter-gatherers subsistence based on the analysis of ecological context in which they live in provide very useful insights into human subsistence behaviour. A detailed review of many of them has been done by Bailey et al. (1989, 1991). Despite the fact that the tropical forests are difficult environment for the hunter-gatherers, there are some populations who still subsist on wild resources alone.

Andaman Islands are one such place where the modern day's hunter-gatherers are found. The Jarawa are one of the five hunting- gathering communities of the Andaman Islands, whose subsistence is still dependent on foraging which consists of hunting, fishing and gathering. Despite being surrounded by the non-tribal population, the relative isolation of the Jarawa on account of hostility between the two has helped them retain their hunting and gathering mode of economy. It exhibits an elementary form of economy which closely resembles the economy of full time hunter-gatherers. The study highlights the subsistence mode of economy in an island situation along with foraging strategies. Here the seasonality of resources, causative factors underlying the setting of base camps and mobility pattern are analysed. Input-output analysis (Lee, 1969) has been used to explain the ecological context of the subsistence economy of the Jarawa. The subsistence economy of the Jarawa presents an ideal case for the application of the input-output analysis for it exhibits close approximation to societies of prehistoric hunter gatherers.

*Methodology*- The Jarawa areas are being visited by since October 1997. But a detailed survey could not be carried out as the situation was not conducive for field work. The lack of knowledge about the Jarawa language was one of the main obstacles. Later on long association with them in the course of field work helped us pick-up communicable understanding of their language. The paper is based on material and information collected through field research of three months in the Jarawa reserve between 2001 and 2002. Between 2003 and 2004, nine shorts visits were made to the Jarawa area with each visit ranging between 4-7 days. It allowed us to update the information. The foraging data on the Jarawa has been collected from the three locations- Thidong, Boiab and Tanmad- between 11-12-01 to 09-01-02, 11-04-02 to 09-05-02 and 11-08-02 to 09-09-02 respectively. It covers the three different seasons - rainy, cool dry, and summer dry seasons. The three phases of study were selected to get information on the availability and seasonality of the resources and mobility pattern of the Jarawa. The foraging data collected from the Boiab territory is excluded as the base camp remained occupied most of the time by the unmarried girls who were least mobile. Secondly first and last day of other two phases are excluded as it does not cover the entire day of activity. Ethnographic study and participant observation were followed to gather the information. For collection of the data on foraging, the diary record method was used. Foraging hours were calculated in terms of man-hours which included the time when an individual left the camp and returned to it. The information on the movement pattern of the Jarawa, who had set on the foraging expedition, was obtained by asking the other Jarawas of the group and also by visiting their locations. During the field work altogether 72 Jarawa camp sites were visited and their locations were recorded by using Global Positioning System device.

## AREA AND PEOPLE

The Andaman and Nicobar islands are the summits of a submarine mountain range lying on the greater tectonic suture zone. This archipelago consists of 352 islands and has a total area of 8249 km$^2$. The four Negrito communities, the Great Andamanese, the Onges, the Jarawa and the Sentenelese are distributed in the five islands of the Andaman group. The Jarawa inhabit the coastal area and adjacent forest in the western part of the South and Middle Andaman islands which is situated between 11$^0$41′

and 12⁰ 45′ north latitude and 92⁰30′ and 92⁰ 46 east longitude. It is characterised by tropical rain forest which may be put into nine categories- giant evergreen forest, cane brakes, southern hill top ever green forest, wet bamboo breaks, Andaman semi ever green forest, Andaman moist deciduous forest, littoral forest, tidal forest, tidal swamp forest (mangrove) and submontane hill forest. The Jarawa territory is a reserved area. Earlier it measured approximately 647 $km^2$ which has recently been increased to approximately 950 $km^2$ (Gazette, 2004). This increase in the territory has only a notional importance for the Jarawa because they have had been using the recently added territories prior to the promulgation of gazette notification. The extension of Jarawa territory from two kilometres to five kilometres in the sea is also of not much help as the Jarawa are not a sea farer community like their counterparts who use out-rigger canoes. However, the good aspect of this notification is that now there would not be any extraction of timber or forest produce from the newly added territories.

**Antiquity of the Jarawa**

The information about Andaman Islands and its inhabitants is found place in the account of sailors, travellers and traders since second century (Mathur, 1968:7). A systematic and detailed account about the islands and its people is found since 1858 when British occupied theses islands second time for penal settlement. But the antiquity of the Negrito populations including the Jarawa in the Andaman Islands is still shrouded in the mystery. In this regard one has to depend on the materials obtained from the excavation of the kitchen midden sites (shell mounds which are an assemblage of shells, pottery, implements, equipments etc. buried in successive layers). On the basis of faunal evidences, the flake, bones shells and stones obtained from the kitchen midden sites of Chouldhari and Beehive Island and their comparison with the blade industry found at different Toalean sites of South-East Asia suggests that the Andaman Islanders would not have arrived latter than 300 B. C. (Man, 1883; Portman, 1899; Holland, 1904; Cipriani, 1968; and Dutta, 1978 and Cooper, 1990).

**Territoriality**

There are three territorial groups among the Jarawa inhabiting the three territories viz. Boiab (Tirur area), Thidong (Middle Strait area), and Tanmad (Kadamtala area). Of these two territories namely Boiab and Thidong are contiguous to each other, punctured by the inland creeks while the third territory Tanmad is a separate island but in the same continuation (Fig.1). In between Tanmad and Thidong, Baratang Island is a buffer zone occupied by non-tribal people. Resource acquisition in a particular territory by a particular group is the basis for grouping the Jarawas in to three territorial groups and demarcating their respective territories. Since the Boiab and Thidong areas are a continuous territory it is a bit difficult to draw a dividing line between the two. In order to solve this problem the huts of the Jarawa of both territories were plotted on the map and it was found that the 12° latitude roughly divide the both territories. It passes through east of Putatang on the eastern side of the Jarawa territory and Petchhleg on the western side. The mobility of the Jarawa is territory specific in relation to hunting and gathering activities. But where the mobility is for socialising purpose as there are inter-territorial marriages and alliances, the impermeability of territorial boundary does not hold true. Thus one observes that the concept of territoriality at subsistence level is very strong in the Jarawa. It is quite natural in a society which primarily subsists on hunting and gathering.

## Population

The Jarawa has a total population of 266 as per the last count in 2002. A territory wise population distribution of the Jarawa shows that there are about 84 Jarawa in Boiab, 78 in Thidong and about 103 in Tanmad area (Table-1). The Jarawa of Thidong area are the smallest territorial group. The family is the smallest unit of the Jarawa society and the territorial group is the largest unit. Within the same territory there are sub groups also. But there is no restriction on the movement of those sub-groups within the territory. Fusion and fission of sub groups is a continuous process which flow from the requirement of foraging.

**Table 1**

| *Territory* | *Male* | *Female* | *Total* |
|---|---|---|---|
| Boiab | 39 | 45 | 84 |
| Thidong | 45 | 33 | 78 |
| Tanmad | 51 | 53 | 103 |

In the Jarawa society the children above the age of 10 starts helping elders to some extent in subsistence activities. However, they become an economically effective person around the age of 15 year. Here the 15 year of age has been considered as dividing line between economically dependent and economically effective population. There are very few individuals above the age of 50 years. But these individuals, too, are active members of the group and are not dependant population. The Jarawa society does not support an economically inactive population except the children. This system of their society flow from the mode of their economy where supporting a large dependent population will be detrimental to their survival.

The adequacy of the area from the viewpoint of man-land ratio suggests that the Jarawa area has a man-land ratio of 0.46 person per km.[2]. The low man-land ratio is offset by the rich coastal region which provides a good amount of marine resources to the population. Besides, being in an island situation the functional resource territory of the Jarawa is even larger than formal resource territory for it includes some small islands also which are close to the Jarawa territory like Bluff Island off the western coast, Baratang Island etc.

**Relation with Neighbours**

The relationship of the Jarawa with the non-Jarawa has a chequered history. It passes through three stages. The first stage was that of indifference during the first penal settlement from 1789 to1796.The relationship came to be characterised by hostility during the second penal settlement (from 1858 onward) when the British tried to tame the Jarawa by force. It happened due to the failure on the part of the British to distinguish the fact that they were facing two different population groups when they took possession of the Andaman Island namely the Aka-bea and the Jarawa. While the Jarawa were indifferent, the Ake-bea were hostile. The British met the hostility with hostility and it turned the Jarawa hostile. The brief period of Japanese occupation added fuel to the fire. The phase of hostility continued till the first half of 1997. In post-Independence period the practice of punitive expedition was abandoned. The first friendly contact was made in the year 1969 (Singh, 2002, pp. 6-12). Thereafter, a team of few individuals would visit the Jarawa once in month at a particular location, would meet them and spend few hours. This continuous effort of almost three decades culminated in September 1997 when a group of unarmed Jarawa came out in open near a non-tribal settlement. It was a significant development as it put an end to the phase of hostility and marked the beginning of the phase of friendliness. The hostile and fleeting relationship of the Jarawa with others has delivered two results; it has helped in protection of the territory and the people, it has also helped perpetuation of ignorance among others about the Jarawa and their physical setting. Their overt defense along their territorial space had patterned mutual avoidance. Such behaviour, on the other hand, created a situation where attempts were made to win them over. Regions of critical food resources, traditional camps sites and areas of their mythic and ecosystem dependent cosmos display the extensive need amongst the Andaman Islanders, both in present and past to maintain its exclusivity by combat, use and occupation (Pandya, 1993). These broad generalisations of territorial behaviour amongst the Andaman Islander serve to briefly illustrate exclusivity and sustenance based on ecological regimes common among such people.

## SUBSISTENCE ECONOMY

Jarawa has a broad spectrum economy which comprised hunting, fishing and gathering. They collect and utilize a wide range of resources. This type of economy has the advantage of reducing the risk of resource paucity.

The resource base of the Jarawa is inclusive of both the terrestrial and aquatic resources.

At cognitive level the Jarawa devide the territory in to five categories namely *pilleh* (sea shore area), *tagidh* (marshy area), *chanhannap* (plain forest land), *tinon* (hilly dense forest) and *wa* (streams, inlets). In fact these five resource zones are the five broad ecological zones providing different suits of resources. The aquatic resources are exploited from *pilleh, tagidh* and *wa* areas while *chanhanap* and *tinon* areas are used for the exploitation of terrestrial resources. The fresh water need is met from *wa*. During the field work about 134 species of plants have been documented as resources for the Jarawa, of which 48 are used as edible resources and others as non-edible resources (Table 2 & 3). The harvesting of aquatic resources is mostly for food purpose. Aquatic resources mostly consist of different varieties of fish, crabs, shells, molluscs, turtle and turtle eggs (Table 4). However, the availability and in some cases density of many of these resources is season specific. The resource extraction by the Jarawa is, therefore, subject to seasonality. There are three broad resource seasons as given below:

1. Mid-March to mid-May (Dry Summer)– It is the season of wild jackfruit collection along with honey. The wild jackfruits are collected in large quantity. The flesh of ripen fruit is eaten instantly. The unripe fruit is roasted in the fire and there after its seeds is taken out. Some of it is eaten immediately and the rest is stored. The stored seeds last till August. The pig hunting is bare minimum during this period.

**Table 2**
**Edible Plant Resources Utilized by the Jarawa**

| | *Availability of Edible Plant* | | | *Resources* |
|---|---|---|---|---|
| *Type of Edible Plants* | *No. of Species* | *Plenty* | *Adequate* | *Occasional* |
| Tender shoots | 4 | 3 | 1 | 0 |
| Tubers (Diascorea sp.) | 3 | 3 | 0 | 0 |
| Fruits | 38 | 16 | 18 | 4 |
| Seeds | 3 | | | |
| (a) Jackfruits seeds | 1 | 1 | 0 | 0 |
| (b) *Cycus rumphii* | 1 | 1 | 0 | 0 |
| (c) *Nipa fruticans* | 1 | 1 | 0 | 0 |
| Honey | 2 | 1 | 0 | 1 |

**Table 3**
**Non-edible Plants Resources**

| *Type of non-edible Plant Resources* | *No. of Species* |
|---|---|
| Medicinal plants | 16 |
| Plants used in hut making | 19 |
| Plants used in ornamentation | 41 |
| Plants used in implements making | 7 |
| Plants used as repellent | 3 |

2. Mid May to November (Rainy Period)– It is the period of rainy seasons which include both the south-west and the north-east monsoons. During this season the thrust is on pig hunting and collection of the seeds of *Cycus rumphii and Nipa fruticans*. The collection of the seeds of *Cycus rumphii* continues till end of October.
3. December to mid-March (Cool Winter)– It is the season of honey gathering and collection of turtle eggs followed by pig hunting. The turtle starts coming ashore for laying the eggs from November. Thus both the turtle hunting together with eggs collection is done between November and February. Though there are certain species of turtles which lay eggs in other seasons also but those are very few. The honey collection begins after the cessation of rain i.e., from December and last till June.

**Table 4**
**Edible Animal Resources of the Jarawa**

| *Type of Animal Resource* | *No. of Species* | *Availability of Animal Resources* | | |
|---|---|---|---|---|
| | | *Plenty* | *Adequate* | *Occasional* |
| Wild pigs | 1 | - | 1 | - |
| Monitor lizards s | 1 | - | 1 | - |
| Aves | 9 | - | - | - |
| Pisces | 29 | 15 | - | - |
| Crustacea | 15 | - | - | - |
| Insecta | 3 | - | - | - |
| Molluscs | 17 | 4 | - | - |
| Grub larvae | 1 | - | 1 | - |

**Quantity and Time of Consumption of the Food Items in the Jarawa**

| *Food Article* | *Quantity (Kg)* | *Hours* |
|---|---|---|
| Meat | 209 | 635 |
| Honey | 185 | 275 |
| Tubers | 185 | 281 |
| Molluscs | 065 | 105 |
| Fish | 025 | 105 |
| Turtle eggs | 010 | 025 |

**Quantity and Time of Consumption of the Food Items in the Jarawa**

| *Food Article* | *Quantity (Kg)* | *Hours* |
|---|---|---|
| Meat | 223 | 647 |
| Honey | 005 | 020 |
| Tubers | 173 | 268 |
| Molluscs | 052 | 108 |
| Fish | 055 | 215 |
| Cycus rumphii | 117 | 225 |

As stated earlier there are numerous edible items procured through hunting fishing and gathering, the Jarawa have a dietary preference for meat, fish and molluscs. This means that when these items are available in plenty, other items are eaten less. Meat is obtained from the game animals. There are only three game animals available in Andaman Islands i.e., pig, monitor lizard and turtle. The feral pig is the most preferred of all items. They are hunted with bow and arrow. Hunting is an exclusively male activity. There is no sanction associated with failure in hunting. During hunting expedition an adult Jarawa expend on an average seven to eight hours. They set out from the camp between 7 AM to 8 AM and returned between 2 PM to 3 PM. Though in case of pig the seasonality does not hold true but between February and May the pig has less fat on their bodies. According to Jarawa during this period pigs turn black and their meat does not taste good. The indirect correlation appears to be that the pig is relished by the Jarawa for their fat. The less hunting efforts in this period is related with lesser fat on the pig body.

Interestingly, the Jarawa do not hunt for the deer which are found in plenty in the Jarawa reserve territory. The apparent reason may be that it is an introduced species. Though there is no definite proof of date as to when deer were introduced. The ignorance about the species appears to be reason for their not being a game animal for the Jarawa. In the Jarawa world view the eating of deer's meat would make them ill. Besides, they do not find the meat of the deer delicious as that of wild pig and monitor lizard.

In the aquatic resources fishes and molluscs are important food resources for the Jarawas. These resources are found in abundance in the coastal region of their habitat and easy to catch. Particularly important are bivalve shells and fishes found in the creek and shallow water near the shore line. Men do the fishing by bow and arrow while women with hands net. Fishing is mostly done by the women. The success rate in both the cases is directly related with size and density of resources. The fish are not only source of protein for the Jarawa but in some cases they supply fat too.

Among the plant resources, tubers, *Cycus rumphii*, jackfruits, and *Nipa fruticans* are the major resources. Along with these, honey is another important item of food procured both by men and women. The Jarawa eat the entire content of a hive including royal jelly and propolis. At times when there is excess collection of honey it is stored also. For this purpose a small trench is dug and bucket of honey is put into it and thereafter covered with soil and leaves. But generally most of the honey is consumed within two to three days of its collection.

Thus the major edible resources of the Jarawa are pig meat, pig fat, honey, mollusc, fish, turtle eggs, tubers, Jackfruits and seeds of *Cycus rumphii* and *Nipa fruticans* though availability of many of these are seasonal

| Week | Mean Group Size | Adult | Children | Man days of Consumption | Man-days of Work | Man-days of Hunting | Meat Out-put (k.g.) | % male Involved in hunting | Work Week | Index of Subsistence |
|---|---|---|---|---|---|---|---|---|---|---|
| Iweek (12-18) | 40.4 (31-42) | 128 | 155 | 283 | 074 | 27 | 83 | 33 | 4.0 | 0.26 |
| II week (19-25) | 51.8 (42-57) | 193 | 170 | 363 | 108 | 29 | 69 | 25 | 3.9 | 0.30 |
| III week (26-01) | 23.7 (10-26) | 089 | 077 | 166 | 050 | 13 | 23 | 25 | 3.9 | 0.30 |
| IV week (02-08) | 15.1 (10-16) | 065 | 041 | 106 | 035 | 11 | 34 | 24 | 3.8 | 0.33 |
| 4 weeks total | 131.0 | 475 | 443 | 918 | 267 | 80 | 209 | 107 | 15.67 | 1.19 |
| 4 weeks average | 32.75 | 118.75 | 110.75 | 229.5 | 66.75 | 20 | 52.25 | 27 | 3.9 | 0.30 |

| Week | Mean Group Size | Adult | Children | Man days of Consumption | Man-days of Work | Man-days of Hunting | Meat Out-put (k.g.) | % male Involved in hunting | Work Week | Index of Subsistence |
|---|---|---|---|---|---|---|---|---|---|---|
| Iweek (12-18) | 47.6 (16-73) | 190 | 143 | 333 | 107 | 48 | 150 | 54 | 3.9 | 0.32 |
| II week (19-25) | 23.3 (16-33) | 082 | 081 | 163 | 044 | 05 | 014 | 13 | 3.7 | 0.27 |
| III week (26-01) | 24.6 (16-33) | 089 | 083 | 172 | 048 | 15 | 032 | 36 | 3.8 | 0.29 |
| IV week (02-08) | 27.0 (23-30) | 105 | 084 | 189 | 051 | 12 | 027 | 23 | 3.4 | 0.27 |
| 4 weeks total = | 122.5 | 466 | 391 | 857 | 250 | 80 | 223 | 126 | 14.8 | 1.15 |
| 4 week average = | 30.6 | 116.5 | 97.75 | 214.25 | 62.5 | 20 | 55.75 | 31.5 | 03.7 | 0.29 |

P* – Pig
M** – Monitor lizard
Mean group size = Total man-days of consumption /7
Man-days of hunting = Total man-days of hunting /Total man-days of consumption

Work week = the number of work days per adult per week.
Hunting week = the number of hunting per adult per week.
Index of Subsistence = Man-days of work / Man-days of consumption

(Table 5 & 6). Apart from them, there are numerous other seasonal fruits. But they are consumed in less quantity and generally at the place of gathering itself. Of major edible resources, it is the molluscs, fish and tuber (*Diascorea sp.*) which are the key stone resources. These resources are found round the year and consumes regularly. The key stone resources allow the population to survive through the lean period (Teborgh, 1986). Though in case of the Jarawa there is no lean season as such except that the availability and density of many major resources are seasonal. On an average the Jarawa expend about 3 hours a day in pursuit of procurement of major resources (Table 4).

In addition, the food gathered is distributed in the family. It is interesting to note that while the meats of game animals are distributed among all the constituent families residing at the camp, the distribution of other foraged resources are within family only. It has an ecological value in it. The most relished and difficult to get items are distributed among them. By doing so the hunter ensures that next time if he fails to get hunt still he can have share in the hunt of other hunters. Besides, the sharing of most prized items help strengthen the social bond among the members of the group.

## FORAGING STRATEGY

The foraging strategy of the Jarawa is a collective response to the harnessing of resources spread over space and time to fulfil their basic needs. In other words it is related with satisfactory collection of food. The people tend to eat easily and abundantly available food items which are at the least distance from the camp. The foraging strategy can be explained in relation to location of the Jarawa camps and mobility patterns.

### Camps

In the process of food procurement the camps (*chadda*) play an important role as the foraging area begins from outside the camp. During course of study about 76 huts of different types and at different locations were visited. Of these, 41 were located along or near the coast while 35 in the forest. On the basis of the size, the camps of the Jarawa can be put into three categories–permanent, semi permanent and temporary camps (Sarkar, 1990, pp. 12-15). Presently, the functions of the first two kinds of camps are almost similar in the post hostility phase. They serve as the base camp. They are large in size and remained occupied for longer period between one to three months. Third type is a lean-to-type hut constructed to spend a day or two in the course of their mobility from one place to another. The base camps of the Jarawa are not randomly distributed over space. Instead the location of a camp at place is dictated by combination of three factors- ecological edges, proximity to drinking water along with easy availability of one of the edible resources and season.

*Ecological Edges*– As stated earlier the cognizance of territory into five broad zones by the Jarawa is in fact the division of space into five broad ecological zones. Each of these ecological zones has different assemblage of resources. Spatially most species, even those that are wide spread in terms of their overall range, are restricted in their living requirements to particular ecological habitats or niches (Winterhalder, 1983). The diversity of species and high productivity of the ecological edges attract human communities because they benefit from association with and exploitation of ecological edges. (Odum, 1971; Turner *et al.*, 2003). It is these characteristics of ecological edges which make them suitable place for location of any camp (Brothers, 1993; Meiners and Pickett Steward, 1999). By locating their camps on the edges of these habitats the Jarawa get access to the resources of two or more than two ecological zones with high resource diversity.

The location of the camp along the waterways and the road is very frequent among the Jarawa. Camping sites of the Jarawa are found on points along streams, inlets, creeks and shore lines. The Jarawa do not have well developed water transportation system like their counter parts who make out-rigger canoes. Instead they make raft of very rudimentary kind, the use of which is to cross the small creek. Therefore, the use of water ways for transportation is not a deciding factor. However, the location near a creek or coast provides them easy accessibility to inter-tidal zone on the seaward side and nearness to wet lands, creeks marshes, as well as forest of various types on landward side. Thus they get access to diverse range resources from different ecological zones.

In the post hostility phase, the proximity to road has become another important factor for location of the camp. It provides them easy access to the vehicular traffic plying on the Andaman Trunk Road. By using the vehicular traffic they are reducing the travel cost in terms of time and are able to exploit the resources of larger area along the road. This phenomenon is more pronounced in the Thidong and Tanmad area.

Availability of water and resources- The setting of the camp at edges is governed by the two factors; first the proximity to drinking water and secondly the availability of one of the resources in plenty with least effort. Access to water for personal use is obviously the key factor. Regarding the latter, it is invariably one or more than one of the aquatic resources which are available in abundance. When the camp has inland location it is used to be bivalve shell followed by fish and in case of coastal location it is different species of molluscs and fish (Figure 1).

Seasons- Seasons play a decisive role with respect to the location of the camp along the coast and in the forest. At any given point of time the Jarawa has between two to three permanent camp sites in any territory. During the rainy season (south-west monsoon) between May to September the permanent campsites along the western coast are avoided as the southwest monsoon winds thrashes the western coast harshly. Consequently the sea remains turbulent and rough on the western side of the islands. On the seaward side the sheltered bay and creeks are ideal location for the camp sites. Inside the forest raised grounds are used for camp sites.

Figure 1: A View of Jarawa ecology and Fishing in Andaman Sea

With on set of cool winter season between November and February, both seaward and landward locations are preferred for setting up the camp. The underlying strategy is to harness the abundantly available seasonal resources namely honey followed by turtle eggs. While the former is available in the forest the latter is found along the coast on sandy beaches.

During the dry summer period the camps are usually located a bit away from the coast in the forest with the purpose of gathering honey and collecting jackfruits. As such the ideal location is generally the forest so that the both the resources could be exploited.

## Mobility Pattern

A combination of factors condition the way hunter-gatherers position themselves over space and make movement. The mobility of hunter-gatherers is broadly of two types: residential and logistical (Binford 1980; Hitchcock 1982; Kelly 1995). In case of residential mobility, the entire group both producers and dependents move from one place to another in their territory. Logistical mobility, on the other hand, is the movement to and from a camp site residential location by an individual or task oriented group for the purpose of obtaining matter, energy, or information. The residential mobility of the Jarawa from one base camp to another is made at an interval of one to two months. The logistical mobility, on the other hand, consists of either daily forays or expeditions of several days or weeks. The foraging expeditions are never more than 15 days at a stretch.

The study in three different seasons reveals that the one-day trip of the Jarawa is within a radius of 10 km. Initially the resources which are at lesser distance from the camp are exploited. With the thinning of resources in the vicinity, they travel longer distances to exploit the resources. However, in case of pig hunting the above-mentioned exploitation of area in a sequential manner does not stand good. Further where the travel requires covering more than 10 km. the either overnight trip is performed or foraging expeditions ranging from few days to two weeks are organised.

The numbers of foraging expeditions consisting of more than five days at a stretch are high in the rainy season and low in dry summer and cool winter. The reason for this high logistical mobility in the rainy season is attributed to the pig hunting. During this season 8 foraging expeditions were performed from Ulia base camp. The reason for less number of longer foraging expedition in the dry summer season is attributed to the fact that the gathering and processing of jackfruits result in their staying at a place for not more than 4-5 days at a stretch when they are away from the base camp. Similarly in the cool winter period the exploitation of honey and turtle eggs require them engaging in few number of longer foraging expeditions. During this season the movement of the Jarawa oscillate between coast and forest. The underlying strategy is to exploit the both the resources. At Alaoethala base camp 4 such foraging expeditions were performed.

On the basis of the frequency of the movement and distance covered, the Jarawa may be divided in three groups. The most mobile group comprised unmarried boys who have been initiated into the hunter hood through the *lepa* ceremony. Even within their territory they move frequently from one camp to another. In fact they help spread the information from one group to another. The least mobile group comprises unmarried girls and widow. They never venture out of their territory alone and generally move with the family units. The family groups, widowers and boys of adolescent age stood in between the two groups.

## INPUT-OUTPUT ANALYSIS

The Jarawa economy demonstrates a close approximation to the economy of true hunter and gatherers. It is completely based on extraction and is characterised by minimum accumulation. It is typified by absence of domestication of plants and animals. The relation between procurement and consumption of food is immediate within space and time. In the Jarawa society every able body person above the age of 14 is an economically active member of the society supporting himself and dependent members. There is generalized reciprocity in terms of sharing of resources with the game animals being shared routinely among the constituent families of a group while the other foraged items are shared within the family. It, therefore, presents a suitable case for the application of the input-output analysis. Here only the subsistence effort has been considered. The nutritional aspect of the analysis could not be attempted due to the inadequacy of data particularly on the minor resources.

Having taken cognizance of the above mentioned points, the input-output analysis has been applied to the data collected on the subsistence effort of the Jarawa. The subsistence effort is a compilation of all days of work carried out by a member of a group within a specified period of time. It has been described in terms of number of days per week per hunter. Here the consumption unit is defined by adding together the total number of effective and dependents members at a camp during a specified period.

The formula used is taken from Lee (1969) as follows:

$$S = W/C$$

Where S = the Index of Subsistence Effort,
Where W = the number of man-days of work and
Where C = number of man days of consumption.

In a self sufficient human group the magnitude of "S", the Index of Subsistence Effort refers to the efforts made for procurement of resources to feed the group.

## RESULTS

The Table 5 is the summary of dairy at Alaoethala base camp in Thidong area. It is the season of honey gathering, turtle eggs collection and hunting. The average group size varies from 15.1 to 40.4. Of the total population at the camp site, 52 percent are active population while the remaining 48 percent are dependent population. The work week varies between 3.8 and 4.0 days a week with average being 3.9 days a week. It means they have 3 to 3.2 days for leisure, socialising and other activities. The Index of Subsistence Effort "S" for four week is 3.0. The "S" value indicates 30 days of work per hundred days of man-days consumption; or each day's work provided food for the worker and 3.3 other persons. The week wise analysis of the table shows that the Index of Subsistence Effort is 0.26 in the first week and it increased to 3.0 in the second and third week. In the fourth week it further rose to 0.33. This increase in the value of 'S' was owing to the onset of the honey collection season which in their case began from the second week of December. Now the subsistence effort of the group was oriented towards the collection of turtle eggs and honey collection. During this season it was observed that decline in the success rate of wild pig hunting on account of their long stay at the same place was off-set by success in the monitor lizard hunting. Of the total adult male population only 27 percent of them were involved in hunting. The hunting accounted for 33 percent of the total man days of work.

Table 6 is the summary of the work diary at Ulia base camp in Tanmad area. It is the period of rainy when pig hunting along with collection of seeds of *Cycus rumphii* is major subsistence activities. The group size varies from 23.3 to 47.6. Of the total population at the camp site, 54 percent are active population while the remaining 46 percent are dependent population. The work week varies between 3.4 to 3.9 days a week with average being 3.7 days a week. It means they have 3.1 to 3.6 days for leisure, socialising and other activities. The average value of Index of Subsistence Effort for four weeks was 0.29 ( 29 work days per 100 consumption days). The value S = .29 indicates 29 man-days of work per hundred man-days of consumption; or each day's work provided foos for the worker and three and half (3.4) other people. A week wise analysis of subsistence index shows, it was high in the first week i.e., 0.32, while in the following three weeks it remained between 0.27 and 0.29. The reason for high value of Index of Subsistence Effort in the first week was due to greater effort made for hunting. In the subsequent weeks less effort was made for hunting owing to less availability of pig on account of intensive hunting operation in the first week. It is evident from the column man-days of hunting which shows that only 32 man-days of work was expended for hunting in three weeks compared to 48 man-days of work in the first week. The percentage adult male population involved in hunting was 31. The hunting accounted for 31 percent of the total man days of work.

## DISCUSSION

The input-output analysis shows that the average value of Index of Subsistence Effort for the Jarawa is 29.5. It means 29.5 days of work per hundred man-days of consumption; or each day's work provided food for for the worker and 3.38 other persons. The average work input varies between 3.7 to 3.9 days a week. If we take into account the man-hours expended towards procurement of major resources it works out to be about 3 hours a day for the Jarawa (table V & VI). It means the Jarawa work about 3 hours a day towards the procurement of major resources and between 3.7 to 3.9 days a week. After subsistence effort they still have between 3.1to 3.3 days left for socializing and other leisure activities. This economically active population constitutes 53 percent of the total population. Of the total adult male population, 30 to 31 percent are involved in hunting. In other words, the subsistence efforts of one third of the total adult male population are oriented toward hunting. Hunting accounts for 31 to 33 percent of the total man-days of work. It means one third of their subsistence effort is made for hunting and the remaining two third for fishing and gathering. This deduction, in turn, is supported by the earlier statement that despite their preference for the meat of game animals, the fish, molluscs and tubers are the key stone resources for the Jarawa.

## CONCLUSIONS

The Jarawas of Andaman Islands are one of the few remaining hunter-gatherers of the world whose subsistence economy is still in the elementary form. The subsistence economy of the Jarawa consists of hunting, fishing and gathering. The hunting is a male activity while the fishing and gathering is done by both the sexes; but there is preponderance of women in the latter activities. The acquisition of food resources is subject to availability, density and distance. The availability and density of resources are subject to seasonality. Broadly there are three resource seasons namely the summer dry, rainy and cool dry. While the summer dry season is characterised by exuberance of honey and jackfruit, the rainy seasons is known for pig hunting and collection of seeds of *Cycus rumphii,* Nipa *fruticans* and cool dry season for turtle eggs, turtle and honey. A number of edible resources are procured by the Jarawa but the meat of the game animals, fish, molluscs, honey, tuber and seeds of Cycus rumphii, Nipa fruticans and jackfruit are the major edible resources of the Jarawa. In the foraging strategy of the Jarawa the location of the camp and mobility of the population play a significant role. The camps are set-up at the transition of ecosystem zones. The underlying strategy is to get access to the resources of two or more than two ecosystems. The mobility of the population allows them to procure the resources spread over space. The Jarawa mobility oscillates between coast and the forest.

The analysis of foraging data suggests that the Jarawa work between 3.7 to 3.9 days a week. In a day about 3 hours (approximately) is expended in pursuit of collection of major resources. It implies that they have sufficient time left for socialising and other leisure activities. The less number of man-days in a week and less number of man-hours in a day points to the fact that there are sufficient resources in the Jarawa habitat to support the subsistence activities of the population.

## REFERENCES CITED

Andaman & Nicobar Administration (2004), *Andaman and Nicobar Gazette: Extraordinary,* A & N Administration, Port-Blair.

Andaman and Nicobar Islands Forest Department (1998), *Forest Statistics,* Vansadan, Port-Blair.

Awaradi, S.A. (1990), *Computerized Master Plan (1991-2021) for Welfare of Primitive Tribes of Andaman and Nicobar Islands,* Andaman Administration, Port Blair.

Bailey, R.C., Head, G., Jenike, M., Owen, B., Rechtman, R., and Zechenter, E. (1989), Hunting and gathering in Tropical Rain Forest: Is It Possible? *American Anthropologist* 91: 59-82.

Bailey, R.C., and Headland, T. N. (1991), Have Hunter-gathers Lived in Tropical Rain Forest Independently of Agriculture? Human Ecology 15: 463-491.

Bellwood, P. (1985), *Prehistory of the Indo-Malaysian Archipelago,* Academic Press, New York.

Binford, L. R. (1980), Willow Smoke and Dogs' Tails: Hunter-gatherer Settlement Systems and Archaeological Site Functions. *Journal of Anthropological Archaeology* 1(1): 4-20.

Brothers, T. S. (1993), Fragmentation and Edge Effects in Central Indiana Old-growth Forests. *Natural Areas Journal* 13(4): 268-275.

Census of India (1931), *The Andaman and Nicobar Islands,* Part-I & II, Vol.II. Central Publication, Calcutta.

Census of India (1981), *The Andaman and Nicobar Islands: General Economic Tables and Social and Cultural Tables,* Part III, A& B, and Part-IV, Govt. of India Press, Delhi.

Champion, H.G. and Seth, S. K. (1968), *A Revised Survey of the Forest Types of India,* Govt. of India publication, Delhi.

Cipriani, L. (1968), *The Andaman Islander,* Weidenfield and Nicolson, London.

Cooper, Z. (1990), Archaeological Evidences for Resource Exploitation in the Andaman Islands. *Man and Environment* 15(1): 73-81.

Danda, D. (1987), The Onges of Little Andaman. *Human Science* 24:89-90.

Dutta, P. C. (1974), *The Great Andamanese Past and Present,* Anthropological Survey of India, Calcutta, pp. 35-38.

Endicott, K. and Bellwood, P. (1991), The Possibility of Independent Foraging in the Rain Forest of Peninsular Malaysia. *Human Ecology* 19: 151-186.

Farb, P., and Armelago, G. (1980), *Consuming Passions: The Anthropology of Eating,* Houghton Miffin Company, Boston.

Gates, D. M. (1962), *Energy Exchange in the Biosphere,* Harper and Row, New York.

Harris, M. (1985), *Good to Eat: Riddles of Food and Culture,* Sinon and Schuster, New York.

Haviland, William (1978), *Anthropology,* Holt, Rinehart and Winston, New York.

Headland, T. (1987), The Wild Yam Question: How Well Could Independent Hunter-gatherer Live in a Tropical Rain Forest Ecosystem? *Human Ecology* 15: 463-491.

Holland, T. H. (1904), Ancient Kitchen Middens in India. *Records of Geological Survey of India,* Calcutta 31 (45) : 107-108.

Kelly, R. L. (1995), *The Foraging Spectrum: Diversity in Hunter-Gatherer Life Ways,* Smithsonian Institutional Press, Washington, D.C.

Keene, A. S. (1981), *Prehistoric Foraging in a Temperate Forest: A Linear Programming Model,* Academic Press, New York.

Kleiber, M. (1961), *The Fire of Life: An Introduction to Animal Energetics,* John Wiley, New York.

Krishnatry, S. M. (1977), *Survival of the Weakest in Retrived from Precipice,* Andaman Adim Janjati Vikas Samiti, Port-Blair, pp. 28-41.

Lal, P. (1976), *The Andaman Islands,* Anthropological Survey of India, Calcutta.

Lee. R. B. (1968), What Hunters Do for a Living or How to Make Out on Scarce Resources? In Lee, R. B., and DeVore, I. (eds.), *Man the Hunter.* Aldine, Chicago, pp. 30-48.

Lee. R. B. (1969), ! Kung Bushman Subsistence: An Input-Output Analysis. In Vayda, A. (ed.), *Environment and Cultural Behaviour,* Natural History Press, New York, pp. 44-79.

Lee. R. B. (1979), *The !Kung San*, Cambridge University Press, Cambridge.

Leontief, W. (1966), *Input-Output Economics*, Oxford University Press, New York.

Majumdar, R. C. (1975), *Penal Settlement in India,* Ministry of Education and Social Welfare, Govt. of India, Delhi.

Man, E. H. (1883) (1975 reprint), *The Aboriginal Inhabitants of the Andaman Islands,* Sanskar Prakasan, Delhi.

Mathur, L. P. (1968), *History of Andaman and Nicobar Islands* (1756-1966), Sterling Publishers Pvt. Ltd., Delhi and Jalandhar, p.- 7.

Meiners, S. J., and Pickett-Steward, T. A. (1999), Changes in Community and Population Responses Across a Forest-field Gradient. *Ecography* 22(5): 261-267.

Odum, E. P. (1971), *Fundamentals of Ecology,* 3rd edn, W. B. Saunders, Philadelphia, PA.

Oliver, W. L. R. (1984), Introduced and Feral Pigs: Feral Mammals Problems and Potentials. Proceedings of Workshop on Feral Mammals, IIIrd International Theoretical Congress, Helsinki, 1982, IUCN, Glano.

Pandey, V. (1993), *Above the Forest: A Study of Andamanese Ethno Anemology, Cosmology and the Power of Rituals,* Oxford University Press, New York, New Delhi.

Pandit, T. N. (1974). Jarawa Story of a Century of Mutual Hostility. *Daily Telegrams,* 16th and 18th March, Port-Blair.

Portman, M. V. (1889/1990), *A History of Our Relation with Great Andamanese,* Vol. II, Asian Education Services, Delhi and Madras, pp. 55-80, 707-709.

Riches, D. (1982), *Northern Nomadic Hunter-Gatherer: A Humanistic Approach,* Academic Press, London, pp. 214-16.

Sahalins, M. (1968), Notes on the Original Affluent Society. In Lee, R. B., & DeVore, I. (eds.), *Man the Hunter,* Aldine, Chicago, pp. 85-86.

Sahalins, M. (1972), *Stone Age Economics,* Aldine, Chicago.

Sahalins, M. (1976), *Culture and Practical Reason,* University of Chicago Press, Chicago.

Sarkar, B. N. (1985), The Jarawa of the Andaman Island: An Anthropometric Study. *Human Science* 34: 186-194.

Sarkar, B. N. (1987), Dermatoglyphic Study of the Jarawa: A Negrito Tribe of the Andaman Island. *Human Science,* 36; 346-358.

Sarkar, J. K. (1987), Befriending the Jarawa: A Challenging Task. *Human Science* 36: 1-12.

Sarkar, J. K. (1989), Endangered Tribes and Their Development in Andaman and Nicobar Islands. *Journal of Indian Anthropological Society* 24: 1-45.

Sarkar, J. K. (1990), *The Jarawa,* Seagull Books, Calcutta.

Sen, P. K. (1962), *Land and People of Andaman,* Post Graduate Book Mart, Calcutta.

Sreenathan, M. (1998), Rhetorical Violence: Language Ideology and Jarawa Hostility. *Man in India* 78: 355.

Sreenathan, M. (2001), *The Jarawa: Language and Culture*, Anthropological Survey of India., Calcutta.

Terborgh, J. (1986), Key Stone Plant Resources in Tropical Forest. *In Soule, M. E. (ed.), Conservation Biology: The Science of Scarcity and Diversity*, Sinauer, Sunderland, Mass.

Turner, N. J., Davidson-Hunt, I. J., and O' Flaherty, M. (2003), Living on the Edge: Ecological and Cultural Edges as Source of Diversity for Social-ecological Resilience. *Human Ecology* 31(3): 431-461.

Whitaker, R. (1988), *Endangered Andaman*, Environmental Service Group, WWF-India and MAB-India, Department of Environment, Government of India.

Winterhalder, B. and Smith, E. A. (1981), *Hunter-gatherer Foraging Strategies: Ethnographic and Archaeological Analysis*, University of Chicago Press, Chicago.

Winterhalder B. (1990), Open Field Common Pot: Harvest Variability and Risk Avoidance in Agricultural and Foraging Societies. In Cashdan, E. (ed.), *Risk and Uncertainty in Tribal and Peasant Economies* Westview Press, Boulder, CO. *Risk and Uncertainty in Tribal and Peasant Economies* Westview Press, Boulder, CO.

Winterhalder, B. (1993). Work, Resource and Their Population. *Man* 28: 321-340.

Yellen, J. E. (1971), *Archaeological Approaches to the Presents: Models for Reconstructing the Past*, Academic Press, New York.

Chapter–23

# Bio-Cultural Adaptations and Evolution in Andaman Islanders

*B.N. Sarkar*

## INTRODUCTION

Evolutionary adaptations are mercilessly judged by nature for survival of species. These evolutionary changes are often sudden, provoked by a beneficial mutation or rapid changes in the environment. In human history a basic ecological process of the transition was from nomadic hunter-gatherer life to sedentary life of food producers. A food producing sedentary life may have been a second choice of prehistoric hunter-gathers for coping with the population increase and food crisis, which began about ten thousand years ago.

Evolutionary outcomes depend not only on those processes that operate within population (e.g. selection) but also on interaction (via gene flow) among population. The study of population genetic theory and of the process of microevolution with human material is very difficult and little actual work has been done. The influence of culture on breeding behavior, through different mating systems, different population sizes or densities, different opportunities for gene exchange and so forth are determine the process of microevolution.

Population geneticists study the genetic constitution populations and how this genetic makeup changes from generation to generation. The continuity of a population through time is provided by the mechanisms of biological heredity. The existence of genetic variation is a necessary condition for evolution. Genetic variation and rate of evolutionary change by natural selection was first demonstrated by Fischer (1930). Variation in gene pools (the aggregate of the genotypes of the entire population) is expressed in terms of either genotype frequencies or gene frequencies.

Culture can be regarded as an aspect of the environment into which each human is born and must succeed or fail, developed gradually by the succession of humans who have lived throughout history. The evidence suggests that cultural traits are, in general, vehicles of genetic survival, and that the heritability of cultural traits depends on the judgments (conscious and unconscious) of individuals with regard to their effects on the individual's inclusive fitness.

Until recently over one hundreds tribes around the world choose to reject contact with outsiders, including the Jarawas and the Sentenelese of Andaman Islands. They are the most vulnerable people on the planet. They have often seen their friends and families die at the hands of outsiders, the unreported massacres or epidemic. Over the decades, several research efforts were conducted on a number of hunting gathering groups all over the world through multidisciplinary researches include ecological, demographic, biomedical, socio-cultural, genetic and behavioral studies. The overall goal of the multidisciplinary approach has been an explorative paradigm, especially with respect to understand the adaptive strategies employ by the hunter-gatherer.

## THE BACKGROUND STUDIES

In view of the above fact, the present paper examines the nature and extent of biological, demographic and genetical variation of the Andaman Islanders particularly the Onge of Little Andaman and the Jarawas of Middle and South Andamans and their micro differentiation in response of cultural, morphological and genetical features over the period of time. The data for the present study was generated among the Onges in 1986 from Little Andaman and the Jarawas in 1999 from South and Middle Andamans (Sarkar 1996, and Sarkar and Sahani 2002). The genetic variations of the Andaman Islanders were also compared with the similar population groups of Southeast Asia namely Semang of Malaysia and Aeta of Philippines.

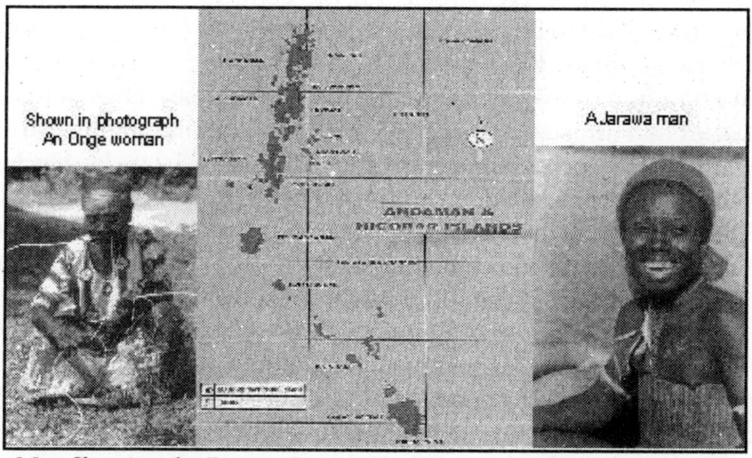


Figure 1: Map Showing the Present Distribution of the Andaman Tribes

The Andaman archipelago is an important corridor (Fig. 1) of ancient human migration and which is the home of a few inbreed 'Negrito' population groups. According to Radcliffe Brown (1948) the Andaman Islanders classified into two broad groups on basis of their linguistic and cultural affinities. The first group, the Great Andamanese included ten tribes of the Great Andaman Islands. Those tribes were basically loose social conglomerates speaking ten different languages. The other group was that of the Little Andamanese including the Onge of Little Andaman Island, the Jarawas of Great Andaman Islands and the inhabitants of the Sentinel Island. The latter two groups of people, Radcliffe Brown thought, migrated at some point of time from the Little to Great Andaman Islands. The Jarawas and the Sentenelese of Andaman Islands are perhaps the last surviving classical example of true hunter gathers of the world.

There is no definite knowledge about the time when the Andaman Islands were peopled first. The earliest evidence of human habitation in the Islands are available in forms of small stone tools, bone and shell artefacts, and potsherds deposited in mounds that are known as Kitchen Middens. Using the method of relative dating, Dutta (1978) suggested that the Mesolithic culture "have possibly arrived in the Andaman Islands sometimes around the beginning of the Christian era". However, Radio Carbon dating, which gives us absolute dates, ranges between 1400 ±100 years B.P. for Beehive Island and 2280 ±90 years B.P. for Chauldari (Cooper 1990). The islands were known to the sailors and travellers become evident from the accounts of the Chinese in seventh century, Arabs in ninth century and Europeans in thirteenth century. Pirates operating in those parts used to capture the islanders and sell them as slaves in those countries (Portman 1899:177).

The region from where the Andaman Islanders arrived and the route of their migration are matters of great controversy. Linguistic affinity between the Andaman Negritoes and the collective group of South-East Asia Negritoes is yet to be established. According to Radcliffe Brown (1948) the Andaman Islands were peopled either by land or by sea route from the Arakan region of lower Burma. The deep-sea researches of Melengraaf (1921) have been utilised by Kaudeen (1939) to interpret the probable routes of migration of the Negritoes into the Andaman Islands. He believed, during the quaternary age there was a fall of 300mts in the sea level, which established direct contact with Burma and facilitated movement of the Negritoes into the islands. But the present physiographic characteristics of the Andaman Sea and the Bay of Bengal Basin floor do not support the contentions of Melengraaf (1921).

Nei and Ray Choudhury (1982) and Omoto (1984) suggested a close affinity between the Philippine Negritoes and their neighbouring Negrito population of South-East Asia than the African pygmies. Biological affinities between the Jarawas, Semangs of Malaysia and Aetas of

Philippines have been suggested with regard to anthropometric (Sarkar 1989) and dermatoglyphic (Sarkar 1987) characteristics. Recently the genomic affinity between the tribes of Andaman islands and the neighboring populations of south east Asia and African Pygmies were reported based on mtDNA and autosomal markers( Kashyap *et al.*, 2003, Thangraj et al., 2003, Barik *et al.*, 2008 and others).

The overall climate of the Andaman Islands is tropical *i.e.*, warm, moist and equable. The proximity of sea and abundant rainfall prevent extremes of heat and the variation of temperature on these islands is rather low (23°C - 31°C).

The Andaman Islanders in general and the Jarawas in particular are primarily depending on animal resources for their sustenance. Plant resources are consumed as a complement to the animal resources. It was observed that the edible plant species are available in various forest types, right from Mangrove Forest to Andaman Semi-Evergreen Forest. The Jarawas depend upon herbal medicines to cure different ailments.

The overall population size of the Andaman Islanders was estimated around 10,000 in 1779 (Dutta 1974), which sharply declined to less than half of it by 1858. Trend of rapid population decline among the Andaman tribes for a period of 1858 to 1981 are depicted in Fig. 2. On the other hand the overall growth of population in the Andaman Islands during the same period presents a contrast picture.

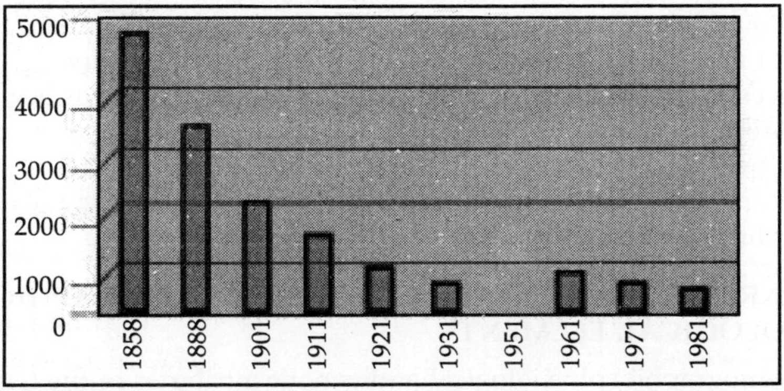


Figure 2: Distribution of the Tribal Populations in Andaman an Islands During 1858–1981

The Jarawas and the Onges have their well-defined society. They are endogamous people, who are not even ready to consider possibilities of violating this rule of marriage. The smallest social unit among them is family; members of a family are husband, wife, and their young children. Those children can be from earlier marriage(s) of the couple or born from their present marriage. A local group consists of several families and some individuals who camp together and move from one place to another while shifting camp. These local groups, however, are not of very permanent nature; they often go through processes of fission and fusion.

The next larger social group is the territorial division; there can be several local groups in one such division. Traditionally the Onge habitat was divided into three geographical regions namely, *Giremekaya* (the northern and eastern coast), *Girerаratwaye* (the southern and western coast) and *Engakwaleye* (thickly forested interior part). Each region was inhabited by a number of local groups or bands of the Onge called *Beyra*. Similarly the Jarawas divide the area under their occupation into three territorial divisions. The northernmost part located on Middle Andaman Island is called *Tanmad*, the southernmost territory is called *Boiab*, and the land lying in between the two is called *Thidong*. Most members of a local group are related to each other either through consanguineal or affinal relations. Thus, kinship plays a significant role in their society. This can be seen in ways the kin extend their cooperation in constructing a small family hut or a large community hut, in foraging activities, in movement from one campsite to another.

Besides, the aesthetic culture of the tribes of Andaman islands mostly among the Jarawas and the Onges until recently are reflected in their ornaments, decoration of their body, chest guard, bow, baskets, song and dance. Traditionally leaves, flowers, shells and clay were used for decoration. Generally females decorate themselves more than the males; however, during pregnancy females do not decorate themselves. The ornamentations are worn as headbands, necklaces, girdles, garlands and armlets.

Although, the Onge has remained largely unchanged genetically, but their diet and life style have become progressively more divergent from their ancestor in the recent past. These maladaptative changes began with the deforestation and rehabilitation programme since 1967 and have been accelerating in recent times. On the other hand the Jarawas are still maintaining their traditional way of life in spite of many changes in their surroundings in the recent years.

## COMPARATIVE EVALUATION OF SOME DEMOGRAPHIC AND PHYSIOLOGICAL ELEMENTS

Some demographic, physiological and genetic attributes of the Onge and the Jarawas are given below to understand nature and magnitude of variation of these tribes. The detailed demographic data comprising age-sex composition, family size, population size of the camp, marital status, sex ratio etc of the the Onge and Jarawa are published elsewhere (Sarkar 1996, Sarkar *et al* 2002). However, in the present discourse a comparative evaluation of such attributes are presented in Fig. 3 and 4. It reveals from the figures that the high proportion of young individuals, a reasonable balanced sex ratio, higher proportion of fertile women and of prospective mothers suggest a progressive trend of population expansion of the present day Jarawas of Andaman Islands in contrast to a marked decline trend of the Onge population of Little Andaman, who came in contact with the outside world earlier.

It is thought the evolution by natural selection produced the 'Functional Design' observed in living beings, known as adaptation. Therefore, sickness and disease pattern can be explained through a cost and benefit analysis of physiological function. In evolutionary medicine, there is a constant race between the body's defence and pathogens. Thus physiological attributes and diseases patterns are also important selective factors of a

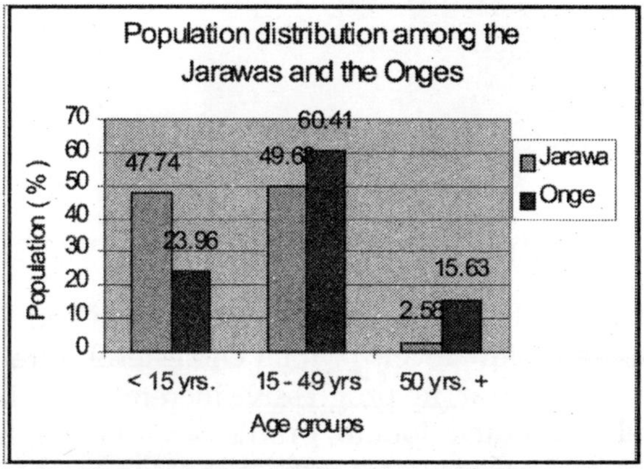


Figure 3: Comparative Distribution of Age Structure of the Onge and Jarawa

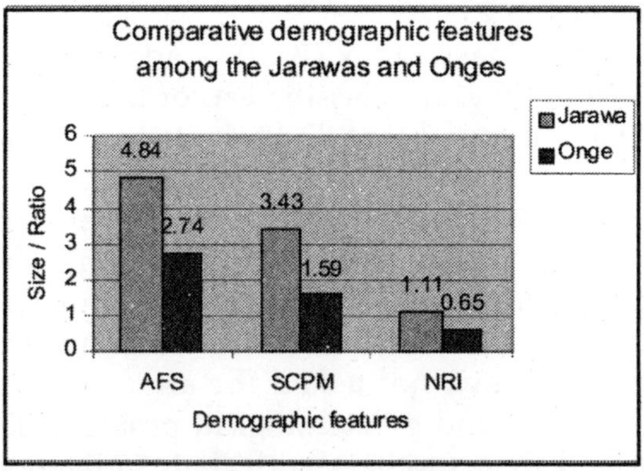


Figure 4: Comparative Demographic Features: [AFS=Average Family Size], SCPM= Surviving Children Pet Mother, NRI= Net Reproductive Index]

population. In this regard, some physiological attributes of the present day Jarawa and the Onges are presented. The mean systolic blood pressure among the Jarawas was 107.60 mm/Hg (male) and 91.88 mm/Hg (female) while the mean diastiolic pressure was 71.70 mm/Hg (male) and 62.76 mm/Hg (female) suggesting low status of blood pressure. It is interesting to mentioned that there is no progressive increment of blood pressure with the age among the Jarawas (Fig. 5). The finding of very low mean blood pressure and lack of elevation of pressure over the age has also been recorded among many African tribes lie the Zulus, the Masais (Scotch and Geiger 1963). However there is an elevation of mean blood pressure both the systolic and diastolic among the Onges are reported after changing

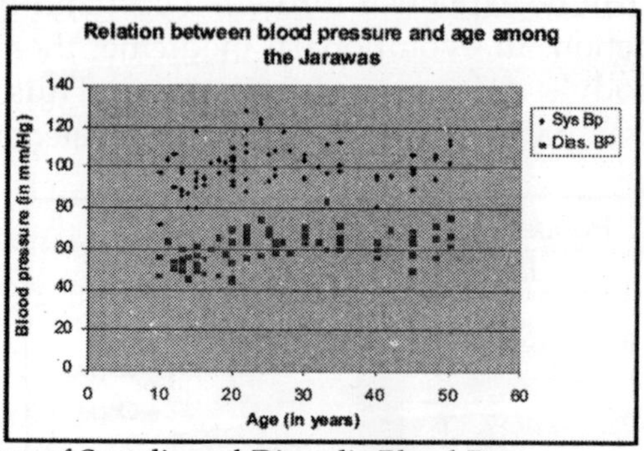


Figure 5: Distribution of Systolic and Diastolic Blood Pressure among the Jarawa

their life style and food habits in recent past (Kumar and Sarkar 1987). Apart for these, extreme low levels of total cholesterol, rare incidence of anaemia and hypovitaminosis, no progressive increment of blood pressure with age, low level of immunoglobulin profiles are some of the significant adaptive responses of this true hunter gather tribes like among the Jarawas. Polyunsaturated fats like Omega3 were abundant in Jarawa diet mainly from marine food chains.

On an average, Body Mass Index (BMI) Grade of 96 adult Jarawas whose age was more than 20 years, classified according to James et al 1988 and Luizz et al (1992) and found that 82.4% Jarawas were in the normal BMI grade, which indicates good nutritional status among adult Jarawas. However only 4.5% Jarawas found to be obese and all were female Jarawas.

Though the Jarawas continue to practice their indigenous system of medicine, utilizing on plant and animal products, in many cases in the recent times they are asking for modern medical assistance from the non-Jarawas. However, they have not asked for any assistance from the outsiders for any obstetrics and gynaecological problem. They prefer to treat the newborns and their mothers with their indigenous system of medicine.

## Microevolution and Gene Diversity

The microevolution is the occurrence of small-scale changes in allele frequencies in a population, over a few generations, also known as change at or below the species level. There are a few basic ways in which microevolutionary change happens. Mutation, migration, genetic drift, and natural selection are all processes that can directly affect gene frequencies in a population. Studies of human population structure and history have tended to use demographic and/or serological data for analysis. To date, studies have indicated that quantitative traits may often be used successfully in studies of human population structure, and show effects of microevolutionary forces on quantitative variation among populations.

The heterozygosity of a population is the measure of genetic variation preferred by most population geneticists. During the last few decades, a considerable number of studies of genetic structure have been reported and mentioned in various reviews (Cannings and Cavalli-Sforza, 1973, Harpending, 1974, Roberts, 1975; Jorde 1980 and others). In India a few studies on genetic structure have been carried out in populations of Orissa, Maharashtra, Andhra Pradesh and Himachal Pradesh( Chakraborty and Yee , 1973; Malhotra *et al* , 1978; Mukherjee *et al* 1979,1989, Pingle *et al* 1981, Papiha *et al* 1982 and others).

The Onges were studied earlier by Gates (1940), Sarkar (1952), Lehmann and Ikin (1954) and Kumar and Mukherjee (1983) with regards to the distribution of ABO blood groups and few other genetic markers among a small limited number of individuals. Thus, the results of the present study and those of the earlier studies provided a unique opportunity to know the temporal changes, if any, in such a small population like the Onge. Apart from these, data on blood groups and

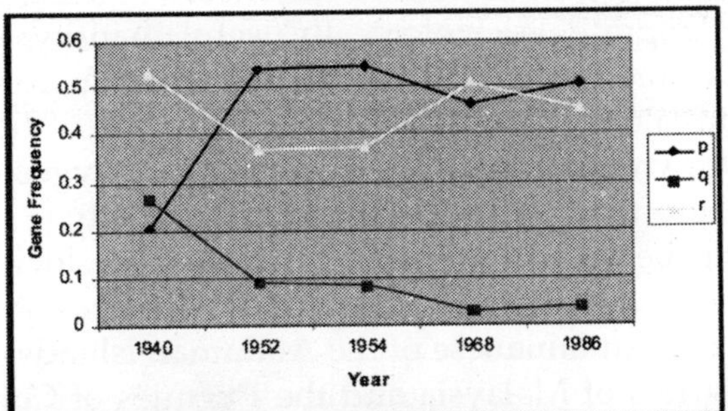


Figure 6: Temporal Changes in ABO Gene Frequencies among the Onge between 1940 and 1986.

some other genetic markers of the Asiatic Negritos namely, the Semang of Malaysia, the Aeta of Philippines (Schebesta 1952; Polunin (1953, Polunin and Sneath (1953), Omoto (1984) and others) as well as the Pygmies of Africa (Cavalli-Sforza 1969, Nirenhuis and Henbrikse, 1986) have also been collected and analysed. These data are most useful for comparison with the present study in order to understand the genetic affinities of the Onge in relation to other Negrito populations for Asia as well as threw Pygmies of Africa.

The Onge are characterized by a very high frequency of $A_1$ gene (0.50) with rather low frequency of B gene (0.03) and complete absent of $A_2$ gene (Sarkar 1996). The Jarawas on the other hand are characterized by only O

(62.79%) followed by only A (37.21%) with regards to ABO blood of 43 individuals so far studied. A trend of temporal increase in the frequency of A gene at the cost of O and B genes is indicated by successive studies among the Onges during 1940 to 1986 (Fig. 6)

Variation in gene frequencies between offspring and parent populations and between local population due to drift have been attributed by several scholars. Birdsell's in 1950 survey in South west Central Australia of 42 tribes showed sharp blood group gene frequency differences which he attributed to drift. Glass et al 1952 showed in their Dunker study was seemed to be drift of MN gene frequencies and Giles *et al* (1966) demonstrated differences in several blood group systems between New Guniea villages of common history and environment, differences which they felt to be due to drift. The changes of gene frequencies in this small Onge population can also be attributed to drift.

The high incidence of *A* gene among the Onges and the Jarawas might be due to random genetic drift operating because of their very small population size and genetic isolation from other populations due to their long geographical as well as biocultural isolation.

## Heterozygosity

The amount of heterozygosity is one of the most common measure of genetic variation and represents a biologically useful quantity. The average heterozygosity is the frequency of heterozygotes averaged over the loci studied. This is equivalent to the expect ed proportion of heterozygote loci in a randomly drawn individual. The average heterozygosity is a more representative measure than locus specific heterozygosity.

The relationship between heterozygosity at three loci have been examined among the four Negrito populations of South east Asia namely, the Onge and the Great Andamanese of the Andaman Islands, the Aeta of Philippines, the Negritos of Malaysia and the Pygmies of Central Africa (Fig. 7 ). It is observed that the heterozygosity level at any specific locus

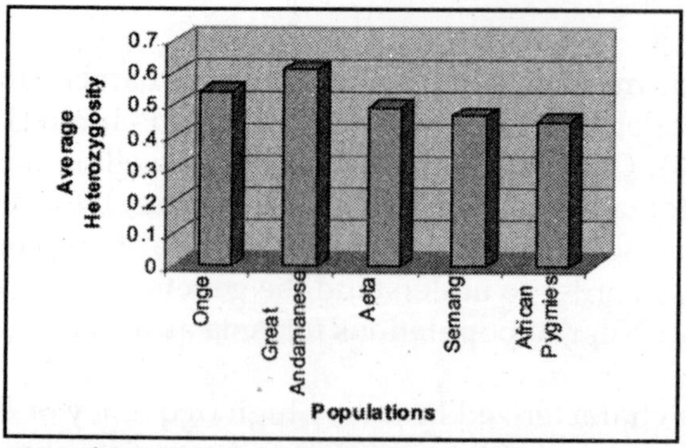


Figure 7: Distribution of Average Heterozygosity (H) among the Asiatic Negritos and the African Pygmies

across the populations do not vary widely. However, a large variability in the heterozygosity level has been found across the loci. This might be due to the monomorphic nature of some of the loci considered where as some other are highly polymorphic.

**Gene Diversity**

The study of nature and extent of genetic differentiation among the sub-populations is of great interest in anthropological genetics. Differentiations at genetics loci among the sub-population may occur because of several factors, e.g., non-random mating, selection, random genetic drift due to isolation etc. A number of studies on genetic differentiation among the various sub-populations have been reported (Morton 1968; Cannings and Cavalli-Sforza 1973, Jorde 1980; Choudhury 1992, Choudhiri 1993 and others).

In the present study the computation of co-efficient of gene differentiation ($G_{ST}$) has been carried out among three Negrito population of southeast Asia namely, the Onge of Andaman Islands, the Aeta of Philippines and the Semang of Malaya Peninsula and the Pygmies of central Africa utilizing four common polymorphic loci viz, ABO, Duffy, MNS and P blood group systems. The gene diversity of total population ($H_T$) is found to be 71.81%, intra-population diversity ($H_S$) 50.4% and the inter-population differences are 21.41% (Fig. 8). The overall coefficient gene differentiation in these populations as revealed by $G_{ST}$ is 0.2981 ± 0.00470. The variance of $G_{ST}$ computed after Chakraborty (1974) is 0.0022. The gene differentiation among the Negrito populations of southeast Asia suggests that overall the level of average gene diversity ($G_{ST}$) is quite high compared to several values reported among many Indian populations.

The distant relationship between the Negritos of southeast Asia and the Negrillos of Africa are also suggested by Nei and Roychoudhury (1982), based on certain polymorphic traits. The genetic affinity based on 21 polymorphic loci , Omoto (1982) suggested that the Aeta of west-central

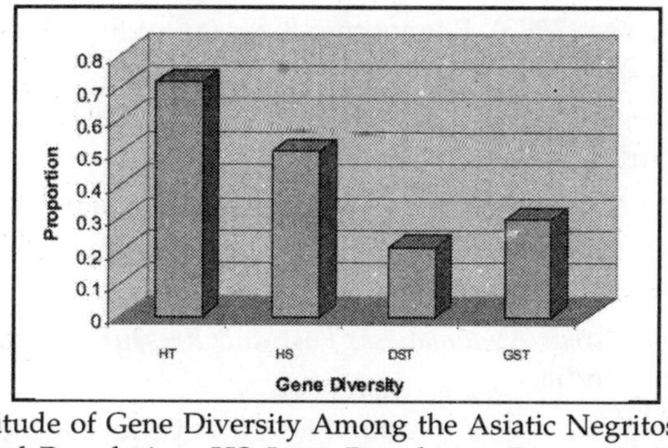


Figure 8: Magnitude of Gene Diversity Among the Asiatic Negritos. [HT–Gene Diversity of Total Population, HS–Intra Population Diversity, DST–Inter Population Diversity, GST–Average Gene Diversity]

Luzan of Philippines are more closely related to Asian-Pacific groups rather than to Africans. He also pointed out that the Aeta and the Semang of Malaysia have a common ancestral stock and evolved in the upper Pleistocene times , probably during 20,000 to 30,000 ybp in the tropical rain forest of Sudaland and developed phenotypic peculiarities through genetic adaptation.

More recently, the improved mtDNA haplogroup M31'32 based on whole genome sequence has permitted the evaluation of hypothesis for the peopling of Andaman Islands (Barik *et al.*, 2008). Thangaraj *et al.* (2003, 2005) suggested that the inhabitants of Andaman Islands are direct descendants of the settlers of the Southeast Asia ~45 kya. Haplogroup 31a1b is exclusively present among the Jarawa and the Onge where as the Great Andamanese sport M31a1a. On the mt DNA lineages, the genetic pool of the Andamanese is likely a product of random genetic drift due to constant relatively small population size and physical isolation of the islands from time immemorial. Further studies would be greatly enhanced by multilocus data, specially autosomal markers to provide insights into population histories and microevolution studies.

## REFERENCES CITED

Barik, SS., R. Sahani, BVR. Prasad, P. Endicott, M. Metspalu, B N Sarkar, S. Bhattacharya, PCH Annapoorna, J Sreenath, D Sun, JJ Sanchez, SYW Ho, A Chandrasekhar and V R Rao (2008), Detailed mtDNA Genotype Permit a Reassessement of the Settlement and Population Structure of the Andaman Islands. *Am. Jr. Phy. Anthrop.*, 136: 19-27.

Cooper, Z. (1990), The Problem of the Origins of the Andamanese. *Bulletin of the Deccan College Post-Graduate & Research Institute (Pune)*, 49: 99-105.

Cannings, C. and L L. Cavalli-Sforza (1973), Human Population Structure. In: *Advances in Human Genetics, Vol.* 4. H Harris and K Hirschhorn (eds.). New York: Plenum Press.

Cavalli-Sforza, L L. (1969), Genetic Drift in an Italian Population. *Sci. Amer*, 221:30-37.

Chakraborty, R. and S. Yee (1973), Phenotypic Bioassay of Five Tribes of Orissa, India. *Hum. Hered.*, 23: 270-279.

Choudhiri, K. (1993), *Genetic Variability in Sixteen Tribes of Central India*. Ph.D. Thesis. University of Calcutta, Calcutta (Unpublished).

Choudhury, A K. (1992), Genetic Structure and Composition of the Shipis: A Small Isolate of High Altitude Himalayas. Ph.D. Thesis. University of Calcutta, Calcutta (Unpublished).

Dutta, P. C. (1978), *The Great Andamanese: Past and Present*. Calcutta: Anthropoological Survey of India.

Fischer, R A. (1930), *Genetical Theory of Natural Selection*. Oxford: Clarendon Press.

Gates, R R. (1940), Blood Groups from the Andamans. Man, 40: 55-56.

Harpending, HC. (1974), Genetic Structure of Small Population. *Ann. Rev. Anthrop.*, 3: 229-243.

Jorde, L B. (1980), The Genetic Structure of Sub-divided Human Populations. In: *Current Development in Anthropological Genetics.* T H Mielke and M H Crawford (eds.).

Kaudeen, W. (1939), Note on the Geographical Distribution of the Pygmies and their Possible Affinities. *Enthnologiska Studier*, 9: 151-175.

Kumar, N. and D P. Mukherjee (1983), A Genetic Study Among the Onge of Little Andaman. *J. Ind. Anthrop. Soc.*, 18: 161-168.

Kumar, S. and B N. Sarkar (1987).

Lehmann, H and E W. Ikin (1954), Study of Andamanese Negritos. *Trans. Royal Soc. Trop. Md. Hyg.*, 48: 12-15.

Malhotra, KC. (1978), Founder Effect, Genetic Drift and Natural Selection Among Four Nomadic Mendelian Isolates. In: *Evolutionay Models and Studies in Human Diversity.* R J Meire (ed.). Mouton: Hauge, pp. 315-324.

Melengraaf, G. A. F. (1921), Modernn Deep Sea Research in the East Indian Archipelago. *Geographical Journal*, London. 57: 95-121.

Morton, NE. (1968), Human Population Structure. *Ann. Rev. Genet.*, 3: 53-74.

Mukherjee, B N, K C Malhotra, S K Das, PP Majumdar and M Roy (1979), Genetic Distance Analysis Among Nine Endogamous Population Groups of Maharashtra, India. *J. Hum. Evol.*, 8: 555-566.

Nei, M. and A. K. Roy Choudhury (1982), Genetic Relationship and Evolution of Human Reces. *Evolution Biology*, 14: 1-59.

Nijenhuis, L E. and I M. Henbrikse (1986), Blood Group Studies in Pygmies and in a Few Bantu Populations. In: African Pygmies. L L Cavalli-Sforza (ed.). Orlando:Academic Press Inc., pp. 181-199.

Omoto, K. (1984), The Negrito: Genetic Origins and Microevolution. *Acta Anthropogenetica*, 8: 137-147.

Papiha , SS, B N Mukherjee, SMS Chahal, K C Malhotra, D F Roberts (1982), Genetic Heterogyneity and Population Structure in North West India. *Am. Hum. Biol.*, 9: 235-251.

Polunin, I. (1953), The Medical Natural History of Malayan Aborigines. *Med. J. Malaya*, 8: 55-174.

Polunin, I and PHA Sneath (1953), Studies of Blood Groups in Southeast Asia. *J. Roy.Anthrop.Inst.*, 83: 215-251.

Portman, M. V. (1899), *A History of Our Relation with the Andamanese.* Calcutta: Govt of India.

Radcliffe Brown, A. R. (1948), *The Andaman Islanders.* Illinois: Free Press.

Roberts, D F. (1975), Genetic Studies of Isolates. In: *Modern Trends in Human Genetics.* AH Emery (ed.). London: Butterworths, pp. 221-269.

Sarkar, S S. (1952), Blood Groups from the Andaman and Nicobar Island. *Man in India*, 33: 245-274.

Sarkar, B. N. (1987), Dermatoglyphic Study of the Jarawas: A Negrito Tribe of Andaman Islands. *Human Science*, 36: 346-358.

– (1989), Anthropometric Study of the Jarawa of Andaman Islands. *Journal of Indian Anthropological Society*, 24: 79-83.

Sarkar, B N. (1996), *Biological Anthropology of the Onge: A Negrito Isolate of Andaman Islands, India*. Ph.D. Thesis. University of Calcutta, Calcutta (unpublished).

Sarkar, BN and R. Sahani (2002), A Demographic and Health Profile of the Jarawas of Andaman Islands. In: *Jarawa Contact: Ours with Them, Theirs with Us*. Mukhopadhyay, K, R. K. Bhattacharya and B. N. Sarkar (eds). Kolkata: Anthropological Survey of India.

Schebesta, P. (1952), Die Negrito Asiens Bd. I, Wien.

Scotch, N A. and H J. Geiger (1963), The Epidemiology of Essential Hypertension,II. *Jr.Chronic Diseases*, 16: 1183-1213.

Thangaraj, K, L. Singh, A Reddy, V Rao, S sehgal, P. Underhill, M pierson, I Frame and E Hagelberg (2003), Genetic Affinities of the Andaman Islanders, A Vanishing Human Population. *Curr. Biol.*, 13:86-93.

Thangaraj, K, G. Chaubey, T. Kivsild, A. G. Reddy, V.K Singh, A.A Rasalkar, L. Singh (2005), Reconstructing the Origin of Andaman Islanders. *Science*, 308: 996.

CHAPTER–24

# On Evolutionism, Progress and Human Development

*Kanchan Mukhopadhyay*

## INTRODUCTION

The Nineteenth Century ideas of social-cultural evolution were closely related to thoughts of progress. Herbert Spencer was the pioneer; he argued the inevitability of transformation of all phenomena from simple to complex, from homogenous to heterogeneous (1862). Extending the idea to human society different possible courses for progressive transition were proposed; from kinship and rank based status to relations based on contract (Maine 1870), from savagery to civilization through barbarism (Morgan 1877), from mechanical to organic solidarity (Durkheim 1893 (1947)). Since early decades of the Twentieth Century Franz Boas and his students rejected the evolutionist thoughts for several reasons. They opposed the ethnocentric stance adopted by some evolutionists and rejected the idea that certain cultures were better than other contemporary cultures in the sense that the former were more evolved. They also discarded the idea that there is some universality in human behaviour and all human societies have to pass through a more or less definite course of transition. They rather argued that the behaviour of an individual makes sense when considered in the perspective of the culture of that person. Sometime later this way of thought came to be known as cultural relativism. This assertion was important in the sense that it acknowledged the merit of distinct cultural forms and denied the inevitability of all non-Western cultural forms to be steamrolled or be devoured by Western forms of cultures.

Since 1930s a group of scholars engaged themselves in salvaging the evolutionist ideas minus the weaknesses of their Nineteenth Century predecessors. They discarded ethnocentrism and racism; they paid attention to empirical archaeological and ethnographic information.

White's 'unilinear evolution' (1959) tried to return to 'scientism' by proposing a mathematical relation between cultural evolution and energy harnessed, but it was not easy to translate the proposed relation into empirical data or vice versa. Steward's approach (1955) had its emphasis on the local, his idea of 'multilinear evolution' recognised the role of the local groups of people actively solving their own problems by adjusting to changing situations; Steward called the process adaptation.

As the process of social evolution is dependent on local history and ecology, it is highly probable that it would follow different courses in different situations. So when a community solves its own problems, generally posed by population and environment, it is not necessary that they evolve at all provided that the conditions do not change significantly. There is no inherent quest for technology perfection that leads to ever-increasing levels of energy efficiency. Hunter-gatherers, horticulturists, and pastoralists can indefinitely remain what they are; if they acquire such technology that can harness more energy, it does not imply that they cannot remain small scale or egalitarian (Johnson and Earle 2000:6). Therefore, it can be said that when the hunter-gatherers, horticulturists, and pastoralists adapt to the changing situations, they do not necessarily change to become something else.

The rejection of typifying human societies on basis of technologies or modes of economy was final. Service (1962) emphasized social organization, while Fried (1967) laid importance to political organization.

"In light of multilinear evolution, such broad organizational typologies recognize that each kind of adaptive solution contains its own possibilities of evolution. The common textbook typology...that even today begins with hunter-gatherer camps or bands and proceeds through horticultural villagers to agricultural states (with pastoralists somehow appended) can be replaced by evolutionary lines that have hunter-gatherers ranging all the way from camps to chiefdoms...with similar ranges for pastoral peoples and agriculturists" (Johnson and Earle 2000:6).

However, the idea of progress or of directional change in anthropological thoughts was not dead. Transformation of 'inferior' forms in to 'superior' ones remained alive not only in the thoughts of common people; in spite of all their emphasis to empirical information and different sorts of theorisation, anthropologists (suspectedly of all hues) kept on contributing to such views in different forms. Kuper (1988) has shown how 'primitivity' remained a core issue in anthropological thoughts since Nineteenth Century. For the Euro American thinkers of that age 'primitivity' was an antithesis to their contemporary society; it was thought to be the original form of human society and the mirror image of the present. In opposition to the contemporary modern society that is characterised by territorial state, monogamous family and private property, the primitive society was described to be nomadic, ordered by blood ties, sexually promiscuous and communist. The primitive man who lacked logical thinking and was believer in magic was bound to progress to a higher mental state and to acquire refined ideas.

No contemporary academic anthropologist would subscribe to the classic account of progress, none of them would venture to explain the huge and varied archaeological, historical, and ethnographic information available today with the idea of primitive society or of primitive man or of their transition into 'higher' forms. But the prototype 'primitive society' persisted through time to the present day. Recent studies on equality and inequality of human societies often adopt an evolutionary perspective, either implicitly or explicitly, commented Beteille (2000:9). It became an ideal type and later took shape of a model. Some of the original ideas, like those related to the early state, survived as orthodoxy; some others like totemism became a special case, still others like kinship theory took shape of elaborate structural transformations, argued Kuper (1988:235). He identified political reasons responsible for persistence of the idea, as it happens with a myth.

"The persistence of a myth is usually explained in terms of its political functions...The idea of primitive society served imperialists and nationalists, anarchists and Marxists. There were certainly some constants. The underlying message was that all societies were based either on blood or on soil. These principles of descent and territoriality were clearly related to ideas of race and citizenship, which were central to political discourse" (Kuper 1988:239-40).

Thus the idea primarily persisted outside the domain of anthropology as a political programme. Once it was suggested that different phases of human history can be perceived in different contemporary human societies, and that we more or less know the future of those who belong to some archaic point of history, what followed was beyond control of the academia. Governments in different parts of the world came up with programmes of assimilation or of integration for the purpose of development of those who were stuck in some history-hole, all such programmes had a sense of direction. And invariably all such programmes were smeared with ethnocentrism, the backwards were the past of the dominants and the dominants were the future of the backwards.

Till 1960s lives of the Australian aborigines were virtually controlled by white Australia through various policies; separating children from their parents and grooming them in custody of the whites was one such policy. In New South Wales alone, these children now known as 'the stolen generations', number between 15,000 and 20,000. It has been argued that such policy was actually camouflaged genocide; its purpose was to destroy the aborigines as a racial group. The policy of assimilation was for individual families, the aborigines were persuaded to share life with the whites in towns. While earlier governments had uprooted the aborigines from their homelands and relocated them to reserves, the assimilation policy tried to close down the reserves, encourage the people to give up seasonal and casual work, and go for regular wage-work. The stations were considered as 'stepping-stones to civilization'. It was believed that the policy would lead the aborigines to a state of 'advancement', and eventually they would fit into the white community.

In contrast to biological absorption, the policy of assimilation sought a social rather than a racial explanation; the focus shifted from biological racial explanations to social factors (Buti, A. 2000).

In South Asia race was a non-issue, there biological extinction of the 'backward' people was never sought. Rather, some social factors determined the popular paradigms of development. According to Bird-David (1999:236) the dominant scheme is based on a traditional way of ranking people and their occupations. Thus the nomadic life of the hunter-gatherers is the lowest form of progress, sedentary life of the agriculturists is placed above that and at the highest level is urban life based on manufacture, commerce, and industry. The material standards of the foragers stand for poverty and backwardness, and their animistic notions are evidences of superstition and ignorance. According to this scheme it is quite logical to help a group of hunter-gatherers to become horticulturists and then agriculturists and then they learn occupations 'more evolved' than agriculture. Bird-David's description of the scheme of arrangement as traditional is quite justified because the common people in India subscribe to such a ranking and treat communities located at different rungs of the arrangement accordingly. However, when subjected to closer examination, the arrangement does not look very traditional and regional; it rather reflects the universal evolutionary scheme discussed above.

Examples drawn from the hunting-gathering communities of India would help us to illustrate our point. They have been considered by both the peasant society and the state as 'backward' and require changing to some 'advanced' state of life. The major difference between the approach of the peasant society and of the state had been that while the former was never very pro-active to bring the change, it was on the agenda of the state to change or develop the people to something better than hunter-gatherers life. We would also consider the viewpoint of the hunting-gathering people also; this we propose to do by noting how they have behaved when confronted with other ways of life, whether they have shown any spontaneous enthusiasm to adapt the same.

The idea of 'original affluent society' assumes that hunting gathering communities are not worried about scarcity of resources, because the resource base they make use of is renewable and abundant for their requirements. It also has been argued that such a situation is impossible in absence of complete or near complete isolation of the people and undisturbed condition of their ecology. Alternatively, more isolated a group of hunter-gatherers and less disturbed is their ecological setting; the probability of their being more attached to their own way of life would be higher. In case the community is exposed to the harsh realities of hierarchical social arrangement where they are relegated to the bottom, if their resource base is depleted or taken away from them, it need not be assumed that they would go for some other way of life on their own. It has been suggested that one possible way of the hunter-gatherers to escape the felt economic deprivation is by withdrawing from the village societies as far as possible and adhere to the view that their own mode of life is much more satisfying (Sinha, D. 1984:85).

## OBSERVATIONS

In the following lines we would examine a few empirical situations and see if the hunter-gatherers feel any spontaneous urge to change their mode of life and if so, whether any directional pattern can be deduced from such changes. We would consider the Nayaka, a people living in the Nilgiri-Wynaad of South India, in the border area between Tamil Nadu, Kerala and Karnataka. Their natural habitat has remained largely undisturbed and accessible for them. Their location in the inaccessible hills has saved them from being run over by immigrants from the plains. Next we would discuss the Birhor; they are found distributed over a wide region of eastern and central India. Though forest resources have been depleted in these regions to a large extent, their patterned movements as nomads along the forest-clad areas over a large expanse have saved them from the brunt of resource depletion to a large extent. The Hill Kharia of Purulia District of West Bengal are a sedentary hunting-gathering people, whose resource base has been severely and irreversibly depleted. They live among peasants; their economy has largely been dependent on the latter.

### The Nayaka

People of this community were found to pursue several economic callings simultaneously. In addition to the hunting and gathering activities, they were doing wage work. A rubber plantation located in Gir Valley was the largest employer of the Nayaka. When the plantation was established in early years of twentieth century, the Nayaka did not show much interest to work there. In those days most of the labourers came from Kerala on seasonal contract, stayed there in temporary accommodations, tapped and smoked the latex and left the valley at end of the season. In 1951 Plantation Labour Act was introduced, this Act abolished contract work and forced the planters to offer permanent employment to the workers and create employment opportunities for their families by introducing coffee plantation. However, immigrant labour became costlier and the Nayaka joined the plantation as wage workers. A subsequent employment structure was introduced in 1964 to protect the interest of casual employees who worked less than fifteen consecutive days each month. Many Nayaka joined the rank of casual workers, as it was not necessary for them to attend plantation work daily.

The Nayaka also worked for a trader commissioned to buy minor forest produce, for the immigrant workers as agricultural helps, for the timber workers as tree fellers and guides. After doing all these Nayaka were found to hunt and gather in a regular manner.

"In fact, in neither time nor space was there any clear demarcation between hunting and gathering and the 'other' pursuits. On their way to work in the plantation – and sometimes even in the course of their work – they occasionally collected forest produce for their own use or for subsequent trade. Sometimes, the plantation superintendent even sent them during their working day... to collect honey for the office. On their way registration point to report for work, Nayaka would sometimes encounter a trader, a neighbour or a timber worker, and spend the day working for him. When they went hunting or gathering, on the other hand, their trails took them in and out of rubber-forested areas, coffee plantations and jungle. They fished in streams that ran within the territorial boundaries of the plantation as well as in the forest" (Bird-David p. 28).

Thus the way the Nayaka were found to integrate themselves into the world of plantation, money, commodities and shops, their own local world of interdependent plantation owner, traders, shop-keepers and themselves, indicated that instead of settling into any new mode of subsistence, they incorporated wage work into their own (Bird-David p. 30).

**The Birhor**

These people were not only found to travel over a large area, they also pursued a wide variety of occupations. Making ropes from creepers and bark and fashioning different artefacts of the rope and selling the same in villages and at markets was their primary occupation. They also hunted monkey and other wild animals for meat, occasionally they hunted monkey for selling the same to the traders visiting their camps. Some members of the community were found to collect medicinal herbs or horns, bones and skins of dead wild animals and sell those items to neighbouring communities as medicines or magical charms. A few worked as agricultural labourers or as magical healers for the peasant villages. Very few were found to beg at villages or at markets (Adhikary, A. K. 1984:21-22).

It was noted that almost every Birhor, irrespective of their age and sex, was much acquainted with forests and their relationship with forest was guided by some ritual and moral obligations. Their knowledge about the larger society, on the other hand, was somewhat segmental and peripheral. However, they tried to maintain good relationship with the villages near which they established their camps by sometimes establishing ceremonial friendship called *phul-saya* with the villagers or behaving as their fellowmen. Though the knowledge of the Birhor about agricultural activities was not very strong, they never denied working as agricultural help for the villagers if asked by them. Even then the villagers ridiculed the Birhor for their way of life, for their eating habits. At market place the Birhor preferred to huddle together. Therefore, all the good manners the Birhor demonstrated while interacting with the villagers were done in a well calculated way to primarily earn economic or material gain. Interestingly, extracting mileage of an interaction with the villagers or traders to maximise economic gain was not treated with moral disapproval in the community. It has been noted that the Birhor, while interacting with others, not only found their ethnic identity at stake, they also lacked a meaningful world of communication. Their humiliating experiences while interacting with the 'larger society' push them to turn back to their own internal solidarity (Adhikary, A. K. 1984:43, 46-7).

**The Hill Kharia**

The forest in the habitat of these people was in such bad shape that food resources previously extracted from forest were severely scarce, hunting and gathering activities could get them only a small part of their food requirement. Their hunting gathering activities were often confined to collection of roots and tubers and hunting snakes. Some activities they carried out could be described as extension of foraging pursuits; they used to fish in river and sell the same at neighbouring villages, collect and sell firewood to peasant households in villages and also at market, collected paddy from burrows of field rats, collected minor forest produces like *biri* and *sal* leaves for selling the same. In addition the Hill Kharia were found to work as agricultural labourers. Though they were participating in agricultural activities since several decades, they were given the jobs of transplanting paddy saplings and of harvesting only. In addition they were cultivating *bajra* in small garden plots. They were also engaged in making craft products like broomsticks, fish-traps made from bamboo, which were sold in local weekly markets. The villagers used to pay them in millet for their products. Excepting sell of the craft products, all other activities had no regularity throughout the year (Sinha, D. 1984: 18-9, 22).

Though the people were working as wage workers, their idea of wage work was found to be different from other neighbouring communities. Being requested by Sinha, an anthropologist doing his field work among the Hill Kharia, the superintendent of a village school gave four Kharia women job of plastering mud wall of school building, which two women from the Bauri caste used to do earlier; the superintendent was even asked by Sinha to pay a higher wage to the Hill Kharia women. Those women took a longer time to do the job, but they did it to great satisfaction of the superintendent, their performance was found to be better than the Bauri ladies. But the same women refused to do the work next year, they said a higher wage should be paid for the job. It was felt that the Bauri women assessed the job in terms of the market principle, while the Hill Kharia women evaluated the job in absolute terms and demanded a wage that should be commensurate with it (Sinha, D. 1984:59).

The economic relations of the Hill Kharia with their peasant neighbours had a striking similarity with the Birhor situation discussed above. It has been observed that the Hill Kharia view their relationship with the peasants as contractual and not to endure beyond a certain time period. Each situation was judged by the immediate economic prospect involved. Even the ceremonial friendship of *phul-saya*, through which kinship relation can be extended beyond one's endogamous group, was found to be used for enhancing economic opportunities by the participants. The Muslim and Muchi traders entered in such relation to gain trust of the Hill Kharia hunters and to keep the other traders out of competition. The Hill Kharias also kept such ceremonial friendship within the confine of economic relation; the *phul-saya* relations were never allowed to become all-encompassing kin relationship (Sinha, D. 1984:58, 60).

The Hill Kharias were caught between two worlds, their resource base had been denuded rendering it insufficient for their survival, they became a group of landless dependents on the peasant society. Hunted by scarcity they tried to find the bare minimum requirements from the village societies, which frustrated them largely (Sinha, D. 1984:86). Their only gain was the new mental state that took them furthest from the 'original affluent society'.

Each of the above mentioned empirical situations shows that the hunting gathering communities, whatever the degree of their interaction with the peasants or planters or traders, have preferred to integrate the other worlds into their own. In case they are made to change their ways, if they are left with no other option but to adopt new modes of subsistence and ways of life, the process of transition might backfire. Surajit Sinha noted that the so-called 'hunting-gathering' communities like Birhor and Hill Kharia are considered by anthropologists as representatives of a more archaic phase of development. He felt that those communities were primarily dependent on shifting cultivation; in response to penetration of caste-based economy and of deforestation in the area, that mode of economy became untenable in the changed situation. The communities reverted back to hunting and gathering; there are many evidences of such 'devolution' or secondary 'primitivization' in cultural patterns and processes among the communities.

Such devolution might occur in other situations to other communities too, if they are subjected to similar kind of exogenous forces.

On most occasions the policy makers failed to look at things from the perspectives of the people themselves or of the anthropologists narrating the empirical situations. Primitivity remained a necessity to assert superiority of not only of Euro American thinkers, but also of the powerful elsewhere. In India some of the Scheduled Tribes are officially designated as 'Primitive Tribals'; most of such people are either hunter-gatherers or used to depend on hunting gathering in recent past. Special welfare schemes were formulated for them, none of which were aimed at strengthening their own way of life, but were meant to make them something else.

The above debate was revived and re-enacted recently, when certain steps were taken to frame a policy for the Ang, popularly known as the Jarawa, inhabiting the Andaman Islands of India. The habitat of the near-isolated islander group of hunter-gatherers was encroached and colonised since late eighteenth century in a systematic manner. The Ang tried to resist the colonisation activities; mostly in form of extraction of forest resources and settling of villages by clear felling forest. After a part of the forest was demarcated for their use, hostility between the Ang on one hand, and the villagers and armed forces protecting the colonial activities on the other, came down considerably. In 1998 the Ang decided to step out of the forest habitat and visit villages, roads and jetties; that was end of hostility and xenophobia. The anthropologists were asked to enquire if food or water scarcity in their habitat has forced them out of forest to seek help. In that case appropriate welfare schemes would be put in operation for them, it was assured. Some of the possible schemes considered by officials and non-official opinion makers at that point of time and earlier were; (1) the Ang be persuaded to take up commercial fishing activities, (2) they be persuaded to take up horticulture (3) all the Ang be gathered at one place and provided with food, water and other basic necessities, (4) they be relocated on some other isolated island, that would protect them from contact with others, that would also make the land under their occupation available for other activities, (5) they be persuaded to take up wage work in their own habitat.

Anthropologists objected to all such suggestions; some of them undertook a study of the people to collect necessary empirical information and a couple of seminars were organised once the report was made available. At the second seminar organised at Port Blair certain resolutions were adopted. The participants debated on whether the highway passing through the Ang territory should be closed down and alternative sea routes be strengthened, whether cultural life of the Ang be intervened with or whether intervention be kept limited to the field of health, whether all road maintenance staff, policemen and other officers be withdrawn from the Tribal Reserve, and whether the Aboriginal Tribe Regulation of the Union Territory be amended to provide stringent punishment for the violators.

The policy that has since been framed for the Ang (Jarawa) of the Andaman Islands by the Central Government of the country has reflected the views and the concerns of the informed anthropologists for the first time in so clear terms. The objectives of the policy are:

(i) To protect the Jarawas from harmful effects of exposure and contact with the outside world while they are not physically, socially and culturally prepared for such interface.;

(ii) To preserve the social organization, mode of subsistence and cultural identity of the Jarawa community;

(iii) To provide medical help to the Jarawas to reduce mortality and morbidity in case of their sudden affliction with diseases which their systems are unaccustomed to;

(iv) To conserve the ecology and environment of the Jarawa Reserve Territory and strengthen support systems in order to enable the Jarawas pursue their traditional modes of subsistence and way of life; and

(v) To sensitize settler communities around the Jarawas habitat and personnel working for the protection and preservation of the Jarawas about the need to preserve this ancient community and to value their unique culture: and life styles.

To achieve the above objectives, the policy document states, the cultural identity of the people would be protected. For the purpose a policy of maximum autonomy to the Jarawas with minimum and regulated intervention shall be adopted. "There shall be no intervention in cultural life of the Jarawas and they will be left at liberty to develop according to their own genius and at their own pace. No attempts to bring them to the mainstream society against their conscious will or to rehabilitate them in separate islands / locations at this stage of their social development will be made." Equal importance has been accorded to protection of their natural habitat. It has been promised that no non-tribal, including the government agencies, will be allowed to exploit the natural resources within the Jarawa Reserve. The notified territory shall be fully and effectively demarcated and no attempt to curtail, reduce or to acquire land there from shall be made, all encroachments shall be removed on priority basis. Stringent arrangements to ensure that such encroachments do not take place in future will also be made, says the document. The only intervention the policy allows is in the area of health care, but under certain conditions. There would be such intervention on basis of advice of experts in the relevant fields only when absolutely necessary, i.e., to save lives. This licence was necessary because time and again the low density hunting gathering communities, when exposed to high density population diseases or to diseases against which they had no immunity, died in large numbers.

The major challenge faced by the policy framed for the Ang would be to find right kind of personnel and the political will to make its implementation possible. In a world dominated and run by hegemonic ideologies the feeble voice of the communities and the anthropologists could be made audible, at least once. It remains a challenge before the anthropologists to come out loud and clear, say what they believe, to the world. Talking to the world would not be enough; we need to change it in favour of the less articulate.

## REFERENCES CITED

Adhikary, A. K. (1984), *Society and World View of the Birhor*, Calcutta, Anthropological Survey of India.

Beteille, A. (1986), 'The Concept of Tribe with Special Reference to India'. *Journal of European Sociology. 27: 297-318.*

Bird-David, Nurit (1992), Beyond 'The Hunting and Gathering Mode of Subsistence': Observations on the Nayaka and Other Modern Hunter-gatherers. *Man* 27: 1, 19-44.

Bird-David, Nurit (1999), Introduction: South Asia in *The Cambridge Encyclopedia of Hunters and Gatherers*, Lee Richard B. and Richard Daly (editors), Cambridge, Cambridge University Press 231-237.

Buti, Antonio (2000), Unfinished Business: The Australian Stolen Generations, *E Law-Murdoch University Electronic Journal of Law* 7: 4

Durkheim, Emile 1893 (1947) *The Division of Labour in Society*. Glencoe, Illinois: Free Press.

Kuper, Adam (1988), *The Invention of Primitive Society: Transformation of an Illusion*. London and New York: Routledge.

Spencer, Herbert (1862), *First Principles*. London, Williams and Norgate.

Sinha, Dikshit (1984), *The Hill Kharia of Purulia: A Study on the Impact of Poverty on a Hunting Gathering Tribe*, Calcutta, Anthropological Survey of India.

Sinha, Surajit (1969), Problems for Research in Social and Cultural Anthropology in India: Perspectives and Suggestions in B. L. Abbi and S. Saberwal (ed.) *Urgent Research in Social Anthropology*. Shimla, Indian Institute of Advanced Study 162-69.

# Index